CALIFORNIA
GARDENING
RHYTHMS

What to do each season to have a beautiful garden all year.

BRUCE, SHARON, AND ERIC ASAKAWA

COOL SPRINGS PRESS
A Division of Thomas Nelson Publishers
Since 1798

For other life-enriching books, visit us at:
www.thomasnelson.com

Published by Cool Springs Press, a Division of Thomas Nelson, Inc., P. O. Box 141000, Nashville, Tennessee, 37214.

Asakawa, Bruce.
   California gardening rhythms / Bruce, Sharon, and Eric Asakawa.
      p. cm.
   Includes bibliographical references and index.
   ISBN 1-59186-084-9 (pbk.)
   1. Landscape plants—California. 2. Landscape gardening—California.
   I. Asakawa, Sharon. II. Asakawa, Eric. III. Title.
SB407.A795 2004
635.9'09794—dc22

                         2004024631

First printing 2005
Printed in the United States of America
10 9 8 7 6 5 4 3 2 1

Managing Editor: Billie Brownell
Designer: James Duncan, James Duncan Creative
Horticulture Editor: Diana Maranhao
Graphic Artist: S.E. Anderson
Cover photograph by Tom Eltzroth; back cover author photo by Lorenzo Gunn

Cool Springs Press books may be purchased in bulk for educational, business, fundraising, or sales promotional use. For information, please email SpecialMarkets@ThomasNelson.com.

Visit the Thomas Nelson website at **www.ThomasNelson.com** and the Cool Springs Press website at **www.coolspringspress.net**

PHOTOGRAPHY CREDITS

Thomas Eltzroth: pages 4, 9, 14, 17 (top photo), 42, 44, 45 (middle and bottom photos), 60, 62, 63 (middle and bottom photos), 96, 98, 99 (all photos), 122, 125 (all photos), 164, 166, 167 (all photos), 178, 198, 201 (top and middle photos), 230, 232, 233 (top and bottom photos), 246, 248, 264, 265 (top and middle photos), 282, 285 (top photo)

Jerry Pavia: pages 17 (middle and bottom photos), 63 (top photo), 180, 181 (middle and bottom photos), 200, 201 (bottom photo), 262, 265 (bottom photo), 284, 285 (middle photo)

Liz Ball: pages 124, 181 (top photo), 233 (middle photo)

Charles Mann: page 8

David Winger: page 16

PhotoDisc Homes and Gardens 2 Stock: pages 5, 6, 7

Brand X Pictures Home and Garden Collection Stock: page 11

Artville Seasons Stock: seasonal tree illustrations

Photo Courtesy of Bruce Asakawa: pages 249 (middle photo), 285 (bottom photo)

Photo Courtesy of Melissa's (**www.Melisas.com**): page 45 (top photo)

Photo Courtesy of Dave Wilson Nursery: page 249 (bottom photo)

TABLE OF CONTENTS

In Our Garden

Why another gardening book? Why not a newsletter? Why not a website? Why not search the Internet for all the answers? The explanation lies in the answer to a question a listener posed during one of our programs. She asked whether there was a source that contained all of our knowledge about gardening, to which we replied, "The closest source would be in our books." Gardening is a very eclectic activity. Ideas, like plants, are gathered from many sources, and there are many paths to a successful garden. When we are writing about gardening, we are describing our personal experiences, both academic and practical. Our books are designed to be used, not put up on the shelf or on the coffee table; if you dog ear the pages of our book within a month, then we have done our job. A book is a comfortable way to disseminate ideas and information, solve gardening problems, and most of all, follow the rhythms of the gardens in California. Except for a few events, rhythms in California gardens follow the same sequence, but there is a timing difference; in the central and northern regions of the state, these events occur a few weeks later in the year than they do in the southern region. So as you read about the time for soil amending, planting tomatoes, or controlling insects, adjust in your mind the time frame, your microclimate, and local variations that might affect the gardening rhythm.

To understand California's seasonal rhythms, it helps to think about its unique geography. California is 770 miles long and 250 miles wide at its widest point. The state lies between 32° 30' and 42° North Latitude. These latitudes north or south of the equator include the cities of Haifa, Casablanca, Kyoto, Sydney, Santiago, and Cape Town. These cities represent regions of the world that have similar climate and growing conditions as California. The 163,707 square miles of land that forms California provide its own set of native plants that can be combined with imported plants (exotics) from all these regions. This means that California is blessed with diversity—diversity in its people, diversity in its geography, and diversity in its plants.

Just as California's people come from every region of the world, the plants that we use for landscaping also come from all reaches of the earth. These imported plants have adapted to the rhythms of their regional weather patterns. Their roots expand rapidly during the period before the rainy season, from November to mid-March. Foliar growth begins about the time of the Vernal Equinox, and most plants quiet their growth through the summer solstice. California also has a wonderful native plant population, which provides a window to the soils below and to the seasonal influence above. Tucked into the northeastern corner of the state, on the edge of the Great Basin, lies the Modoc Plateau, where ponderosa and pinyon pines grow in soils weathered from metamorphic rock strewn from volcanic activity eons ago. The world's tallest trees, the coastal redwoods, live on a thin veneer of soil along California's northwest coast, capturing water though a process called fog drip.

On the western slope of the Sierra Nevada, the world supply of straight, dense, and aromatic wood for pencils is harvested from California's incense cedar. Its young branches and foliage are also woven into decorative cedar roping for the holidays. The sole species of palm tree endemic to California is the California fan palm, found near the extreme western end of the Sonoran desert in Riverside and Imperial Valley. One of the oldest living plants, the creosote bush is from the upper Mojave Desert.

Weather is also an important influence in the seasonal variations of California. The weather emanating in the Pacific Northwest surges southward through Oregon's southern Cascades before entering California's northern tier of counties. Late in summer and in early fall, winds storm through Weed and Redding into the northern Sacramento Valley. When there is a high-pressure cell over Utah and Nevada's Great Basin, the air heats up, rises, loses its moisture, and accelerates as it descends in a south-westerly direction. This weather phenomenon is similar to the Foehn of Switzerland, the Mistrals of France, and the Chinooks of the eastern Rockies. Unless hydrated thoroughly before they arrive, these hot dry winds desiccate landscape plants.

In addition to weather conditions, rhythms denote other patterned movements that are always recurring. By observing these rhythms, the events in the garden

become more predictable, easier to manage, and much more enjoyable. Daily rhythms affect our gardens. The dominant daily rhythm is the rising and the setting of the sun. Some plants grow, flower, and set seed in response to day length (the number of hours of daylight). For example, there are short-day and long-day onions; the long-day onions do well in the northern tier of states where the long hours of summer daylight bring the bulbs to maturity. Short-day onions fare better in the southern regions of the country where there are fewer daylight hours during the growing season. The diurnal activities of butterflies and nocturnal activities of moths are initiated by the rising and the setting of the sun. The alternating sexual responses of avocado flowers are initiated by daylight, darkness, and temperature.

Other rhythms are longer; the monthly waxing and waning of the moon gives rise to planting cycles of root crops and leaf crops. There are the seasonal rhythms of summer, autumn, winter, and spring and the growth rhythms of seed, leaf, flower, fruit and egg, larvae, pupa, and adult. Most garden events are repetitive; if we anticipate these events, we increase our chances for gardening successes—we become garden wise. For example, after the last spring frost, vigorous, lush, new growth emerges from latent buds. The succulent new growth becomes a feeding ground for aphids. The aphids secrete honeydew that attracts ants. The ants harvest the honeydew. When the honeydew inundates the foliage, black sooty mold develops. But by anticipating the seasonal rhythm, the cycle can be avoided.

Rhythms in the garden can be rapid or sluggish. One of the quickest rhythms in a garden is the life of the mayfly (*Dolania americana*). The female of the species lives less than five minutes after her final molt, during which time she mates and lays her eggs. Another fleeting rhythm is that of the frenetic activity that occurs in the vernal ponds that form on the coastal mesas during the seasonal rains. The shallow pools of water host the truest form of ephemeral community. On dense, expansive, clayey soils, they teem with life for a few weeks; then before the moisture evaporates, insects, amphibians, grasses, sedges, and other life forms mate or pollinate and return to a state of dormancy until the next rainy season. This clayey, expansive, and almost impenetrable soil is the same type of soil many of us find in our gardens.

On the other hand, one of the slowest and limiting rhythms in the California landscape is the development of soils. Whether or not the soil in your neighborhood is from sedimentary, metamorphic, or igneous rock, it takes centuries, if not eons, for it to develop. Soil is different than dirt. Forty plus years ago, in my (Bruce) soils class at Cal Poly, Pomona, dirt was defined as the debris that was swept under the rug, and soil was the thin veneer of weathered rock, organic material, microorganisms, air, and water that provides nutrients and a medium for roots to develop. As space shuttles pass over the earth, the astronauts have taken thousands of land mass images. It is distinctly clear where the deserts are, where the population centers are, where the rivers flow, and where the vegetation flourishes; these photographs point out to the geologists, agronomists, and biologists where to study that thin veneer of soil at the top of the earth's crust that supports life. An interesting side note about growing plants in certain California soils is that soils borne of ancient, metamorphic serpentine rock in the central part of the state actually limit the kinds of plants grown there. Pushed to the surface from deep within the earth's crust, this rock contains high levels of magnesium and has weathered over time to become serpentine soils. High levels of magnesium are toxic to most plants, resulting in fewer than 100 species able to survive in serpentine soils.

Some rhythms hesitate as they progress, as if there were syncopation. The brown garden snails, as slow as they are, can become slower, surviving drought conditions through a process called estivation. They are capable of developing membranes over the opening of their shells that protects them and keeps them from desiccating. In this state of inactivity, they can survive for several years until moisture conditions are again suitable, at which time their membranes dissolve and they become active again.

Even mathematical rhythms express themselves in nature. The most perfect and infinite visual rhythm is the graphic representation of the Fibonacci series. The series is an infinite progression of numbers, each of which is the sum of the preceding two numbers, for example: (1), 1+1= (2), 2+1= (3), 3+2= (5), 5+3= (8), 8+5= (13). Graphic representation of this numerical progression is found in the golden rectangle, the golden section, the golden spiral, and the golden mean. Its ratio of 1:1.61803399 is found in the spiral pattern of sunflowers, pinecones, pineapples, dandelion seedheads, lupine leaves, and many other natural structures, such as nautilus shells.

Many rhythms are symbiotic; others are parasitic. One of the most remarkable partnerships is the one between a unique group of beneficial fungi called mychorrizae and that of their host plants. The fungi serve their host plant by increasing the absorbing root's capacity to gather water and nutrients, while the host plant provides nourishment for the fungi as it uses the sun's energy to manufacture carbohydrates. The relationship works remarkably well. As an interesting sidebar to this relationship, it should be noted that coniferous or cone-bearing plants have a host-specific relationship with mychorrizae fungi. In other words, there is a specific fungus that is associated with a specific conifer.

Though populations of specialized fungus occur naturally in the soil around the plant, there are commercial formulations that accelerate their population quickly. Organic soil amendments, fertilizers, and soil conditioners are also available with added mychorrizae.

Among the parasitic relationships that occur in our gardens are those of predacious insects and controlling, chewing, sucking, and rasping insects. Several years ago, Californians experienced the arrival of the unwanted eucalyptus longhorn borer. For decades, eucalyptus trees were never susceptible to insect attacks. It was thought that the essential oils of the eucalyptus made it impervious to insect infestation, but this was not true. Once the borer became established, it did not have any natural predators, so thousands of trees died. A contingent from the University of California traveled to Australia to find a parasite or predator to control the borer. From "the land down under," they found a wasp that laid its eggs in the larvae of the borer and, when the eggs hatched, the wasp larvae consumed its host, limiting the next generation.

Water is the driving force behind the rhythm of sustainable landscapes. From floods to droughts, from verdant greens to desiccated browns, sustaining our landscapes depends on water. The path of California's history parallels the availability of water. From the snow packs of the Sierra Nevada and the Southern Cascades, our water flows into the reservoirs that feed the Sacramento and San Joaquin rivers. Water is also gathered and directed into the California, Los Angeles, and Colorado aqueducts, moving its liquid gold hundreds of miles into the reservoirs of central and southern California before it is distributed for agricultural, commercial, and residential use. If it were not for California's interdependent water distribution system, our landscapes would revert to chaparral and desert within the next generation. Another factor to be taken into consideration when water is discussed is that the state of California is in a very seismically active part of the world and much of the distribution system crosses some of the major fault lines. What does this have to do landscaping? The first two restrictive uses of water in times of scarcity are car washing and irrigating our landscape plants.

We embrace the concept of sustainable landscapes. There have been times in the past when our state's water resources were so limited that watering landscape plants was not an option, and since history tends to repeat itself, it seems prudent to prepare for a likely future. Planning ahead for a sustainable landscape is not so different than following the traditional design process. Both need to resolve conflicting issues of form following function, budgets and building codes that limit creativity. The major distinction is a matter of emphasis placed on the selection and installation of plant material. The idea is deceptively simple. After the selected plants are established, they should be able to sustain themselves for two or three growing seasons without supplemental irrigation. Their survival would rely solely on seasonal rainfall.

Only two considerations are needed to develop a sustainable garden. The first is to select the right combination of plants, those that fill the functional and

cultural needs of your garden design. The second is to position the plants where they can optimize their growth. In short, it is the right plant in the right place. These two considerations include the steps necessary to establish the right plant and to select a location that optimizes the plant's potential. Once the right plants are selected, positioned, and established, they fend for themselves during adverse conditions, such as periods of drought, desiccating winds, and searing heat, freezing cold, or torrential rains. In the case of drought, they might not look their best after a prolonged period of dryness, but they should be resilient and flourish once more when water is available.

The concept of a sustainable landscape is to group the plants that need the least amount of water in the most strategic locations. These plants, including trees, are the first-tier plants and the most important groupings. Once first-tier plants become established, they remain viable through one or two seasons of drought. They might not look good, they might even defoliate, but if they are the right plants in the right places, they will resume their growth when conditions become supportive. Second-tier plants sustain growth with deep irrigation once a month during the growing season, and third-tier plants perish if they are not irrigated at least once a week.

To make appropriate decisions about first-, second-, and third-tier plants, survey your neighborhood for plants that have been growing for at least ten years. Take photographs of the plants you do not recognize, and ask your local garden center or botanical garden representative for identification. To make sure your plant selections have the best chance for survival under adverse conditions, prepare the soil so that its volume approximates 50 percent soil structure (silt, sand, clay, and organic material), 25 percent air, and 25 percent water. Soil serves as an easily accessible reservoir of moisture and nutrients. This includes developing a soil texture that encourages the expansion of root systems. An ideal soil has a loam texture, about 40 percent sand, 40 percent silt, and 20 percent clay. Loam soil should be blended with 20 to 30 percent organic material such as compost, wormcastings, humus mulch, peat moss, or planting mix. Once the right plants are selected for the right spots in the best soil environment, your sustainable landscape will survive the seasonal rhythms of scarcity, as well as abundance.

One event that has always reminded us of nature's rhythms happened years ago in the Medusula Grove of the Bristle Cone Pine Tree preserve in the White Mountains, south of Mammoth. The grove is at an elevation of 12,000 feet and is north and east of the mountain town of Big Pine in the Owens Valley. This is an area as isolated as a place can be, where wind chill drops the temperature far below what living things should have to endure and blasts of searing wind carve away the soft wood of pine trees, exposing the tougher grain. In this inhospitable setting, we spied a very determined wooly caterpillar inching its way across our path with a sense of urgency. Earlier at the state park information center, a ranger explained to us, with a twinkle in his eye, that the woolly caterpillar anticipates winter weather conditions and dons a pure black coat if the winter is to be severe, but chooses to wear a brown coat when the winter will be mild. He was wearing a black coat, and that year, there was no need for snow-making machines in Mammoth. Whether the caterpillar's ability to anticipate weather is the stuff of urban legend, much like Puxatawny Phil, we will never know for sure, but it is a woolly tale about a creature attuned to the changes in nature.

For us, the term rhythm describes the repetitive flow of events through our gardens. There is a natural cadence that repeats itself, and if we observe carefully, the rhythms become more defined and we begin to understand and then anticipate the seasonal change. But most California seasons are never as defined as the specific days or months of a calendar. Most important is to use the information in this book as a guideline. If there is one reality we have learned during the past fifty years talking on the radio to gardening aficionados and visiting many wonderful gardens of the world, it is that there is never just one way to be successful at gardening, but if you care for your plants based on your observations, rather than the calendar, chances are your garden will flourish.

The most influential force that affects the natural rhythms in our gardens is the sun. The sun is the life force for all flora and fauna. Its rhythms are punctuated by the vernal and autumnal equinox and summer and winter solstices. In California, the sun's traverse begins spring by moving northward from the Mexican border to the Modoc plateau. Progressively through the seasons, the sun initiates the events that occur in our gardens. By observing these patterns, the natural rhythms become more predictable, which will assist in anticipating events in your garden.

YEAR-ROUND RHYTHMS

- Snails and slugs appear when it's cool and humid.
- Root crops should be planted under a new moon.
- Leaf or vining vegetables should be planted under a full moon.
- It might rain when insects become more active; when bees return to their hives; when birds fly lower in the sky or when frogs croak louder.

Turn the page for other Natural Rhythms.

Great Gardening!
—Bruce, Sharon,
*   and Eric Asakawa*

NATURAL RHYTHMS
OF CALIFORNIA

SPRING

- The departure of migrating birds....indicates the end of the rainy season.
- Red tail hawks court in early spring....signals the last freeze day is nearing.
- California poppies bloom in spring....the seasonal rains have ended.
- Aphids appear from nowhere and multiply geometrically....ants are sure to follow.
- The orange beaks of the bird of paradise blossoms appear....you know it's spring or autumn.
- When nasturtiums bloom....summer is right behind.
- Carpets of pink blossoms on rosea ice plant....signal the end of spring.
- Cherimoyas, the fruit of the gods....defoliate in spring.
- May gray and June gloom....invites mildew and rust.

SUMMER

- Parasitic dodder twines over native shrubs....the fire season is here.
- Dry, hot, north easterlies remind us....plants should be watered the day before.
- Figs and peaches ripen....green fig leaf beetles emerge.
- Fragrant Madagascar jasmine are blooming....look for mealy bugs.
- Birds of paradise cease blooming....it's time to divide and transplant them.
- St. Augustine turf turns to straw....chinch bugs have arrived.
- Dichondra leaves shows striations....flea beatles have arrived.

AUTUMN

- Annual bluegrass starts to grow....cooler weather is approaching.
- Larvae of the green fig leaf beetle....consume degrading compost.
- Ripening persimmons....herald the holiday season is approaching.
- High pressure cells over the great basin....precede seasonal dry winds.
- Liquidambars displaying fall color....mark the autumnal equinox.
- St. Augustine grass turns to straw....look for chinch bugs.
- The rainy season begins....the cool-season weeds emerge..
- Bracts of poinsettias turn holiday colors....it's time to spray fruit trees with dormant oil.
- When the woolly caterpillar dons a heavy coat....a severe winter is coming
- Autumn's harvest moon rises....it's time to mulch the ground.

WINTER

- The clusters of pearly white eggs of snails and slugs....tell us to destroy them when we find them.
- Pomegranates persist even after the foliage has fallen....it's time to set rat traps.
- Pyracantha, holly, and cotoneaster berries redden....squirrels are hibernating.
- When 'Pink Mink' proteas bloom....apply humic acid and saponin to the soil.

CHAPTER ONE

California Annuals

Annuals bring serendipitous bursts of color to permanent plantings. With their vividly painted faces and interesting shapes, sizes, and scents, they also attract pollinating birds, bees, and other insects. While there are differences in growth, bloom, and seed cycles, most annuals have evolved to survive during the brief growing season from the time the snow pack melts until summer or autumn winds dry out the landscape. In mild-winter areas, many act like perennials. Annuals more than compensate for their short lifespan by helping define the rhythms of the seasonal garden. Cool-weather selections—such as Iceland poppies and pansies—grow and blossom during winter and spring. Heat-loving cosmos and four o'clocks are summer through fall replacements. Some—such as coleus—may even last through winter if protected from the cold. Less expensive and less permanent than shrubs, trees, and perennials, annuals allow for greater experimentation and frivolous fun. Use them to brighten a shady area, fill in blank a space, or cover a spent bulb bed. With a bit of planning, annuals can provide that extra sparkle from spring through fall—or even the entire year in mild-winter regions.

Most Californians garden year-round, especially when it comes to annuals. Unless we live in a Jack Frost zone, we sow seeds or plant our posies in fall and early spring; fertilize, water, and amend with mulch in spring; deadhead through summer, and continue to dig around during winter. As gardeners, we tend to fiddle with our landscapes. Depending on the season or our mood, we first can't seem to get enough of a plant and then we grow bored with it, only to become enamored with other plants.

With annuals, we can be as fickle as we please—adding instant color here, changing bedding plants there, and filling in bare spots wherever our discerning eyes land. Annuals are relatively easy to grow, are inexpensive, and can easily be replaced two, three, or more times a year. With a bit of effort and planning, they will offer up a symphony of color for just about every month of the year, especially in mild-winter regions.

Our short list of "favorite" annuals is meant to offer something a bit out of the ordinary, and we hope you "dig them" enough to try a few that are new to you.

ANGELONIA
Angelonia augustifolia

Angelonia resembles a cluster of miniature orchids on upright spikes with glossy-green, needlelike leaves; it flowers in colors of rose, plum, blue, lavender, white, and combination stripes and bicolors. Although it loves high temperatures, once cold weather sets in, angelonia will die back—but don't be surprised if it "springs" back to life when warm weather returns.

S. America / Zones 8 to 11 / full sun / height 18 to 36 inches / width 18 inches / flowers spring to autumn

INDIAN PEA
Lathyrus sativus azureus

Indian pea is so stunning that Mother Nature must have decided it would be almost criminal if it were also blessed with fragrance. Azure-blue, wing-shaped flowers outlined in a deeper blue veination and tinted with a touch of deep rose at their center decorate stems of dark green foliage. Indian pea grows well in inland heat as well as along cooler coastal areas.

E. Europe and India / Zones 7 to11 / full sun, part shade / height 36 inches / width 72 inches / flowers late spring to summer

SPURRED SNAPDRAGON
Linaria reticulata 'Flamenco'

From clumps of fine-leafed, grasslike foliage emerge hundreds of small, bicolor blooms that are a vibrant maroon-red with gold and orange throats. Spurred snapdragon is drought-tolerant once established, adaptable to most soil types, and tends to be resistant to snails and deer. For eye-popping displays of color, plant 'Flamenco' in full sun and deadhead regularly.

N. Africa / Zones 8 to 11 / full sun / height 18 to 30 inches / width 12 inches / flowers spring to autumn

SPRING

California's earthy foothills shed their blankets of dusty gray and native tan to cover themselves in serene greens. Against this verdant backdrop, California poppies spring to life, nodding in homage to the return of mild temperatures.

PLANNING

Stroll through public gardens and visit retail garden centers for ideas about annual varieties, new cultivars, colors, and sizes for expected—and even more important, unexpected—choices appropriate for your landscape.

Keep writing in your garden journal; note important information such as last frost date, amount of spring rainfall, numbers and types of annuals purchased or started from seed, and bedding plant sites. You'll be glad to have this information next year.

Decide if you want to keep your current annual beds, expand them, or start new ones at a different location. Think inside or outside the box when making your plans.

- Consider the architecture of your home and your own personal style.
- Formal annual beds and borders are designed in a more linear fashion with plantings inside square or rectangular shapes.
- Informal beds and borders are characterized by more meandering, flowing, and natural planting patterns.
- Create swathes of color beside walkways, driveways, fences, walls, along the house, or bordering the street.
- Tuck annuals among trees, shrubs, and bulb beds or snuggle them in a lawn area.

Wait until the ground has defrosted or dried out a bit from the rains before shoveling and preparing new or established flower beds. Digging in permafrost or muck is no fun.

Purchase annual bedding plants after the last frost date has come and gone in your area. An unusually sunny, breath-of-spring day can trick us into thinking that balmy weather is here to stay. Review your garden journal notes from last year to make sure you are not planting warm-season annuals too early. If you still can't help yourself, monitor the evening weather forecasts and if predicted temperatures fall in the 30s, be prepared to spray with an antitranspirant or cover them with cotton sheets.

PLANTING

Begin planting annuals into your garden after you observe annual weeds, such as dandelions, beginning to grow or after the possibility of a late frost has passed. Along the coastal areas of California, frosty weather is not expected past St. Patrick's Day, March 17. If you live inland or at higher elevations, frost is possible later in the year. To find out your region's historical temperature patterns, review your own garden journals or contact your local University of California Cooperative Extension Office.

Try to control yourself and wait before planting cold-sensitive plants such as Indian peas (a relative of the sweetpea), four o'clocks, coleus, calibrachoas, cosmos, and angelonia until warmer spring temperatures are here to stay.

ANNUALS

Once Jack Frost has left your region, it's time to acclimate those seedlings that you germinated indoors during winter to outdoor life; see pages 37 to 39 for directions on starting from seed. When the seedlings are about 4 inches high or the seed leaves give way to 2 to 4 pairs of *true leaves* (the first two leaves that appear are cotyledons and the true leaves appear above them), "harden" them by taking them outdoors for longer and longer periods during the day in a warm, protected location before bringing them back indoors for the night. If they are not hardened off before being planted directly in the garden, they could be damaged from the sun, wind, or cold. Along the coast where temperature fluctuations are rare, acclimating plants by hardening them is not as critical. Seedlings can be left outdoors in a wind-protected area without bringing them back indoors in the evening. For inland and mountain regions, start 2 weeks before they are to be transplanted and set them outdoors in a wind-protected, shady location. Each day, increase the time spent outdoors before bringing them back indoors in the evening. Also, gradually increase the sun exposure if the plant requires full sun to develop. Just like us, sudden and excessive sun exposure leads to sunburn. Do not move your tender seedlings outdoors during windy days or when temperatures dip below 45 degrees Fahrenheit. Start the first day by leaving them outdoors for 1 to 2 hours; each day extend the time for longer periods until they are left outdoors from 10 to 12 hours. Near the end of the second week, they should be hardened enough to stay outdoors in a wind-protected area overnight.

To transplant, dig a hole slightly bigger than the pot's size, gently hold the soil surrounding the seedling, carefully turn the container sideways and tap the bottom of the pot until the plant comes out. If the plant is stuck, run a knife between the container and soil. Do not hold the seedling by its stem while removing or placing it in the hole. Handle the seedling by its rootball, gently place it in the hole, fill with soil, and lightly tamp the soil around it. Pinch back the tip growth to encourage the development of its root system. Generally, seedlings mature in a month, and continue to bloom for another two months.

Before planting seeds directly outdoors, prepare and amend your annual planting beds so that the soil is loam or sandy loam;. see page 307 to read about ideal soil textures. Dig a shallow trench at the depth recommended on the seed packet, partially fill with an organic soil mix or your own loam soil, sow the seeds, and cover them with the rest of the soil. Sow slightly more seeds than suggested to prevent unsightly bare spots due to non-germinating seeds. You can always thin out any excess sprouts.

Summer annuals are sold in cell-packs at retail nurseries during spring. Make sure the soil has been properly prepared and amended; read pages 307 to 308 on soil preparation. Here are a few tips to give them a good start in your garden:

- Select plants that are short and stocky with dark green leaves.
- Make sure all the cells are filled with plants. If any are missing, it may mean they died from disease or neglect.
- Avoid cell-packs with plants whose roots are growing out of the drainage holes. These plants are already root-bound and will not transplant very well.
- Plant during a cloudy day or in the late afternoon to give them time to recover from transplant shock before being exposed to hot sun.
- Water the cell-pack first so the individual plants slide out more easily.
- Carefully turn the cell-pack sideways;

remove each plant by gently crumpling the cell, gingerly pushing the plant out with the eraser end of a pencil or chopstick, and letting gravity do the rest.

- If the plant is stuck, run a knife between the soil and the container.
- Gently separate any matted roots without damaging them.
- Dig a planting hole deep enough so that the new soil level is the same level as that at which the plant was previously growing.
- Yanking the plant out of the cell pack or handling the plant by its stem can cause root or stem breakage. Instead, handle by the rootball.
- Fill in around the roots with soil, tamp lightly, and water in gently with a solution of a root stimulator or an organic planting solution rich in humic acid and micorrhizal fungi (beneficial fungi that keep the soil healthy).
- Pinch back the young plant tips to stimulate root growth.

Container planting for spots of spring color is another way to bring the season into your garden, decks, patio, and poolside. See Summer Planting.

WATERING

California's rainy season extends from November to the middle of March and in a perfect world, there would be a gentle soaking rain between 3 and 5 a.m. every Monday and Friday morning. Since this cycle doesn't exist in the real world, supplemental watering is necessary. It is important that soil moisture be kept at what is called "field capacity." Think of soil as a sponge; field capacity is like the amount of water the sponge can hold before saturation causes the excess water to drip out.

The best time to water is early morning or late afternoon. If fungal diseases such as rust or mildew are problems, water annuals in the early morning so that any water splashed onto the foliage has time to dry out during the day.

As temperatures warm and daylight increases, growth accelerates and plants require additional moisture. Monitor the soil moisture around newly planted annuals every other day or until the absorbing roots grow sufficiently enough to supply adequate moisture and to support the plant's structure.

Fungi such as water molds can damage plant roots if the water does not drain through its root zone. Avoid root rot by keeping the soil porous enough so that it drains well (see page 32 on soil amendments).

Do not allow newly sown seeds to dry out. Water daily, using a spray nozzle with a fine-mist setting or a spray bottle and be careful not to wash away the soil, exposing the seeds. Daily misting keeps the soil around the seeds evenly moist until the seeds give way to true leaves. Allow the surface to dry out before watering again (it feels dry to the touch about 1 inch below the surface).

It is a bit tricky striking the right chord between too little and too much water. Learn by observing and let your fingers teach you how and when to water. Most annuals wilt and eventually collapse when watered too infrequently or break off from their roots if watered too often. Petunias, calibrachoas, Indian peas, and coleus are notorious water-needy annuals, while others such as celosia, cosmos, moss rose, spurred snapdragons, and sunflowers tolerate drier conditions once they are established. After annuals have established their root systems, water them thoroughly and allow the soil surface to dry before watering again. Test with your fingers; if it feels dry to the touch 1 to 2 inches below the surface, water again.

FERTILIZING

Transplanting solutions such as a root stimulator product or an organic planting solution (1-3-1 NPK) with humic acid give annuals a boost by encouraging the development of their root systems.

Apply an organic liquid fertilizer (12-12-6 NPK) monthly; begin 2 to 4 weeks after planting. If your time is limited, consider using a controlled-release fertilizer or connecting a liquid fertilizer injection system to your sprinklers. Depending on the manufacturer, controlled-release fertilizers last 4 to 6 months, while water-soluble organic fertilizers are applied more frequently. Organic fertilizers are utilized by the plants as they need them and controlled-release fertilizers are delivered to the plant in small doses. Both types prevent rapid vegetative growth, which often causes leaf burn. It also takes the worry out of fertilizing plants that are light feeders such as cosmos and globe amaranth.

Fertilize annuals in containers every 2 weeks with a water-soluble organic fertilizer or about once every 4 months with a controlled-release food.

A granular fertilizer is another feeding option for annuals, but do not drop any on the plants because it will burn them. Water the fertilizer in as soon as it's applied and wash off any residue that accidentally spills on the plants. Follow the manufacturer's directions for frequency of application.

MAINTAINING

Once annuals are established, cultivate the soil surface to keep it from crusting. This allows air and moisture to move in and out of the surface of the soil and also prevents weeds.

If frost is imminent, mist an antitranspirant over your annuals; the coating provides insulation from the cold. If they have sturdy enough stems, you can protect them from the cold by covering them with a cotton sheet or with a loose covering of straw. Never use plastic because the cold goes right through plastic.

Before preparing a new planting bed for annuals, eradicate any weeds prior to reconditioning the soil by applying glyphosate, a non-selective, systemic herbicide. For a more benign control—and if you have the time—solarize the soil (refer to the glossary for a definition of "solarizing").

Do not use a pre-emergent weed control if you are growing annual plants from seeds sown directly in the soil. Wait until the annual seeds are germinated and their root systems are established before applying pre-emergent weed controls. These products work on *all* seeds, not just on weeds.

Towards the end of spring or beginning of summer (depending on when the seed heads have formed), collect heirloom seeds for next year's supply of cool-season annuals. It is best to collect ripe seeds just before the flowers disperse them. Begin checking the seeds a couple of weeks after the flowers have faded and harvest them when they feel dry to the touch. They are the most viable and are likely to germinate without extraordinary effort. Seeds usually develop in casings. It is a good idea to collect only unopened, dry seed casings because they have usually protected the seeds from disease and insect infestation. Place the casings in a paper or cloth bag (never in a closed plastic container because the casings will sweat) and put the casings in a tray. Place the tray in a sunny location until the casings split open, allowing easy seed extraction. Small seeds take 7 to 10 days to dry, while large seeds need about 2 weeks. Put the seeds in a paper envelope, label the envelope with the name of the annual and the date of storage, and store them in a glass jar with an airtight lid. Since fluctuations of temperatures can harm seeds, set the jar in a cool, dry, dark location or refrigerator until it is time to plant. Be aware that hybrids do not replicate true to form, so unless you want to roll the botanical dice, don't collect seed from hybrids. It is not necessary to collect seeds from self-seeding annuals such as alyssum and nasturtiums.

Pinch off any budded or open flowers and pinch back the tip growth of newly purchased annual bedding plants. It may seem like cruel and unusual punishment for such young plants just starting out in your garden, but it keeps the energy flowing towards development of their root systems and vigorous growth.

Encourage continued growth and reblooming by removing faded flowers (deadheading) from established annuals weekly (unless you are saving seeds). Regular deadheading before seeds are formed is a small price to pay in order to keep Iceland poppies, primroses, and petunias on the flower production line. Or plant self-cleaning annuals such as four o'clocks, calibrachoas, and pansies if you dislike deadheading chores. A few annuals such as alyssum and moss rose bloom as soon as growth occurs and usually do not need deadheading or pinching back.

Pinch back stem ends to prevent annuals from becoming too open, leggy, or floppy. It also enables new growth to emerge at points lower down the stem.

If annuals are damaged by a late frost, do not prune them back until new growth shows. The location on the stems where new growth occurs indicates the point where the stem is still viable. Of course, if the stems turn black and collapse, start over with new plants.

Select cold-tolerant annuals such as alyssum, cornflowers, dianthus, pansies, and violas over the more frost-tender annuals like celosia, marigold, and zinnia if there is a history of late spring freezes.

PROTECTING

If your garden is being invaded by opossums, raccoons, rabbits, or squirrels use a live trap available at agricultural supply stores or retail garden centers to snare the critters. Then you can move them to another location or to an animal shelter. Identify the critters by their footprints. Moisten the soil surface near the damaged plants, lightly rake the surface, then be patient.

Use a physical gopher trap or poisonous bait if your garden is being invaded by gophers. If you decide to use the bait, read and follow the instructions. Where moles are a problem, use a guillotine mole trap. In a single season, we trapped and relocated over 60 ground squirrels to less residential areas because they were undermining the stability of a slope in our yard. Raptors such as red tail hawks, owls, golden eagles, kestrels, and harriers are good guys because they help control the rodent population.

Water molds are soilborne fungi that are active year-round in water-saturated, heavy clay soils. They invade the root systems of plants and prevent them from absorbing moisture and nutrients. The damage is very easy to identify. Look for brown, mushy, and decaying roots. At the point where the stem of the plant becomes a root system, which is usually at ground level, the stem looks as if a person took a thumb and forefinger and pinched the stem together. If you touch a plant that has been invaded by water molds, the top of the plant may appear fine but when touched, it falls over. Pull up the infected plants, throw them away in the trash, and solarize the soil.

Prevention is the best control for water molds. Increase the porosity and organic content by blending compost, humus mulch, worm castings, or comparable amendment into the soil. Planting in raised beds containing porous, highly organic soil also reduces or eliminates standing water in the root zones. While preventative measures are the first line of defense, it may be necessary to use chemicals. Aliette® (Fosetyl-A1) is most effective if used in the early stages of infection, but should not be used too often because fungi develop resistance to continual applications.

To save time, money, and frustration, control insects early. The appearance of aphids is astounding. One day there are only a few, the next day it seems there are thousands of them. Actually aphids multiply geometrically because they are parthenogenic, so they can reproduce sexually and asexually. Washing aphids off with a strong stream of water is a benign, but effective, way to control their population. Releasing lady beetles, lacewings, and mantids or using biodegradable and natural insect controls are also excellent controls. You can obtain these controls at garden centers or by mail through regional insectaries.

Monitor and control insect pest activity by using pheromone traps, available through regional insectaries or garden centers.

Leafhoppers, scales, thrips, and other chewing, sucking, or rasping insects are miniscule but mighty terminators of annuals. Get rid of them for up to one year by applying a systemic pesticide containing the active ingredient imidacloprid and following the label directions. For an organic approach, syringe the pests off with a stream of water, use a synthetic pyrethroid (synthetic compound similar to liquid extracted from chrysanthemums), or use a garlic-based insecticide. Spraying with water, pyrethroids, or garlic-based insecticides are direct contact controls and must be used whenever new infestations land on the plants. Horticultural oils are effective direct contact suffocants. Use when there is no rain predicted within 72 hours of application or when temperatures are below 75 degrees Fahrenheit.

Subterranean cut worms and grubs are ugly, grayish-brown, hairless caterpillars that destroy absorbing roots, which causes plants to wilt or even sever seedlings at ground level. Cut worms are larvae of night-flying moths and grubs are larvae of beetles; they curl up their fleshy bodies when disturbed. They come to the surface when you are digging around the garden or watering deeply. Apply a season-long granular or liquid grub control containing the active ingredient imidacloprid. **Caution:** Do not use this control near annuals intended for culinary purposes such as nasturtiums or pansies.

Snails and slugs slither, slime, and dine on fresh spring plants. Decollate snails—which are permitted in counties south of Kern County, but always double-check with your county agriculture department to verify—are available at retail nurseries and insectaries as a beneficial control because they devour juvenile brown garden snails and their eggs as well as slug eggs. Once the garden snails and slugs are under control, decollates will continue to feed on decomposing organic material, but they will not attack most plants (they might go after some seedlings if their "protein" source is gone). 100 decollate snails are usually sufficient for an average-sized yard and 1,000 are sufficient per acre. Refresh their population every 2 to 3 years. Iron phosphate is another effective, organic control, but do not use decollate snails if you're applying iron phosphate.

ANNUALS TO PLANT IN SPRING

PLANT NAME	START FROM
Alyssum	seeds or pony packs
Baby's Breath	seeds or 4-inch pot size plants
Calibrachoa	color packs or 4-inch pot size plants
Candytuft	seeds, pony packs, or color packs
Celosia	pony packs or color packs
Cosmos	seeds, pony packs, or color packs
Four o'Clock	seeds or pony packs
Globe Amaranth	seeds or pony packs
Iceland Poppy	color packs or 4-inch pot size plants
Impatiens	seeds, pony packs, or color packs
Indian Pea	seeds
Lobelia	seeds or pony packs
Marigold	seeds or pony packs
Moss Rose	seeds or pony packs
Nasturtium	seeds
Nemesia	color packs or 4-inch pot size plants
Pansy	4-inch pot size plants
Petunia	seeds, pony packs, color packs, or 4-inch pot size plants
Phlox	seeds, pony packs, or color packs
Primrose	4-inch pot size plants
Snapdragon	seeds, pony packs, or color packs
Spurred Snapdragon	seeds or 4-inch pot size plants
Sunflower	seeds or 1-gallon size pots
Sweetpea	seeds or pony packs
Viola	pony packs or color packs
Zinnia	seeds or pony packs

SUMMER

Sunflowers are the floral soul mates to summer's languid, humid days. Rather than peeking shyly from the protective cover of dappled light, they bask in the full sun turning their heads to follow it across the azure sky.

PLANNING

If you live along the coastal areas, summer temperatures are a fun time to putter in the garden, but in the hotter inland valleys, plan your annual planting and preparation activities before the onset of blistering summer heat and dry, desiccating winds.

Terracotta containers filled with colorful annuals add a splash of informal charm to gardens and patios, but plastic containers retain moisture better. Potting soil should "breathe" (meaning it should drain well), not pots. In containers that breathe, plants dry out almost daily in hot summer weather and often collapse. Before planting annuals in porous, clay pots, coat the inside with an asphalt emulsion or terracotta sealer available at your local home improvement store or garden center.

Loll under the shade of a sheltering tree, sip a frosty glass of lemonade, and "journal" in your garden notebook. Jot down the varieties of summer annuals planted, the successes, disappointments, and new ideas inspired from vacation visits, strolls through public gardens, and newspaper and magazine articles.

Paste photographs of your landscape and other gardens into your journal. Don't forget to include any news and magazine clippings that have been accumulating in the "save for future garden plans" pile.

Summer is vacation time for children and grandchildren. Pass on the tradition of family gardening and set aside a space for a child to call his or her own. By definition, an annual lives its entire life in one season; because of this quick growth and development, a child can observe its complete cycle over a few weeks. Be there for help and guidance, but let them choose what to plant inside their plot. It may be an all purple garden (petunia, morning glory, angelonia) or other favorite color or a garden that attracts butterflies and hummingbirds (marigolds, impatiens, zinnias) or a scented garden (four o'clocks, chocolate cosmos, phlox). With encouragement, children are enthusiastic gardeners. Even toddlers can dig holes and plant large seeds such as sunflower. Older children can transplant seedlings, pick off bugs, release beneficial insects such as ladybugs, and begin to identify different plants. Everyone, young and old, knows how to splash in mud puddles and make mushy mud pies. Purchase some inexpensive, child-sized tools and buckets and let them dig in the dirt, smell the flowers, watch bugs, or look at leaves. Gardening with children teaches us that structure is not nearly as important as living life. In turn, give your children and grandchildren a garden that is a haven from the hustling, bustling pressures of life.

PLANTING

Remove cool-season annuals such as pansies, violas, primroses, and Iceland poppies if you haven't done so already. Fill in the spaces with hot-weather color, plants that thrive and fill out quickly in the summer sun. No matter where you live in California, summer months are perfect to display petunias, calibrachoas, cosmos, angelonias, and four o'clocks front and center. Coleus are an old-time favorite for those shady nooks, but many recent cultivars tolerate full sun and come in a rainbow of brilliant colors.

To avoid the hurdles of growing annuals from seeds during summer, it is generally better to plant them from bedding plants. Insects, diseases, rodents, birds, and other pests abound during summer and inflict damage on tender seedlings. Also, immature plants are no match for intense heat or dry winds.

Some exceptions to this general rule are the more robust sunflowers, marigolds, and zinnias. They can still be sown outdoors because they germinate quickly and grow like weeds. Prepare the soil as recommended on page 32. Follow the planting directions specified on the seed packet and tamp the soil with a trowel or your hand to make sure the seeds and soil are set firmly in place.

At the end of summer, start seeds of winter annuals such as dianthus, Iceland poppies, pansies, snapdragons, stock, and violas and they will be ready to transplant by midfall.

When buying bedding annuals during summer, it is important to select plants that are not rootbound. Annuals that are transplanted with thickly matted, rootbound roots do not readily absorb moisture and may collapse as a result. Pass on those fully opened, larger, and older flowering annuals with roots sticking out of their containers' drainage holes, a definite sign that they are rootbound. Opt instead for younger starter plants that have little or no flowering buds and whose roots are still contained in their cell packs or pots.

Spruce up your summer garden with hanging baskets and container plantings. Line wire baskets with sphagnum moss, fill with an organic potting soil, and plant cascading petunias, alyssum, and verbena. Tuck in angelonias, coleus and, in shaded areas, impatiens for welcome spots of color. Select containers with drainage holes in the bottom and cut out pieces of screening or coffee filters to place over the holes. This keeps the potting mix from washing out. Researchers have learned that gravel, rocks, or shards of broken pottery placed over the holes do not improve drainage. For containers and baskets, adding a water-holding polymer to the potting soil mix can reduce the frequency of watering by as much as 50 percent. Follow the manufacturer's directions closely because water-retentive polymers turn into a gel and "runneth over" if you add too much. Just as in bedding areas, plant taller annuals such as cosmos, zinnias, and sunflowers towards the center or back of the container, followed by medium-height plants such as phlox or baby's breath, lastly, add low-growing or cascading varieties such as calibrachoa around the edge. Make sure you have planted annuals with similar light, water, and fertilizing needs. Most annuals are water-thirsty and heavy feeders, but some varieties are drought tolerant when mature, such as celosia, cosmos, dusty miller, amaranthus, and verbena. Dianthus and impatiens thrive under shade, but cockscomb, sunflowers, and zinnias love their faces in the sun all day long.

WATERING

When spring turns to summer, the evapotranspiration rate increases. This means it's time to adjust your irrigation clock to keep the soil moist, but not saturated. Test the soil periodically and in different areas, by pushing a pointed shovel into the ground and pushing the soil up; if the soil is damp, wait 2 to 3 more days before deep soaking the area. Learn the watering needs of summer annuals. Coleus and impatiens prefer shady areas and usually tolerate wetter soil conditions, but once established, dusty miller, marigolds, and sunflowers prefer soil on the drier side.

For newly sown seeds, do not allow the soil to dry out. Mist daily or even more frequently during hot, dry spells until the seeds germinate and their true leaves appear. Once the seedlings begin to grow, decrease the frequency of watering, but still keep the soil moist. Refer to Spring Watering.

During the hot summer months there is a tendency to water our plants every day or even two or three times per day. When mature plants are watered deeply, their roots reach downward, thus remaining cooler. But, if plants are lightly spritzed, their roots tend to grow near the soil surface and may shrivel during hot weather. Also, deep watering about once a week conserves water, builds healthier plants, and saves time. During hot, dry windy conditions, it is necessary to water more frequently. The best time of day to water is early morning or late afternoon, but if fungal diseases such as mildew are attacking your annuals, water only in the early morning. One method to prevent fungus such as mildew from developing is to water at ground level rather than from above so moisture does not get on the leaves.

The general guideline for watering any outdoor plants is to deep soak if one inch of rainfall has not fallen in the last week. If you have clay soil, the rule of thumb states to water if two inches of rainfall has not fallen; one inch applies to loam soils. In most areas of California, one to two inches of rainfall per week during summer is unlikely. Our hot, dry summer months are incentives to consider drip irrigation or soaker hoses.

For containers or annuals planted in sandy soils, water more frequently. During the hottest weather, it is almost impossible to overwater container plants. While it is a common recommendation to water container plants in the early morning, recent studies show morning watering stresses plants and retards growth. When plants are watered in the afternoon, their rate of photosynthesis increases and their growth accelerates as much as 70 percent more than morning soakings. Apparently, plants respond to cool dips during the heat of the day (anytime from noon to 6 p.m.), just like us.

Ask a garden-savvy neighbor or hire a professional to water your thirsty plants while you're on vacation. Make sure he or she understands that container plants need to be watered daily during periods of hot days and warm evenings, unless they have been planted in a soil mix with water-retentive polymers. When polymers are used, containers can be watered every 2 or 3 days during peak summer heat.

FERTILIZING

Beginning in early summer, fertilize bedding annuals every month with a complete liquid organic plant food (12-12-6) with humic acid added to its formula or hand broadcast a complete, granular, organic fertilizer onto the cultivated ground. After applying a granular fertilizer, thoroughly water the area with a fan sprayer attached to a garden hose. Wash off any residue that drifts onto the foliage and flowers. Spray liquid fertilizers uniformly across the planting bed directly on the foliage.

Just like people, plants need a balanced diet to flourish and remain healthy. Whether your annuals are heavy or light feeders, seedlings, or mature bedding plants, organic fertilizers are preferable because they form a storehouse in the soil, soil fertility is increased for the long-term, and they are released gradually to the plant as it needs nutrients.

Most chemical fertilizers offer high doses of nitrogen, phosphorous, and potassium (NPK), but do not include vital humic and amino acids as well as organic materials, which also support the life of beneficial microbes and micronutrients. The beneficial microorganisms in the soil enable nutrients to become available to plants as their root systems need them. Organic fertilizers maintain soil fertility by supplying organic matter, improving soil structure, and releasing nutrients gradually. Most chemical fertilizers are salt- or acid-based and formulated to be fast acting. Since plants cannot absorb such a high concentration of NPK, a residue is left behind in the soil, which decreases soil fertility and suppresses beneficial microbial populations. For gardeners seeking convenience, a controlled-release chemical fertilizer is a good compromise because the NPK nutrients are released slowly and it remains effective for 4 to 6 months. Containers need more frequent fertilizing because potting soil is porous, which allows water to drain well. This also means nutrients leach more rapidly from the soil. To compensate, fertilize every two weeks at $1/2$ the concentration recommended by the manufacturer for chemical or synthetic fertilizers, or use a water-soluble organic food at the recommended full strength every two weeks. A controlled-release fertilizer is another ideal option for container-grown annuals because they slowly release nutrients over a long period and do not need to be reapplied for another 4 to 6 months. Select a slow-release fertilizer that includes trace elements as well as basic nutrients, or use organic fertilizers with humic acid.

MAINTAINING

Towards the end of summer, stop watering annuals that are losing their growth and blooming momentum and replace them with cool-season annuals for fall. Some warm-season annuals will come back to grow and bloom again if they are clipped back. Petunias, calibrachoas, and angelonias are great bloomers from late spring until frost.

If the weather permits and summer annuals such as zinnias, cosmos, marigolds, and rudbeckias continue to grow and flower, pinch back their stem ends and seedheads to encourage compactness and continued growth.

A sudden rainstorm can knock down taller annuals. Wait a day to see if they are "down for the count" and if they are, try to get them back into an upright stance. If they can't stand on their own, support them with stakes. Now is also a good time to stake those lanky sunflowers so they won't flop during windy or rainy days.

To keep shallow annual roots cool and retain moisture, mulch the soil surface with a $1/2$ to 1-inch layer of worm castings, humus, or compost. Make sure the mulch is distributed away from the stems (about 2 to 4 inches) to prevent the stems from rotting.

After seedlings have formed two sets of true leaves, thin them out to improve air circulation and plant vigor.

New generations of weeds love to pop up and flourish in annual flower beds. Long daylight hours and the heat of the summer sun make this an ideal time to solarize the soil of fallow bedding plant areas. You can also make toast of weed seeds by using a corn gluten-based mulch or pre-emergent weed control if you are planting annuals from bedding plants rather than from seed.

Deadhead and pinch off yellowed or damaged foliage once a week to keep annuals well groomed and flowering.

If annuals are leggy or bloom-impaired, cut them back and they should start up their flower factories in 2 to 3 weeks. Petunias, baby's breath, calibrachoas, nemesias, and angelonias appreciate snipping and grooming. Pinch off the tips of coleus and other foliar annuals to encourage a fuller, bushier growth habit. Some plants such as impatiens are self-cleaning, meaning they shed their dead blossoms on their own, but others such as petunias and marigolds need to have their old flowerheads snapped off.

PROTECTING

Marigolds are often recommended as a rabbit and gopher deterrent. In our experience, traps, bait, or kitty cats are much more effective. Bloodmeal is another common deterrent to keep deer, rabbits, and squirrels away, but it must be reapplied after a rainy period. A biennial *Euphorbia* commonly known as gopher purge exudes a milky latex in its leaves, flowers, and roots supposedly causing one heck of stomach ache or even death if a gnoshing gopher eats enough of it. Unfortunately, reputed controls such as gopher purge, castor bean, oleander plants, flooding, moth balls, sonic vibrators, and Juicy Fruit™ chewing gum are all remedies that are the stuff of urban legends rather than scientific fact. Manual traps, gopher baits, and natural predators are the tried-and-true gopher terminators.

Slugs and snails thrive in summer. Control them with iron phosphate or decollate snails. See Spring Protecting.

Inspect annuals for leafminers, thrips, caterpillars, aphids, mites and other chewing, sucking, and rasping insects. If there are no plants with edible parts in your annual bed or if you don't plan to eat any of the edible ones, use a granular, systemic insect control. Caterpillars are the larvae of butterflies and moths that chew on foliage voraciously. Fortunately there are beneficial bacteria, such as *Bacillus thuringiensis* (also known as Bt) that disrupt the digestive system of caterpillars causing the creepy crawlers to starve themselves to death. Botanicals are plant-derived controls such as pyrethrum, rotenone, and azadirachtin that have been synthesized for pest control. They are effective against destructive insects such as adelgids, aphids, whitefly, scale, mites, and thrips, but not against caterpillars or leafminers; they usually require repeated applications. Horticultural oils are highly refined petroleum products that act as suffocants when sprayed directly on scales and mites. Do not spray horticultural oils during the heat of the day. Wait until late afternoon or early evening.

Hordes of greenhouse whiteflies plague warm-weather gardeners. They are miniscule $1/16$-inch winged insects that congregate under leaves and then flit out in clouds whenever their havens are disturbed. Carefully lift a leaf and you can spot them hiding underneath. Since whiteflies proliferate rapidly between egg and adult stages, they are very difficult to control. Once their eggs hatch, the microscopic larvae suck on plant juices, weakening the plant and excreting sticky honeydew that is ambrosia to ants. If you spot a beginning infestation before hordes of colonies establish themselves, try sticky yellow traps for greenhouses and patios (available at retail nurseries) or release beneficial insects such as ladybugs or the parasitic wasp, *Encarsia formosa,* sold at insectaries or garden centers. Insecticidal soap, horticultural oil, or garlic-based organic insecticides are also appropriate remedies, but must be reapplied about once a week until the whiteflies are gone. It is also important to get rid of the ants because they move the whitefly larvae from plant to plant as they harvest their honeydew like dairy farmers. Destroy ant colonies with boric acid ant bait or an organic contact product containing d'limonene (citrus oil).

Twice the size of common whiteflies, giant whiteflies deposit their eggs in a circular pattern underneath leaves; their larvae excrete so much honeydew it resembles streams of white, cotton candy hanging from leaves. They are one of the most persistent pests and if horticultural oil or garlic-based insecticides are ineffective, use the systemic insect control imidacloprid. This control is absorbed by the plant's roots and transported into the plant's canopy. **Caution:** Do not apply on plants that are for culinary use. Apply all pest controls according to label directions.

Rust is a fungus that appears as rusty-brown, powdery pustules, primarily on foliage. It weakens the plant and—if left unchecked—the annual could suffer an untimely death. Space plants for good air circulation. Since dry foliage impedes the onset of rust, water at the base of the plant rather than overhead and water in the early morning to allow wet leaves enough time to dry out before evening. Remove any diseased foliage, on the plant or on the ground, and throw it away in the trash. Once established, rust is a challenge to control. Organic controls to combat rust are safe to use such as the extract from lemon myrtle, *Backhousia citriodora.* There is even a tea made from lemon myrtle. As a last resort, fungicides such as Triforine™ or Daconil™ are listed as controls for rust on annuals. Follow the formulator's instructions and wear protective apparel such as goggles, face masks, gloves, long-sleeved shirts, and long pants. If the plants are covered with rust, it is probably better to pull them up and dispose of them in the trash.

Mildew is a fungus that starts on the topside of leaves and looks like white, powdery patches. Its spores thrive in dry weather and spread by wind. Mildew saps plant nutrients causing foliage, and even the entire plant, to die. Good air circulation is a must to prevent mildew. Allow enough space between plants and remove infected leaves on the plant as well as those that have fallen on the ground. Spray with a benign control such as an antitranspirant, Neem oil, or a lemon myrtle oil extract. Daconil™ is a chemical fungicide and should be used according to the formulator's directions. Wear protective clothing when applying chemical fungicides.

ANNUALS TO PLANT IN SUMMER

PLANT NAME	START FROM
African Daisy	color packs, 4-or 6-inch pots, or 1-gallon size plants
Ageratum	pony packs, color packs, or 4-inch pot size plants
Alyssum	seeds, pony packs, or color packs
Amaranthus	color packs or 4-inch pot size plants
Angelonia	color packs or 4- or 6-inch pot size plants
Baby's Breath	4-inch pots or 1-gallon size plants
Calibrachoa	pony packs or 4-inch pots
Cockscomb	color packs or 4-inch pot size plants
Coleus	color packs or 4- or 6-inch pot size plants
Cosmos	color packs or 4-inch pot size plants
Dianthus	pony packs, color packs, or 4-inch pot size plants
Dusty Miller	pony packs, color packs, or 4- or 6-inch pot size plants
Four O'Clock	seeds, pony packs, or color packs
Impatiens	color packs or 4- or 6-inch pot size plants
Lisianthus	color packs or 4- or 6-inch pot size plants
Lobelia	seeds or pony packs
Marigold	pony packs, color packs, or 4-inch pot size plants
Morning Glory	seeds or pony packs
Petunia	pony packs
Phlox	pony packs or 4-inch pot size plants
Pinks	pony packs, color packs, or 1-gallon size plants
Sunflower	color packs, 4-or 6-inch pots, or 1-gallon size plants
Verbena	color packs
Wax Begonia	4- or 6-inch pot size plants
Zinnia	pony packs or color packs

AUTUMN

Fall is California's second spring bearing gifts of flowers, flowers, and more flowers. Even with so many choices, pansies are impossible to ignore with their painted faces in every imaginable color, shouting "pick me, pick me!"

PLANNING

Keep a record of temperature variations in your yard over several years and note important events such as heat waves and early frosts. Identify microclimates in your garden and the plants that survive or flourish in those particular areas. There are bound to be spots that are cooler or warmer than the rest of your garden. On a cool autumn day, settle down with a hot cup of apple cider and think about what you really loved in your annual flower beds, what did not work out, and what changes you would like to make. Then write these thoughts down before you begin planting existing flower beds or creating new ones. In most areas of California, the soil is still cozy enough for cool-season annuals to snuggle in, expand, and take hold. Study the sun and shade areas in your garden; trees and tall shrubs continue to grow and light conditions can change as a result.

Decide whether you want to replace those shabby or spent summer annuals with cool-season annuals. If the answer is "yes", then select plants in coordinating colors with the established annuals or be prepared to start all over with a new color palette. Don't forget that autumn or winter annuals are effective when planted in hanging baskets and pots. Ornamental peppers in brilliant yellows, oranges, reds, and purples provide fall pizzazz in containers and jazz up winter-white stocks and snapdragons.

Keep old cotton sheets handy in case there is a forecast of early frost. They are easily removed during the day when temperatures have warmed up.

If your area experiences a few bouts of frosty temperatures in autumn and you want to start a new planting bed anyway, purchase rolls of landscape fabric from retail nurseries. They are handy to use for bedding plants and provide an extra 2 to 4 degrees of protection.

PLANTING

Now that the temperatures are milder and the air is turning cooler, it is a pleasure to dig and discard spent plants and flowers and replace them with the more burnished or quieter colors of fall and winter. Replant or add cool-season annuals to your pots.

A good fall cleaning reduces pest and disease problems that flourish in plant debris. Renovate the soil by turning it over and begin blending in a preplant fertilizer such as cottonseed meal at a rate of 2 pounds per hundred square feet, soil sulfur at a rate of 1 pound per hundred square feet, humus mulch at a rate of 2 cubic feet per hundred square feet, worm castings at the rate described on the bag, and gypsum at a rate of 10 pounds per hundred square feet. If the soil pH is as high as 8.5, make the initial gypsum application at a rate of 6 pounds per 100 square feet. Calcium chloride products are now available that are easily applied compared to gypsum (32 ounces of calcium chloride cover up to 1,000 square feet depending on soil and pH conditions). Rake the surface smooth, remove large rocks and large clods, saturate the soil with water, and let the soil settle. Once it has settled, rake it smooth one more time and it's ready for replanting.

Pansies, violas, johnny-jump-ups, stocks, snapdragons, Iceland poppies, ornamental kale, and ornamental peppers are available at your local garden center in cell- or pony-packs. Plant them now so that their roots will have time to establish before cold weather sets in. Pinch off the flower buds and tip growth to redirect more energy into root development. The plants will also be fuller and form more blooming stems. Make sure the soil has been tamped down to remove air pockets. Air pockets allow cold air to reach tender roots and possibly freeze them. Refer to Spring Planting.

Plant your cool-season seedlings in autumn for mature blossoms by the winter holidays. Read about transplanting seedlings in Spring Planting.

Save money by taking cuttings of your warm-season annuals, rooting and planting them outdoors next spring. Annuals such as coleus and impatiens are very easy to propagate by cuttings. Snip 4- to 6-inch length cuttings just below leaf nodes (the point where a leaf forms). Take cuttings in fall before cold weather sets in. Strip off most of their leaves and all of their flowers (allowing energy to go to root development). Do not place the cuttings in water because proper root development needs moisture and air circulation. Since there is no air circulation in water, stems and roots are susceptible to rot. Instead, plant cuttings in sterile mediums such as vermiculite or perlite to retain moisture and permit airflow. Before planting, dip the cut ends in a rooting hormone, mist the cuttings and the medium with tepid water, and place a plastic bag over them until they have established roots. Avoid direct contact between the plastic and the cutting and find a warm spot that has indirect light. Bottom heaters for plant propagation also encourage faster rooting. Identify the annual by labeling popsicle sticks or plastic labels with a permanent marker. Use sterilized plastic pots (washed in 1 part bleach to 10 parts water) or resealable plastic bags to plant your cuttings. Refer to Winter Planting for information on the "baggie method."

Many people prefer to replace their annuals by shopping for them in season at retail nurseries, but for those who don't mind the extra effort, many annuals can be overwintered. Cosmos is one of them. Dig up the cosmos roots in autumn after their bloom cycle is complete and place them in a plastic pot. Store in a cool dry area such as a garage or basement and plant again in spring. If they are planted in containers, move them to a dry protected area (under a deck for example) and stop watering. When spring arrives, replant in full sun and begin watering again.

WATERING

As the rhythms of fall become more apparent, the ambient temperature declines, the day length shortens, and the rainy season commences, which means you don't have to be out in the garden to water your annuals as much as during summer. (Santa Ana winds, drought, and high temperatures conditions can still make their appearance during autumn.) Moisture is still required, but at a lesser amount. Pick out a couple of spots in your yard where annuals are growing, one in full sun and the other shaded. Monitor the soil moisture at the two locations every few days and water when the soil is dry to the touch (down to a depth of 2 to 4 inches). The shady areas should not need to be watered as frequently as those in full sun. Be vigilant about watering needs during Santa Ana conditions of low humidity and high temperatures or extended periods of drought. If you are still in doubt, invest in a tensiometer (water meter) to guide you.

Water newly planted annuals thoroughly to collapse any air pockets. Thereafter, water every other day so that their shallow root systems receive adequate moisture. Within two weeks, new foliar growth should begin. Thereafter water deeply so the plants do not dry out and their roots grow downward rather than outward. Pansies, ornamental kale, Iceland poppies, stocks, and snapdragons need a constant supply of moisture to flourish. This applies to most fall annuals planted directly in the ground. In containers, they dry out more rapidly; during hot weather they need to be watered every day. Overwatering is rarely a problem for container plants unless the drainage holes are plugged.

Keep the soil around cuttings moist but not soggy. If excessive moisture condenses on the plastic covering, open or vent it to allow the soil and the cutting to dry out slightly.

Let your fingers guide you when it comes to watering seeds, seedlings, and cuttings. If the soil or planting medium feels dry to the touch, water thoroughly.

FERTILIZING

Use a root stimulator solution when transplanting annuals from containers to give them a head start in their new beds.

Although organic fertilizers are less effective during the cool season because the activity of soil microorganisms that make the nutrients available to the plants slows, they remain beneficial to growing plants and keep your soil healthy. For these reasons, use organic fertilizers about once a month during autumn. Organic foods with humic acid also help to fortify new plantings for future bouts of freezing weather. Another option is controlled-release feeding in encapsulated form. This type is not only a slow-release form of chemical fertilizer, but it only needs to be applied once every 3 to 6 months.

MAINTAINING

Collect heirloom seeds for next year's supply of summer annuals before digging them up. See Spring Maintaining for seed collection information.

Many annuals such as cosmos, four o'clocks, and alyssum are eager reseeders as long as care is taken not to disturb the soil too much when pulling up the parent plants. The seeds will sprout next spring and reward you with free plants.

Mulching with a 1- to 2-inch layer of humus, compost, or worm castings is a fine idea to maintain an even soil temperature around your fall annuals, but do not pile the mulch close to their stems. The stems might rot if mulch is piled up against them.

If some annuals develop persistent fungal disease, it is best to pull them up, remove the surrounding mulch, dispose of plants and mulch in heavy duty trash bags, and replace with fresh humus, compost, or worm castings. Otherwise the fungus could persist through the cooler seasons and come back to haunt spring and summer annuals again. Remove and dispose of container plants—as well as the soil—

if they are suffering from severe insect infestations or disease. Then clean the containers with a solution of 1 part bleach to 10 parts water and scrub them inside and out. Rinse with clear water and set out to dry; they will be ready for fresh organic potting soil. Cover the drainage holes with a fine wire mesh or coffee filters before filling the pots. To conserve water, add water-retentive polymers to the potting medium, but follow the manufacturer's directions.

Continue to pull up spent summer annuals such as sunflowers and use them to replenish your compost piles. Even better, cut off the old flower heads and place on a saucer for an autumn bird buffet.

Remove the spent flowers of your cool-season annuals such as pansies, violas, and johnny-jump-ups to encourage vigorous growth and prolong the bloom cycle. Pinch back plants that are beginning to look scraggly or leggy such as begonias or impatiens for a fuller, tidier appearance. Snip off any discolored or damaged leaves and remove any dead plants. Dead plants are havens for insects and diseases.

PROTECTING

Dig out young weeds as they appear so that next season's weeding will not be as tedious. As a preventative, protect newly planted and established annual beds and borders from weeds by using a mulch that contains corn gluten. It stops weed seeds from germinating and serves as a fertilizer. If you're planting annuals from seeds, do not use a corn gluten or pre-emergent product.

Since most regions of California experience mild weather and even bouts of hot, dry conditions during fall, pests continue to thrive and damage plants. Control caterpillars with Bt (*Bacillus thuringiensis*) or hand pick and squish if damage to annuals is extensive. Keep an eye out for spider mite infestations, aphids, beetles, mealybugs, scale, and whitefly; control them with a strong stream of water from a hose or use a garlic extract organic insecticide, insecticidal soap, or horticultural oil (in the case of scale). Add worm castings to raise the chitinase levels in plants (an enzyme that disintegrates chitin, the exoskeleton of insects). Sucking insects are repelled by the taste of plant juices with elevated chitinase levels, similar to our reaction of drinking sour milk. Systemic insecticide is another alternative if there are no plants with edible parts nearby. Use baits or traps to get rid of gophers in the flower beds. For snails and slugs, use iron phosphate or decollate snails (if they are permitted in your county), but do not apply iron phosphate if you have decollate snails.

ANNUALS TO PLANT IN AUTUMN

PLANT NAME	START FROM
Alyssum	seeds or pony packs
Annual African Daisy	4- or 6-inch pot size plants
Annual Phlox	color packs
Baby's Breath	4-inch pot size plants or 1-gallon size plants
Calendula	pony packs
Cineraria	color packs or 4- or 6-inch pot size plants
Columbine	4- or 6-inch pot size plants or 1-gallon size plants
Dianthus	color packs
Foxglove	4- or 6-inch pot size plants or 1 gallon size plants
Hollyhock	6-inch pot size plants or 1-gallon size plants
Iceland Poppy	pony packs or 4-inch pot size plants
Johnny-jump-up	pony packs or color packs
Larkspur	4- or 6-inch pot size plants
Lobelia	pony packs or color packs
Nasturtium	seeds
Nemesia	4-inch pot size plants
Ornamental Kale	4- or 6-inch pot size plants or 1-gallon size plants
Ornamental Pepper	color packs or 1-gallon size plants
Paludosum Daisy	4- or 6-inch pot size plants
Pansy	seeds, pony packs, or 4-inch pot size plants
Primrose	4-inch pot size plants
Snapdragon	pony packs
Stock	pony packs or color packs
Sweetpea	seeds, pony packs, or color packs
Sweet William	color packs
Viola	seeds, pony packs, or color packs

WINTER

It is the season of endings when evenings quickly cover the garden in black velvet. Lucky for us, cascading clusters of sweet alyssum and spires of stock blossoms provide moon-beams of light without disturbing winter's quiet slumber.

PLANNING

Winter provides a respite from many gardening chores and allows time to write in your journal. Jot down the high and low temperatures, amount of rainfall or snow, and list the annuals that are still thriving in your garden. Ask Santa for a high-low outdoor thermometer and a rain gauge if you don't already have them.

This is a good time to make plans for projects like a raised bed for specialty cut flowers. Raised beds are easier to maintain because they are less prone to weeds and, if designed with a maximum width of 4 feet, easy to reach and harvest the flowers.

Order seed and plant catalogues and review your own garden journal about plant successes and failures in order to better plan the coming year's annual plantings. High-light any new introductions in the catalogues or visit online websites for annuals, such as **www.all-americaselections.org**, to try some different varieties. Part of the fun of gardening is to incorporate new as well as standard themes in the landscape and annuals make a big impact compared to their relatively low cost.

If you want a head start on the annual planting season, start seeds in cell-packs (seed starter kits), peat pots, or expandable peat pellets (which contain fertilizer and fungicides to control damping off disease) where they can be easily protected from frost. Most annual seeds will germinate within two weeks. The starter plants should be set out into the garden after the last possibility of frost has passed; they will mature in about six weeks and continue to bloom for another eight weeks. See Planting for details. Check out the list of easy-to-start seeds on page 41.

Germinating seeds indoors makes it easier to maintain an average air tempera-ture between 65 and 70 degrees Fahrenheit. Suggested supplies for seed propagation are:

- Well-draining, organic potting soil or a soilless mix for starting seeds.
- Heating mat to keep the soil tem-perature at 70 degrees Fahrenheit.
- 2-inch diameter peat pots or expand-able peat pellets, called Jiffy 7's, which contain starter nutrients and a fungi-cide to control pathogens such as damping off. Since peat pots or peat pellets degrade readily, they can be planted directly into the ground without taking the seedlings out and possibly damaging their tender roots.
- Cart with grow lights if there is insuf-ficient natural light in your home.
- Nurseries commonly sell their starter plants in six-cell plastic containers. They are usually thrown away after the plants are removed, but they can be sterilized (wash with one part bleach to 10 parts water) to prevent any spread of fungal or bacterial disease and reused to plant seeds. These work well when you only have a few seeds to plant.

Carefully read the information listed on seed packets, especially when they should be started before planting them outdoors. 6 to 8 weeks is the usual time frame for most annuals. Among this group are ageratum, celosia, and dusty miller. Sow impatiens, petunias, and snapdragons about 10 weeks before outdoor life. Early germinators include cosmos, marigold, sunflower, and zinnia—they only need about 4 weeks before facing the great outdoors. To take the guesswork out of when to sow seeds indoors, count back from the last average frost date in your area and chart the start dates of your selected seeds. Do not sow them before that date because seedlings get leggy and weak if they are grown too long indoors. Allow an additional 2 weeks to "harden" your tender seedlings before transplanting them outdoors (read Spring Planting guidelines).

Some specialty hybrids may take more or less time than their generic cousins, so carefully check the seed packet.

Double-check for any special requirements. Many seeds such as morning glory and sweetpeas require scarifying (scratching or nicking the seed with a file or sand paper to help germination), while others such as varieties of wildflowers need stratifying (the process to overcome dormancy by cold treatment, usually wrapping seeds in a moistened paper towel, placing them in a resealable plastic bag, and setting in a refrigerator's vegetable bin for about a month).

Seed packets also tell you everything you should know about planting depth, amount of light, and whether or not the variety needs light or darkness for germination. Annual seeds that prefer light include four o'clocks, petunias, snapdragons, sunflowers, and ageratums. Those that grow in darkness are celosia and globe amaranth. Some annual seeds germinate in light or dark conditions such as cosmos, dianthus, marigold, sunflower, and zinnia.

Just like milk cartons, look for a seed packet's expiration date. Last year's date may affect the seed's viability. To determine whether or not they are past their prime, place about 10 seeds on a moistened paper towel, fold the towel in half, and put it in a sealed plastic bag. Set the bag in a warm location such as on top of the refrigerator. Check periodically up to 15 days. Determine the germination percentage by counting the number of sprouted seeds. For example, if 5 or 7 seeds sprouted, then that rate is 50 to 70 percent. If this is the case, sow the seeds more thickly than recommended to compensate for the lower germination percentage. Discard the seeds into a compost pile when germination is less than 50 percent.

PLANTING

In regions where winter temperatures are not severe or along coastal areas, winter annuals for color is still a happy option, but bear in mind that they will bloom a bit later than those planted towards the end of fall. Plant winter annuals in containers if the ground is too saturated. Iceland poppies, pansies, primroses, and violas make ideal container plants. Read Summer Planting for more details on container planting.

To plant seeds in containers for indoor germination, use an organic, well-draining potting soil mixture. Seed depth recommendations given on seed packets can be followed as long as these soil conditions are followed, but if the soil is heavier, plant the seeds slightly shallower than the directions (this also applies to outdoor planting). A good rule of thumb for planting depth is: the smaller the seeds, the shallower the depth of planting. If there are no directions, plant seeds at one to three times the greatest seed diameter. For most seeds, it is best to cover with soil rather than pushing them into the soil because novice and many experienced gardeners have a tendency to plant seeds too deeply. Use a pencil, popsicle stick, or chopstick; using a permanent marker, draw measurement lines in $1/2$ inch increments, up to 4 inches, for a simple seed hole maker. Premoisten the soil in the pot or seed-starter tray, poke a hole at the recommended depth, then cover the seeds with more soil and lightly mist the surface with water. A gentle spritzing keeps the seeds from washing away. Label with the name of the plant and the planting date. Cover the container with plastic and place where the temperature is between 68 to 75 degrees Fahrenheit or use a heating mat manufactured for starting seeds. If there is insufficient sunlight indoors to germinate seeds that need light, use grow lights and leave them on 24 hours, 7 days a week, until the seeds sprout.

Our radio co-host, John Bagnasco, introduced us to the "baggie method," an economical way to propagate seeds indoors. Using a permanent marker, label the bag noting the type of plant and date sown. Fill $1/3$ of a resealable plastic bag with perlite or vermiculite, moisten the medium (but do not get it soggy), distribute your seeds on the surface, and thinly top with more vermiculite or perlite. The number of seeds varies depending on their size and the size of the bag, but for average-sized seeds plant 4 in a sandwich bag and up to 12 for a gallon-sized bag. Mist lightly with tepid water, seal the bag, and place in a warm location. If it needs light to germinate, place on a windowsill. Open the bag up periodically if condensation covers the interior surface to prevent mildew or damping off. Lift the seedlings out when they have developed two sets of true leaves and transplant into 2-inch peat pots.

Some annual varieties, like poppies and violas, are difficult to sow because their seeds are so fine. To make planting easier, mix seeds with $1/4$ cup of fine sand in a plastic zip-lock bag and shake thoroughly. Fold a piece of note pad paper in half and sprinkle some of the sandy seed mixture in the crease. Distribute the seeds evenly by lightly tapping the paper over the pot filled with moistened, organic, fast-draining potting soil or soilless seeding medium. Gently mist with a spray bottle filled with water.

Most annual seeds will germinate within two weeks to a month. After germination comes the ruthless part. Carefully follow the thinning instructions on the seed packet. Otherwise your plants will become stunted from overcrowded conditions.

WATERING

Adjust watering to accommodate slower growth, cooler weather, and increased rain. Plants do not grow as fast in winter because of the shorter days and higher humidity. To avoid overwatering, change the settings on the irrigation system's timer. Although winter is considered part of the rainy season in California, look for areas in your garden that are not exposed to rain such as under eaves, patio covers, or tree canopies to make sure those areas receive supplemental watering. Turn off irrigation systems and drain the lines and valves in regions where freezing weather and snow is common.

Water indoor seedlings and cuttings with tepid water, 65 to 70 degrees Fahrenheit, and use a spray bottle to mist the planting medium until seeds or cuttings germinate. Make sure the containers are not sitting in water and do not overwater.

To water or not to water, that is the question. If too dry, seeds won't germinate and roots will shrivel, but if too wet, seeds and roots rot. Feel the soil and if slightly dry, water thoroughly. Remember cuttings and seedlings need to be kept moist, not soggy.

FERTILIZING

Wait about two weeks after planting outdoor winter annuals before fertilizing with an organic food. Then fertilize them one more time in late winter. Use organic fertilizers because they increase the health of the soil and do not encourage rapid, soft, frost-tender plant growth. If a chemical fertilizer is your preference, then select a controlled-release food and one that contains trace elements as well as basic nutrients.

Apply a 1- to 2-inch layer of compost over the soil of your annual beds and borders to stabilize the temperature of the soil and to suppress weeds. Another alternative is corn gluten mulch to moderate soil temperature and to provide nitrogen for winter annuals.

Winter rains dissolve and leach salts out of the root zone. To enhance this process, apply calcium chloride with a hose-end sprayer. By dissolving and leaching salts, calcium chloride along with winter rains help nutrients become more readily available to plants.

Fertilize young indoor seedlings with an organic, water-soluble food following the manufacturer's directions after they have their second set of true leaves (the first two leaves that appear are seed leaves or cotyledons and the true leaves appear above them). For chemical fertilizers, mix at $1/4$ to $1/2$ the recommended rate to avoid salt burn or fast vegetative growth before the roots are properly established.

MAINTAINING

Once the holidays are over, a time of welcome quiet arrives. Take advantage by setting up a potting work bench to store cell packs, pots, compressed peat planting tablets, plant tags, hand tools, marker pens, gloves, and other important garden supplies and accessories. Clean, sharpen, and repair gardening tools such as cultivators, clippers, rakes, and trowels or take them to a garden tool specialist.

After a cycle of freezing and thawing, look for signs of heaving (plants pushed out of the ground) among pansies, violas, primroses, ornamental kale, and other winter annuals. If they have been pushed out of the ground, their roots will dry and they will be exposed to future freezing temperatures. Pack the soil back around their roots and add extra mulch, but do not mulch close to their stems (mulching too close to their stems encourages rotting).

To recycle spent annuals, pass them through a shredder or chop them up with a pair of clippers or a shovel and put them in a compost bin.

If you need a breather from the hustle and bustle of holiday preparations, take a break and putter outdoors on a pleasant day. Remove any discolored foliage from your annuals and pick up any fallen flowers. Deadhead spent flowers to encourage annuals to expend their energy towards continued flower production and plant vigor. During winter, fewer plants are in bloom and colorful winter annuals provide a welcome relief from an otherwise dreary landscape and hectic life.

PROTECTING

Move container plants away from cold winds or heavy rains into protected areas such as covered patios, under houses eaves, or under the sheltered canopies of trees. Don't forget that if they are out of the rain, they will need regular supplemental watering.

Although pansies, violas, snapdragons, Iceland poppies, stock, and flowering kale love winter, extended periods of freezing temperatures can cause damage and sometimes kill them if protective measures are not taken. Alleviate damage from frost conditions by a one-time spraying of winter annuals with an antitranspirant, loosely spreading straw over the annual bed, or temporarily covering the plants with a cotton sheet (removed as the day warms up). Set up stakes or wire cages around your annuals and drape the covering over the frame to avoid touching the plants (otherwise the cover can damage them).

Young seedlings are susceptible to damping off, a fungal disease caused by overwatering. If they collapse suddenly, throw them away in the trash and start over using only new or sterilized containers (washed with a solution of 1 part bleach to 10 parts water) and a sterile potting medium. When working with plants, make sure your hands are clean and place the pots where there is good air circulation.

Once seeds have germinated indoors, reduce room temperatures to 60 to 65 degrees Fahrenheit or move them to a sunny room that can be shut off from the warmth of the rest of the house. If using grow lights, raise the light fixture about 6 inches above the seedlings. Protect seedlings from the midday sun if they are placed in natural light.

As the weather warms near the end of winter, insects may appear on your outdoor annuals. Use imidacloprid, a systemic insecticide to control and prevent insect infestations for up to one year, or select an organic insecticide that is safe to apply around pets, humans, and plants with edible parts. Organic insecticides should be reapplied once a week until the insects have disappeared.

If you find insects on indoor seedlings or cuttings, take them outdoors and spray with an organic, garlic-based insecticide or insecticidal soap (although they are completely safe to use, they might make a mess or stain your floor or furniture). When the plants have dried, bring them back indoors. Repeat applications once a week for three weeks or until the infestation is gone.

Foraging deer, mice, rats, and rabbits can be discouraged from feeding on winter annuals by putting out olfactory repellents or spraying regularly with a dilute solution of d'limonene (d'limonene is a major component of the oil extracted from citrus rind).

Winter rains soften soils and allow gophers to become more active. Before they destroy your flower beds or annual borders, use poisonous baits or set manual traps.

Put out snail and slug bait stations filled with iron phosphate or release decollate snails (if permitted in your county) near the end of winter. Decollate snails prey on immature brown garden snails and decomposing plant material. Do not apply snail bait if decollate snails are present.

If crabgrass is prevalent in your garden, the seeds will blow into annual beds and germinate when the weather warms. Control crabgrass for 3 to 4 months with a pre-emergent that contains the active ingredient, trifluralin.

ANNUALS TO PLANT FROM SEED IN LATE WINTER

Ageratum	Candytuft	Impatiens	Nicotiana	Statice
Bachelor Button	Clarkia	Lobelia	Petunia	Stock
Bells of Ireland	Forget-me-not	Linaria	Phlox	Verbena

CHAPTER TWO

California Citrus

I'll never forget my first drive through California's citrus belt. My parents (Bruce) purchased a new, 1949 Dodge Meadowbrook for our cross-country trek from Ohio to California. It came with a new-fangled, fluid drive—predecessor to the automatic transmission—but it could only accelerate about as fast as an elderly cow. We drove the length of Route 66 at a snail's pace, but it was a grand tour. As we drove through Southern California, the fragrance of flowering citrus trees swooshed through the open windows, saturating the air with a sense memory that I still recall today. The California citrus industry has a long history; in 1873, the Washington navel orange arrived in Riverside, California. William Saunders sent three trees from Bahia, Brazil, to Luther and Eliza Tibbets of Riverside to evaluate their suitability in southern California. Two trees survived the journey and became the cornerstone of a multi-billion dollar industry. One of those trees still thrives in downtown Riverside and has been designated the "Parent Navel Orange." Although the seas of citrus groves have been replaced by suburban housing, a hint of the past is still evident. Citrus trees still mature in many home gardens along California's citrus belt.

In Our Garden

Citrus are plant nomads who have been brought from other parts of the world in the form of hundreds of varieties and subspecies. They have taken root and made themselves at home in the sunny warmth of our golden state.

Whether standard, semidwarf, or dwarf, with fruit as petite as kumquats or as gargantuan as pumelos, whether as grotesque as a 'Buddha's Hand' or as gorgeous as a 'Navel', as tangy and spicy as mandarins or as acidic and aromatic as lemons—all thrive in many home gardeners' landscapes throughout California. For small-space gardeners who do not have the luxury of wide-open orchards, ultra-dwarf citrus trees are the perfect answer to their dilemma. Traditional citrus are available and are the perfect size for courtyards, decks, and balconies.

Whether used as an ornamental focal point in the landscape or planted in an orchard, citrus trees are much more than fruit-bearing nuggets of sunshine: They are canopied providers of shade, dense purveyors of privacy hedges, floriferous creators of heavenly perfumes, standard exemplars among specimen trees, and glittering stars of winter orchards and containers.

BUDDHA'S HAND CITRON
Citrus medica 'Buddha's Hand'

'Buddha's Hand' is highly prized in China and Japan as a symbol of happiness, longevity, and good fortune. It has an intensely aromatic citrus fragrance with little or no flesh that permeates the home for days. The thick, bumpy rind is grated and used in salads, added to vinegar infusions, and even candied.

Asia / Zones 10 to 11 / full sun / height 10 to 14 feet / width 5 to 10 feet / harvest autumn or year-round in frost-free zones

MEIWA KUMQUAT
Fortunella crassifolia 'Meiwa'

Kumquat fruits are eaten whole—rind and all. For regions that are too frigid for other citrus, plant kumquats. Where summers are warm and humid, kumquats produce fruits that are even sweeter and juicier. We prefer to grow 'Meiwa' because of its soft, sweet-as-candy rind and spicy-sweet, lemon-yellow flesh.

China / Zones 8 to 11 / full sun / height 7 to 10 feet / width 7 to 10 feet / harvest winter to spring

OWARI SATSUMA MANDARIN ORANGE
Citrus unshiu 'Owari Satsuma'

Satsumas are easy to peel, hardy, ripen early, and are seedless. None are more cold-hardy than the Satsuma mandarins. They also grow well in more Mediterranean climates where the summers have negligible rainfall and the humidity is low. The fruits are delicately sweet and good-sized with a flat shape, unless left on the tree too long after they're completely ripe. If held too long, the fruits become puffy and lose their flavor.

China / Zones 9 to 11 / full sun / height 4 to 16 feet / width 4 to 16 feet / harvest autumn to spring or through summer, depending on zone and cultivar

SPRING

The rhythms of California's spring move northward as the fragrant blossoms of lemon and orange trees unfold. The open flowers invite dancing bees, to collect its nectar and move its pollen to neighboring flowers.

PLANNING

The first and most important decision is where to locate your tree. Preferred sites have full sun, are protected from wind, and have free-draining soil. Full sun maximizes the foliage, which ultimately increases the sweetness of the fruit. Citrus trees should be exposed to a minimum of eight hours of full sun every day. A wind-protected location encourages pollinators to linger in the tree's canopy longer, setting more fruit. Fabricating a windbreak 6 to 10 feet high on the windward side of a citrus tree deflects the wind just enough to create a less windy and warmer microclimate around it. Refer to Summer Maintaining for more details about constructing a wind baffle. A frost-free location prevents cold damage to the tree's canopy. Of course, for every rule there are exceptions. Exceptions to the frost-free preference are cold-tolerant kumquats that withstand temperatures as low as 10 degrees Fahrenheit, and calamondins and grapefruits that survive short periods of freeze (to 28 degrees). Sweet oranges prefer warm to hot days and cool nights. If you live in a neighborhood where temperatures dip into the 30- or 40-degree range, select a location 6 to 10 feet in front of a heat-reflecting, south-facing wall, where the earth absorbs and stores the heat during the day and then radiates the heat during the night. Blanketing the ground above the root zone with 2 inches of heat-absorbing mulch also helps maintain soil warmth.

Containerized dwarf citrus trees can also be grown indoors if there is sufficient light, humidity, and air circulation. If you are considering remodeling your home and you live in an area where the temperatures become extremely cold, incorporate a solarium into the redesign. Wouldn't it be great to build a l'orangerie (glass house) to grow exhibition citrus trees, such as the 'Cara Cara' navel orange, in large planters?

When planning for the success of a citrus tree, free-draining soil helps avoid most problems caused by soil-borne pathogens. If the soil is too dense or too clayey, lacking in organic content, and not free-draining, amend the soil with compost, humus, or similar organic matter. Adding organic material provides drainage, air movement, and an environment for beneficial microorganisms to multiply. If amending is impractical, consider planting in containers or raised or terraced planting beds.

Select plants such as African blue basil, Hall's honeysuckle, and red apple ground cover to attract bees and birds to pollinate the citrus blossoms.

Avoid growing citrus trees over or near septic systems unless they are in containers. Toxic materials that are found in cleaning compounds and pesticides might gravitate into leach fields or seepage pits, absorbing into the citrus tree's root system and into the fruit.

Determine the size and form of the citrus trees that are right for your yard. They are available as standard, semidwarf, or dwarf. The standard citrus (tree form) trees grow to heights of 12 to 20 feet and should be planted 15 to 20 feet on center; semidwarfs grow 8 to 15 feet and should be spaced 10 to 12 feet on center, and dwarf citrus (bush form) grows to a height of 6 to 10 feet and should be spaced 6 to 8 feet on center. These on-center dimensions apply both to rectilinear and triangular planting patterns.

Plan your citrus-growing area to accommodate three varieties of dwarf citrus in a single planting pit (3 to 4 feet on center); if you want more citrus varieties, select salad citrus trees. Salad citrus have multiple varieties grafted or budded onto a single rootstock. For example, growing a 'Washington' navel orange, a 'Valencia' orange, and a 'Minneola' tangelo on the same rootstock is a way to enjoy three varieties from a single tree in a limited space. But if a 'Eureka' lemon is one of the varieties grafted onto a salad citrus tree, its vigorous growth eventually dominates the other varieties, so pruning is necessary to keep its growth pattern proportional to the others.

Select a citrus tree that has a symmetrical canopy with healthy green foliage and no broken branches, as well as roots that are not rootbound. If you purchase a containerized citrus tree, don't pick it up by the trunk, the jarring might loosen and damage the rootball. California's rainy season begins in midfall and ends in midspring. The ideal time for planting citrus trees is in early spring after the last frost date.

PLANTING

Excavate a planting pit three to four times the diameter and one to one and a half times the depth of the rootball. Pile the soil to one side, and create four straight sides—in other words, make a rectilinear hole in the ground. Assuming that the native soil is denser than the soil in the container, the rectilinear form of the pit will direct the roots towards its corners, then into the original soil, rather than circling around and around in a cylindrical planting pit. Scratch the inside surface with a cultivator; that also helps direct the absorbing roots into the native soil.

Formulate your own soil for backfilling; blend $1/3$ sand (or coarse perlite), $1/3$ soil (salvaged from the planting pit), and $1/3$ organic material (such as compost, humus mulch, or worm castings). These ingredients, blended together, provide sufficient porosity and moisture-holding capacity for air to move in and out of the root zone and moisture to be available when the plant requires it. Heavy, dense, and clayey soils restrict roots from optimizing their ability to absorb nutrients and moisture, and limit beneficial aerobic microorganisms, such as mycorrhizal fungi, from helping roots to absorb water and nutrients. Ideally, the soil that citrus trees are planted in should have a loam texture (about 40 percent sand, 40 percent silt, and 20 percent clay).

Determine the pH of the soil at the selected location before you plant your citrus trees. Refer to page 307.

Construct a 4- to 6-inch-high berm around the tree to form a watering basin. The radius of the basin should be 10 to 20 percent wider than the radius of the tree's drip line. The soil surface in the basin should slope away from the tree's root flare (the area where the root system becomes the trunk of the tree) and toward the toe of the berm. The sloping surface keeps the irrigation water moving away from the trunk, encouraging the root system to expand outward.

Thoroughly soak the planting pit around the rootball immediately after transplanting a new citrus tree, and then apply a root growth stimulator containing alpha-naphthalene acetic acid (NAA) or indolebutyric acid (IBA). Apply three times, one week apart. These growth regulators encourage new absorbing roots to develop.

WATERING

Irrigate citrus trees to replenish moisture lost through evapotranspiration (moisture evaporating from the surface of the root zone and transpiring from a plant's canopy). Soil moisture should be maintained so the trees have sufficient moisture to prevent foliage from wilting. Watering infrequently and deeply benefits citrus trees much more than frequent light watering.

Avoid over-irrigating because the majority of citrus trees do not tolerate water-saturated soils. If the soil is too wet, pathogens such as water molds will invade a citrus tree's vascular system, restricting the movement of water, nutrients, and carbohydrates. If this doesn't kill the tree, it certainly weakens it, resulting in poor-quality fruit.

Determine how quickly water percolates through the soil. The percolation rate is a factor in determining how often and how much to irrigate citrus trees.

Be aware of seasonal rain patterns; the rainy season in California is from fall to mid-spring. In spring, as precipitation decreases, supplemental irrigation is necessary for citrus trees to grow and develop. If the soil texture is sandy loam, apply 4 to 6 inches of water to the watering basin every seven to ten days. As conditions change, increase or decrease the application intervals.

FERTILIZING

Feed citrus trees with a complete organic fertilizer four times a year. The first application should be made in late winter or early spring, before the flush of growth begins. The second application should be made after the tree blooms and the fruit sets and develops to $1/2$ inch in diameter. The third application should be made in early summer, and the last application, if necessary, should be done in early fall to winterize the tree. Use the formulator's recommendations for application times and rates.

An alternative fertilizing program for 'Washington Navel' orange trees would be to follow a fertilizing routine that applies 1 pound of actual nitrogen (N) per year for each mature three- to four-year-old tree. For instance, if you are using fertilizer containing 10 percent nitrogen, the first application should be in late winter or early spring and should have 50 percent ($1/2$ pound) of the yearly allocation of nitrogen. The second application should occur when the fruit develops to $1/2$ inch in diameter and should have 25 percent ($1/4$ pound) of the allocation. The last 25 percent ($1/4$ pound) should be applied in early summer. If a citrus fertilizer has a blend of ingredients totaling 10 percent nitrogen, it requires 10 pounds of that fertilizer to provide the 1 pound of *actual* nitrogen for the year. The first application requires 5 pounds of that fertilizer to provide $1/2$ pound of actual nitrogen; the second and third applications require $2^1/2$ pounds each of that fertilizer to provide the remaining $1/2$ pound of actual nitrogen per application.

Natural sources of nitrogen include bloodmeal (13-0-0), cottonseed meal (6-2-1), bone meal (3-15-0), and kelp meal (1-0.1-2). They all work well as nutrient sources, especially as the weather warms.

Although nitrogen (N) is the primary element that is required the most and needs to be replenished regularly, for convenience's sake, a complete organic fertilizer with an NPK of 7-4-2, 5-3-1, or 12-12-6 can benefit your citrus trees if phosphorous or potassium levels are at low levels. By combining humic acid with the fertilizer, beneficial microorganism activity increases in the root zone and makes the soil healthier. Distribute the fertilizer at the base of and inside the berm comprising the watering basin and water thoroughly.

If you use organic fertilizers, supplemental nitrogen can be added to your basic formula by blending bloodmeal to the mix. Of the most common micronutrient deficiencies in citrus trees, zinc (Zn) is the most frequently encountered. The symptoms for zinc deficiencies are yellowing interveins and smaller leaves near the ends of the branches. To correct this problem, spray the tree with a foliar application of chelated iron/zinc.

Identify nutrient deficiencies in citrus trees by observing the location, progression, and patterns of the color changes in the canopy's foliage. If the lower leaves of your citrus tree become light-green, then turn yellow, and then fall to the ground, the problem might stem from a deficiency in one of the primary nutrients such as nitrogen, phosphorus, and potassium (NPK). Primary nutrients readily move (translocate) from the root system to the top of the tree's canopy, so their deficiencies show up in the lower inside leaves of a canopy. Since secondary and micronutrients do not readily translocate, their deficiencies show up as chlorotic foliage in the canopy from the top down. Of course, the most accurate way to define the deficiency is to make a leaf analysis (testing is routine for an agricultural supply house). For homeowners, avoid primary nutrient deficiencies by using a complete organic fertilizer every another month from late winter to late summer.

To prevent secondary or micronutrient deficiencies, foliar feed with a water-soluble blend of chelated micronutrients derived from seaweed. This technique of fertilizing is called the "shotgun" method and is designed to cover everything.

Compare and record the foliage, flower, and fruit quantity and quality of the citrus using different fertilizers. Continue using whatever yields the best results for your particular conditions.

Use a controlled-release citrus fertilizer if adhering to a rigid fertilizing schedule is too demanding. The fertilizer's semipermeable coating will meter an even amount of nutrients to the citrus plant each time it is watered for four months.

MAINTAINING

Maintain a 2-inch mulch blanket under the tree's canopy. A mulch blanket stabilizes soil moisture, moderates soil temperatures, and suppresses the weed population. The mulch should be porous enough to permit air to move freely in and out of the root zone. Mulches such as compost, humus, cocoa mulch, and those containing corn gluten are ideal for covering the root zone. Avoid using materials such as pine wood chips unless they have added nitrogen to compensate for the nitrogen used by soil microorganisms. If the mulch blanket dries and crusts, break the crust apart by cultivating the surface. Also apply the mulch covering starting 6 inches away from the root flare out to the drip line of the canopy. Do not mulch up to the trunk of the tree because moisture accumulates and may cause disease problems.

Cull the fruit early in its development if there is a bumper crop. When conditions are ideal, citrus trees set an enormous quantity of fruit. When this happens, most citrus trees can't possibly hold and bring all of the fruit to maturity, so the trees protect themselves by self-culling the fruit when it is about a half-inch in diameter. The process, called *June drop*, helps the remaining fruit to be sweeter and larger. Other influences can accelerate June drop, for example, repeated fluctuations in temperatures or repeated fluctuations in soil moisture. June drop can be mitigated by thinning. In a cluster of five fruits, remove two, allowing enough space for the remaining fruits to develop to optimum size.

If a layer of mulch is around the tree, hand-pulling weeds as they emerge should not be such a chore. You can also apply a pre-emergent weed control around the tree and out to its drip line to prevent the germination of any weed seeds. Use a pre-emergent product containing corn gluten, an effective and organic control. Follow the directions on the package for application amount and frequency.

Pruning citrus trees is necessary only to:

- prune out freeze-damaged branches just above the point where there is new growth
- maintain shape by selective branch removal, not by shearing, which produces a dense growth pattern at the ends of the branches
- lower the tree's canopy to a manageable height (8 to 12 feet), shortly after the possibility of frost has passed, usually early spring
- remove water sprouts (errant vertical growth at the top of the tree's canopy)
- thin a dense canopy so sunlight can reach the tree's interior to stimulate latent buds to begin growing

- remove interfering, diseased, dead, or declining branches

Heavy pruning of citrus is generally not necessary, but there are a few times you should pull out the old pruning saw, bypass pruning shears or wooden handled loppers, and give the tree a good whack! One of those times is when you see rapidly growing suckers at the base of the bole (trunk) or on or near the root flare, but below the graft union. Dig down to expose their points of origin; then prune them off. Spray the exposed wounds with a sucker-stopping product. Tree wound sealers available at your local garden center also suppress sucker regrowth.

PROTECTING

Protecting citrus trees from pests is easier than correcting problems caused by pests. Be alert for the changes in the weather pattern. In early spring, as the ambient temperature warms and the hours of daylight increase, citrus trees begin to show signs of awakening. Latent leaf and flower buds begin swelling and soon show color. Along with the signs of renewal, look for signs of damage and destruction.

Aphids can easily be controlled by introducing predacious lady beetles, lacewings, and big-eyed bugs or by washing them off with a stream of water and by eliminating the ant population. Ants farm the aphid population by moving them from one location to another. As the aphids suck the sap from citrus leaves, they excrete honeydew, which is harvested by the ants. Control aphids early because they are parthenogenic, meaning they are able to clone themselves, geometrically increasing their numbers.

Brown garden snails hibernate in the earth during winter, where they can deposit up to eighty eggs. When the snail population emerges from hibernation in late winter through early spring, they are voracious. This is the most effective time to use snail bait. During hot and dry weather, brown garden snails develop a membrane over their shell's opening which keeps them from desiccating. The process is called *estivation* (a state of dormancy during prolonged hot and dry periods). They become active again in fall until it becomes too cold, at which time they hibernate. In the milder regions of California, brown garden snails are found foraging in and around citrus trees throughout the year; once they find their way up into the canopy of the tree, they feed on leaves and fruit for months, at which time they must be removed by hand. If they still reside on the ground, block them from moving up the tree's trunk by wrapping a fluted, 4-inch-wide, copper foil band around the trunk, 12 inches above the ground. Or if your county permits, introduce decollate snails into the landscaping near your citrus trees. They will attack, kill, and consume immature brown garden snails without damaging your landscape plants.

Control brown soft scales by applying horticultural oil, and use predacious mites to control citrus red mite. Read Summer Protecting for more detailed information.

Citrus woolly whiteflies and giant whiteflies are persistent threats to citrus trees. They deposit their eggs in circular patterns on the underside of citrus leaves.

When their eggs hatch, their larvae damage citrus trees by sucking sap from the foliage; this is followed by secretions of honeydew that is harvested by ants. If giant whitefly infestations persist, white streams resembling cotton candy appear on the underside of the leaves, leading to a fungus infestation called black sooty mold. The extent of the damage caused by the larvae and fungus is aggravated by ants harvesting the honeydew for food and transporting the whitefly larvae to other locations on the tree. Control the whitefly larvae population by introducing parasitic Encarsia wasps, lady beetles, lacewings, and big-eyed bugs into the tree's canopy or by applying Neem oil, horticultural oil, insecticidal soap, or garlic extract solutions. You should also prevent ants from traveling up by creating an ant barrier. Dust ant control powder near the base of the trunk, or apply a 4-inch band of sticky gel, 1 foot above the ground, on the trunk of the tree.

Citrus thrips feed inside in the flowers of citrus trees. Their piercing mouth parts penetrate the petal surfaces, causing the flowers not to open and, in most instances, causing them to fall. Other thrips use their piercing mouth parts to penetrate leaf surfaces and suck out the sap. Heavy infestations of these thrips cause stippling and a silvery sheen on the top and bottom surfaces of citrus leaves. Exposed thrips can be controlled by applying botanicals (derivative of naturally occurring plants) such as ryania, sabadilla, or garlic oil.

SUMMER

Patience and prudence produce the flavors of oranges and lemons. Not rushing the cadence through the doldrums of summer, nor neglecting the needs during the maturing of citrus will reward all with sweetness and health.

PLANNING

Stay informed of short-term weather changes so steps can be taken to moderate moisture and heat stress on your citrus trees. We have found that the most efficient way to stay on top of changing weather patterns is to access the National Oceanic and Atmospheric Administration (NOAA) website. Local weather reports are also very helpful. When dry, hot winds are predicted, schedule planting or transplanting citrus trees at a later date.

Contact your county agricultural department to learn about the long-term climatic conditions for your region.

Schedule a reliable person to irrigate your citrus trees when you plan to go on an extended vacation. The person should also be provided with a sketch that identifies the trees that need special attention.

PLANTING

Plant citrus trees twenty-four hours after a thorough watering. This delay gives the tree sufficient time to become completely hydrated and reduces transplant shock. Planting container-grown citrus trees during summer should not be a problem. If the planting time is early summer and the tree is still booming or is laden with maturing fruit, remove the flowers and fruit before planting. The energy of the plant is then directed into reestablishing its root system rather than maturing the fruit. See Spring Planting.

If you have limited space, grow dwarf citrus trees in such containers as half-barrels or 15-gallon black plastic nursery containers. Make sure there are at least four 1-inch drainage holes at the bottom of the side wall. Use a potting soil that is porous and free-draining, with 20 to 30 percent organic material, such as compost, humus, or worm castings.

If you decide to plant citrus trees in summer, use a tank sprayer to spray the canopy with an antitranspirant, especially when weather forecasts predict hot, dry winds. The rapid moisture loss through the leaves, called transpiration, causes the leaves to wilt and sends your tree into transplant shock. If you live in the high desert (Mojave) or the low desert (Sonoran) where temperatures reach 120 degrees Fahrenheit, use 55 percent lumite shade cloth to protect sapling citrus trees from scorching.

Apply a root stimulator containing indolebutyric acid (IBA) or alpha-naphthalene acetic acid (NAA) to give your newly planted tree a head start.

WATERING

Irrigate citrus trees in summer to replenish the reservoir of soil moisture. The best time to irrigate citrus trees is late in the afternoon or early in the morning. Both of these times permit the tree to hydrate, avoiding moisture stress during the heat of the day. If there is a choice, late afternoon is preferable.

React quickly when a citrus tree folds its leaves as if praying for water. It is most likely under severe moisture stress. The moisture content in the leaves keeps them upright. When the moisture volume in the leaves falls below a critical point, the leaves' cellular structure collapses and they wilt. If the wilting is severe, even a slight breeze will separate the leaves from their twigs. To maintain the necessary moisture for optimum canopy growth and fruit production, monitor the soil moisture by using a tensiometer (moisture meter) or use a soil probe to sample the soil in the root zone to a depth of about 2 feet. If the tensiometer or probe indicates that the first foot is drying, water again. When the moisture content is low, increase the frequency and amount of water. For an established citrus tree growing in a sandy loam soil, fill the watering basin twice every seven to ten days.

Maintain a 2-inch blanket of mulch over the root zone to help reduce evaporation from the soil surface.

FERTILIZING

In late summer, test the root zone soil for pH (acidity or alkalinity). Use a pH test kit available from your local garden center. The results of the test provide information on how much and how often corrective materials should be prescribed. The testing for salt levels results in a measure of electrical conductivity (EC) and should be tested by a commercial soils laboratory. In most cases, a simple pH test is sufficient. If the pH is high (alkaline), begin correcting by applying calcium chloride (CaCl) or gypsum (CaSO4). Refer to page 307 for application rates. Both formulations work to flocculate (form aggregates of) the soil particles. Forming aggregates creates spaces, permitting movement of water, air, nutrients, and roots.

Feed citrus trees one last time, after the fruit develops to about 60 percent of its optimum size. For most citrus varieties, this application should be between early and midsummer.

MAINTAINING

Construct a wind baffle 6 feet away from the canopy, on the windward side of the tree if it is growing in a breezy location. A baffle is a wind deflector constructed of three 8-foot posts with plastic sheeting secured between the posts and positioned to protect the tree from wind, creating a microclimate on its lee side. It also alleviates rapid moisture loss due to rapid air movement across the surface of its leaves.

Keep the foliage of citrus trees at least 6 inches off the ground to prevent snails, slugs, and ants from slithering or parading up through the leaves.

Shore-up the berms around the watering basins because they tend to erode away during the spring rains. The berm that creates the watering basin should be 4 to 6 inches high and have a radius that extends 10 percent beyond the drip line of the tree. An alternative for the earthen berm is a large circle around the base of the tree, formed from curved sections of cast concrete. The sections are designed to make circles of various diameters.

For weed control information, read Spring Maintaining.

Fasciated, rigid, fast-growing, and thorny stems emerging from within the citrus tree's canopy are different from the rest of the plant. This abnormal growth, called a chimera or sport, produces fruit very different from the fruit of the parent tree. Whether to let it grow or to prune it out is your decision. Many new and tasty citrus cultivars such as the 'Cara Cara' navel orange was developed as a result of a chimera. Part of the fun of gardening is waiting to see what new plant might develop from a parent. The experience is almost as rewarding as raising a child!

Drop (lower) the canopy of citrus trees during mid- or late summer if it has become impractical to harvest the fruit without climbing a ladder. It is precarious to climb a ladder, lean out, and pluck oranges from a tree branch 15 to 20 feet in the air. Lowering the tree's canopy after the majority of the fruit has been harvested is the ideal time to do the deed, but even if you are not able to harvest all the fruit, it is better to reduce the tree's height. We try to keep the height of our citrus tree at about 8 feet, a practical height that allows us to stand on the ground and reach the fruit safely with a fruit picker. Other than lowering the tree's canopy, little pruning is needed on the outside of the tree.

Observe the developing fruit. If there are too many in each cluster, cull the fruit to make space for the remaining ones and to protect the bearing limbs from excessive weight. For example, if there was an enormous set in spring and a bumper crop was maturing during summer, selectively remove 20 to 40 percent of the fruit.

Remove suckers growing from the tree's root system, from the root flare, and from the area below the graft union. These suckers originate from the rootstock and do not produce viable fruit. As a general rule, it is not necessary to seal the exposed area where the sucker has been removed. A natural barrier called a callus develops, however, in some cases where diseases and insects are widespread; cover the wound with a commercial sealant to create a barrier over the wound. Keep in mind, however, that sealing often slows the natural callusing process.

Remove or reduce the height of water sprouts, which are thorny, rapidly growing vertical stems emerging from older branches. They do not produce fruit but are useful in providing additional foliage for photosynthesis. If the water sprouts have grown well beyond the canopy, prune them back to a point just inside the perimeter. If the canopy is healthy with lots of foliage and fruit, remove the entire water sprout. See Spring Maintaining, also.

PROTECTING

Protect the bark of young citrus trees from the scorching summer sun. Apply interior, white, water-soluble latex paint from the root flare to the first or second scaffold. Once dried, the white surface will protect the tender trunk from scorching by reflecting the sun's rays.

Control summer disease and insect pests. First, attempt to remedy insect infestations on citrus trees with natural controls. For citrus red scale (which appear as reddish oval bumps on the rind), use a suffocant like horticultural oil or garlic extract, or release aphytis wasps (available at insectaries and garden centers that carry beneficial insects). Lady beetles are the predacious insect of choice for brown soft scale, or you can spray with a suffocant or garlic extract. Delphastus beetles or garlic extract help keep whiteflies under control. Keep citrus thrip populations in check by introducing predatory mites or by applying a garlic extract insecticide.

For navel orange worm, introduce goniozus wasps or apply *Bacillus thuringiensis* (Bt) before the larvae bore into the fruit in early summer. Once they make themselves at home inside the fruit, most remedies are ineffective. Discard the infested fruit.

Introduce colonies of decollate snails to prey on immature brown garden snails. When they have eaten their way through the snail population, the predator decollate snails will feed primarily on decomposing organic material. (Check with your county agricultural department before ordering because many counties in northern California do not allow the use of decollate snails.) You can also control snails and slugs by attaching a 2-inch-wide band of copper around the trunk of the tree. Iron phosphate is another effective organic molluscicide to use around plants with edible parts and safe to use around small children and pets, but avoid using it if you have distributed decollate snails in the area.

Control roof rats with poisonous bait placed in a bait station to keep it away from pets, birds, and small children, or use manual traps. A sure sign of roof rat damage is a hollowed-out, rounded hole, 2 to 3 inches in diameter on the side of the fruit. For mice, poisonous baits in bait stations, sticky paper traps, or manual traps are effective.

Larger critters that are causing damage to your fruit trees, such as burrowing rabbits and squirrels and foraging skunks, raccoons, and opossums, can be trapped in a live-animal trap and relocated to a more wilderness-friendly area. Check with the state department of fish and wildlife to find out where you can release the critters.

If you are declaring war on pocket gophers, your arsenal ranges from manual gopher traps and bait and gas bombs to feline hunters. Do not funnel exhaust fumes from your car, flood with water, stick wads of gum or balls of cut hair inside their tunnels. They are usually ineffective against buck-toothed marauders, but a hungry pet gopher snake or king snake might be just the answer.

Set guillotine traps, the best "gotcha" method for moles. Moles are insectivorous, not herbivorous. They do eat plant parts, but cause a great deal of tunneling damage.

PRUNING TIPS FOR ALL PLANTS

Plants are pruned to develop structure, to enhance character, and to improve purpose. Structure is achieved by managing growth; for example, removing diseased, dead, and dangerous wood. Capturing character by pruning selectively enhances a plant's appeal. Improving purpose is gained by pruning to optimize function: visual screening, soil binding, flowering, and fruiting. These goals are accomplished by using thinning and heading cuts.

Thinning cuts opens a plant's canopy to lower a plant's height, to reduce the weight on branches, and to stimulate new growth. Thinning can increase flowering and fruiting.

Heading back (also called *shearing*) can increase the density of a plant's perimeter thereby improving its ability to provide shade or screening. Heading cuts remove current or one year old shoots down to a bud or stub. It's used for training young trees, pollarding, and shaping flowering trees and hedges.

See pages 229, 261, 293, 298, 302, 306, and 309 for more pruning information.

AUTUMN

The chill of autumn is the downbeat for change. Tangelos, kumquats, and calamondins don their orange winter attire, the weather cools, and daylight dwindles but the summer store of sweet sugar stays secure.

PLANNING

When selecting citrus trees, ask yourself the following questions: Do I have the right location for them? Will these varieties grow well in my neighborhood? Do they look healthy? Is the foliage a uniform, glossy green? Are there signs of pest damage? Do they look malnourished? Are their roots protruding from the drainage holes, indicating they are root-bound? How much will it cost? Providing the cost is within your budget, choose the tree that answers all these questions to your satisfaction.

Test mandarin oranges, navel oranges, blood oranges, and kumquats as the weather cools. Lemons, both 'Meyer' and 'Eureka', sporadically blossom and set fruit all year long. Grapefruits on the average take eighteen months to mature, so it is normal to have two crops on the tree at the same time.

Record the events that might affect the quality of the fruit. Most events are repetitive, and if they are anticipated, it is much easier to avoid the problem than it is to cure a problem. When a citrus cultivar or variety is supposed to taste sweet, but you get lip puckers instead, several "souring" causes may be responsible. Mother Nature reigns supreme over temperature, humidity, and overcast days, but we can solve nutrient deficiencies, proper irrigation, and insect and disease problems.

PLANTING

Early fall is the last time during the year that citrus trees should be planted in the ground unless you live in a frost-free area. Select a full-sun location because the sun's warmth will bring the citrus to maturity (10 feet in front of south-facing walls are excellent locations). See Spring Planting.

WATERING

Shore up the tree's watering basin in anticipation of the rainy season. As daylight decreases and average temperatures cool, citrus slow their growth rate and require less water. If you are growing citrus trees in loam soil, extend the watering interval to once every ten to fourteen days. Keep in mind that as citrus fruit mature, soil moisture should always be available; the moisture content should not fluctuate. If rainfall keeps the soil moist, supplemental irrigation might not be necessary.

Be aware of the hot dry winds that originate in the Great Basin and blow across southern California and the hot dry winds that come from Oregon's southern Cascades and blow down into northern California. They can desiccate a citrus tree in hours. When winds are predicted, irrigate your trees at least twenty-four hours before they arrive.

Water containerized citrus trees when the soil surface is dry to the touch. It is almost impossible to overwater a potted citrus tree. All the gravitational water moves down and out of the root zone. One important caveat to this watering procedure is that if the container is placed in a saucer and the saucer fills with water, the water will saturate the soil and the roots will rot. If you need a saucer to catch the water, place two bricks on the saucer and place the container on the bricks.

FERTILIZING

Winterize citrus trees by applying sulfate of potash (0-0-50) fertilizer, following the package directions and distributing evenly around the inside perimeter of the berm, and then give it a good soaking. Potassium is the primary element that regulates the moisture content in plants, increases cold tolerance, and improves branch strength. For citrus trees growing in a half-barrel or similar-sized container, distribute a half-cup of sulfate of potash evenly over the soil surface and water in thoroughly.

Towards the end of fall, stop using fertilizers containing nitrogen. Nitrogen encourages new and tender growth, which is susceptible to cold damage.

MAINTAINING

Keep a 2- to 4-inch blanket of mulch over the soil in the irrigation basin. This blanket stabilizes the moisture content in the root zone and the soil temperature. It also helps control the weed population. As the mulch blanket decomposes or becomes part of the soil, it must be replenished with additional humus mulch.

The cool autumn weather triggers the orange coloration of citrus fruit, but it is the Valencia orange's response to warm summer weather that causes regreening. Regreening doesn't harm the fruit; in fact, the fruit will continue to mature normally. The only difference is that the fruit will not regain its intense orange.

To control weeds, refer to Spring Maintaining.

Autumn pruning is not necessary, but remove all mummified fruit (shriveled, hard, moldy fruit) from the trees' canopies and pick up and discard any fruit on the ground.

PROTECTING

Trap, transport, and release those pesky ground squirrels in places far away from your citrus trees. Autumn finds squirrels very active in citrus groves because they are stashing food in preparation for winter and spring. If ground squirrels are doing no harm to your plants or your landscape, leave them alone, but if their tunneling is compromising your slopes or damaging your foundation, roof, or plants, control them by using live traps and safely release them away from your garden. Live traps also control rabbits, squirrels, raccoons, skunks, and opossums. Check first with the state department of fish and wildlife to find out where you can release them.

Control pocket gophers with manual gopher traps, gopher baskets, feline hunters, and certain plants. Plants such as gopher purge, angel's trumpet, narcissus, amaryllis, hippeastrum, and squill manufacture natural toxins that rodents learn to avoid. There is little success using fumes from a car's exhaust, wads of gum, balls of cut hair or sonic repellents, but gopher snakes and king snakes are very effective.

Also see Summer Protecting for additional information regarding pests.

WINTER

Through sizzling summer heat and winter freezes, the Parent Navel orange tree has its own rhythm. For more than 120 years it has lead its progeny, creating one of the nation's most prosperous citrus crops.

PLANNING

During the holiday season, citrus trees are still available at local garden centers, and they make ideal gifts. Most garden centers in California have an excellent inventory of dwarf citrus trees to choose from, many with fruit on them.

Collect all your notes, or if you kept a journal, review the entire year and decide what problems can be prevented for next year. Also include additional citrus trees you might want to put on a wish list to be planted in the ground or in containers.

PLANTING

Remember that a dwarf citrus tree planted in a redwood tub or a half-barrel is an everlasting holiday gift. Drill eight 1-inch-diameter drainage holes and use a complete potting soil for planting.

WATERING

Reduce the irrigation frequency and quantity to adjust to lower water requirements by the tree, but when you do water, the best time of day is early in the morning when there is no wind and the humidity is high.

Adjust the irrigation clock to keep the soil in the root zone moist. If there is sufficient rainfall to wet the soil to a depth of 2 feet, turn off the irrigation system, but if there is a dry spell, monitor the soil with a tensiometer or soil probe. Turn the system

on if the tensiometer or probe indicates that the first foot is becoming dry. Also look for any cracks in the surface of the soil or beginning signs of leaf wilt. Monitoring the soil moisture is critical because it is easy to overwater during the cool season unless they are growing in containers. Container plants dry out more quickly than plants in the ground.

FERTILIZING

If the foliage at the top of the tree appears to be chlorotic where the intervein is yellow and the veins are green, it is probably a secondary or micronutrient deficiency. To correct this problem, foliar feed the tree with a mixture of chelated micronutrients.

General fertilizing is not necessary during winter because it encourages tender growth that may be damaged.

MAINTAINING

Maintain a 2- to 3-inch blanket of humus mulch in the watering basins or surrounding the surface of the citrus tree (keep the mulch 2 to 4 inches away from its trunk) if there are no basins out to the drip line. This mulch covering conserves water, keeps the root system warm, and suppresses the weed population.

If you grow dwarf citrus in containers, install casters under the tubs and roll them into a protected area or cover the citrus with an old cotton sheet (never plastic) to protect against cold weather.

When a hard freeze is predicted, insulate the bud union or graft point by temporarily mounding soil on the trunk of the tree to a height that covers the union, or wrap the area with 6-inch-wide gauze tape. Remove the mounded soil or wrap when the last freeze is over.

Weeds may still be a problem, particularly where winters are mild. Pull them out whenever they appear, or apply a corn-gluten-based preemergent to prevent seed germination.

Do not prune citrus trees in winter because it might stimulate frost tender growth. When the canopy sustains freeze damage, do not prune the damaged section back until new buds begin to grow (usually in spring). This growth activity indicates how far into the canopy the damage was sustained. Then prune back the branches to a point just above the new growth.

Allow citrus fruit to remain on the tree because the fruit stops ripening as soon as it is removed. Many times there will be two crops of fruit on the tree at the same time, but for the highest quality citrus, the latest crop should be removed before the tree blossoms and sets its next crop.

PROTECTING

Spray citrus trees with a horticultural oil. This clean-up spray helps control spider mites, citrus red scales, and mealybugs that overwinter in the cracks and crevices of a citrus tree's bark and fruit.

If there is a freeze and the temperature dips below 25 degrees Fahrenheit, damage to citrus trees is almost inevitable. There will be freeze damage to the entire exposed portion of the canopy. The damage occurs when the moisture in the leaf freezes, expands, and shatters the cellular structure of the leaf. When the moisture thaws, the leaf structure collapses and the frozen portion of the tree turns black. This condition is not a pretty sight. If a black frost is predicted, commercial growers fog their trees with water two or three times during the night. The water freezes, insulating the foliage because the temperature of ice never falls below 32 degrees. To protect citrus from ordinary freeze damage, spray with an antitranspirant to coat the leaves and insulate them from the cold. Also, mulch to stabilize the soil temperature. If it is a dwarf tree, cover it with a cotton (not plastic) sheet or string Christmas lights on it.

Look for signs of roof rat damage. Citrus fruit, exotic fruit, and avocadoes are all susceptible to foraging rats. They eat the innards of fruit, leaving an empty sack of rind with a symmetrical entrance hole. Cover the trunk with a 2- to 3-foot-long smooth metal or plastic sleeve to deter them. The sleeves are available at most agricultural supply stores, but if tree limbs rest on the ground or touch other structures, such as fences, rats will find a way to the fruit. Other controls include spring-loaded rat traps or rat bait. If you decide on bait, place it in a bait station to protect pets, small children, and birds from the poison.

Control black sooty mold by eliminating infestations of sucking insect and the larvae of the citrus woolly whitefly. During winter, apply garlic, Neem, or horticultural oil, according to the formulator's label instructions.

CHAPTER THREE

California Drought-Tolerant Plants

When you mention drought-tolerant landscaping, most folks think of cacti, succulents, and creosote bushes planted on rolling mounds of earth with gravel covering the barren spaces. There are, however, many other options for creating a drought-tolerant landscape.

Plants have developed unique methods of coping with a lack of moisture. Some shut down totally, completing their reproductive cycle before soil moisture is depleted. They conserve water by developing deep root systems, curling their leaves, and using a method of respiration called Crassulacean Acid Metabolism (CAM) where the stomata close during hot, dry days and open during cool, humid nights. Finally, some plants tolerate a lack of water, becoming limp and barely surviving, only to miraculously recover when moisture becomes available. Indigenous plants offer a striking range of color for the drought-tolerant landscape. Diverse plant groups have adapted well to California's seasonal rhythms of wet winters and dry summers. They all can be very useful in designing an easily maintained drought-tolerant landscape.

In Our Garden

Our golden state not only hosts its own native California plants, but is also a hospitable haven for a wide variety of plants from other Mediterranean climates, such as South Africa and Australia. These plants are tough and adaptable to wet winters and dry summers. They are also lush and colorful when paired with Italian, Spanish, or mission-style architecture.

Limited water supply, recurring drought, and dry summers are some of the challenges and blessings of living in our golden state. Fortunately, there are many native and Mediterranean plants that are not only water-efficient, but also add unique beauty and provide welcoming bird, bee, and butterfly habitats to our California gardens. When planning a new landscape or renovating part of an existing one, consider plants that do not require much water or maintenance, and yet are just as colorful and interesting as more water-thirsty plants.

We hope the following three selections from our garden will inspire you to incorporate more drought-resistant plants that are also known for their "oohs-and-aahs" beauty.

BUTTERFLY BUSH
Buddleja davidii

While we labor over our summer roses, fluttering butterflies, fuzzy bumblebees, honeybees, and ruby-throated hummingbirds linger over clusters of delicate, fragrant, spiked flowers on a nearby butterfly bush. Its upright structure provides a picturesque silhouette in winter, serves as a colorful screen in warm seasons, and it's both salt- and cold-tolerant.

China and Japan / Zones 5 to 10 / full sun, part shade / height 4 to12 feet / width 6 to 20 feet / flowers in summer

MATILIJA POPPY
Romneya coulteri

Matilija poppy is known as the "fried egg" plant because of its huge 4- to 9-inch diameter, chalk-white flowers with golden eyes. Its blooms are the largest of any plant native to California. Matilija poppy branches support five to eight crepe paper-textured blossoms. Because it tolerates many soil types, different weather conditions, and needs no summer water once established, these gray-green giants can be invasive and are not recommended for small gardens.

California / Zones 7 to 10 / full sun / height 8 to 10 feet / width 3 feet / flowers in summer

PROTEA
Protea species

Protea flowers are named after Proteus, the Greek god who could assume many different forms. Their enticing charms range from massive, 8- to 12-inch King or Queen proteas to the smaller creamy-pink, fuzzy black-fringed Pink Mink (*P. neriifolia*). Cut flowers last up to four weeks and can be kept as a semi-permanent flower when dried. Proteas require more care to establish, but their diverse beauty and forms are worth the extra effort.

S. Africa / Zones 9 to 10 / full sun / height 3 to 40 feet / width 4 to 40 feet / flowers depending on variety

SPRING

California's hillsides painted in palettes of muted grays, tans, and dusty olives dissolve in the warmth of spring sun. Lilacs and poppies awaken and fill the empty spaces with brush-strokes of hazy blues and vibrant oranges.

PLANNING

Average annual rainfalls in California vary greatly from region to region: Redding traditionally receives 33 inches; San Francisco normally has 20 inches; San Diego receives a mere 10.77 inches; Los Angeles County is anywhere from 13 to 20 inches. Periodic droughts are a way of life for California. Since the 1920s, droughts spanning several years have occurred in the Sacramento and San Joaquin valleys from 1929 to 1934, 1976 to 1977, and 1987 to1992. Another drought lasted from late 1999 through 2004, south of Sacramento. During that period, the average for San Diego was below its average rainfall by as much as 5 to 7 inches. Additionally, much of the state relies on the Sierra Nevada snowpack, particularly during summer. If Northern California's mountains experience light snowfall and a warm, dry, early spring, water supplies are compromised even more by a lack of snow, early thaw, and runoff.

Unlike other natural disasters such as floods, earthquakes, and fires—which require an immediate response with little time to prepare—the good news/bad news is that droughts occur slowly over a number of years. Rather than forget about the bad times during the years of plentiful rainfall, plan to incorporate plants that adapt to arid environments into your landscape design as a first line of defense against extended periods of dry weather.

Xeriscape is a word that has become part of the popular vernacular for water-conscious gardeners. It was coined and trademarked by the Denver Water Department in 1983 so that their carefully developed "Seven Principles of Xeriscape Landscaping" would remind everyone that the principles and the term, Xeriscape, would be forever linked together. In 1986, the trademark was transferred to the National Xeriscape Council, Inc., a non-profit entity that serves as a source of information about Xeriscape landscaping and as a support for the development of Xeriscape demonstration gardens across the United States.

The seven Xeriscape landscaping principles are:
- start with a good design
- improve the soil
- limit lawn use
- choose low-water need plants
- water efficiently
- mulch
- practice good maintenance

These guidelines promote the idea that water conservation in the landscape is not "zero-scape" gardening. Instead they provide alternatives that are just as exciting as water-thirsty plants with an endless variety of flower and foliar color and texture.

Despite the efforts of water departments and other water conservationists, myths abound when it comes to drought tolerant plants. They are not just prickly cacti sticking out of concrete or gravel beds, nor are they limited to the blah color spectrum from lackluster brown to gloomy grey. Instead of barren landscapes and wind-swept sand dunes, water-thrifty plants create colorful and beautiful gardens with lower water demands. Besides stunningly colorful or fragrant California natives, many exotic species with similar low water and fertilizer needs native to Australia, New Zealand, South Africa, and the Mediterranean are adaptable to our soil and climate. For example, flannel bush and California lilac pair very well with Mediterranean lavender and South African red-hot poker. When you combine natives with these compatible out-of-towners, you lengthen the flowering season and brighten up the landscape.

There are additional reasons to consider drought-tolerant plants. Many such as sage and lavender have resins that saturate the surrounding air with their fragrance on sultry afternoons, encouraging you to inhale nature's aromatherapy and exhale all of life's tensions. Others are nectar and seed factories that advertise their bounty to birds and butterflies. Butterfly bushes, proteas, and tower of jewels will lure so many winged flutterers, your garden may look like a wildlife refuge. Water-efficient shrubs, perennials, and trees will quiver with the activity of finches, hummingbirds, sparrows, butterflies, hover flies, honey-bees, and other beneficial birds and insects.

Drought-tolerant species are also problem-solvers. Mahonia, coyote bush, New Zealand flax, manzanita, or sumac stabilize slopes. If there are swaths of dry shade, bush anemone or Pacific Coast iris will happily bloom for you. Near wind-swept coastal areas and salt spray, butterfly bush or lemonade berry are ideal choices. For high elevations at 6,000 to 7,000 feet,

flannel bush has survived for 60 million years while meeting additional challenges such as dry, granitic slopes and rocky ridges. If your garden is filled with rocks and serpentine soils, Siskiyou lewisia provides petite, daisylike flowers growing from rosettes of greenery. Rock purslane and elephant bush are attractive water-efficient succulents that thrive in the desert and other areas that average fewer than 10 inches of annual rainfall.

As for the prickly cactus, there are so many different cactus species and other succulents that generalizations about them are impossible. They offer thousands of possibilities for architectural interest, color, and texture. To learn more in-depth knowledge on succulents or cactuses, contact your local chapter of the USA Cactus and Succulent Society of America, visit retail nurseries specializing in them, or visit arboreta that offer desert plant displays. For those who want to establish a collection of cacti and other succulents, join a local club or society because their insights in growing these plants in your area will be most helpful. The same advice applies to all drought-tolerant plants. Local clubs, organizations, retail nurseries, arboreta, and public water-conservation gardens offer a wealth of knowledge in successfully cultivating drought-resistant plants for the landscape.

While walking by an untended hillside or hiking in the backcountry, snap photos of interesting plants growing "wild" and take them to your retail nursery or closest botanic garden for proper identification. If you do decide to "go native" and walk on the wild side, buy them from a retail store specializing in native seeds. Populations of native plants and their seeds need to be left alone in the wild if they are to survive. Mother Nature's panoramic displays of wildflowers and grass species at Bear Valley (Colusa County), Carrizo Plain (eastern San Luis Obispo County), and Antelope Valley inspire gardeners to recreate nature in their backyards. What Mother Nature accomplishes so easily, requires more study and effort on our part. Many native plants have unique niches and needs for successful germination and growth. Learn not only what wild things grow easily near your home, but also where and with what other plants. Write down if they are growing in open areas, or a sheltered nook; if they are thriving along streambeds or peeking out among rocky outcroppings; if their faces are in full sun and facing south or if there are in cooler, moister, north-facing hillsides; and if they are solitary plants or growing in groups with other species. Natives to consider include bush anemone, California lilac, coral bells, Matilija poppies, and woolly blue curls.

If your property has a wilderness view, take advantage of the "borrowed scenery" and select the same plants that are thriving at the edges of your landscape—manzanita, sage, and flannel bush. Use drought-tolerant varieties in mass plantings, clustered groups, or drifts separated from water-hungry plants. Cultural compatibility is of primary importance in determining if they grow to maturity or end up in a compost heap. Consider the cultural requirements of the largest plants first because they set the stage for the space.

Before selecting plants, analyze the soil. 80 to 90 percent of drought-tolerant plants that are available for home landscapes prefer a full sun location with deep, porous, free-draining soil. They have an excellent chance to grow successfully as long as they have a well-drained site, sufficient light, and moderately fertile soil. Even though many drought tolerant plants grow in alkaline soils, a slightly acidic soil is preferable.

A pH of 6.5 to 7.0 optimizes nutrient availability. Read Annuals Autumn Planting on soil preparation for more details.

If the color and texture of the native soil changes in the area to be landscaped, conduct a percolation test in each of the different areas; if the percolation rate is substantially slower than 1 inch per hour, dig a wider planting pit to accommodate the slower percolation rate. For more information about testing the percolation rate of soil, see page 308.

PLANTING

Plant California natives and other water-thrifty varieties from autumn through early spring in mild-winter climates, but in frostier regions plant them in spring. Cool (not freezing) temperatures and rainy weather help establish drought-tolerant and native plants.

Sow seeds in the open ground as soon as the danger of frost is over. Then lightly cover them with soil. Read Autumn Planting for more information on planting drought-resistant natives and exotics from seed and Winter Planting for indoor seed germination.

If planting a containerized drought-tolerant plant, dig the planting pit to promote rapid growth of its root system so that the roots extend deeply into the soil. Create a rectilinear-shaped pit (to discourage roots from circling themselves) and scratch its interior surfaces with a cultivator (to direct the absorbing roots into the native soil).

Match the texture of the excavated soil to the texture of the soil in the rootball of containerized drought-tolerant plants. If the excavated soil is denser than the soil in the rootball, blend in organic compost, organic planting mix, worm castings, or a comparable humus material into the excavated soil. The final backfill mix should be about 30 to 40 percent organic material.

To prevent water from accumulating around the plant's base, set it about $1/2$ to 1 inch above the finished level around the surrounding soil. Most drought-resistant plants need good drainage and are prone to fungal root rot if water is allowed to collect and settle around the trunk or main stem.

Build a watering basin around trees or large shrubs twice the diameter of the canopy of the plant and by forming a berm 4 to 6 inches high. For smaller shrubs or perennials that are clustered close together, watering basins with berms are not as practical, but they still require well-draining soil.

At planting, thoroughly water with a solution rich in humic acid or apply it in granular form and water it in thoroughly; then use a root stimulator with alpha-naphthalene acetic acid or indolebutyric acid three times, two weeks apart.

Some native plants known for their drought tolerance and which are in bloom during spring are:

■ Beard-tongue (*Penstemon* species) are found from the mountains to the desert. Plant in full sun along the coast and partial shade inland. Most of these perennials are drought tolerant and pest- and disease-free, but require well-draining soil. For medium, tall, or sprawling beard-tongue, space about 18 inches apart. Usually they live 3 to 4 years, but their colorful bell-shaped spikes of flowers in blue, red, pink, salmon, rose, deep purple, lavender, peach, and white are a welcome sight from spring to summer. Since native beard-tongue dislikes too much water or soil that is too rich, select hybridized beard-tongue when mixing with regularly irrigated and fertilized garden plants.

■ Bush anemone (*Carpenteria californica*) is an evergreen shrub that bears scented clusters of alabaster-white flowers with yellow centers from late spring to summer. Native to the Sierra Nevada foothills, it does well in shade or sun and grows 4 to 6 feet tall. Space it approximately 4 to 6 feet from other drought-tolerant shrubs. On the coast it needs little or no water once it is established, but inland it may need supplemental watering particularly during the hot, dry summer and fall.

■ California lilacs (*Ceanothus* species) come in many shapes and sizes from ground covers to small trees. A few species lose their foliage in cold weather, but most remain evergreen. Their signature blue or white blooms occur in late winter or early spring. They perform best in full sun with well-drained soil. Once established, they do not like summer watering and typically live 5 to 10 years. Do not plant them near water-thirsty plants.

■ California poppy (*Eschscholzia californica*) grows in all zones of California. It is California's state flower and now comes in a variety of cultivars of varying colors (red, white, pink, orange and gold) and compactness. Plant in full sun and start from seed in early spring or fall. They bloom about the middle of spring or later, depending on the winter and spring rains and the warmth of the season. To extend their bloom, deadhead regularly.

■ Coral bells (*Heuchera* species) bear petite white or pink flowers on 17- to 36-inch-tall stems. Many make excellent ground covers in partial to full shade. They are not as drought tolerant as bush anemone or California lilac, but are still considered moderate water users.

■ Flannel bush (*Fremontodendron californicum*) bears large lemon-gold blossoms in spring and often repeats its flower season in fall. For more information, read Autumn Planting.

■ Matilija poppies (*Romneya coulteri*) are giant perennials, 8- to 10-foot-tall plants with up to 9-inch wide crepe papery-white flowers and golden-yellow centers. Found naturally in coastal arroyos from Santa Barbara to northern Baja, they adapt to all zones in California. They bloom in late spring through early summer and thrive with little to no water once established.

■ Oregon grape (*Mahonia aquifolium*) grows along the coast and inland foothills from British Columbia to Northern California. It grows well in sun or shade and tolerates frost and arid conditions. In spring it bears lovely sprays of yellow flowers.

■ Pacific Coast iris (*Iris douglasiana*) is found along the Pacific Coast from Northern California to Santa Barbara. Their elegant flowers bloom in a rainbow of colors in spring. They grow 1 to 2 feet tall and flourish in rock gardens, meadows, and woodlands.

■ Siskiyou lewisia (*Lewisia cotyledon*) come in varieties that bear lovely striped red, orange, yellow, and pink daisylike flowers above a rosette of leaves. They are excellent in rock gardens. They need excellent drainage and should be in full sun to light shade. Although they tolerate some winter cold, they cannot survive prolonged periods of wet, freezing weather.

■ Cacti and succulent plants provide another fascinating facet to the drought-tolerant garden with their texture, glaucous skins, showy flowers, and intricate, symmetrical spine or leaf crown patterns. The majority of cacti are endemic to the mountains, deserts, and tropical rain forests of the Americas—from Canada to Argentina—and to the drier regions of the American West. Cacti are usually leafless with thick-skinned stems morphing into cylinders, pads, or joints that serve as water reservoirs. Spines commonly cover most cacti to protect them against browsing wildlife. Their brilliant, colorful blossoms are often followed by edible fruit. At maturity, their sizes range from miniature to gigantic (up to 50 feet) making some ideal for containers or rock gardens and others as stand-alone landscape beacons. Cacti are thought to be the ultimate desert survivors. It is a common misconception that if you plant them in pure sand and full sun, they never need much water or nutrients. While most survive under such harsh conditions, they thrive with a bit more care. Many such as prickly pear cactus can live off their inner reserves through several years of drought in their natural habitat. However, they become susceptible to root rot, sunburn, splitting, cracking, and bacterial infections if not properly cared for in an urban landscape.

Although all cacti are succulents, not all succulents are cacti. Succulents have leaves, stems, or roots that serve as sources of moisture during periods of drought. Many are native to primarily desert or semidesert parts of the world such as Mexico and South Africa, but several *Sedum* and *Sempervivum* species hail from cooler areas nestled among rocky ledges and slopes. In mild-winter climates, the majority of succulents are ideal in water-conserving landscapes or in containers. For areas prone to frost, select succulents that tolerate lower temperatures or plant the more cold-sensitive ones in containers where they can be moved easily to more protective areas. As with cacti, large succulent species make impressive statements in the garden such as the monstrous *Agave americana* (century plant), *Aloe arborescens* (tree aloe), and *Crassula ovata* (jade plant). For more diminutive species in containers or in rock gardens, include *Echeveria elegans* (hen and chicks), *Lithops* (stoneface or pebble plants), and *Sempervivum arachnoideum* (cobweb plant). Succulents are most attractive when properly maintained, but survive extended periods of drought by shedding their leaves, shriveling up, or losing their vibrant color.

Most cacti and succulents can be planted anytime if there is sufficient heat and light to encourage strong root development, but it is best to plant or re-pot them during the warmer months of spring and summer when they are in their growth cycle. The big "however" is there are always exceptions and it is best to learn about each plant's special cultural needs. Spring is the best time to propagate cacti and succulents by cuttings unless they are species that grow during fall or winter. Detach a single leaf or stem and let it callus over for 2 to 3 days. To avoid the possibility of root rot, place the cutting against the edge of a pot and allow the stem end to touch the potting medium rather than burying it. Set the pot in a zip-lock bag (if it is a small pot) or cut the bottom of a 2-liter plastic soda bottle and place it over the potted cutting for an instant greenhouse. Water sparingly until new growth is evident. In time, roots will form and grow into the planting medium and small leaves will develop. Keep the cuttings in a warm, protected location away from direct sunlight. Many species of succulents and cacti produce pups or small plants at the base of the mother plant. Pull or cut these offsets, allow them to dry for 2 to 3 days and plant them the same as cuttings. Since pups divert energy from the parent plant, removing them helps the main plant to develop into a large single specimen. Wait until the offsets are well-rooted before planting them directly in the landscape. In most cases, these water-thrifty icons must be planted in a

well-draining medium with equal parts coarse sand, organic material and native soil, sandy peat or in a commercial cactus mix. When transplanting, try to keep some roots attached to the plant, but do not be too concerned about losing part of the root system. New roots regenerate quickly if planted in a well-draining medium that is moist, but not soggy. Also plant them away from high-traffic areas, especially those with sharp needles or spines.

Light requirements vary because many cacti, succulents, and other drought-tolerant plants are protected by the shaded canopy of an overhead shrub or tree in their native habitats. As a broad guideline, cacti need at least four hours of bright light, preferably morning sun while most leafy succulents can flourish with fewer hours of strong sunshine. Until the plant is well-established, protect from direct sunlight with a shade cloth to avoid sunburn. A new root system must develop before the plant is able to take up adequate moisture.

Many Mediterranean, South African, Australian, and other exotic natives adapt well to California's soil and climate conditions. Try these:

■ Butterfly bush (*Buddleja* species), planted from a 4-inch pot in the early spring will rapidly grow 3 to 4 feet during its first year and stretch out to 8 to 10 feet by its second. As long as there is good drainage, *Buddleja* is an ideal choice for naturalizing large areas or covering hillsides because it is so fast growing and thrives even in poor soil, Since there are species native to China, Japan, Chile, Texas, East Indies, Himalayas, and Mexico, there is bound to be a butterfly bush adaptable to your local climate. Hummingbirds, butterflies, and other beneficial insects will thank you for their intoxicating, nectar-rich flowers.

■ Coast rosemary (*Westringia fruticosa*) is native to Australia and flowers from the middle of winter to spring in colder areas, but almost year-round in milder regions. Refer to Autumn Planting for more information on coast rosemary.

■ Plant *Echium* species in spring or fall at least 6 to 10 feet on center, from 4-inch to 1- or 5-gallon containers. The two most popular species found in California are pride of Madeira (native to Madeira, *E. candicans* or *E. fastuosum*) and tower of jewels (*E. wildpretii*) from the Canary Islands. Both require full sun and tolerate poor soil as long as there is good drainage. To encourage the rapid development of deep roots, create watering basins for these giants at least 6 feet in diameter with 6-inch high berms. If you are planting other companions in a grouping, then forego the basins but expect a slower development of the roots and the plant. Hardy to 25 degrees Fahrenheit, they are also excellent for coastal gardens.

■ *Phormium* are native to New Zealand and make dramatic evergreen perennials with swordlike leaves. New Zealand flax and other varieties of *P. tenax* are tough plants that survive with little or no water, coastal winds, poor soil, and hot weather, but they cannot tolerate poorly drained soil or freezing temperatures. Depending on the variety, their fast-growing, swordlike leaves can stretch 3 to 9 feet and spread out to twice the height of their upright leaves. *P. colensol* and hybrid crosses between *P. tenax* × *P. colensol* tend to be more finicky. They require more water, particularly in hot, inland areas, and need to be planted where there is afternoon shade. When purchased at retail nurseries, many look like they will remain small, but they are usually very fast-growing and need plenty of room to stretch out. Whether they are variegated, solid green, bronze, purple, or red, flax plants create striking focal points in the landscape, among other perennials and shrubs, slopes, and around pools or ponds.

Perhaps no family of flowers and foliage from the Southern Hemisphere is more spectacular that the family Proteaceae, which has 42 genera and more than 800 species in Australia and 14 genera and over 330 species in South Africa. The first time you see one, you understand immediately why they were named after Proteus, the Greek god of the sea who could change his form at will. Since the family of Proteaceae is named after the genus *Protea*, it has become common practice to refer to *Banksia, Leucadendron, Leucospermum, Protea, Telopea* and other members of the Proteaceae family as proteas. Although botanists may disagree, we also find it simpler to refer to the various genera of the Proteaceae family as proteas. Their primary blooming periods are fall, winter, and spring, but a few such as the king protea (*P. cynaroides*) continue flowering into summer. In frost-free climates there are many that bloom year-round such as *Banksia integrifolia, B. ericifolia,* and *Leucadendron floridum*. In regions that are cool with heavy winter frosts, it is best to plant proteas during spring, after the danger of frost is over. This gives young plants sufficient time to establish, acclimate, and grow a reasonable size before "Old Man Winter" casts his icy wand across frosty areas.

Before you add proteas to your list of "must haves" for your garden, understand that they are not easy to grow. Although generalizations are difficult for such a diverse genera and species, the majority of proteas prefer good air movement and well-drained, acidic soils (about 6.5 pH) that are low in nutrients. Some notable exceptions to acid preference are *P. obtusifolia* and *P. repens* because they grow naturally in slightly alkaline soils with a 7.5 pH, but even these exceptions will do fine in mildly acid soils. Most members of the Proteaceae family are usually found in sandy, gravelly, or rocky soils. For gardens with heavy clay soils, plant proteas in raised beds or on top of hillsides and slopes. Proteas thrive in mild climates and low humidity. Some withstand short periods of frost, but expect damage to the tender foliage and flowers of species such as *P. neriifolia* and *P. cynaroides*. Heat lovers such as *Leucadendron* and *Leucospermum* species survive temperatures in the 90s and above, as long as there is adequate supplemental irrigation.

Rock purslane (*Calandrinia grandiflora*) is a Chilean native that blooms nonstop from early spring until late fall with 2-inch, hot pink flowers suspended from 24-inch stems emerging from silvery-blue rosettes of fleshy leaves. Winter is its resting season. Plant this perennial in full sun to partial shade surrounded by well-drained soil in a frost-free area. If temperatures dip below freezing, plant it in a container and move it to a more protected location during periods of frost. It is propagated by cuttings or seed. For propagation tips, refer to propagation tips of cacti in this section.

WATERING

All native and drought-tolerant plants require regular water the first year or two. To help develop deep roots, water new plantings deeply and thoroughly once a week (less frequently along the more humid coastal areas, more often in deserts or wherever sandy soil conditions exist) during periods of meager or nonexistent rainfall. As plants become established, reduce the frequency. When selecting water-conserving plants, remember "drought tolerance" refers to the plant's ability to survive drought *once it is established*.

Compared to tropical plants, mature drought-tolerant plants require less moisture during warm seasons. Keep the irrigation system that waters drought-tolerant plants isolated from the circuits that water lawn areas and other plants that require more frequent irrigation. Sprinkler irrigation systems are either hose-end or permanent underground systems and apply large amounts of water in a short time. For permanent systems, adjust the sprinkler heads to spray large droplets of water instead of a fine mist to avoid excess evaporation or wind drift. Avoid spraying water directly on top of plants that are susceptible to crown rot, such as Siskiyou lewisia or rock purslane.

Drought-tolerant plants survive extended dry periods when they have developed roots systems that tap deeply into the native soil for precious moisture. Drip systems are designed to deliver water in a specific area via emitters, bubblers, or spray heads placed at every plant. The soil is gradually saturated to a deep level with little or no surface evaporation. This encourages the development of deep roots by allowing water to percolate down into the soil where it remains for several weeks. For alkaline soils, the drip method is a safer way to irrigate with water containing high amounts of salts.

Deep watering with a garden hose is also practical when there is a watering basin surrounding the plant. The basin serves as a reservoir allowing the water to slowly percolate into the soil. If a basin is impractical (particularly for clusters of medium to small-sized plants), and you do not have a drip system, set the garden hose slightly away from the base of the plant and allow it to trickle for a few hours. This works well when they are in specific designated areas and enables more opportunities to keep a watchful eye over them. Withhold watering for 7 to 10 days, but look for any sign of temporary wilt—a good clue that it is time to thoroughly water again.

Once plants have developed deep roots, they can survive 2 to 3 weeks between watering. Irrigate at a low flow rate allowing the water to percolate down into the deep root zone.

Do not allow any runoff from surrounding plants with higher water requirements to reach the drought-tolerant plantings.

Clay pots or containers that breathe are perfect for drought-resistant plants, but plants dry out faster than those planted directly in the ground. Pay more attention to container plants and water more frequently. Stick your finger into the top inch of the soil and if it is dry, water again, especially when they are in the growth cycle.

Water newly planted succulents and large specimen cacti sparingly until their roots begin to grow. After 4 to 6 weeks, their roots should be developed enough for a thorough soaking; then allow them to dry between watering intervals. Most cacti and succulents do not develop deep root systems because in their native habitats, rainfall becomes available in sudden downpours. Their shallow root systems enable them to suck up water very quickly. A general hint for watering established cacti and succulent plants is: Soak the soil thoroughly, similar to a thunderstorm, then wait until the soil dries out before watering again.

Refer to Summer Watering for advice for newly planted proteas. Supplemental watering is needed to establish proteas, especially if spring rainfall is below normal.

Once established, water Siskiyou lewisias lightly because they are native to the rocky crevices of the Klamath region in northern California where rainfall is minimal.

FERTILIZING

Light feedings are best for most native and drought-tolerant plants because they are adapted to growing in conditions without supplemental fertilizers. Apply a complete organic fertilizer every 45 to 60 days during the growing season or use a controlled-release fertilizer. Follow the manufacturer's directions for amount and frequency (usually about once every 90 to 120 days) if using a controlled-release product. Organic nutrients and controlled-release foods provide the essentials, but at a slower rate than typical chemical fertilizers. Excess amounts of potent chemical fertilizers promote leafy growth and increase a drought-tolerant plant's thirst for water.

Plants endemic to nutrient-poor soils such as proteas need little, if any, fertilizers. Refer to Autumn Fertilizing for specific information.

Although succulents and cacti planted directly in the landscape can also exist without any fertilizer, they thrive and look much better if they are fed a water-soluble organic food every 45 to 60 days beginning in spring after the danger of frost has passed. Chemical controlled-release fertilizers specifically formulated for cacti and succulents that also contain a range of trace elements or micronutrients are another appropriate option during the growing season. Depending on the manufacturer, controlled-release foods are generally applied every 90 to 120 days. Avoid chemical fertilizers with high concentrations of nitrogen, phosphorous, and potassium because they can cause the tips of leaves to turn brown, indicating root and leaf burn.

For container specimen and potted seedlings that are just beginning their new lives outdoors, feed them at half strength every time you water during spring's warm weather. Continue to feed them at this dilution rate while they are in their growth cycle or until they are transplanted into larger containers or planted directly in the garden. Then follow the feeding schedule for established plants.

MAINTAINING

A key element in drought preparedness is to spread a 2-inch layer of mulch evenly around the soil surface, beneath and around plants. An organic mulch of straw, ground bark, humus, worm castings, or compost insulates the roots protecting them from fluctuations of hot and cold temperatures. It also reduces water evaporation, facilitates water and fertilizer penetration, and prevents excess runoff. During decomposition, mulch increases the beneficial microbial activity and provides nutrients for a healthy soil as well as for the plants. Add more mulch when the layer thins out from decomposition.

Use finer-textured mulch for annual and perennial plants, ground bark or other medium-textured mulch around shrubs and trees, and bark nuggets (for proteas in particular) for windy areas or along pathways. Spread mulch around an entire planting bed or mulch individual plants out to their drip lines (the area where water drips off the outermost branches). Keep mulch 3 to 6 inches away from plant stems, crowns, and trunks to prevent rot and to keep pests from using the mulch as hiding places.

Since the crowns of succulents and borderline succulents such as *Lewisia cotyledon* are susceptible to rot, mulch around their crowns with 1 to 2 inches of pea gravel.

Collect ripe seeds and store for outdoor sowing in fall and indoor sowing in winter. Allow the seedpods to ripen on the plant before harvesting; if collected too early, they may not be viable enough for successful germination. Clean off any chaff or pulp from fleshy fruits or pods (chaff and pulp often cause seeds to rot), allow them to dry, and dust them with a fungicide to prevent damping off. Put them in a clean jar or envelope and store them in a cool, dry place such as the garage or closet.

Pull weeds before they go to seed and use a pre-emergent weed control to prevent future weed seeds from germinating in the garden. Plants such as Bermuda buttercup (*Oxalis* species) are a major problem because they spread by seed and by bulbs. Cut the tops off and dig up their bulbs to reduce their spread or use a pre-emergent for about one year prior to planting native grasses, perennials, or annuals. Do not use a pre-emergent control if you intend to plant seeds in that area; instead, dig out the weeds or use a systemic weed-killer containing over 40 percent glyphosate herbicide.

If an alien plant has sprouted in your garden, find out if it is invasive by visiting these websites: **www.invasivespecies.gov** and **www.invasiveplants.net.** To establish a native plant meadow successfully, the most important chore is to eradicate any invasive nonnative species, because they tend to crowd out less vigorous natives.

Efficient and properly maintained irrigation systems can reduce water consumption by 30 to 50 percent. Check the irrigation system 2 to 3 times a month to adjust the timing to accommodate current weather conditions.

Judicious pruning promotes vigorous and healthy plants, but be mindful of any special needs. For example, it is generally best to limit or thin shrubs to no more than $1/3$ their total height, but cut Matilija poppy stems down to the ground in winter or it will resprout from the rootstock the following spring. Also consider the flowering habit of the plant you are pruning. Most California lilac species bloom from buds at the ends of new growth and if pruning back their plants by $1/3$ includes all of the new tip growth, then there will be no blooming buds in spring. Prune after their flowering cycle and leave branches over 1 inch in diameter alone. By doing so, you may be able to extend their bloom period because it forces new growth which will also bloom. To control their growth, pinch back the tips of the new shoots during the warmer months of spring and summer. For flannel bush, *Fremontodendron californicum*, it is best to remove $1/3$ to $2/3$ off each new shoot in early spring once the plant is well established. Hard pruning by $2/3$ increases flower production and controls flannel bush's notoriously gangly size and rangy habit. After taking into account pruning needs of specific plants, trim for shape whenever the flowering period has ended, and deadhead spent flowers to prolong the flowering cycle and to divert plant energy from seed production into foliar and bud growth.

Butterfly bushes are rampant growers and look best in naturalized settings. Clip off their spent flowers for a tidier appearance because they rarely drop their dead blossoms. In more formal areas, they can be gussied up by lopping off their weeping side branches in early spring and leaving a cluster of tall, stately center stems. Their bare columns may look temporarily forlorn, but within a few weeks of mild spring weather they will be covered with fresh, new growth and form stunning panicles of blossoms. Another choice is to continually shear its side branches, leaving a single main trunk and training the top growth so that it is in the shape of a tree. *Buddleja alternifolia*, fountain bush, is ideally suited to "tree training" because it grows to about 8 feet and its weeping branches droop like floral sprays of water in a fountain. *B. crispa* is better pruned back to the ground in regions of winter freeze. Unlike B. *davidii*, B. *crispa* is perfect for smaller gardens. Whatever species or cultivar you select, butterfly bushes are tough and can be pruned just about anytime, particularly in mild winter climates. But spring and early summer is the best time to prune them way back. During the growing season, you will probably interrupt the flowering cycle for a bit, but being such fast growers, they will flower again in a relatively short period of time.

When New Zealand flax flowers are spent, cut out the flower stalks. Old, faded leaves should be pruned out down to the base of the plant to maintain a neat appearance. Watch out for color reversions of variegated or special colored varieties. Remove any reversions by cutting out their crowns down to the roots or else they will eventually take over the original clump. To propagate, remove pups from the mother plant or divide the large clumps. Then transplant into a well-draining planting medium.

PROTECTING

Keep drought-resistant or native plants healthy by watering, fertilizing appropriately, and protecting them from poor drainage and weeds. Basic preventative measures protect them from insect infestations and diseases.

Spring rains and warmer temperatures act as alarm clocks for "sleeping" snails and slugs. If you notice slime trails among your plants use an organic molluscicide with iron phosphate or hand pick and squish. They hide during the heat of the day under the cool, moist shade of ground-hugging plants. Hunt them down when they are hiding or grab them when they come out during spring rains or warm spring evenings. Decollate snails are available for Southern Californians at local garden centers or insectaries. They search out and feed on juvenile brown snails and leave your established plants alone.

New growth attracts sucking insects such as aphids, scale, and mealybugs. Mealybugs have oval cottony coverings and cluster together in clumps. Scale are pinhead-sized insects that resemble tiny limpet shells. Their shells are actually hard coverings that protect the insects underneath. Aphids come in all colors and cluster together in tight groups along stems and on leaves. For minor infestations, blast them off with a strong stream of water or wear gloves and strip them off by hand. When these little suckers are out of control and there are no neighboring plants with edible parts, use a systemic insecticide product, or use a garlic-based or Neem oil insecticide as an organic alternative. Spider mites are practically invisible to the naked eye, but they spin white webs matted close to the plant's surface. Insecticides are ineffective against spider mites because they are not insects; to control mites, spray with a miticide. Sap-sucking insects and mites impair growth, leave unsightly blemishes or scars, and create opportunities for secondary viral, bacterial, and fungal infections that often prove fatal to the host plant. Systemic or organic insecticide and miticide treatments begun in early spring are effective preventative measures against these plant suckers.

Rats, mice, and other foraging creatures can cause considerable damage to plants. If poisons are used to deal with these pests, put the toxic product in bait stations that are safe to use around small children and pets. Also, dispose of the remains of the poisoned dead animals so that beneficial predators such as owls and hawks are not poisoned.

There are deer-resistant plants that do well in a water-conserving garden. For example, the spiky leaves and bitter sap of aloes discourage both animals and insects from dining on them.

Fungal diseases thrive in damp soil and often enter the plants through cuts and wounds made by insects and animals. Dark discolorations and soft spots on drought resistant plants such as cacti and succulents are signs of rotting tissue usually caused by poor drainage or too much water. Make sure drought tolerant plants are separated away from plants with higher water demands and improve drainage so that there is no standing water around the plants. Also treat with a broad-spectrum fungicide appropriately labeled to treat cacti and succulents as well as drought-resistant natives and exotics. Remove infected parts with a sharp, clean knife or clippers and dispose of them in the trash.

If there are weeds among your wildflowers in spring, cut them with a lawn mower set 8 to 10 inches high, once in midspring, and once in late spring, along the coast from Crescent City to San Diego. In the Sacramento and San Joaquin valleys and more inland areas, mow once in early spring and once in midspring.

SUMMER

Fountains of butterfly bush flowers are beckoning butterflies, hummingbirds, and bees to sip from their nectar goblets. Just like us, the lazy days of summer encourage their alfresco dining against the backdrop of heavenly ambrosia.

PLANNING

Plan a trip through the countryside. Summer months are excellent times to see many California natives in bloom including: California fuchsia (*Zauschneria californica*); Cleveland sage (*Salvia clevelandii*); Matilija poppy (*Romneya coulteri*); scarlet monkeyflower (*Mimulus cardinalis*); and woolly blue curls (*Trichostema lanatum*). California fuchsia is only 1 to 2 feet tall, but its bright orange-red flowers in late summer or early fall more than compensates for its size. It survives on little to no water in partial shade to morning sun. A shrubby perennial that adapts to most climates except freezing weather, its prolific tubular-shaped flowers attract hummingbirds from summer until late fall. Cleveland sage is an evergreen with whorls of 1-inch long lavender to dark-blue flowers. Against a backdrop of gray-green evergreen leaves, it thrives in full sun with little water. Scarlet monkeyflower has brilliant scarlet, 2-inch long, tubular flowers on 2^1/$_2$ feet tall plants that are hardy in sun or shade. If there is little or no rainfall, however, they need regular water. Woolly blue curls is a shrub found from Monterey to San Diego along the coast and in inland coastal foothills. It bears violet-blue, trumpet-shaped flowers amidst lime-green foliage. Native to coastal scrub and chaparral on dry slopes, it grows 4 to 6 feet tall and displays its brilliant flowers from the end of spring to late summer.

Butterfly bushes are in full bloom. If you have never seen them before, look over all the cultivars available at your local nursery, arboretum, or botanical garden. Hundreds of petite flowers are arranged along bottle-brush spikes in hues of yellow, purple, magenta, blue, pink, lavender, or white. Their color, fragrance, and nectar are butterfly and bee magnets for the garden. If temperatures climb over 90 degrees Fahrenheit, the opened flowers will remain on the stems as vibrant in color as ever, but new blossoms will hold off until temperatures cool a bit. For the hotter inland valleys, this means their peak flowering beauty occurs during spring and fall.

Make notes of other less-thirsty perennial plants such as aster, coreopsis, gaillardia, and rudbeckia whose summer colors might coordinate with your other plants. Consider kangaroo paw, Russian sage, sea lavender, and creeping thyme to add texture to a water-wise landscape.

PLANTING

Cacti and succulents can be planted in spring and summer, unless a particular genus or species has a different growing season. Read more under Spring Planting. For potted succulents, choose containers that are wide and shallow. Many succulent cultivars tend to spread wide rather than to stretch tall. Unless you have the patience to wait for the succulents to fill in all the blank spaces, set them close together for an impressive display. If one succulent overpowers its companions, just keep cutting it back until the others have a chance to catch up. Depending on the species and varieties, deeper containers may be more appropriate. Make sure they are planted in quick-draining soil. A cactus mix that is 50 percent pumice is ideal unless typical rainfall averages over 10 inches per year. In this case, use a mix with even more pumice or add perlite.

Other drought-tolerant plants can be planted in summer, but transplant shock is a common problem where hot and dry weather conditions prevail. Undeveloped or damaged roots cannot supply enough moisture to foliage, which causes wilting and stress. Wait until early autumn to reduce the possibility of transplant shock unless you live along the coast where summers are typically cooler and milder. Even along the coast, hot spells are known to come on suddenly during summer. Spray the plants with an antitranspirant and apply a root stimulator three times, once every two weeks to help them survive transplant shock.

Mid- to late summer is a better time to prepare the ground for fall planting. Add organic matter such as humus, compost, peat, shredded pine bark, or worm castings maximizing the ability of the soil and plants to absorb and store water in the bedding areas and individual planting holes. Till in 4 to 6 inches of organic material to a depth of 18 inches for trees, shrubs, and perennial flower beds.

Break up the ground and pulverize dirt clods thoroughly to prepare an area for annual wildflower seeds. Although Mother Nature does not prepare the soil as we do in our landscapes, she sows tons more seeds and can afford to be wasteful. Wildflowers need much more help in the cultivated garden.

WATERING

Summer watering is a top priority except for many established California natives and other mature drought-tolerant varieties. The more you include and establish drought tolerant plants, the less you need to irrigate.

Watering frequency depends on prevailing soil, temperature, and humidity conditions as well as whether or not a plant is established and considered drought tolerant. Refer to Soil Rhythms, page 307. Do not overwater established native or drought-tolerant plants. Allow them to dry out before watering again. After about 2 years in the landscape, water-thrifty trees and shrubs only need supplemental irrigation once every 2 to 4 weeks in mild-summer regions. Even in the inland areas or other hot, dry regions of California, watering may only have to be increased to once every 2 weeks. However, the first summer of a drought-tolerant plant's life in a garden requires watering—as often as twice a week and sometimes more frequently—when it is really hot and dry. In containers, they need a thirst-quenching drink every other day and when temperatures reach the 90s or higher, every day. Read more under Autumn Watering.

During summer, irrigation water tends to bead and roll along the surface of the soil, rather than wetting it and percolating through the root zone. If this is happening when you begin to water, apply a surfactant or wetting agent about once a month if the soil is sandy. For clay soil, every 45 to 60 days should be sufficient. This application will break the surface tension and water will penetrate the soil much more efficiently.

Whether watering with a hose-end sprinkler or permanent system, water early in the morning or early evening to prevent waste through evaporation, particularly during the hot, dry summer or fall.

Established butterfly bushes should be watered about once or twice a month during summer.

Water cacti and succulents once or twice during the warmer summer months if the summer is particularly hot and dry and if spring did not produce much rainfall. Check the surrounding soil with a trowel to determine when the soil is dry around the root zone and if a good drenching is in order. Older, established plants prefer deeper, less frequent watering, but newly transplanted ones need more frequent, light watering schedules. You know cacti and succulents are receiving enough water when their leaves, pads, or branches remain pretty and plump. Decrease watering most cacti and succulents towards the end of summer to encourage winter dormancy.

Potted succulents, cacti, and other drought-resistant plants survive on neglect in mild, coastal climates, but they look better and remain healthier with regular watering wherever summer temperatures hover in the 90s or above. For those in containers, it is difficult to overwater them during a hot, dry summer.

Depending on the variety, some established California lilacs (*Ceanothus*) require complete dryness during summer while others, such as the coastal ground cover types, do better with occasional summer irrigation if located away from the fog belt. To locate the species best adapted to your region's conditions, stay with tried-and-true varieties sold at your local nursery.

Water *Echium* regularly where summers are hot and dry, but little or no water is necessary in mild, coastal regions.

Proteas are tough once they are established, but they require water about twice a week during their first summer. After the first year they do not need much watering if they are varieties that are listed as drought

tolerant. Established plants usually need supplemental irrigation only in summer. When temperatures climb over 90 degrees Fahrenheit and dry winds and sunlight are intense, they may have to be watered every other day, especially those in sandy soils or in containers. Under such conditions, an automated drip irrigation system with a single emitter placed near the base of each established protea plant is ideal. Proteas planted in the ground prefer deep watering around their bases instead of overhead sprinklers. Overhead sprinkling encourages fungal disease and burns tender foliage in the bright summer sun. If conditions remain mild and the preceding winter and spring seasons provided normal rainfall, then decrease the frequency to once every 7 to 10 days. Bear in mind that sandy or gravelly soils drain very well and dry out faster than heavier soils. When summer days begin to sizzle, water proteas in containers daily.

FERTILIZING

Feed with organic fertilizers every 45 to 60 days or chemical controlled-release fertilizers according to the manufacturer's directions. Also read Spring Fertilizing.

If foliage on the outer canopy show signs of chlorosis (leaf veins stand out green and the intervein areas are yellow), then it is probably a sign of secondary or micronutrient deficiency. Secondary plant nutrients include calcium, magnesium, and sulfur. (The major plant nutrients are nitrogen, phosphorus, potassium, carbon, hydrogen, and oxygen.) Micronutrients are zinc, iron, manganese, copper, boron, molybdenum, and chlorine. To remedy a deficiency, spray the plant with a blend of chelated micronutrients.

Refer to fertilizing proteas under Spring Fertilizing.

Continue to fertilize potted cacti and succulents with a water-soluble, organic food at half strength every time they are watered during the warm summer months (or use a chemical fertilizer that is specifically formulated for cacti and succulents). Feed cacti and succulents in the landscape mid- to late summer. Many cacti and succulents go dormant in late summer or fall. Discontinue fertilizing to encourage dormancy and continue to feed only those plants that continue to grow during fall and winter. Refer to Spring Planting for examples of plants that are in their growth cycle during fall and winter.

MAINTAINING

Monitor the moisture content to make sure there is adequate drainage so that there is no standing water in the root zone. If there is standing water, dig a dry well (pit) away from the plant that is deeper than the root zone. This allows excess water to gravitate towards lower elevations.

Maintain 2 inches of humus or compost over the surface of the watering basin to conserve water, keep the weeds down, and stabilize soil temperature. If the top layer of material has decomposed to less than 2 inches, add more. Mulching away from the base of the plant by at least 4 inches keeps the trunk or main stem dry. It also prevents fungi from entering through the plant's openings in its stem or trunk.

Unless it is in an area where seeds are to be planted, look for products containing corn gluten. Corn gluten suppresses weeds and decomposes into food for the plants. Continue to eliminate any weeds, especially where you plan to plan California natives from seed. Hand pull, dig out, or spray the weeds with a systemic weed killer. Thoroughly water the area where you want to sow California native seeds for several weeks prior to fall. As more weeds germinate, knock them down with a systemic or dig them out. The more time and effort spent on keeping the area weed-free, the better the chance for your fall-planted wildflower seeds to germinate and flourish next spring. Once the weeds have been eliminated, smooth out the soil, and break up any chunky dirt clods.

Compost piles work even faster in hot weather. Keep them turned and moist. Save coffee grounds or tea leaves and add them to the compost pile. Their acidity will "heat" up the compost pile even more.

Mulch proteas with heavier bark mulch.

Collect and store wildflower seeds in a cool, dark, dry place. Keep them in storage until fall. Read Spring Maintaining for more information on collecting, cleaning, and storing seeds.

To control rampant or leggy growth, the general rule is to reduce the size of the plant by 20 to 40 percent. It is important to learn about the dos and don'ts when it comes to pruning a specific plant. Many scrub brush plants such as coyote bush tend to get scraggly and woody after several seasons. Cut them back hard with a heavyweight pruner or with a mower. For blooming drought-tolerant plants, wait until their flowering cycle is over before pruning.

Cut away any dead, damaged, or diseased branches and clip off any interfering branches for shape. Lace dense interiors by thinning out any branches with skimpy or browning foliage. Lacing allows more sunlight into the centers of plants encouraging bushier and healthier growth.

To encourage more blooms, deadhead spent flowers. Unless you are keeping the seeds to grow new plants, deadhead the spent flowers so that the energy of the plant is directed into growth and in more flowers production rather than into seed development. An exception to this rule is a biennial plant, such as the tower of jewels (*Echium wildpretii*). Once the 6 to 10 feet columns of flowers are spent, the parent plant produces seeds to perpetuate itself and then dies. New plants will emerge unless the seeds are dug out. The perennial shrub, pride of Madeira (*Echium candicans*), should have its panicles cut once the flowers are spent for a tidier appearance.

Some species of butterfly bush such as *Buddleja alternifolia*, *B. asiatica*, and *B. globosa* need to be pruned after blooming in late spring or early summer. If they are in a natural, rather than a more formal landscape, it is not necessary to be so obsessive about clipping them. Read Spring Maintaining for more detailed information on pruning butterfly bushes.

Hairy, cone-shaped seedpods emerge after flannel bush flowers are spent. If you find them unbearably ugly, cut them off, but wear protective gloves and clothing because they can irritate sensitive skin.

Mature foliage of New Zealand flax may fade with age. Cut off old foliage when the younger leaves show more color. If the new shoots are reverting to plain green, prune them off at the base.

While a few *Westringia fruticosa* remain a diminutive 3 feet tall, most coast rosemary cultivars need room to grow to their full potential of 5 to 6 feet tall and 5 to 10 feet width. Prune off the dead and diseased wood, but do not shear off too much off the healthy growth. Pruning takes away from the large, billowy nature of coast rosemary.

PROTECTING

Once the weather warms from spring through summer and often into fall, whiteflies begin collecting on the foliar undersides of plants such as butterfly bush, flannel bush, Matilija poppy, and tower of jewels. Use a systemic insect control for whitefly, an organic garlic-based control, or Neem oil. Organic controls need to be reapplied about once or twice a week, until the whitefly problem is gone, but a systemic lasts between 6 weeks to a year, depending on the product. Also add a 1-inch layer of worm castings around the plants to increase the beneficial microbe population in the soil, making the plants healthier.

White, cotton-candylike streamers on leaves is evidence of giant whitefly. The most effective control is a systemic shrub insect killer specifically labeled for giant whitefly. A single application protects about one year.

Order beneficial insects such as ladybugs, lacewings, praying mantis, predatory mites, and wasps from a mail-order insectary or buy them at your retail nursery. They will control the "bad bugs."

If you spot ants marching up and down your plants, first get rid of the aphids. The ants are trekking up your plants to feed on the honeydew secretions of aphids. Read more under Spring Protecting. Stop ants in their tracks with a sticky trap or set out bait stations containing boric acid. They will take the boric acid back to their nests and, in time, the entire colony will be killed.

Summer gloom (overcast days) is a perfect environment for powdery mildew. Combat the "fungus among us" by washing off the foliage in the early morning to remove spores or by spraying with a product containing organic lemon myrtle extract.

Phytophthora is a fungus commonly known as root rot that particularly affects drought-tolerant plants when they have been overwatered in heavy clay soils. Plants showing early symptoms of poor growth, yellowing foliage, and wilt should be treated immediately with an application of compost tea (read Herbs and Vegetables Spring Protecting for more information on compost tea) and a water-soluble solution of humic acid. Both help increase the beneficial microbes and oxygen supply in the soil. If the plant continues to die back, dig it up and allow that area to remain fallow and dry for 2 to 3 years. Another alternative is to add a granular humic concentrate into the soil, apply a 1-inch layer of worm castings, and water it in with compost tea. Wait until the following spring before planting and repeat the soil treatment again with the humic concentrate, worm castings, and compost tea. This regimen has helped combat phytophthora in many instances.

Stem borers, thrips, mites, scale, and various beetles are major pests of proteas. Spray with an organic, garlic-based insecticide at least once a week for three weeks or until the infestation is under control or use a systemic insecticide with imidacloprid every 12 months. For mite control, use a miticide.

Read Spring Protecting for deterrents against rodents, deer, raccoons, possums, rabbits, squirrels, and other critters.

DROUGHT-TOLERANT NATIVES

Achillea, Yarrow (perennial)	*Mahonia aquifolium*, Oregon grape (shrub)
Aquilegia formosa, Western columbine (perennial)	*Mimulus* species, Monkeyflower (perennial)
Arctostaphylos species, Manzanita (shrub)	*Penstemon* species, Penstemon (perennial)
Baccharis pilularis, Dwarf coyote bush (shrub)	*Pinus* species, Pine (tree) (also non-native species)
Ceanothus species, California lilac (shrub)	*Platanus racemosa*, California sycamore (tree)
Cercis occidentalis, Western redbud (shrub or tree)	*Quercus agrifolia*, Coast live oak (tree)
Eschscholzia californica, California poppy (perennial; often grown as annual)	*Romneya coulteri*, Matilija poppy (perennial)
Fremontodendron californicum, Flannel bush (shrub)	*Sequoia sempervirens*, Coast redwood (tree)
Heteromeles arbutifolia, California toyon shrub)	*Umbellularia californica*, California laurel (tree)
Lewisia cotyledon, Siskiyou lewisia (perennial)	*Washingtonia filifera*, California fan palm (tree)
	Zauschneria californica, California fuchsia (perennial)

AUTUMN

 Toasty warm soil, shorter days, and cooler evenings are the familiar drumbeats of autumn. Plant your native and drought tolerant selections to these rhythms, but be wary of the staccato notes of the Santa Ana and Chinook wind section.

PLANNING

This is the time when nurseries have a wide selection of native and drought-resistant plants. Since not all native plants are drought resistant, do your homework before making your selections. Some are endemic to streambeds and require copious amounts of water, while others adapt well to summer watering but can also go dry if necessary. Still others can only survive if winters are wet and summers are completely dry. Some natives such as flannel bush do not appreciate any summer water, but others such as Western columbine and monkeyflowers tolerate some irrigation. Find out if the plant you're considering appreciates a dry, full-sun location; sunny with water; dry shade; or shade with water. Avoid making the wrong selections by visiting a native plant or drought-tolerant plant specialty nursery. You can also find appropriate plants at botanical gardens such as Theodore Payne in Sun Valley, Rancho Santa Ana Botanic Garden in Claremont, and Strybing Arboretum and Botanical Garden in San Francisco. Local native plant societies and water districts are other sources for valuable information.

Since turfgrasses require more frequent watering and maintenance than most water-thrifty plants, don't interplant them. Place low-water need selections such as ceanothus or Matilija poppy on the outer perimeters of your yard and keep your thirstier plants closer to the house.

Review all your notes about drought-tolerant and native plants and decide which ones you will be planting in fall. Leaf through seed and plant catalogues. Check with your local nurseries to make sure they will have your choices in stock. If not, see if you can place special orders so that they will be available later.

PLANTING

In mild-winter climates you can plant natives or drought-tolerant plants just about any time, but fall and early spring are the best seasons. In autumn, these plants transition into the garden with greater ease, especially after the hot, dry Santa Ana winds and Chinooks blow away. The ground is still cozy enough for their roots to dig in and expand and the cooling air soothes the trauma of transplanting. Fall planting allows enough time to actively grow during the upcoming winter and spring rains so that they can withstand the hot and dry conditions of summer. For cold-winter regions, autumn is also the best time to plant, if it is at least six weeks before the ground freezes. If not, wait until spring after the last frost.

If the ground was not prepared during summer, prepare now before planting to ensure excellent drainage. Read soil preparation under Spring and Summer Planting. Most drought-tolerant plants prefer to be planted on sloping ground, raised beds, or containers.

There are a few simple tricks to transplanting California native and other water-wise plants. First, purchase them from a specialty nursery, retail garden center, or public garden from staff knowledgeable about drought-resistant and native species. Before taking them home, check the bottom of the containers. If roots are coming out the bottom, they are probably rootbound and will not transplant very well. You can also slide a plant carefully out of its container; if the roots are tightly matted, put it back, do not take it home. Buy 1-gallon size containers or smaller, because younger plants adapt more quickly to transplanting conditions. Raised beds or tops of slopes are better sites to plant water-thrifty plants if the soil is clayey. Dig an 18-inch deep hole (depth depends on the species; follow the recommendations of the nursery staff), fill it with water, and allow to drain out. Water the plant thoroughly before transplanting, then gently remove the plant from its container and set it in the hole. Don't treat it roughly because it has delicate, easily broken roots and crowns. Plant so that the top of its rootball peeks about 1 inch above the surrounding soil. If the crown is buried, it increases the chance of rot. Backfill with native soil blended with amendments to match the soil around the rootball, and lightly tamp the soil down with your hands. Refer to Spring Planting for specifics on constructing a watering basin for large plants. Cover with a 2-inch layer of organic mulch for insulation against temperature fluctuations (hot and cold) and water retention. Mulch the area around plants susceptible to crown rot with pea gravel. Then soak deeply and thoroughly.

Autumn is also the perfect season to plant native California seeds such as California poppies and other wildflowers. Plant the wildflower seeds you recently purchased or collected and stored from last spring and summer. Stay away from generic "wildflower" mixes that might include plants native to other regions of the United States or the world; look for packets containing only California natives. Successful germination and growth is much higher when planting wildflower seeds that are "homegrown." Consult your local native plant nursery or University of California Cooperative Extension Office for specific methods for germinating native and other drought-resistant plant seeds. Some need scarification (nicking the seed with a rough file or sandpaper); others do best with a warm water soak; some require cold stratification (storing in the refrigerator for 1 to 3 months in a seed-starting medium in a plastic bag); others may need scorching (the most challenging method). Mix seeds with 50 to 75 percent fine sand to distribute the seeds easily and more evenly. Broadcast the sandy seed mixture by hand or by spreader and lightly rake them in so they have direct contact with the soil, about $1/16$ to $1/8$ inch deep for optimum germination. For larger areas such as meadows, it might be easier to scatter a thin covering of organic potting soil, humus mulch, worm casting, or compost over the seeds instead of raking them into the soil. Plant individual wildflower or grass species in swaths about 50 to 100 feet long and 20 feet wide. This replicates more closely the pattern in their native habitat and makes for a spectacular spring show, but planting California mixes is fine too. Although it is commonly recommended to sow 5 to 10 pounds per acre, native wildflower or grass seeds will have a much better chance if you spread 50 pounds per acre or 1 quart of seeds for 200 to 500 square feet. Annuals usually germinate within 2 to 4 weeks and perennials sprout within 4 to 8 weeks.

There is a difference between California natives and their cultivated or hybridized varieties. Many of the cultivated forms were developed to thrive in our irrigated urban and suburban gardens; natives are more attuned to rangeland, foothills, mountains, and coastlines where they grow naturally. The California poppy is a great example. Considered a perennial, it is treated as an annual in cold-climate areas, and reseeds itself year after year. Unless the native poppy flowers are deadheaded regularly, they quickly go to seed. For natural hillsides or for a water-thrifty country garden look, the native poppy is an excellent choice. Since it is illegal to collect seeds or to dig up native plants in the wild, visit a retail nursery for your supply. If you want the true orange California poppy, make sure it is labeled *Eschscholzia californica*. Sow the seeds directly where you want them, because California poppies do not transplant very well. California poppy is adaptable to most climate zones, provided it receives full sun and is planted in fairly well-draining soil. For more manicured gardens, the cultivated or hybridized poppy would do much better. Be careful where and what kind of poppies you plant because the cultivated or hybridized newcomers can genetically swamp the native poppies growing in their natural habitat. This is true for other cultivated or hybridized versions of California native plants.

Seeds of native and drought-resistant flowering perennials, shrubs and trees are best started in containers and planted in the ground later. Use nursery flats or small plastic pots with drainage holes that have been sterilized in a solution of 1 part bleach to 10 parts water. Commercial, organic potting mixes are ideal because they are sterile and free of weeds. Scatter the seeds over the soil or place in shallow furrows and topdress with 1/4-inch layer of fine grit or commercial potting mix. Use a spray bottle to moisten the surface without disturbing the seeds. Keep it moist but not soggy by misting the surface regularly and placing it in a protected location away from direct sunlight. After the second set of true leaves appear, transplant to another flat or individual 2-inch pots so that the seedlings will have more room to grow. Wait another 7 to 10 days before exposing the seedlings to increasing amounts of light over a 2 to 3 week period. Introducing them to full sun without conditioning them burns their tender foliage, much like what happens to us when we spend several months out of the sun and spend the day at the beach without sunscreen. Allow 6 weeks after the second transplanting before planting them in the ground or into 4-inch pots. Some trees and shrubs, especially those with large seeds, can be successfully germinated directly in the ground. California lilac and flannel bush can grow in place from seed, but it may take 3 to 5 years from seed germination to flowering maturity. In the case of tower of jewels, birds, gravity, and wind disperse the seeds to germinate on their own. If their seeds germinate early enough in fall, they may flower by the following spring. For successful plantings from seeds, be sure to prepare the soil, protect the tender plants from animals, maintain a proper watering and fertilization regimen, and keep the surrounding area weed-free.

When California natives and other drought-resistant plants are propagated from seed, they may be mistaken for weeds in their early development. Plant a few seeds in a containers with appropriate labels so you can properly identify them in your landscape. You can also start seedlings in containers before transplanting them in the ground. Since many such as California poppies do not appreciate having their roots disturbed, plant the seeds in peat pots. They can be planted directly in the ground without taking them out of the containers. For best results, make sure the soil texture in the ground is the same as the soil texture in the peat pots.

Some seeds require "smoke signals" in order to properly germinate. For example, protea and many other seeds from the area around Cape Fynbos (the Cape Floral Kingdom of South Africa) germinate only when you recreate conditions similar to the rainy season after a fire. Smoking the seeds involves burning Fynbos plant material in a plastic tent and suspending the seeds over the fire. Fortunately there is no need for the home gardener to set bush fires or establish smoking tents. There are paper disks impregnated with the chemicals found in bushfire smoke known as smoke seed primers. When they are soaked in a solution of these chemicals, it "tricks" certain seeds into germinating. *Protea*, *Leucospermum* (pincushions), and *Leucadendron* seeds have a very difficult time growing among dense Fynbos shrubs because as seedlings they are competing for sun and nutrients. But after a fire, there is no competition for sunlight and the soil is rich with nutrients. How do the seeds know when it is safe to come out after a fire and during winter rainfall? When the first rains dissolve the ash on the soil's surface, it is a "smoke signal," a cue to break seed dormancy. Sow the "smoked" seeds in seed trays or a plastic baggy filled with 2 parts coarse river sand, 2 parts peat, and 1 part vermiculite or perlite. Moisten the soil mixture and plant the seed to a depth equal to its size. If using the baggy method, zip up the bag and place indoors by a window with bright, indirect light. Periodically open up the bag if excess beads of moisture begin to

collect on its surface. Set seed trays outdoors in partial shade and water with a mister. Never allow the soil mixture to dry out completely in the seed tray or the plastic bag. If you have alkaline or brackish water, use deionized water (steam-iron water) available at the grocery store. Depending on the species, the germination period is between 1 to 3 months. First the cotyledons appear, followed by the true leaves. Transplant them to a full sun site during late winter or early spring, when there is no danger of frost, into a similar, well-draining potting medium. 1-gallon black plastic pots with drainage holes are sufficient until the young plants have grown sufficient root systems and are established enough to be transplanted directly in the ground.

If you have neither the time nor inclination to germinate proteas from seed, purchase them in 1-gallon pots. Autumn and early winter are the prime times to plant proteas in mild-winter locales. This gives them an opportunity to nestle their roots into the surrounding soil before the dry summer months. Plant in a sandy loam soil or decomposed granite in full sun with good air circulation. Dig a hole 2 to 3 times the diameter and depth of the original pot and fill it with water. Allow the water to soak in before setting the plant in the pit. Backfill so that it is at the same level as it was in the container or slightly above the surrounding soil level. Tamp the soil down and add more water to moisten the area around the plant. For heavy clay soils, mound the soil, mix in compost and gypsum to break up the clay, and plant proteas on sunny slopes. If you are planting more than one, space them about 6 to 10 feet apart depending on the species. Most proteas dislike being crowded because they need good air circulation to avoid fungal diseases and spindly, scraggly growth (especially in warm humid climates). Although some proteas withstand neutral to alkaline soils, they usually appreciate acidic soil. Contact your local nursery or arboretum to find out more about your local soil conditions and which proteas are best suited for your area. The arboretum at University of California Santa Cruz has sections devoted to proteas. The Los Angeles Arboretum, Huntington Botanical Gardens, Quail Botanical Gardens, The San Francisco Botanical Garden at Strybing Arboretum, and the protea garden at Escondido's Wild Animal Park offer good examples on where to plant and how to combine these plants with other compatible companions for interest all year long. Do not plant proteas among plants that need regular fertilizing or in old flower beds that have been previously fertilized with phosphorous.

Although much of the planting advice for drought-resistant or native plants has been covered in Spring Planting, the following provides a few reminders that are important to keep in mind when considering specific plants.

■ Butterfly bush (*Buddleja* species) grows from 5 to 15 feet depending on the species or cultivar and blooms heavily during summer with tightly knit panicles of purple, magenta, pink, or white nectar-laden flowers. Although it does best in full sun, it tolerates partial shade and seaside exposures. Depending on the species and the climate, the butterfly bush is evergreen, deciduous, or semievergreen. *B. davidii* adapts to a wide range of climates from USDA zones 5 to 10, but flourishes where there is excellent soil drainage and the weather is dry.

■ Some species of *Ceanothus* are endemic to other states or to Mexico, but the majority are California natives. Since they grow naturally on rocky slopes, they require soil that drains very well in the garden. Some California lilacs stand tall at 6 to 9 feet, while others measure their height in inches but have a spreading girth of 5 to 15 feet, and several others remain a compact, bushy 2 to 4 feet. Typically they are evergreen, but some defoliate in cold weather. There are so many species and hybrids available it is best to seek the advice of a nursery retailer knowledgeable about California natives for the selections most appropriate for your neighborhood.

■ Coast rosemary (*Westringia fruticosa*) is native to Australia but adapts very well to California. Depending on the cultivar, it remains a compact 3 feet or expands up to 5 to 6 feet and 5 to 10 feet wide. This shrub tolerates little to moderate amounts of water, salt spray, and is insect-resistant. It flowers from spring through midwinter in colder climates and year-round in mild winter regions. The best time to plant coast rosemary is in the fall season for most areas of California or in early spring for regions with winter frost. Once established, coast rosemary is hardy to 25 degrees F. For best growth, provide light, well-drained soil, and full sun, but coast rosemary tolerates some shade and seaside conditions.

■ Flannel bush (*Fremontodendron californicum*) stands as tall as 15 feet and spreads 12 feet wide. In addition to plenty of elbow-room, it needs very good drainage, but adapts to a variety of exposures. Planting on a hillside or slope is ideal. Once established, it can take the cold down to 5 degrees Fahrenheit. Plant in fall to get it well established before the warm summer season. When planted in full sun with good drainage, it bears large lemon-yellow flowers from early to midspring and sometimes repeats for a shorter bloom period in autumn. It is a good choice for a sprawling, informal hedge on dry, rocky hillsides or espaliered against a sunny wall. Do not plant near walkways because its fuzzy stems can be irritating to those with sensitive skin.

■ To propagate a Matilija poppy, dig up an established clump and carefully move it to a new home. Plant the poppy at the same depth and orientation as its original home and in well-draining soil. You can also propagate by root cuttings. Gingerly dig around the mother plant with a shovel or trowel and pick out roots with diameters the size of pencil widths and with obvious bud development. Take several cuttings for good measure. Put them in a plastic baggy filled with moist potting soil to keep them viable if you are not planting them immediately. Plant them 1 inch deep in soil with excellent drainage. Set the root cuttings horizontally. If the soil is clay-textured, read Soil Rhythms, page 307, on soil preparation. Water the ground thoroughly and let it settle overnight before adding a 3- to 4-inch layer of sand on the prepared surface. Plant the roots 2 inches deep in the sand. This permits root growth between the sand and the clay. If you mix the sand into the clay soil, the clay becomes even denser in texture. Water so that the soil is moist, but not soggy. When the cuttings begin to grow and sprout, begin watering regularly until they are well established.

■ Many species of succulent plants and cacti may be propagated by division. Usually the best time to divide is when the plant is dormant and dry, typically in fall or winter. Refer to Spring Planting for information on exceptions to fall or winter dormant cacti and succulents. Divide thick, tuberous branching roots with a sterile knife into two or more pieces. Dust the cut surface with a fungicide and allow the cuttings to callus over. Plant each piece in a commercial cactus mix and water very little until new growth is evident. To learn more about propagation techniques including division, planting with offsets, cuttings, and grafting, contact your local cactus and succulent society or arboretum.

Refer to the Spring and Summer Planting for additional information on New Zealand flax, rock purslane, Siskiyou lewisia, and tower of jewels as well as other California natives and exotic water-thrifty plants.

WATERING

One abiding truth about watering plants, whether drought-tolerant or not, is that all new seedlings or transplants need time and adequate water to establish their root systems. Do not just plant and forget about them. Water new plantings thoroughly and gently after burying them in place. Fill each hole with water and allow it to drain completely before setting plants in; then give them extra moisture around the sides. Where there is little or no rainfall, supplemental irrigation is necessary. Keep the soil moist but not soggy. For the first year or two, water every other week along the coast; inland, water as often as once a week. Keep in mind, these are general guidelines and water needs vary according to species, soil type, exposure, and location. Clay soils need less water than sandy soils.

During heavy rainfall, if there are basins built around trees and large shrubs, open a section of each basin to drain off excess water. Watch the plants; if they are stressed or withered during the growth or bloom cycle, continue irrigation. It takes about 1 to 2 years before a newly planted water-thrifty or native plant can develop a root system large and deep enough to withstand drought. When they are nursery grown, their natural ability to root deeply in the soil to reach water trapped far below the surface is limited. Once their root systems are established, they will survive quite well on winter rains and an occasional summer watering.

Water the seed beds or containers lightly and frequently, about once a week, to keep the area moist until seeds have germinated. To avoid washing the seeds out, sprinkle lightly with a mister or set your containers directly in 1 to 2 inches of water until the surface of the soil feels moist to the touch.

There is a fine balance between not watering enough and overwatering. For young seedlings with just one or two pairs of true leaves, check as often as once a day for signs of wilting. When in doubt, stick your finger up to the knuckle down into the dirt every few days. If it feels dry to the touch, water thoroughly and wait until it is dry again before watering. It is important to let the soil moisture—not the calendar—be your signal for watering. After three weeks, seedlings should be strong enough to survive without so much monitoring, unless there is a spell of hot, dry weather. For trees and shrubs, decrease water after the second year and by the third year, no additional watering should be necessary. Wean drought-tolerant perennials off supplemental watering by the end of the first year and with annuals as quickly as 4 to 12 weeks depending on the regularity and amount of rainfall.

New transplants of drought-tolerant shrubs should be watered about once a week with approximately one gallon of water per week during cool months. If there is a hot, dry spell, water twice or possibly three times a week but allow the plants to dry out a bit between watering cycles. If there is plentiful rain after planting, take time off from watering and let Mother Nature care for them.

Since most drought-tolerant plants prefer wet-dry cycles, set up a drip system for the most efficient watering regime. Place a single dripper 2 inches from the stem until the plant is mature (about 2 to 3 years for shrubs and trees and 1 year for perennials) at a rate of one gallon per hour. Once the plant reaches maturity, remove the original dripper and set up two drippers, one on either side at 6 inches from the stem to accommodate its increased size.

It is often recommended that cacti and succulents receive no water from fall through early spring. Although this is one way to prevent winter rotting, it may not be the best advice when there is low humidity, wind, and little rainfall. It certainly is the wrong advice for cacti and succulents that are in their growth cycle during the cooler months of the year, particularly when there is a dearth of rainfall. Since these conditions stress the plants and leave them susceptible to other problems, it is wiser to use common sense. If it has been unseasonably warm and there has been no rainfall, a light watering may be just the right thing to do for your plants. However, some established succulents such as elephant bush or elephant food (*Portulacaria afra*) should be kept as dry as possible until the first rainfall because when they are stressed from lack of water, they tend to bloom more profusely in late autumn.

FERTILIZING

Never feed proteas with chemical fertilizers or manure. They have very sensitive root systems and burn easily when there are too many chemical nutrients, especially phosphates: Phosphates kill proteas. It is usually not necessary to feed proteas because they are native to nutrient-poor areas. If they are planted in sandy soils or containers, use a fertilizer specifically formulated for Proteaceae or feed them an organic food such as fish emulsion or kelp (at $1/2$ the recommended strength) or a slow-release fertilizer appropriate for native plants.

Avoid planting proteas in former vegetable gardens or orchards where fertilizers have normally been applied.

Many species of cacti and succulents go into dormancy during autumn or winter. When their growth cycle stops, they should not be fertilized. There are exceptions such as certain species of *Aeonium*, *Crassula*, and *Epiphyllum* that have growth cycles during fall through winter.

Refer to Spring Fertilizing for general feeding recommendations.

MAINTAINING

Although we may provide the most optimum conditions for a plant and fertilize and water when they should, sometimes a plant will suddenly die for no discernable reason. Now is a good time to take out the dead ones and replace them.

More than likely, however, their premature deaths are due to poor drainage, improper watering, diseases, or insect infestation. Refer to Spring Planting, Maintaining, and Protecting for more information.

Monitor the moisture content to make sure there is adequate drainage so that there is no standing water in the root zone. Tree sap bleeding from trunk openings and root rot is caused by an excessive amount of moisture in drought tolerant trees, shrubs, and perennials.

Do not dig or cultivate around a protea because it dislikes having its root system disturbed. Newly planted larger proteas may need staking to prevent them from rocking and rolling in the wind and suffering root damage as a result. Stake at an angle away from the trunk to avoid root damage and tie the plant loosely. Of course, it is preferable to select smaller plants that establish and fill out quickly without the necessity of stakes.

Use coarse bark or cocoa mulch around proteas. Gardeners with shredder machines can use a mulch of shredded protea branches, clippings, and spent flowerheads.

If weeds or exotic seedlings are beginning to overtake the wildflower seedlings, it might be best to dig everything under and start over because wildflower seedlings cannot compete against a heavy influx of weeds or other exotics.

Wear protective gloves, particularly when handling fuzzy, thorny, or prickly plants or those that ooze sap because they irritate and damage sensitive skin.

For new plantings, mulch the surface with 2 inches of organic material and replenish the surface mulch of established plants to protect them from the cooler evening temperatures in autumn. For succulents, cacti, and drought-tolerant plants that are susceptible to crown rot, maintain a 1- to 2-inch layer of pea gravel.

When Matilija poppy leaves turn yellow and brown towards the end of autumn, cut the statuesque plants down to 4 to 6 inches or all the way to the ground. New growth will come from the roots during winter rains.

Prune proteas to maintain a well-shaped and compact plant for ease of care as well as harvesting foliage and flowers. *Banksia* species like their branches trimmed for shape only in order to encourage new growth. Primarily remove their old flowers and seed cones. Most *Leucadendron* species need to be pruned when their colorful bracts have faded and before new growth has begun. If they become leggy, wait to prune them back severely to the stump in spring for bushier new growth. Prostrate species need only a light trim to snip off seedcones. *Leucospermum* do not need much pruning except for shaping and for removing spent flowers. If they are pruned too hard back into the previous year's growth, they may not send out new growth again. *Protea* species also do not need much pruning with the exception of *P. cynaroides* (the king protea). King proteas are able to produce new vigorous shoots from a stump. When clipping for shape, make sure you leave enough leaf growth behind the cuts and do not go too far back into old wood. For more compact habits, prune the current season's growth off with the spent flowers to encourage the development of lower shoots. Similar to *Leucadendron*, *Telopea* species appreciate an annual hard pruning right after flowering and before the start of new growth. Remove the entire flowering stem to develop multiple shoots from the base of the bush. This results in more flowering stems on a bushier, more compact plant.

Snip off any browning, outer foliage of Siskiyou lewisia to encourage good air circulation around its root crown.

PROTECTING

If birds or four-legged critters settle in to snack on freshly planted seeds or newly emerging sprouts, net the entire area or use a floating horticulture blanket.

As the days shorten and the evenings cool, many plants in the wild begin to go dormant, encouraging deer to visit gardens for food. Plant deer-resistant plants such as the *Ceanothus × hybrida* 'Blue Sapphire'. For other deer resistant plants, read Winter Protecting.

When digging planting pits, line them and cover the surface with wire mesh to prevent gophers or moles from tunneling into and destroying the new drought-resistant plants. Surround young plants with a wire cage if deer or rabbits are a problem.

Most insect infestations should abate during the cooler months of fall. Refer to Spring and Summer Protecting for advice.

DROUGHT-TOLERANT NON-NATIVE PLANTS

Acacia species, Acacia (shrub or tree)	*Cotoneaster* species, Cotoneaster (shrub)
Arbutus unedo, Strawberry tree (shrub)	*Dodonaea viscosa*, Hopseed bush (shrub)
Banksia species, (shrub)	*Echium candicans*, Pride of Madeira (shrub)
Buddleja species, Butterfly bush (shrub)	*Echium wildpretii*, Tower of jewels (shrub)
Calandrinia grandiflora, Rock purslane (perennial)	*Eucalyptus* species, Eucalyptus (tree/shrub)
Callistemon citrinus, Bottlebrush (shrub)	*Grevillea* species, Grevillea (shrub/tree)
Campsis radicans, Trumpet vine (vine)	*Juniperus* species, Juniper (shrub/tree)
Cedrus deodara, Deodar cedar (tree)	*Kniphofia uvaria*, Red-hot poker (perennial)
Ceratonia siliqua, Carob tree (tree)	*Lagerstroemia indica*, Crape myrtle (shrub/tree)
Chamelaucium uncinatum, Geraldton wax flower (shrub)	*Lantana* species, Lantana (perennial)
Cistus species, Rockrose (shrub)	*(See page 95 for more non-native plants)*

WINTER

Poinsettia bracts brighten the winter garden as daylight quickly races to pass its baton to twilight. Like Dylan Thomas, they "Do not go gentle into that good night" and stubbornly flaunt their vibrant colors.

PLANNING

After a brief and glorious Indian summer, easterners and midwesterners get out their thermals and button up to prepare for cold and icy weather. Most Californians, however, look forward to a typically mild, rainy season in winter, but wise gardeners have long memories and recall periods of earth-cracking droughts and torrential floods. We need to remember the whimsical weather patterns that define California as well as the uncertainty of rainfall.

Whether starting a brand new landscape or partially renovating a water-thirsty garden, start learning more about your local climate and the unique microclimates in your yard by gathering and recording temperatures and rainfalls in a journal. Areas around your home, under established trees, shrubs, and roofs, and along fences and walls may provide warmer, drier microclimates than sites atop a breezy hillside or in a canyon portion of your yard. Consult with your local water department or University of California Cooperative Extension Office for information relating to drought-tolerant landscaping.

Go to your local library or search the Web for sites to help you with ideas and information about drought-tolerant garden designs and plant selections. Visit water conservation gardens and sign up for workshops or seminars at a nearby university, community college, botanic garden, arboretum, adult education, or garden center.

For those with limited time, hire a landscape architect or designer who is knowledgeable about native and drought-tolerant designs.

Make a rough sketch noting the existing trees, shrubs, beds, and current structures. Determine your budget for any changes in plants as well as what changes may be made in terms of maintenance and water requirements. Depending on your budget and time, a new design can be implemented or an existing garden modified over several years, rather than the "all or nothing" approach.

The plant lists on pages 81 and 90 are not meant to be complete, but will help provide some ideas for water-wise gardening.

For frost-prone locales, select genera and species that grow naturally in colder habitats. There are species of proteas, for example, that stand up to heavy winter frosts such as the mountain-dwelling *P. venusta* as well as *Leucadendron salignum*. Some cold-hardy cacti and succulent species belonging to the genera *Opuntia*, *Echinocereus*, *Pediocactus*, *Rebutia*, *Agave*, *Yucca*, *Sedum*, and *Sempervivum* tolerate freezing temperatures and dry humidity for varying lengths of time. Many California lilacs, coast rosemary, flannel bush, and Matilija poppy are cold tolerant, while others may grow back after winter freezes such as New Zealand flax (*Phormium* species) and still others remain dormant until spring.

California coastal areas are generally frost-free, but many plant species cannot tolerate sea-sprayed winds and salt-laden soils. Some seacoast-hardy plants are: butterfly bush (*Buddleja*), rockrose (*Cistus*), cotoneaster (*Cotoneaster*), Matilija poppy (*Romneya coulteri*), tea tree (*Leptospermum*), coast rosemary (*Westringia fruticosa*), tree aloe (*Aloe arborescens*), pride of Madeira (*Echium candicans*), *Phormium* species, and *Yucca* species.

Along the central valleys or inland deserts, dry winds and sweltering summers cause many drought-tolerant plants to wilt except these: many species of butterfly bush, California lilac, succulents, cacti such as elephant bush (*Portulacaria afra*) and *Opuntia*, flannel bush (*Fremontodendron*), *Phormium*, and tower of jewels (*Echium wildpretii*). But where summer temperatures commonly rise above 90 degrees, they are happiest planted where there is partial shade or morning sun and afternoon shade.

Even rocky, gravelly regions provide hospitable havens for butterfly bush, many cacti, succulents, wildflowers, flannel bush, some members of the Proteaceae family, and Sikiyou lewisia.

PLANTING

It is still okay to plant California natives and other drought-resistant species in mild-winter regions directly into the ground, but for cold-winter areas wait until spring or early fall.

Sowing drought-tolerant native and exotic annuals and perennials from seed outdoors is possible in frost-free regions of California, but the plants will tend to be smaller by spring. Refer to Autumn Planting for sowing seeds.

Starting plants from seed indoors takes a bit more effort and patience, but successfully raising them from infancy indoors to teenagers outdoors can be satisfying. Read the seed packets carefully because some need treatments to soften or break their seed coats in order for their embryos to emerge, particularly those with hard seed coats. Refer to starting seeds in Autumn Planting.

Some seeds are so tiny they are easier to sow if mixed with fine sand first. Then put them in an envelope or return them to the seed packet and sprinkle the seeds evenly over the planting surface by gently tapping the seeds out of the packet.

Most species of cacti and succulents germinate quite successfully if sown indoors during winter. It allows them a full year of growth before they become dormant the following winter. Some have their growth cycle during the cooler seasons of fall and winter and rest during late spring and summer. Sow those cool-season growers in spring and summer. A soilless, commercial cactus or growing mix provides an optimum environment for growth and helps prevent disease and insect infestations because the commercial mediums are sterile and porous enough for proper root aeration. Also avoid mixes that are high in humus because those tend to retain moisture longer; most succulents, cacti, and other drought-tolerant plants hate wet feet. Do not use plain sand because it is too fine to provide good drainage and definitely keep away from seaside sand because of its high salt content. Individual containers for each species is the most practical because some seedlings will grow faster and will need to be plucked out and repotted, while the slower-growing ones can remain in the same container. Since the majority of cacti and succulents are notoriously slow-growing, sow them in small 2- to 4-inch pots. 10 to 15 seeds fit nicely in a 2-inch pot or double that number in a 4-inch pot. Most need light to germinate and prefer a shallow covering of $1/4$ inch of fine potting mix or grit. Spray the planting medium thoroughly without dislodging the seeds or submerge the bottoms of the containers in a couple of inches of water for 45 to 60 minutes and allow the excess water to drain out. The seeds should germinate in 4 to 12 weeks, but because of their slow growth many cacti and succulent seedlings resemble small peas even 6 months after germination. Often it takes 2 to 4 years before they reach 1 to 2 inches in diameter, but the taller columnar species typically grow more quickly. Since they have fine root systems that are easily damaged, do not transplant them until they become crowded. Lucky you if you have a temperature-controlled greenhouse or propagator to set your pots in winter. Otherwise, place them in closed plastic bags and air them out periodically if excess moisture collects on the surface. 70 to 75 degrees Fahrenheit is an ideal soil temperature range to germinate most plants from seed. Keep the soil warm by using a plant heat mat or keep them in a warm room. Once the seedlings emerge, remove them from the propagator or plastic bags and keep them in an area with bright indirect light near a south-facing window or provide artificial fluorescent gro-lights. When the seedlings are large enough to handle (as soon as 8 to 12 weeks and as long as two years depending on the particular cactus or succulent), lift them from the container and gently pry them apart without bruising their fragile roots. At this stage of development, even cactus spines are soft enough to handle without wearing gloves. One inch or larger seedlings should be planted in 2-inch pots, but smaller ones thrive much better if planted in rows in flats or seed trays spaced apart at twice their diameter. Continue growing them in trays or flats until they become crowded enough to

deserve their own separate pots. Commercial cactus mixes are recommended whenever cacti and succulents are transplanted.

Transplant other drought-tolerant seedlings into larger containers if they become too crowded and keep them indoors if the outdoor temperatures are below 65 degrees Fahrenheit. Handle the fragile seedlings carefully by removing the individual plants with a spoon or your fingers. Do not pick up the fragile seedlings by their stems, instead carefully lift them and gently grasp them by their leaves or roots. Repot the seedling at the same depth and into the same type of potting medium.

It is just as important to use a well-drained planting mix when transplanting outdoor California natives or drought-tolerant plants from one container to another. Adding perlite or pumice provides additional help against saturating, winter rains.

WATERING

While seeds are germinating or seedlings are emerging, keep the planting medium evenly moist, but not soggy. Young seedlings do not have drought-surviving characteristics and should be watered regularly.

Hold off watering newly transplanted seedlings for a few days. This gives them time to settle in their new pots and heal any damaged roots. Then water and return them to a place with bright, indirect light indoors if the outdoor temperatures are still below 65 degrees Fahrenheit. Allow them to dry slightly between watering intervals.

Do not overwater outdoor drought-resistant plants, especially if winter rains arrive. If rainfall is below normal, supplement just enough to keep the plants from shriveling. Most water-thrifty plants do not like wet feet and cold conditions during winter. If there has been a drought and the plants appear shriveled and stressed, then water when temperatures are above 40 degrees Fahrenheit at night. If they appear plump and healthy, leave them alone, particularly those that are dormant during winter.

Drought-tolerant plants are at risk when there is an unseasonably wet winter. When the pores of the soil are filled with water, soil-born fungi called water molds invade a plant's roots and vascular system, which interferes with its ability to lift moisture and nutrients into its canopy, eventually killing the plant. Dig temporary drainage ditches so that rainfall will not collect and stand around the root zones. Also, apply compost tea and any product rich in humic acid directly on the soil to kill the anaerobic bacteria (the bad, oxygen-sucking bacteria) and increase the population of aerobic bacteria (the good, oxygen-supplying bacteria).

Check for faulty sprinklers, emitters, and irrigation lines and repair them.

FERTILIZING

Knowing a specific plant's growth and rest cycles as well as other cultural requirements provides the necessary guidelines for proper care such as a feeding regimen. Do not fertilize any drought-resistant or native plants that rest during winter. Some exceptions include many species from the genus *Crassula* and *Dudleya*. Since they are in their growth cycle during the cooler months of winter through early spring, feed them a water-soluble organic food every 45 to 60 days or a controlled-release chemical fertilizer at the beginning of their growth period.

Begin feeding seedlings when they develop their second set of true leaves. Succulent or cactus seedlings should also be fed shortly after they emerge. Since young seedlings have tender growth, feed them with a balanced, liquid organic fertilizer diluted to $1/4$ strength every time they are watered (use an organic fertilizer that contains trace elements to provide the major and minor nutrients necessary for healthy seedling development).

MAINTAINING

Winter rains encourage weeds to germinate. Apply a pre-emergent prior to the rainy season to suppress weeds before they appear and eliminate future weeding chores from your life.

Although most butterfly bushes can recover after a freezing winter, it is best to protect the crown with a 3- to 6-inch layer of mulch in zones 5 to 9. Where winter temperatures remain above freezing, they stay evergreen and their crowns do not need protection.

If winter temperatures typically dip below freezing in your area, protect New Zealand flax, rock purslane, elephant bush, and other frost-sensitive specimens by planting them in containers and moving them to a more sheltered location away from icy winds such as under the eaves of the house, against a sunny wall, in a greenhouse, or indoors (far from heating vents but near a window with bright, indirect sunlight).

Shelter drought-tolerant container plants by moving them under the eaves of the house or indoors to protect them from excessive rainfall. Do not forget about them once they have been moved, because if they begin to dehydrate and shrivel they will need supplemental watering. Check up on them at least every 7 to 10 days.

There is little need for pruning in winter. For the most part, prune off any dead, diseased, or interfering branches or stems.

An exception is that many species of butterfly bush (such as *B. asiatica* and *B. davidii*) freeze to the ground in winter, but recover to bloom the following summer, similar to perennials. When the canes aboveground are dead, prune them to the ground after the last winter frost. In mild-winter climates, B. davidii and B. crispa need to be pruned back hard (almost to the ground for B. crispa) in winter before spring growth begins for increased flower production and more compact growth.

To control the size and shape of drought-tolerant plants that continue to grow during the cool season, a light trim might be a better course of action. Severe pruning sometimes ruins a plant's character such as the coast rosemary (Westringia). If you must prune, just prune its tips.

The colors and variegated patterns of New Zealand flax and other Phormium species intensify during cool weather. Cut off any shoots that are old and faded, to the base of the plant. Younger shoots tend to be more colorful than the older ones, but if the younger shoots are showing signs of color reversion, cut them off too.

PROTECTING

Protecting drought-tolerant or native plants against browsing deer, particularly during winter when there is less for them to eat in the wild, is difficult. Provide physical barriers such as wire enclosures, use olfactory repellants, and select plants that are deer-resistant. "Deer-resistant" is a relative term depending on the plant's toxicity as well as the individual deer's culinary palate and level of hunger. The following are some suggestions:

- Beard-tongue (Penstemon species)
- Bush anemone (Carpenteria californica)
- Butterfly bush (Buddleja davidii)
- California lilac (Ceanothus, primarily small-leaved species or hybrids)
- California poppy (Eschscholzia californica)
- Century plant (Agave americana)
- Coyote bush (Baccharis pilularis)
- Manzanita (Arctostaphylos species)
- Matilija poppy (Romneya coulteri)
- Monkeyflower (Mimulus species)
- Oregon grape (Mahonia species)
- Rock rose (Cistus species)
- Spanish bayonet (Yucca species)
- Stone crop (Sedum species)
- Tower of jewels (Echium wildpretii)

DROUGHT-TOLERANT NON-NATIVE PLANTS

Lavendula species, Lavender (perennial)	Punica granatum, Pomegranate (tree/ shrub)
Leptospermum species, Tea tree (shrub/tree)	Quercus species, Oak (tree)
Leucadendron species, Leucadendron (shrub)	Rosmarinus species, Rosemary (herb)
Leucospermum species, Pincushion (shrub)	Schinus molle, California pepper (tree)
Olea europaea, Olive (tree)	Senecio cineraria, Dusty miller (perennial)
Phormium species, New Zealand flax (shrub)	Stenocarpus sinuatus, Firewheel tree (tree)
Pinus species, Pine trees (tree) (also Native species)	Telopea species, Waratah (shrub)
Pistacia chinensis, Chinese pistache (tree)	Westringia fruticosa, Coast rosemary (shrub)
Plumbago auriculata, Cape plumbago (shrub)	Wisteria species, Wisteria (vine)
Portulacaria afra, Elephant bush or elephant food (succulent)	Xylosma congestum, Xylosma (shrub)
Protea species, Protea (shrub)	(See page 90 for more non-native plants)

CHAPTER FOUR

California
Ground Covers

Ground covers are on the bottom rung of the planting ladder. They are stepped on, neglected, and often forgotten. They harbor snails, slugs, gophers, snakes, and ground squirrels. On the positive side, they control erosion, act as fire barriers, attract bees for pollinating orchards, are lawn substitutes, and can even be used for strictly decorative purposes. Aesthetically, ground covers provide the foundation for a landscape design. Foliar carpets—such as blue star creeper—perform double duty by providing welcome bursts of floriferous color. Others, such as Corsican mint, release a refreshing fragrance when stepped upon. Moss rose and sea pink add a lovely touch of color. Many landscaping ground covers are originally from South Africa, Australia, and the Mediterranean. Climate and soil types in these regions are similar to those in California, allowing these imports to acclimate easily. Native plants are also used, especially for bank planting. Creeping boobialla is one of the most attractive and effective solutions for sloping banks, and it provides an excellent firebreak. While trees may teach us to reach for the heavens, it is the foliar and floral carpets that keep our feet firmly planted on the ground.

Ground covers encompass a wide range of low-growing plants that not only blanket unsightly bare areas of ground quickly and sometimes aggressively, but they also prevent erosion of the soil, give dimensional variety in the garden, provide buffers against fire, unite shrubs and flower beds in the landscape, replace higher maintenance lawn areas, inhibit weeds, and edge pathways.

Among our favorite ground-hugging succulents is the moss rose. It is an annual that stands 8 inches high and spreads a modest 6 to 12 inches, but there is nothing modest about its flowers. Lance-shaped, plump green leaves attached to fleshy, reddish stems serve as a background canvas to blooms of single or double, 3-inch rose look-a-likes. Moss rose greets summer heat in dazzling "hot" colors or in cooler tones. Moss rose is at home in hot, dry places—spreading around rock gardens, meandering along pathways, and spilling over the edges of flower beds and borders.

Whether in a sunny location or shaded shelter, ground covers soften a landscape, hide and stabilize barren soil, offer shelter and food for wildlife, and provide fire-retardant buffers—keeping us "grounded" to the underlying rhythms beneath our feet.

BLUE STAR CREEPER
Pratia pedunculata

Blue star creeper's low-growing, mat-forming habit makes it easy-to-manage and its pastel blue to whitish blooms resemble twinkling stars. Despite its dainty appearance, it's very cold hardy and spreads easily. As long as it is watered regularly during warm weather, blue star creeper is perfect as a filler between steppingstones, along pathways, or cascading over rocks.

E. Australia / Zones 8 to 10 / full sun, part shade / height 3 inches / width spreading / flowers late spring to autumn

CREEPING BOOBIALLA
Myoporum parvifolium

Creeping boobialla may have an odd-sounding name, but it's fire-resistant and weed-suppressing. Semi-succulent foliage, low care, and drought tolerance make it an excellent ground cover choice. In season, it's covered with waxy, white, star-shaped flowers that smell of honey. By autumn, tiny, sweet-tasting purplish berries that attract birds and four-legged critters replace the spent flowers. Its only downside: it cannot withstand any foot traffic.

SW Australia / Zones 8 to 10 / full sun / height 3 to 6 inches / width 6 feet / flowers spring to summer

TRAILING GAZANIA
Gazania rigens

Trailing gazania is tough, spreads indefinitely, and serves as a graceful edging along walkways, driveways, and in front of, or tumbling over, walls and fences. Gray-green, felted foliage grows in a rosette pattern. Although the foliage is lovely, its main attraction is its daisylike flowers in a rainbow of colors. They show off their 3-inch heads of yellows, oranges, reds, and golds, or brilliant combinations.

S. Africa / Zones 10 to 11 / full sun / height 6 to 8 inches / width trailing / flowers spring to summer or year-round depending on variety

SPRING

Slumbering slopes wait patiently through the long nights of winter. Their patience is rewarded when ice plants smothered with blankets of sparkling lavender, hot pink, yellow, and magenta flowers boldly announce the arrival of spring.

PLANNING

If you are confused about the term "ground cover," you are not alone. Sometimes ground cover refers to wood chips, bark, stone, and even plastic—all kinds of inert stuff. This chapter is about *plants* that cover bare ground to unify or soften the areas between the house, walkways, patios, and other hardscapes. Ground covers influence the perception of space and serve as firebreaks. They can also serve as a colorful mosaic on a prominent bank and as an erosion control stabilizer. When properly grown, established, and maintained, they help prevent the growth of weeds and serve as lawn replacements, especially in shady areas and where tree roots are close to the surface. Without pruning, some ground covers can stand up to 4 feet tall; others remain a 1-inch mat. Turf grass comes in only a narrow range of greens, but ground covers offer a rainbow of choices, including many shades of green, as well as Olympian gold, silver, and bronze, as well as red, blue, purple, and variegated. Their forms and textures are equally varied: clumping, vining, or sprawling; succulent, woody, shrubby, or herbaceous; annual, biennial, or perennial; deciduous, evergreen, or semievergreen. Their foliage can be fine or coarse, soft as feathers or prickly as needles.

With so many choices, here are some "ground rules" to consider:

Select only a few varieties because too many different ground covers in the garden can create a cluttered or mish-mash appearance.

Choose ground covers in scale with the site. Use larger specimens for more expansive areas and smaller varieties for more intimate spaces. Corsican mint (*Mentha requienii*) or blue star creeper (*Pratia pedunculata*) are ideal fillers between steppingstones, bordering pathways, or spilling over rock gardens, but creeping boobialla (*Myoporum parvifolium*) and many juniper cultivars spread their girth from 6 to 10 feet and are better suited for wide-open slopes, embankments, or snuggling up against massive boulders.

Two words: companion planting. When combining other trees, shrubs, perennials, or bulbs with ground covers, make sure they will live together in peaceful harmony. Their growth and maintenance requirements need to be complementary, not incompatible. If you combine a vigorous, thirsty spreader such as English ivy with a slower growing, drought-tolerant California lilac, the more aggressive ivy will probably over-run, smother, and eventually kill the California native.

Look at the site you want to cover and assess the condition of the soil: sandy or clayey; free-draining or compacted; alkaline, acidic, or neutral pH. Read Soil Rhythms on page 307. Then determine whether the location is full sun (at least six hours of direct sunshine per day), partial (receives morning or afternoon sun), or heavy shade (little, if any, direct sunlight).

Find out the hardiness zone of your neighborhood, and make sure it matches the hardiness designation of a particular ground cover. Gardeners know, however, that several unique microclimates can exist, either man-made (swimming pools, ponds, sidewalks, roads, foundations) or natural (higher elevations, lower slopes, bare open land), affecting soil conditions, air temperature, sun and wind exposure, snow cover, and humidity. Determine all the distinctive climatic niches in your garden, and select accordingly. For example, shady areas on the north side of a home can deflect freezing or drying winds more effectively than a sunny, open southern exposure.

Visit displays at your local arboretum or botanical gardens, contact your local UC Cooperative Extension office, compare ideas with neighbors, and talk to your knowledgeable nursery retailer for appropriate ground cover suggestions.

Before making your final decisions, understand that ground covers are not necessarily low-maintenance replacements for high-maintenance lawns. Ground covers are not magic carpets. Depending on the genus, species, or cultivar, most take time to develop, and the bare spots need to be weeded until the ground cover reaches maturity. Even when they do fill in, some slow-growing ground covers such as Corsican mint or moss rose (*Portulaca grandiflora*) can be overrun by Bermuda grass, oxalis, and other weedy warriors.

To cover an area quickly, few plants can outpace ivy (*Hedera* species). For areas too shady for lawns, consider Japanese spurge (*Pachysandra terminalis*) or baby's tears (*Soleirolia soleirolii*).

Give preference to perennial rather than annual ground covers, particularly for expansive spaces, because of the time, cost, and effort needed to prepare the sites and to maintain the plants.

Ground covers that begin to flower in spring are blue star creeper; carpet bugleweed (*Ajuga reptans*); creeping boobialla; sea pink (*Armeria maritima*); and trailing gazania (*Gazania rigens*).

A few more spring bloomers to consider:

■ Ice plants are fast-growing succulent ground covers that used to all be lumped together under *Mesembryanthemum*, but are now reclassified under many different genera, such as *Carpobrotus*, *Delosperma*, *Drosanthemum*, and *Lampranthus*. They are most effective in expansive carpets, covering slopes and coastal bluffs and bearing brilliant magenta, red, pink, orange, yellow, lavender, or white flowers typically from midwinter through early summer. The common trailing ice plant (*Lampranthus spectabilis*) features 2-inch-wide pastel-pink, cherry-pink, red, or purple blossoms blanketing their gray-green foliar mats from late winter to spring. Choose your favorite colors when they are in bloom at your local garden center.

■ While the majority are ideal for erosion control and make effective fire-resistant barriers, do not plant the Hottentot fig (*Carpobrotus edulis*, formerly known as *Mesembryanthemum edule*) on steep banks. It becomes waterlogged during heavy seasonal rains and often slides down hills, taking the soil with it. For steep slopes, select the rosea ice plant (*Drosanthemum floribundum*); it remains 6 inches tall and spreads out very well. Plant these South African natives in well-drained soil with full sun, and water just enough to keep their fleshy foliage plump and happy. Ice plants are damaged when temperatures dip to 25 degrees Fahrenheit, but survive periods of drought. Depending on the genera, species, and cultivar, plant them 12 to 24 inches apart.

■ Periwinkle and dwarf periwinkle (*Vinca major* and *V. minor*) are from Europe and western Asia. These vinelike creepers do not climb, but cover the ground quickly and are efficient ground covers for erosion control. Periwinkles flourish under the canopy of shallow-rooted trees; they show off their violet flowers mainly in spring, but often through summer and fall. The larger species have bigger leaves, grow up to 2 feet, and tend to be invasive in protected, shaded areas. *V. minor* is the "mini-me" version of *V. major*, but its 4- to 6-inch growth is less aggressive. They resist drought once established, thrive in rich, well-drained soils, and prefer a 6.5 to 7.0 pH. Space larger species 24 to 30 inches apart and the dwarf species 18 inches apart. Plant in shade to partial shade, unless the climate is mild year-round; then they can be set out in full sun.

■ Red apple or baby sun rose (*Aptenia cordifolia*) has heart-shaped, emerald leaves and bears a profusion of purple to red flowers in spring and summer. It performs best in full sun, but provide partial shade in the hottest climates. Use this South African ice plant relative in rock gardens or on slopes, but if you are allergic to bees, plant it away from pathways. Their flowers are bee magnets during spring and summer. Space red apple 8 to 12 inches apart, and plant them in acidic to neutral, well-drained soil. Once red apple is established, water primarily during periods of heat and drought.

■ Spring cinquefoil (*Potentilla neumanniana* or *P. tabernaemontani*) bears buttercup-yellow, 1/4-inch flowers in spring and summer. Its bright-green foliage stands just 3 to 6 inches, but spreads and covers the ground quickly. Despite its delicate appearance, spring cinquefoil is a tough, resilient

ground cover that tolerates some foot traffic and serves as a cozy blanket for bulbs. Plant this perennial European native in partial shade where summers are very hot, but provide full sun for other areas. Cinquefoil is not fussy as long as there is good air circulation and the soil is well drained with an acidic to neutral pH.

■ Woolly yarrow (*Achillea tomentosa*) is named for its woolly-haired leaves. In late spring through autumn, dense clusters of small, yellow flowers emerge from gray, aromatic, fernlike foliage that stands 6 to 12 inches tall. Yarrows resist drought well and love hot, dry, sunny sites, as long as they have a well-drained, sandy loam soil. Plant them 12 to 16 inches apart. Originally from Europe and western Asia, yarrows survive in just about every climate in California, with very little care. More ground cover suggestions are listed under Summer, Autumn, and Winter Planning.

PLANTING

Once the last day of frost has passed, spring is an ideal season to plant ground covers.

Remove the existing weed population in your future ground cover home with a systemic herbicide or by digging them up and throwing them in the compost or trash. Water the area thoroughly to encourage any remaining weed seeds to germinate; once the seeds sprout, dig them out again and dispose of them. If Bermuda grass is present (or other grasses that spread by runners), do not hoe and till the soil because this helps spread them even more; instead, use a systemic herbicide or solarize the area using 4- to 6-millimeter clear plastic.

Prepare the planned ground cover area to a depth of 6 to 12 inches by incorporating an organic soil amendment such as

PLANT SPACING CHART (Square-foot Coverage per Flat)

Spacing inches on center	50 plants per flat	64 plants per flat
4 in. oc	5 sq. ft.	7 sq. ft.
8 in. oc	22 sq. ft.	28 sq. ft.
12 in. oc	50 sq. ft.	64 sq. ft.
18 in. oc	112 sq. ft.	144 sq. ft.
24 in. oc	200 sq. ft.	256 sq. ft.
30 in. oc	312 sq. ft.	400 sq. ft.

humus, worm castings, or compost at a rate of 1 to 2 cubic yards per 1,000 square feet. Rake the soil surface until smooth, and water the area thoroughly. To prevent weeds, spread out a weed-control landscape fabric, cut holes at the recommended intervals, and then plant in the holes (see the above Plant Spacing Chart).

It is difficult to prepare the ground when it comes to banks that have loose soil. Instead, put down landscape fabric or jute netting before planting. Landscape fabric provides the additional benefit of weed control, but both the fabric and jute netting reduce the eroding effects of pelting raindrops. Cut holes in the fabric or netting where plants are to be set. You can use a 2-inch diameter by 12- to 16-inch long auger attached to a portable electric drill. This is an efficient hole-drilling tool for planting ground covers grown in flats. Drill planting tubes 2 inches in diameter and 8 to 10 inches deep, at the recommended spacing for your particular plant. Amend the soil to be used to backfill the space around the rooted cutting; use about 30 percent organic material. Mix $1/3$ sand and $1/3$ organic compost or humus mulch to $1/3$ native soil. Place the rooted cutting over the hole, and backfill until the plant is at the same depth as it grew before. Gently tamp down the soil around the roots, and form a berm or lip of soil in the front of each plant to catch and hold water.

Transplant all ground covers, whether on slopes or on level sites, at the same depth as they were in the containers. If planted too deep, the plants will be susceptible to rot; if too shallow, the soil will be insufficient for the roots to properly attach or absorb moisture.

Spreading ground covers are usually available in 1-gallon containers, in 2- to 4-inch pots, or in flats as well-rooted cuttings. Flats contain fifty to sixty-four rooted cuttings and are the least expensive. Rooted ground covers tend to grow in a dense mass, so it is easier to use a clean knife to carefully cut them into 2-inch squares before serving them up like pieces of cake and installing them at the recommended spacing. If you decide to plant your ground cover as rooted cuttings from flats, calculate the square footage of the planting area and determine the number of plants necessary for coverage. The farther apart you space them, the longer it takes to blanket an area, but if planted too close together, the ground cover becomes overgrown and requires more maintenance.

When it comes to random versus triangular or square spacing, consider the following: Random plantings are less time consuming, but they do not fill in evenly; triangular and square spacing patterns are more organized in appearance and cover evenly. If they are planted in parallel rows in a square pattern, the plants above, below, and across are equal from each other. Staggering plants in parallel rows creates a triangular pattern so that they are all equidistant from each other.

Creeping shrubs are woody, low-growing ground covers with long, spreading branches. They are most readily available in 1-gallon containers; give them a wide berth when planting because many, such as creeping boobialla (*Myoporum parvifolium*) and 'Calgary Carpet'® juniper (*Juniperus sabina* 'Calgary Carpet'®), expand 6 to 15 feet when mature. Shrub ground covers are often the tortoises of the plant world, some taking years to fill in the spaces. Lay down a fabric weed barrier, cut out the planting holes at recommended intervals and depths, and plant with prepared backfill (read Spring Planting for mixing backfill). Another alternative is to apply a pre-emergent and water it in after there are signs of new growth on the plants. A 1- to 2-inch layer of organic mulch surrounding the shrubby spreaders also helps control weeds and protects the root zones from severe temperature fluctuations.

Immediately after planting, use a water-soluble or granular soil conditioner containing humic acid and a root stimulator containing indolebutyric acid or alpha-naphthalene acetic acid. A root stimulator helps prevent transplant shock and jumpstarts root development when applied three times, two weeks apart.

Most perennial ground covers that form an expanding crown can be divided when mature to increase stock, revitalize plants, and maximize flower production. For example, woolly yarrow should be divided every two to four years when they become overcrowded and less floriferous. On the other hand, ground covers with deep taproots or single central stems are usually better candidates for stem or root cuttings. Spring is the ideal time to divide plants, especially for cold-winter regions, because plants have a full growing season to develop new root systems and produce growth at their crowns. Divide only healthy plants that are free of pests and diseases; then shred and compost the old growth. Young, vigorous side-shoots near the outer part of the clumps are most suited for division and for replanting. Lift the plant with a fork or spade, and try to get as much of the root zone as possible. If the rootball is tightly matted, set two garden forks with their backs together in the clump's center and pry them apart. It is often simpler to set the clump in a bucket of water, wash the soil off from the roots, and separate the individual crowns. Each clump should be divided into no more than three to five shoots. Clumps that are too small do not spread very well the first year after replanting. As long as the weather remains mild, some spring-flowering ground covers can be divided later in summer, after their blooms are spent, or during fall. If you wait until summer or autumn, keep new divisions well watered during prolonged dry spells.

WATERING

Thoroughly water ground covers immediately after planting. Deep soaking helps collapse any air pockets that were created during the initial planting. Water newly planted ground covers at a depth of $1/2$ to $3/4$ inch every day for the first two to three weeks. Extend the watering interval to every other day for two to four more weeks until the ground cover roots into the surrounding soil. Most ground covers establish in about three months and then won't need to be monitored as closely as before. Once the roots are established, water only when needed and keep in mind that too much water can lead to root rot. Use the finger test: If the top inch feels dry to the touch, then water again to a depth of $1/2$ to $3/4$ inch. Also watch for signs of foliage wilting during midday, a signal the roots are dried out. After the first year, spring watering may not be necessary at all if rainfall is sufficient.

Keep a watchful eye over ground covers that were planted last autumn. They are still in their "adolescence" and do not have fully mature root systems. If there is little spring rainfall, make sure these youngsters are watered regularly.

Shallow-rooted plants such as carpet bugleweed need regular watering about once every seven to ten days, depending on spring rainfall.

Irrigating ground cover plants on a slope requires patience. Initially, the soil on the bank should not dry out. Ensure minimal runoff by hand watering with a fogging nozzle attached to the hose. This method disperses water without excess runoff. To save time and avoid hand watering, use an action-reaction sprinkler on the ring stand (such as a portable Rainbird™ sprinkler) or an automatic sprinkler system with heads designed to apply a low volume of water over a longer period. Set out clean tuna or cat food tins (any shallow tin cans will do) at different locations of the ground cover to determine the amount of time needed to deliver $3/4$ to 1 inch of water. The next time you water, set the timer on your automatic sprinkler accordingly or turn off the action-reaction sprinkler manually.

FERTILIZING

Beginning in spring, use a complete, liquid all-organic fertilizer once every four to six weeks to establish new plantings. For established ground covers, apply once every six to eight weeks during the growing seasons of spring through summer. Water-soluble organic fertilizers applied with a hose-end sprayer move into the soil readily without causing any damage to tender growth foliage. Established stands of thick ground cover, as well as young plants, tend to burn when granular fertilizers settle on their leaves. Granular organic or controlled-release chemical fertilizers can be used if they are watered in thoroughly and washed off the foliage. Depending on the formulation, reapply the controlled-release fertilizer every three to six months.

MAINTAINING

Monitor newly planted ground covers, and wait till there is new growth showing before applying a pre-emergent herbicide. Since the herbicide is nonselective, do not use if sowing wildflower or other seeds around the ground cover. For established ground covers, use the granular pre-emergent weed control in late spring.

If you forget to apply a pre-emergent weed control, remove weeds as soon as they come up. Weeds are much harder to control once they are established, and it is crucial to keep the ground cover free of weeds until it can fill in all the blank spaces. Hand-pull weeds before they reseed. If weeds are growing in the bare spots or if the weeds are taller than the ground cover, put on a pair of rubber gloves and wear cotton gloves over them. Then saturate the cotton glove with the systemic and spot treat the weeds. This prevents any solution from dripping on the ground cover. If you have damaged any ground cover while stepping on it to get to the weeds, monitor its recovery. The damaged areas may have to be replanted. Remember, the longer the ground covers take to fill in, the longer your commitment to weed and mulch any bare spots.

To control Bermudagrass, crabgrass, and foxtails in beds of English ivy, red apple, trailing gazania, or rosea ice plant, use a post-emergent herbicide with sethoxydim as the active ingredient.

Mulch the spaces between new or establishing ground covers with a 1- to 2-inch layer of organic material such as humus, worm castings, compost, pine needles, or cocoa hulls to disrupt the germination of weed seeds by blocking out sunlight. Organic mulch also helps maintain moisture, and protects roots from fluctuating hot or cold temperatures encouraging faster root development.

Remove any dead leaves or debris that have collected on top of established or newly planted ground covers. If this is not practical or safe because the ground cover has completely filled in, does not withstand foot traffic, or is on a steep slope, wash off the foliage with a strong stream of water.

Once a newly planted ground cover reaches 4 to 6 inches, pinch back the tips of new growth by 1 inch to encourage new growth at a lower level and ultimately a denser growth pattern on the ground. Clip off spent flowers to encourage stronger foliar growth and prolong the bloom season. Pinching and deadheading are labor intensive and recommended prima-

rily for level or smaller, confined sites and for ground covers that withstand foot traffic such as the fast-growing Corsican mint and carpet bugleweed. Avoid stepping on ground covers such as creeping boobialla and sea pink because they cannot tolerate any foot traffic. Pinching and deadheading are also impractical for steep slopes or large areas.

Prune back aggressive ground covers to prevent them from climbing into shrubs and trees or spreading into the root systems of existing shrubs and trees. If the ground covers are beginning to invade other territories, cut them back at least once during spring with an edging tool or dig a shallow trench to confine their growth.

Spreading perennials propagate via stems that take root above the ground as they expand or via underground roots (rhizomes) that sprout new shoots as they spread out. Often they are jammed too close together and tend to grow a bit thin on top and develop a thick, woody, thatched mat as they age. To rejuvenate, mow their surface with a rotary lawn mower calibrated at its highest setting during their growth cycle and after their flowering spikes are spent in the warm spring months. Bag the clippings and throw them away, share them with a neighbor, or root them and plant in any bare spots. For irregular, rocky, or steep slopes, use weed whackers or string trimmers, but stay clear of tree trunks or the stems of larger shrubs. Creeping St. Johns wort (*Hypericum calycinum*), dwarf coyote bush (*Baccharis pilularis*), dwarf periwinkle, trailing gazania, and dwarf yarrow (*Achillea* species) all appreciate an occasional "mow" hawk or "string" cleaning. Rake up the cuttings because decomposing and dried cuttings are havens for insect pests and diseases and are dangerous fuel sources.

GROUND COVERS

Spring-flowering ground covers such as baby's tears, blue star creeper, coprosma (*Coprosma × kirkii*), and creeping thyme (*Thymus serpyllum*) should be cut back after their flowers are spent. A regular haircut encourages new, more vigorous growth, keeps them tidy, and prevents them from overstepping their boundaries.

Summer- and fall-flowering ground covers can also be pruned back in spring, but do not remove more than $1/3$ of the branch lengths. It might weaken the plants and leave them open to insect infestation and disease problems.

Lightly shear manzanita (*Arctostaphylos* species) tips immediately after blooms are spent to encourage more branching and to keep it neat and dense. If it mounds and goes "bald" in the center with age, prune selected branches no more than 50 percent and cut only into leafy wood. This plant does not come back from bare wood.

Woolly yarrow and many other flowering ground covers germinate their seeds easily if their spent flowers are not clipped and left alone. Unless you want the flowers to go to seed, cut off the old blooms to divert the energy back to the plant itself.

PROTECTING

Ground covers offer cozy homes for many garden pests, including gophers, mice, rats, and other wild things. Manual traps leave no doubt when the pest has been nabbed. If poisons are used, make sure they are in child- and pet-safe bait stations. Try not to tromp around the ground cover too much, especially if it does not tolerate foot traffic.

A warm, moist spring brings new life to snails, slugs, earwigs, and sowbugs. Natural molluscicides and insecticides are preferable to chemical remedies. For snails and slugs, use iron phosphate or decollate snails (not both). Decollate snails dine primarily on immature brown garden snails and decaying organic matter. They are available in southern California and certain San Joaquin Valley counties, but are illegal elsewhere because they may prey on certain protected native snail and slug species. For earwigs, sowbugs, and slugs, roll up a newspaper, moisten it, and set it out in the ground cover. They love moist, newspaper homes. The next morning, throw them away in the trash, paper and all. Grapefruit and orange rinds are another safe way to attract and get rid of these creepy crawlies.

Caterpillars are the larvae of moths and butterflies and come in a variety of colors and sizes. When they are found feeding on ground cover foliage or stems, pick them off by hand or use an organic spray, *Bacillus thuringiensis* (Bt). Bt disrupts the caterpillar's digestive system, causing it to die from starvation.

Aphids and mealybugs are also attracted to many ground covers, especially when there is tender, new growth. They suck sap from leaves and stems, weakening the plants. Aphids are tiny insects ranging from pale green to black that cluster under leaves and stems. Mealybugs are grayish white $1/8$-inch suckers that cluster in the same manner as aphids. It is common to find ants with aphids or mealybugs because ants harvest their honeydew (aphid and mealybug excretions). Use an organic insecticide such as a garlic-based type to control aphids. Set out ant bait stations to get rid of the ants. Systemic insecticides are another option as long as there are no plants with edible parts nearby.

Mites are difficult to see with the naked eye, but they leave whitish webbings on leaves. Since they are not insects, a chemical formulated for mite control is best, or use a horticultural oil to suffocate them (the oil is just as effective against aphids and mealybugs). To prevent leaf burn, spray the oil during cool, overcast days or during the late afternoon when the weather is warm and sunny. Beneficial insects can also be used to control aphids, mealybugs, and mites. Some beneficial insects to consider include: lacewing, twelve-spotted lady beetle, looper parasite, mealybug destroyer, parasitic wasp, big eyed bug, ladybird beetle, scale destroyer, Western predatory mite, beneficial mite, and beneficial nematodes. Contact an insectary (cruise the Internet for websites) or your local garden center for more information.

Scales look like tiny limpet shells and are difficult to control when they remain under their shell coverings. A systemic insecticide is very effective at this life cycle stage, but do not apply it near plants with edible parts. In early spring, there is a short window of opportunity to control these suckers when they are out of their protective shells and crawling around. Horticultural oil is a safe, organic, and effective suffocant, but only when scales are in their crawling stage. Repeat spraying to kill any successive populations of crawlers.

Powdery mildew is a fungus that produces powdery patches on the foliage; its spores are spread by the wind to other healthy plants. A severe infestation interferes with the plant's nutrient uptake ability, causes yellow discoloration, and may kill the plants. Spring provides two of the most favorable conditions for powdery mildew: humidity and warmth. If left unchecked, mildew can decimate a ground cover in a few days or weeks. Spray with an organic fungicide that contains lemon myrtle oil extract, or use a chemical fungicide labeled for use on your affected ground cover.

COCOA MULCH

To use cocoa hulls as a mulch, spread an even layer of 1 to 2 inches with a rake and stamp it down. A fine spray of water activates a natural gum, binding the hulls into a loosely, knitted porous mat that retains moisture. It also deters snails, slugs, and most cats, while filling the air with the aroma of chocolate without the calories. There is an important caveat: When purchasing cocoa hull products, make sure the manufacturer stipulates on the bag that the hulls have been heat processed and cleansed without the use of chemicals and is 100 percent free of cocoa butter. The heat and cleansing processes eliminate theobromine, a chemical found in cocoa butter. Theobromine is toxic and often lethal to dogs and other domestic animals, such as horses, affecting their central nervous systems, hearts, and kidneys. If the bag does not list this vital heating and cleansing process, warranting that it does **not** contain theobromine, it is not safe to use around dogs, horses, and other domestic animals.

SUMMER

Crickets play their leggy violins while frogs croak their throaty love songs. Capture the essence of summer evenings by listening to their sultry music and breathing in the heady fragrance of star jasmine.

PLANNING

Study potentially suitable ground cover sites from midsummer to early fall because these are the most stressful times for plants. Understanding how high temperatures and lack of water affect these areas will help you make better decisions about ground cover selections. Visit public gardens to see which ground covers can and cannot stand up to high temperatures.

Visit water conservation gardens to learn about native or exotic drought-tolerant ground covers that thrive in your area. Once these ground covers mature, you won't have to worry as much about their survival during periods of drought.

If new ground cover beds are adjacent to open space or woodland sites, design a watering system so that there is access to hose bibs about 50 feet apart (the average length of a watering hose). Summer is a critical season to keep ground covers properly hydrated, and accessible water is very important during California's fire seasons from summer to fall.

Think about designing fire-retardant buffer zones 30 feet away from the house and other structures wherever possible. Although there are no fireproof plants, many resist fire because of high-moisture or low-fuel content. *Fire resistance* is a relative term, and California's intense firestorms of 2002 proved that *everything* can burn, given the right conditions. Low-growing, high-moisture-content ground covers, such as ice plant (classified under many different genera such as *Carpobrotus, Delosperma Drosanthemum,* and *Lampranthus*) and several species of stonecrop or sedum (*Sedum acre, S. album, S. anglicum,* and *S. spurium*), are among the many succulent perennials that have the greatest fire resistance. Where winter temperatures dip below freezing, many stonecrop species exhibit excellent frost hardiness and most ice plants tolerate temperatures down to 32 degrees Fahrenheit for short periods without too much damage. Make sure the soil drains well, and water succulents as often as once a week during periods of hot, dry Santa Ana or Chinook winds. During most other weather conditions, water succulent ground covers just enough to keep their foliage from becoming shriveled and withered. On the other hand, if they are properly planted, fed, and watered, ice plants and other succulent perennials can become aggressive invaders. Make sure they remain where you want them; cut them back whenever they step out of bounds.

Low fuel volume is defined as the amount of fuel a plant supplies to an approaching fire. In simple terms, the size and height of a plant matters. A ground-hugging creeping boobialla (*Myoporum parvifolium*), emerald carpet manzanita (*Arctostaphylos* 'Emerald Carpet'), or dwarf coyote bush (*Baccharis pilularis*) that stands 6 to 12 inches tall contributes very little fuel compared to an average-sized shrub or tree. Proper watering and maintenance are key elements in retaining fire-resistant or low-fuel-volume characteristics. If a low-growing ground cover dries up or builds up dead wood from neglect, it loses its low fuel volume and becomes a fire hazard. See Spring Maintaining also.

Rather than planting during the hottest and driest months of the year, spend this time properly preparing the soil for planting ground covers in autumn. Refer to Spring Planting for soil preparation guidelines.

Cool thoughts of shade are always pleasant on a sunny summer day. The following are ground covers that can tolerate shade: blue star creeper, carpet bugleweed, Corsican mint, and sea pink. They prefer full sun along the coast, but need partial shade further inland.

Baby's tears (*Soleirolia soleirolii* or *Helxine soleirolii*), Japanese spurge (*Pachysandra terminalis*), and sweet violet (*Viola odorata*) are shade-loving ground covers that prefer rich, well-drained, acidic loamy soil. From the western area of the Mediterranean, baby's tears grows to only 2 to 4 inches tall, but spreads to infinity and beyond. Its dainty leaves and creeping stems provide a lush carpet that does not tolerate foot traffic, but its vigorous growth keeps damage to a minimum. For good coverage, space baby's tears 10 inches apart. To control its invasive nature, plant baby's tears in small, easily confined spaces, such as underneath ferns and other shade-seekers.

Japanese spurge is endemic to Japan and China, but adapts to a surprising array of different climates and tolerates deep shade, even under trees. It has compact 8- to 12-inch growth with shiny forest-green leaves. Some cultivars are edged in creamy white. For best results, plant in slightly acidic soil amended with humus, compost, worm castings, or other organic material. Space them 10 to 12 inches apart; then thin them out when growth becomes woody with age.

Sweet violet is native to Europe, Asia, and Africa. It grows up to 8 inches tall, spreads 18 inches wide, and propagates by seeds and runners. Perfumed, delicate flowers tinted in shades of violet, rosy-pink, or white appear in spring, contrasting beautifully with their heart-shaped, deep-green leaves. Plant in partial to dense shade except where summers are cool; sweet violet tolerates more direct sun.

Many fragrances infuse the warm summer air, but few can compare to star jasmine (*Trachelospermum jasminoides*). Commonly thought of as a climbing twiner, this Mediterranean native becomes a spreading ground cover, 2 feet tall and 10 feet wide, with a bit of tip-pinching and no means of support. Glossy, dark-green leaves provide a lush background for a plethora of clustered white flowers that perfume the air when planted under open canopied trees and shrubs. Grow in full sun except in the hottest inland regions, and provide good drainage. Space plants 5 feet apart for ground cover, and supply water on a regular basis.

If you have not already done so, take a soil sample to your local garden center or soil-testing lab for a thorough analysis. Information about which nutrients are present and which are lacking, as well as the soil pH, helps you make better decisions about soil preparation, amendments, and fertilizers.

Before taking a summer vacation, ask a garden-savvy neighbor or friend to water your plants, especially if you are gone longer than two weeks or if the ground cover was planted this past spring.

PLANTING

Late spring through early summer is a good time to root clippings snipped off many perennial spreaders such as ice plant and red apple. Set up a tray of peat pots or use a flat. Fill with a commercial potting mix, such as cactus mix, or combine 2 parts vermiculite or perlite to 1 part sterilized potting soil. Dip 3- to 6-inch-long tip cuttings in a rooting hormone. Remove any foliage that might be buried below the soil line. Insert one cutting in each peat pot, or space fifty to sixty-four cuttings evenly in a flat. Water thoroughly; then set them in a protected, lightly shaded spot. Cover with a sheet of plastic, and check daily to make sure the cuttings do not dry out. If temperatures remain mild and rainfall is abundant, the plastic covering is unnecessary. They should root in ten to thirty days. Test by tugging gently to see whether the roots are taking hold. Once rooting has begun, puncture holes in the plastic sheet to allow more air circulation. Remove the cover after new foliage emerges, and pinch back their tips by 1 inch seven to ten days after the plastic is removed to encourage more branching.

Ground covers such as blue star creeper, carpet bugleweed, and English ivy form plantlets by developing roots along their stems. Simply cut off the ends that have rooted and replant them in other bare spots or wherever they are needed. Make sure you give them a dose of root stimulator three times, two weeks apart.

Most perennial ground covers with woody stems can be propagated by layering. Bend stems horizontally to the ground in spring or early summer when the sap is surging and the stems are flexible. At the point where the stem is in contact with the soil, cut a shallow 1/2-inch sliver along the bottom of that stem. Remove all leaves and stems from behind the cut, and pin it securely with a U-shaped piece of wire. Stake the rest of the stem from the layered point, turn it upward, and tie loosely around the stake. Cover the nicked stem with 1 inch of organically amended backfill soil (refer to Spring Planting), and add a water-soluble root stimulator containing indolebutyric acid or alpha-naphthalene acetic acid three times, two weeks apart. When roots form at the point of soil contact and new growth emerges, clip off the rooted cutting from the mother plant; allow it to remain in place or transplant to a container or another location. Layered plants often take up to one year to root. Follow the planting and care guidelines for propagated plants under Spring Planting.

Once the cuttings, plantlets, or layered plants have rooted well, they can be planted directly in the garden, provided temperatures are no higher than 75 to 80 degrees Fahrenheit. If summer temperatures are above 80 degrees, wait until the cooler fall season to transplant them. In cold-winter climates, wait until the danger of frost has passed and the *soil* has warmed to 55 degrees before planting in spring. Soil thermometers are available at retail nurseries or agriculture supply stores.

WATERING

Water ground covers early in the morning when there is no wind, humidity is at its peak, and water pressure is high. If you have an automatic system, adjust the timer so that the sprinklers turn on between 3 and 5 a.m. For hand watering, irrigate as early as possible.

Deep watering established ground covers is necessary only during long, hot, dry summer days. Shallow-rooted ground covers are more likely to stress during dry, hot periods and may need more frequent supplemental watering. Drought-resistant varieties with deeper roots may not require much supplemental watering. Plants in full sun or on slopes dry out more quickly than those in the shade. Monitor the soil moisture level down to 4 to 6 inches; if it feels dry, water until the soil is wet to a depth of 6 to 10 inches, depending on the particular plant.

Spring-planted ground covers need supplemental irrigation if there is little or no rainfall. When the soil feels dry to the touch, water down to about 1 inch. Refer to Spring Watering for newly planted ground covers.

FERTILIZING

Feed with a complete, liquid organic fertilizer every forty-five to sixty days during the growth and bloom cycles. When fed water-soluble or granular organic fertilizers, established ground covers do not develop as much soft, vegetative growth that is so susceptible to insects and diseases. For the most convenient application, use a metered, hose-end sprayer. A granular organic food or chemical controlled-release fertilizer is another sound alternative, provided any residue is washed off foliage immediately after application. Depending on the formulation, chemical controlled-release feedings are used every three to six months.

For containerized cuttings, plantlets, and air-layered plants, fertilize once a week with a complete, liquid organic fertilizer diluted to $1/4$ the normal rate. After four to six weeks, increase to $1/2$ the normal dilution rate; apply the regular recommended dilution rate when they have been transplanted directly into the ground.

MAINTAINING

Replenish mulch around newly establishing plants so that there continues to be a 1- to 2-inch layer. Keep mulch away from plant stems and crowns to avoid rot problems. If weeds still break through the mulch, pull them out by hand, but use a systemic herbicide if Bermuda or other stoloniferous grasses are spreading throughout your ground cover. Check the label because most herbicides have temperature guidelines. Read them carefully, and follow the directions. Since systemic herbicides harm ground covers, apply the herbicide with a paintbrush or use the glove method described under Spring Maintaining.

The downside to low-maintenance ground covers that grow and spread rapidly is they can just as quickly move out of their defined area and take over neighboring shrubs, annuals, and perennials. Pay attention to the fast-spreading trailing gazania, just about any ivy, including English ivy, periwinkle and dwarf periwinkle, and succulents such as ice plant or stonecrop, and keep them under control. Once they escape from their boundaries and establish themselves elsewhere, a systemic herbicide may be the only solution.

When leaves turn black and the plant centers appear dead or wilted, it may be crown rot. Pull on the plant; if it comes out easily or falls over, remove the infected plants. Crown rot is a fungus that usually occurs when there is poor drainage. Stop watering the area to dry the soil. Solarizing accelerates the drying-out process and is most effective during hot, sunny summer months. After the soil has dried, improve drainage by adding more organic material, such as humus and compost. Cover the surface with worm castings, and water it in with a water-soluble humic acid concentrate or use a granular form of humic acid. Also soak the soil surface with a compost tea. All these remedies encourage the proliferation of mycorrhizal fungi, aerobic bacteria, and other beneficial microbes. They in turn improve the health of the soil and plants by improving soil texture, oxygenating the soil, and making nutrients more readily available to the plant root systems. At the same time, the anaerobic bacteria population (microbes that live in unhealthy, oxygen-deprived soils) dramatically decreases. Read Soil Rhythms on page 307 for more details.

Cut back ground covers that are overstepping their boundaries, and save the tip cuttings to root more plants.

In small, easy-to-reach areas, snip off dead, diseased, or insect-damaged leaves.

Clip back the tendrils of periwinkle and star jasmine after blooming to encourage denser growth or to control their growth.

Annual ground covers such as hybrid cultivars of moss rose often reseed themselves, but do not necessarily come up the following spring true to seed (meaning they may not display the same characteristics as the original plant). Prevent them from seeding by clipping off the spent flowers if you prefer the original plant's features, but allow it to reseed if you enjoy Mother Nature's surprises.

PROTECTING

To protect newly planted and tender ground covers from grazing deer, rabbits, or skunks, use an olfactory repellent, motion-activated sprinklers, or live traps (for the smaller critters). Check with your local fish and wildlife agency to determine whether trapped animals can be released in more wilderness-friendly areas. If their grazing problems are causing too much plant damage, contact your animal control center for advice or hire a licensed professional.

Use manual traps or bait to get rid of gophers and a guillotine trap for moles. Their tunneling destroys ground cover plants, leaving large swaths of empty space that will need to be replanted.

Spider mites, aphids, scales, mealybugs, slugs, snails, and other creepy crawlers remain active during summer. For insect and pest controls, refer to Spring Protecting.

Grasshoppers are frequent summer visitors; they can be caught by hand and destroyed. Use contact insecticidal sprays containing carbaryl or cyfluthrin only when grasshoppers are visible in large numbers and causing considerable damage. Grasshoppers flit from plant to plant and then fly or hop away, making them difficult to spray on contact.

Like all plants, when ground covers are grown under optimum conditions, they are less susceptible to diseases and pests. Frequent applications of chemical remedies to keep ground covers healthy serve as big, red-light signals, indicating environmental problems. Odds are the ground covers are not adapting to their current hardiness zone, exposure, soil, or light condition. Your plants will be much healthier and more resistant to diseases and pests if the underlying site problems are corrected.

AUTUMN

Summer's slide into autumn might go unnoticed except for the gusts of wind and the smell of falling leaves. Boston ivy and other creepers turn shades of burgundy, red, orange, and yellow and tumble like acrobats in the wind.

PLANNING

Besides spring, fall is one of the best times to dig in and plant. Think about planting more drought-tolerant ground covers because they not only conserve water but do particularly well when planted in autumn. Woolly yarrow, periwinkle, ice plant, and stonecrop are covered in Spring and Summer Planning. Creeping boobialla is featured in the ground cover selections on page 99. Some others to consider include creeping rosemary (*Rosmarinus officinalis* 'Prostrata'), dwarf coyote bush (*Baccharis pilularis*), and certain manzanita species (*Arctostaphylos*).

Creeping rosemary is a Mediterranean native with neat, aromatic foliage on trailing stems that look lovely on gentle slopes, tumbling over retaining walls or rocks, along walkways, and as a dwarf hedge. This plant stands about 2 feet tall and spreads 4 to 8 feet; pale-blue flowers appear in fall and continue blooming through spring on last year's growth. Although it withstands slightly alkaline soils, it does best in acidic to neutral soils in full sun with good drainage. Plant rosemary from 1-gallon pots, and space them 2 feet apart for good coverage in a moderate period. Along the seashore, creeping rosemary remains lush with very little maintenance. It also thrives inland if watered moderately and fed with a light, organic food two to three times a year.

Dwarf coyote bush is another short, but wide-spreading, woody ground cover prized for its drought- and fire-resistant characteristics. Along the coastal and desert areas, it tolerates salt spray and high temperatures and serves as a fire buffer around building perimeters and a slope stabilizer on steep slopes. The fast-growing evergreen has attractive, deep-green, serrated leaves with summer-bearing pale-yellow flowers. Plant this coastal Northern California native from a 1-gallon sized container, and space it 4 to 6 feet apart. It flourishes in full sun with well-drained soil that is acidic to neutral. Water regularly for the first year, but once it is established, little or no supplemental water is needed near the coast. It looks perkier inland if watered once a month, especially if there is little or no winter-through-spring rainfall. Periodically wash dust off the foliage. Since female plants produce messy seeds, select males when possible.

Although many manzanita species are treelike shrubs, there are species that are creeping ground covers. Most manzanitas are known for their leathery, dark-green, teardrop-shaped leaves that turn bronze or reddish brown in fall and winter. By late winter or early spring, these western natives become green again and bear pink or white urn-shaped flowers at the ends of their branches. The flowers are replaced by green fruit in late summer, often turning red or brown in fall. Their twisted, rust-red, reddish black or purple-tinged branches can stretch to mats 12 feet wide, but they stand only 8 to 14 inches tall. Little Sur manzanita (A.

edmundsii), 'Emerald Carpet' (*A. densiflorus* 'Emerald Carpet'), pine-mat manzanita (*A. nevadensis*), dune manzanita (*A. pumila*), and bearberry (*A. uva-ursi* 'Point Reyes' and *A. u.* 'Woods Red') are just a few to consider for their drought resistance, low growth habit, and seasonal beauty. Make sure they are planted in acidic, well-drained, sandy-textured soil, and space 1-gallon pots about 2 feet apart. Consistent care and maintenance of newly planted drought-resistant plants is very important. Read the chapter on drought-tolerant plants also.

Walk around your neighborhood and look for ground covers that in autumn turn brilliant colors, such as the yellow, orange, and wine-red saturated colors of Boston ivy (*Parthenocissus tricuspidata*), the deep aubergine hues of purple-leaf winter creeper (*Euonymos fortunei* 'Coloratus'), and the crimson and burgundy leaves of the Virginia creeper (*Parthenocissus quinquefolia*). Before planting them, ask your neighbors what ground covers they recommend and what problems they have experienced with their plants.

PLANTING

After the hot, dry Santa Ana and Chinook winds depart, milder weather returns to California. Don't be afraid to plant store-bought evergreen creepers and spreaders, as well as any rooted cuttings or divisions that you potted up during the past spring or summer. As long as you live in frost-free locales, autumn is an ideal time to buy and plant a wide variety of ground covers while the soil is still warm from the summer sun. If you live where winters are frigid, wait until spring before planting, but for the rest of you, fall is the second planting season.

Do your "ground work" first before planting to give your plants the best chance

to survive and flourish. Most plants, including ground covers, need well-draining soil. Adding organic materials is a must for clay or sandy soils. If a plant died in the area you are replanting, do not set in a new plant until you have resolved the problem. Perhaps the previous plants were ill-suited for the light or temperature conditions. If they were inappropriate, substitute a ground cover better adapted for those conditions. Often soilborne diseases remain in the soil and infect the new ground cover. Properly prepare that site by adding concentrated humic acid in water-soluble or granular form, as well as compost tea, to rejuvenate the planting site. Review Spring Planting for soil and site preparation guidelines.

If you are only adding or replacing a few ground cover plants, it is not necessary to till a large planting site. Simply dig a hole bigger than the rootball. Carefully remove the plant from the container; if the roots are matted and rootbound, loosen the ones around the outer perimeter of the ball. Make sure the ground cover is planted at the same depth as it was in its original container.

Take a few extra precautions if planting towards the end of autumn. Make sure the soil around the roots has been tamped firmly enough and watered sufficiently to collapse any air holes that might allow cold temperatures to enter and damage the plant's root system. Add at least a 1- to 2-inch layer of humus, compost, pine needles, cocoa hulls, or worm castings around a newly planted ground cover to insulate it from temperature extremes.

WATERING

Water fall-planted ground covers thoroughly and continue to water frequently during their first three months as transplants, especially if weather conditions remain hot and dry. Monitor them two to three times a week; if the soil feels dry to the touch down to 1 inch, then water again. Check on spring-planted ground covers about once a week when there is no rainfall. Avoid overwatering plants, especially in clayey soil, because roots left in standing water are prone to root rot. Refer to Spring Watering for more details.

Even though temperatures cool during autumn, it is still important to water established evergreen ground covers thoroughly before the rainy season. Prepare plants for the colder months of winter, and protect them from leaf burn (common during cold weather) by keeping them well watered during fall. If the preceding summer was warm and dry, water mature ground covers about once a month, but if the summer was cool and humid, water only once or twice during the entire autumn season.

After feeding the ground covers their "winterizing" fertilizer, water thoroughly to move the nutrients into the root zone.

FERTILIZING

A fall feeding is necessary to maintain your ground cover's vigor and to "winterize" or protect it from the colder conditions of the winter season. Winterize ground covers by applying potassium in the form of sulfate of potash (0-0-8), kelp meal, or greensand in early autumn at a rate designated by the formulating company. Adequate levels of potassium elevate the sugar levels in a plant's system, which in turn increases its ability to weather harsh winter conditions.

Avoid chemical fertilizers that are high in nitrogen because nitrogen stimulates new and frost-tender growth. It also harms beneficial microorganisms in the soil.

MAINTAINING

Since manzanitas and other drought-resistant plants are typically slow-growers, be prepared to keep the open spaces between them well mulched and weed-free until they blanket the ground completely. Weeds continue to invade gardens even when the days shorten and the weather cools. Maintain a 1- to 2-inch layer of mulch around new plantings to keep out uninvited weeds, but do not spread mulch over the crowns of ground cover. Hand pull or dig out weeds before they become too entrenched, and spot treat stoloniferous Bermuda grass with a systemic herbicide. Refer to Spring Maintaining for application methods. Future weeding problems will be resolved if you apply a pre-emergent herbicide around ground covers before the winter rainy season.

To encourage more spring blooms and control the spread of vigorous growers such as sweet violet and Japanese spurge, cut the runners off or shear any excess, rangy growth in autumn.

If a lot of deciduous trees are dropping their leaves over evergreen ground covers, use a leaf blower to keep them from smothering your ground huggers. Netting is another remedy, especially for small areas. Cover the ground cover with a net; when the leaves fall into it, pull the net and turn the captive leaves into compost.

To rejuvenate periwinkles or encourage thicker growth, mow them with a rotary mower calibrated at its highest level.

There are no other pruning duties for early fall except to clip off any remnants of spent flowers from ground covers and to prune off dead, damaged, or diseased portions of their leaves and branches. By late fall, wait to prune until late winter or early spring after the danger of frost has passed. Cold temperature could damage plants pruned so late in the season.

PROTECTING

Besides aphids and spider mites, scale infestations can be very damaging to ground covers. The young have protective white to tan shells that resemble limpet shells. They feed all year and lay their eggs from late winter to late spring and again late summer to fall. The fall generation damages ground covers and other plants the most because the plants are already weakened from the summer heat and dryness. Their honeydew attracts ants and serves as a host to black sooty mold. Treat with an organic insecticide containing garlic extract, and mix with horticultural oil for a suffocant. Systemic insecticides are also effective if there are no plants with edible parts nearby. Use a horticultural oil or chemical miticide to control spider mites. When spraying with oils, apply during the late afternoons or early evenings. Hot, midday sunny conditions can cause leaf burn.

Hungry deer become more brazen during late fall and winter when food becomes scarce. Use an olfactory repellents, or for smaller areas, set up a series of posts surrounding the ground cover and tie monofilament line chest-high. When they brush against the line, it tends to spook them because they cannot see it. Also try motion-activated water sprinklers. Since deer become accustomed to the different remedies, try alternating them for longing-lasting controls. Spray plants with 2 ounces of d'limonene (orange oil) mixed with 1 gallon of water over plants that are being eaten by deer, rabbits, and mice. Apparently, nibblers find the taste unpalatable and leave the plants alone. Since it is pure orange oil, the product is food-grade-safe and can be used on edible, as well as ornamental, plants. During warm, sunny days, spray the oil in the late afternoon or early evening to prevent scorching of the foliage.

Caterpillars are still munching their way through fall gardens. If there are lots of chewed leaves, use *Bacillus thuringiensis*, an organic insecticide known as Bt. Read about grasshopper control under Summer Protecting.

STOPPING ANTS IN THEIR TRACKS

At times, ants can drive you crazy! But don't let the ants get in your pants. Control ants outdoors by baiting them with a sugar solution laced with boric acid. The ants will transport the bait down into their nests, destroying the colony. The recipe for ant baiting is as follows:

- Prepare 6 plastic margarine containers (with their lids) by cutting 4, 1-inch-diameter holes, equally spaced, 1 inch above the container's bottom.
- Cut sponges into pieces that will loosely fit into the containers (approximately 4 inches × 4 inches each).
- Dissolve 2 cups of granulated sugar into 2 pints of boiling water.
- Add 2 tablespoons of 100% boric acid.
- Place 1 piece of sponge into each container as the solution cools.
- Pour the mixture onto the sponges until the sponges are saturated.
- Replace the lids. Place the bait stations near the ant's nests and wait.

Even mild California winters can be slim-pickings for our resident wildlife. Creeping boobialla, low-spreading manzanita, and junipers serve up a welcome winter smorgasbord of brown, purple, and red berries for browsing and pecking creatures, great and small.

PLANNING

Winter is an excellent time to assess the "bare bones" of your yard, when many trees and plants are resting and few flowers are blooming. Are the spaces between your house, walkways, decks, patios, pools, stairways, fences, or other hardscape features effectively blending into and highlighting your existing landscape? Or are the plants standing apart like forlorn sentries from the architectural components of your property? The right ground cover can help solve the aesthetic tug-of-war between hardscape and landscape. Ground covers also soften the stark contrast between trees and shrubs, encouraging the eyes to take in the "big picture," the highs, mediums, and lows of the landscape. Steps, decks, and fences become less mundane and more dramatic when accented by ground covers with colorful foliage and interesting texture. Tuck a notebook and pen in your pocket, and write down anything you notice or want to improve.

Hillsides, slopes, and banks can be stabilized and highlighted by the unique characteristic of a specimen ground cover. Shrubby soil stabilizers such as 'Calgary Carpet' juniper or 'Emerald Carpet' manzanita perform double duty by capturing the eye with their foliar sea of bluish or rich green color.

There are low-growers that endure light foot traffic, making them ideal for edgings along pathways and borders, as fillers between steppingstones, and mounded in rock gardens. Despite their small stature, many withstand a wide range of temperatures. These are worth reviewing when making plans for small spaces.

■ Blue star creeper is endemic to Australia and mats the ground with 2- to 3-inch tall, $1/2$-inch-wide evergreen leaves. From late spring through autumn, pale blue or white blooms twinkle like stars against their dark-green foliage. In cooler, coastal climates, plant it in full sun, but where summers are particularly hot, find a shadier spot with filtered light. As long as the soil drains well, blue star creeper withstands acidic to alkaline soils. Space plants at 8- to 12-inch intervals in spring for good coverage. Water regularly during warm weather, and the plants will continue to send out new roots through their nodes.

■ Carpet bugleweed (or carpet bugle) does well in partial shade inland or full sun along the coast. It spreads quickly via runners, similar to strawberry plants each spring, and blue, violet, or pink flowers form on 6-inch spikes from late spring through summer. Depending on the cultivar, foliage colors vary from bronze-purple to variegated hues of cream, pink, burgundy, and green to splashes of red, yellow, and white mixed with green. Although tolerant of heavier, clay soils, this European native does best in well-drained, slightly acidic soils. Plant in spring or early autumn, about 1 foot apart, and keep the plants well watered because of their shallow root system.

■ Cinquefoil or spring cinquefoil (*Potentilla neumanniana*, syn. *P. verna* 'Nana' or *P. taberaemontani*) is a petite, but hardy, fast-spreading cover with rooting stems. In spring and summer, bright-yellow flowers bloom and contrast with emerald leaves. Cinquefoil is also a good blanket for bulbs. Plant cinquefoil in early spring, and space the plants 12 inches apart in good draining soil.

■ Creeping thyme (*Thymus serpyllum*, syn. *T. praecox arcticus* or *T. drucei*) can grow up to 3 inches high and spread as much as 3 feet wide, bearing masses of tiny purple flowers in summer against a backdrop of dark-green leaves. As an aromatherapy bonus, their foliage releases a pleasant, light fragrance when crushed. Typical of many Mediterranean natives, it needs well-drained soil and full sun.

■ Baby's tears (*Soleirolia soleirolii* syn. *Helxine soleirolii*) is another low-mat ground cover that creates a lush, green carpet for shade, but crushes easily with the lightest footstep. Because of its vigorous growth and aggressive root system, it will recover quickly from footstep damage and may even revive in spring despite freezing weather, as long as the soil drains well. Plant in spring wherever there is shade or partial shade, and space it 10 inches apart for small areas.

■ Salt-tolerant ground covers fill an important landscape niche for seaside gardens. Sea pink (*Armeria maritima*) and trailing ice plant (*Lampranthus spectabilis*) are popular choices as well as beach straw-

berry and coprosma (Also read the ground cover featured selections on page 99 and Spring Planning).

■ Beach strawberry (*Fragaria chiloensis*) is found on seaside bluffs of North and South America and along the Pacific Coast beaches. It is a plant for all seasons with delicate white blossoms in spring emerging from dense, 6- to 8-inch mats of deep-green leaves. In fall, it bears $3/4$-inch bright-red fruit that is more ornamental than tasty; by winter, their serrated foliage morphs into reddish hues. In spring or fall, plant them in full or partial sun, provide good drainage, and space 12 to 18 inches apart.

■ Coprosma (*Coprosma* × *kirkii*) hails from New Zealand, stands 12 to 24 inches tall, and is 4 to 6 feet wide. Small chartreuse leaves are set close together on long, straight, prostrate stems. It is a tough woody ground cover for slopes and tolerates a wide range of soil and climatic conditions including salt spray, ocean winds, and drought, once established. Plant in full sun along the coast, and provide light shade further inland if summers are hot and dry.

Since winter requires less of your time in the yard, take a gardening class, catch up on your garden magazine and catalogue reading, surf the Internet, and check out ground cover books at the library to glean plant ideas for your landscape.

PLANTING

Planting during winter is not recommended unless you live in an area that is frost-free, with moderate day and evening temperatures no lower than 65 degrees Fahrenheit. If there are wide swings between evening and daytime temperatures, wait until spring to plant.

Annual and some small perennial ground covers can be started from seed indoors, but many are quite challenging because of the application of certain treatments, such as chilling, burning, or scarifying the seed coat to break dormancy, as well as the specific timing of collecting, storing, sowing, and germination. Some seeds take several months or years to successfully germinate. For the novice gardener or anyone who has the patience and time to spare, try planting a ground cover seed that is readily available in seed packets at the local retail garden center. Determine when seedlings can be safely moved outdoors in your area, and count back the weeks needed to germinate and grow a particular plant according to its packet. Do not start them too early indoors because it often results in spindly, weak plants that will not be vigorous growers when transplanted in the garden. Fill a planting tray or individual pots within $3/4$ inch from the top using a commercial planting medium. To prevent disease, make sure the containers are sterile. Use new containers or wash old ones in a solution of 1 part bleach to 10 parts water. For very small seeds, add a $1/2$-inch layer of vermiculite. Tamp down the moistened planting medium firmly, creating a uniformly flat surface. Follow the directions on the packet, and plant according to the recommended spacing and depth. Usually the planting depth is about two times the diameter of the seed. Sow in furrows 1 to 2 inches apart at a depth of $1/8$ to $1/4$ inch. If seeds need darkness for germination, cover them lightly with a $1/4$-inch layer of the same planting medium, dry vermiculite, or fine, sterilized sand (not beach sand). Sow large seeds into cell packs or individual 2- to 4-inch pots, two to three seeds per unit, and thin to allow the strongest seedlings to develop. To avoid dislodging the seeds, mist thoroughly with a spray bottle or set the pots in 1 to 2 inches of water for about an hour and allow them to drain. If you do not have a plant propagator or temperature-controlled greenhouse, place a clear plastic bag over the flat, cell pack, or pot, keeping the plastic about 1 to 2 inches from the soil. Until germination, maintain an even amount of moisture (not soggy). Annual seeds usually need their planting medium kept at 70 to 75 degrees Fahrenheit for germination. Special commercial heating mats are available for seed propagation at retail nurseries if minimum soil temperatures are not possible. Seeds of hardy perennials do not need as much heat and will germinate in soils between 60 to 70 degrees. Keep the container out of direct sunlight. As soon as the seedlings appear, remove the plastic and continue to water if the medium feels dry. Thin seedlings, and plant them into individual containers as soon as the first set of true leaves appear. Place the seedlings in bright, indirect light (a south-facing window is perfect), or use special plant-growth lamps. Hang the lights 6 inches from the plants, and turn them on for about sixteen hours each day. Raise the lights to accommodate seedling growth. Label the seed with the name of the plant and the date of sowing. The seedlings can go outside in spring after the last day of frost has passed. Over a seven-day period, gradually increase their time spent outdoors; this is known as "hardening them off" (acclimating the plants to outdoor conditions). Allow them to remain outdoors for two hours the first day, four hours the next, six hours the third day, but wait until the seventh day before keeping them outdoors through the night. Once they have hardened off, they can be planted directly in the ground.

GROUND COVERS

WATERING

During normal winters, supplemental watering is not necessary, but when rainfall is below normal and the temperature is above freezing, water ground covers thoroughly.

For seedlings that are germinated indoors, keep the medium moist by misting or soak the container in 1 to 2 inches of water for an hour, then drain thoroughly.

FERTILIZING

Take a holiday from fertilizing ground covers during winter.

For indoor seedlings, wait until the second set of true leaves appears. Then fertilize with a water-soluble organic food at $1/4$ the normal dilution rate once a week until they are ready to be transplanted outdoors in spring.

MAINTAINING

If fall-planted ground covers heave out of the soil due to freezing temperatures, gently replant them right away rather than waiting until spring. Cold weather dries and damages tender roots.

Apply a pre-emergent weed control in winter before the rains arrive if you forgot to put it down in fall.

Evergreen ground covers are damaged when their foliage has been exposed to a very dry and cold winter. Apply antitranspirant towards the end of autumn or early winter, before the first frost, the waterproof coating should last all winter.

Remove any dead or diseased wood and foliage. Shear off any foliage or branches that have been damaged.

Mow or shear spring cinquefoil and beach strawberry in late winter or early spring (where winter freezes are common,

wait until spring) before new growth and flowers appear; this results in a more groomed appearance and removes any dried or brown leaves.

PROTECTING

Late winter is when food is scarce for wildlife, particularly if there was drought the preceding summer. They may turn to ground covers as their snacks of choice. Manual traps are effective against mice and rats, as well as poisoned bait set in child- and pet-proof bait stations. There are commercial olfactory repellents for deer and rabbits. The only permanent solution against voracious deer might be to build an 8-foot fence surrounding your property.

If you did not use horticultural oil during fall to control overwintering pests, apply when temperatures are above 45 degrees Fahrenheit with no rainfall predicted for the next seventy-two hours.

Root and stem rot occur in heavy, poor-draining soils and are most common during the rainy season. The fungus gains access through the roots and crowns of plants, rotting them and causing them to wilt and die. Since it spreads to other plants from contaminated tools and splashing water, sterilize any tools each time they come into contact with diseased plants (use a product specially formulated to sterilize tools instead of dipping them in a bleach solution, which can rust the implements if not dried completely), drain off any standing water, and apply a layer of wood chips or cocoa husks around the ground cover where practical. Allow the soil to dry out between watering intervals, but when rainfall is plentiful, it is simpler to pull out the infected plants and dispose of them in the trash.

CHAPTER FIVE

California Herbs
and Vegetables

Surprisingly, fewer than two dozen species of plants provide the world's staple foods. Nicolay Ivanovich Vavilov, an icon in the world of plant genetics, identified eight world regions—now called Vavilov Centers—where those plants evolved. The vegetables that sustain the world's population all originated in those centers. By identifying, evaluating, and classifying plants, Vavilov laid a cornerstone of the science of plant genetics.

Thanks to George Shull, a pioneer plant hybridizer, the seeds available from local garden centers are the result of meticulous scrutiny. Only hybrid varieties that are adaptive, productive, or have other desirable qualities are reproduced for seed. The downside to this process is loss of diversity because plants change from generation to generation, developing strengths, weaknesses, and uniqueness.

Herbs are plants valued for medicinal, savory, or aromatic qualities. Essential oils or essences are concentrated in their flowers, seeds, fruit, foliage, bark, or roots—and it is these parts that researchers explore, looking for the next miraculous cure or the perfect herb to create a recipe worthy of culinary immortality.

In Our Garden

Herbs can be found in a variety of plant types—trees, vines, shrubs, herbaceous perennials, annuals, and biennials. Adding to the confusion, they can also be used for medicinal, culinary, or ornamental purposes. Even vegetables have an identity problem. Radishes, carrots, celery, and lettuce are seedless and are—botanically speaking—vegetables. But if they contain seeds such as cucumbers, squash, beans, peppers and tomatoes, are they fruits? Botanists say "yes," but the common perception is that they are *all* vegetables—seeded or unseeded.

Growing herbs and vegetables is a splendid excuse to get your hands in the dirt. In most areas of California, Mother Nature is particularly kind, allowing us to grow an extensive array of fresh food throughout the year. The limits are bounded only by our imagination. We hope the following chapter will heighten all your senses and encourage you to stretch the boundaries of your edible garden.

AFRICAN BLUE BASIL

Ocimum kilimandsharicum × *O. basilicum purpureum*

African blue basil's maroon-streaked stems, dusty purple-veined green leaves, and beautiful plum-colored flower bracts are blanketed with dainty lavender-pink florets. During summer, it blooms hard and is highly fragrant, with an intense aroma that can be used in sachets, potpourris, or cut-flower arrangements. The spicy flowers and leaves impart a mouth-watering, complex flavor.

Africa / Zones 10 to 11 / full sun, part shade / height 3 to 5 feet / width 3 to 5 feet / harvest spring to autumn

CHILE PEPPER

Capsicum chinense and *Capsicum annum*

For a mildly hot, good-flavored, and ornamental pepper, 'Black Hungarian' is a fine choice. Sturdy plants with green foliage veined in purple and lovely deep-lavender flowers produce 3- to 4-inch black jalapeno-shaped fruits. If you would rather try the hottest chile, then plant 'Red Savina' registering a scorching 577,000 Scoville units. Most of the heat in chiles originates in their seeds and white membranes, so cut these out.

S. America / Zones 9 to 11 / full sun / height 36 to 42 inches / width 10 to 18 inches / harvest summer to autumn, depending on variety

EGGPLANT

Solarum melongena

It is believed that eggplant derived its name from the fact that early varieties were white and egg-shaped. A seed breeder from India developed 'Indian Baby', a variety that produces small, 1-ounce eggplants with a bright, reddish-purple color. 'Indian Baby' is very popular in Indian and Southern Asian cuisine as a stuffed delicacy. Among the Japanese eggplants (Nasubis), 'Kurume Long' is a late-maturing, glossy-black type with 9-inch, zucchini-shaped fruit and a deep-purple calyx. The skin is thin and tender, and the flesh is sweet.

SE Asia, India, and Africa / Zones 8 to 11 / full sun / height 18 to 48 inches / width 18 to 24 inches / harvest summer

SPRING

Flights of fancy butterflies flit about, fat striped bees bumble by, and lizards skitter over rocks announcing the end of frosty weather. Asparagus tips finally wake up and peek out of their beds to witness spring's ruckus.

PLANNING

Herb and vegetable gardening is an activity suitable for a variety of sites. The size of the garden can be the entire area of a yard; it can surround an enclosed patio; it can be plantings in an array of sundry and assorted containers gracing an atrium or solarium; and it can even be a planter box on a windowsill. The idea is that crops can be grown just about anywhere, as long as there is sufficient light, good air circulation, a suitable temperature range, nutrients, plenty of water, and tender loving care. Whether your herb and vegetable garden is going to be on a west-facing balcony in Richmond, in an enclosed patio next to the ocean in Santa Monica, on a slope behind a home in Fallbrook, or on an estate in the Napa valley, you can thoroughly enjoy harvesting the rewards of your efforts.

Organize your edible garden by recording your ideas in a notebook or journal. Include recollections of past selections, problems as well as successes, and decisions about current varieties. Of all the rhythms in your garden, growing herbs and vegetables, and the events that are associated with them, come closest to being predictable. For instance, many vegetables react to day length, such as long-day and short-day onions. A short-day onion begins forming bulbs when days are twelve to fourteen hours long, but a long-day variety demands fourteen to sixteen hours. Since the longest day, even in Northern California cities such as San Francisco, Monterey, and Mendocino, is about $14^{1}/_{2}$ hours, long-day onions are best left to southern parts of the country.

Survey your garden for a location that provides sunshine from sunup to sundown. Sunlight is the energy source for photosynthesis, the process of manufacturing carbohydrates (starches and sugars) by plants. A basic rule to remember is this: the more sunshine, the higher the quality of the herb or vegetable and the greater the quantity to harvest. Tweak this rule depending on where you live and the light needs of your selected plants. Many herbs and vegetables produce poorly in the shade, especially tomatoes, but cool-season crops such as lettuce, spinach, and cabbage tolerate some shade. If the sunshine is too intense, particularly in the desert and inland areas, even heat-loving tomatoes are susceptible to scalding.

If you can't find enough sunny space in your garden, borrow some by joining a community garden. Community gardens offer the added advantage of meeting other gardeners and learning from each other.

You should know the soil pH because pH determines the availability of nutrients. As a guideline, if your vegetable garden soil has an acidic pH of 6.0 to 6.5, it is ideal for 98 percent of all the vegetables. If the soil tests between 7.5 to 8.2 pH, begin acidifying the soil by adding additional organic material (humus, compost, worm castings) and soil sulfur at a rate of 2.5 pounds per 100 square feet. The correction occurs gradually because it takes time for the beneficial soil microorganisms to process the soil sulfur and organic materials. Retest the pH every four to six weeks, and reapply more organic material and soil sulfur until the pH is in the acidic range.

Once a site is selected, consider raised planting beds. They are space efficient and maintenance timesavers. Planting beds are also water-wise because only the beds are watered, not the paths. If your native soil is poor, you can better control the soil-building in beds, instead of an entire yard. Design the planting beds on a sheet of graph paper with a $1/4$-inch grid ($1/4$ inch equals 4 feet). We recommend rectilinear planting beds for herbs and vegetables. The long axis is oriented east to west, to take advantage of the full sweep of the sun. Make the short sides narrow enough for you to easily reach into the middle of the bed without walking on it. As a result, the soil remains light and fluffy, which is much healthier for roots to develop and grow. Beds measuring 8 or 12 feet long and 4 feet wide are ideal for care and harvest convenience. It is also simpler to construct the beds since the standard lengths for lumber are in multiples of 8, 10, and 12 feet. Design walkways between beds so that they are wide enough to accommodate a wheelbarrow.

Vegetables and herbs are ideal container plants if space is limited. Combining herbs that require similar moisture, sun, and nutrients makes their maintenance easier and increases their chance for survival. Thirsty gotu kola and shiso plants tolerate partial shade, but unthirsty French lavender, rosemary, and thyme make better companions in the sun. African blue basil, angelica, and stevia are also sun worshippers, but they prefer to have their own roomy pots all to themselves. Although small-leafed herbs such as thyme and mint do well in window boxes or planter bowls, most vegetables

need 1-gallon-sized or larger pots, and standard tomato plants perform best in 15-gallon containers. Hanging pots and containers on stairways and on the edges of decks are also sun-catchers in confined spaces. Bok choy, purple cabbage, Swiss chard, lettuce, dwarf tomatoes ('Micro Tom', the smallest tomato in the world, needs only a 2- to 4-inch pot to fruit), and radishes are lovely decorative accents in pots. To cover arbors, use peas, pole beans, and scarlet runner beans.

There is also no rule against interspersing vegetables and herbs among ornamental plantings especially when there is insufficient room or sunshine for a separate vegetable and herb garden. Treat your vegetables and many of your herbs as annuals and plant them among your more permanent ornamental plantings. When the herbs and vegetables are past their prime, replace them. Lettuce, cabbage, and parsley can be harvested and replanted throughout the cooler months of the year, and perennial vegetables such as artichokes and garlic can be camouflaged by annual flowers when they are going through dormancy and are not up to snuff on the beauty meter. Combine cutting flowers or plants with edible flowers among your vegetables. Many herbs such as rosemary, African blue basil, and lavender are known for their lovely, fragrant flowers and combine beautifully with ornamentals and veggies. Variegated thyme, rosemary, French lavender, and sage make themselves at home among drought-tolerant ornamentals.

Follow special guidelines for rooftop gardens or container plants on decks, porches, and stairways. Consider hiring a structural engineer to determine how much extra weight your roof can withstand and whether foot traffic would cause damaging leaks. Containers need to be large enough for the selected herbs or vegetables. Some may require only 6 to 10 inches of depth, such as basil, cilantro, peppermint, radish, thyme, and dwarf cherry tomatoes. While beans, kale, squash, tomatoes, cabbages, and cauliflowers need 18 to 24 inches to keep their roots happy and healthy, oregano, sage, carrots, Chinese cabbage, and Swiss chard prefer their roots to be in 10 to 15 inches of soil. Make sure the containers have drainage holes; do not place pots directly on wooden stairs or decks. Elevate them with blocks or other methods to keep the wood dry. Do not use heavy garden soil to fill the pots. Select a lightweight, well-draining, pest-free potting soil.

Visit your garden center, and look through all their seed racks for your standard favorites and for some interesting new ones, especially heirlooms. Heirloom vegetables are open-pollinated varieties, meaning when they are grown from seed, they will come back "true to type" exactly as the parent plant. Do not plant heirloom vegetables belonging to the same family close together, because they may cross-pollinate and produce a hodge-podge of progeny. Seeds from a hybrid variety, however, will either be sterile or will not exhibit the same characteristics as its parent. Refer to page 156 for seed-saving tips. Most heirlooms existed before the 1950s, before hybridization. Some actually date back before recorded history, but the real reason for the resurgence of heirlooms is because of their diverse, mouth-watering flavors, shapes, sizes, and colors. They offer a link between those of us in the present to the generations of gardeners that preceded us from all corners of the earth. Maintaining this horticultural tie to the past also preserves genetic diversity that might be critical to feeding the world's future population. Tomatoes are among the most popular heirlooms with annual tomato-tasting festivals and events held throughout California in summer and early fall. Many other heirloom vegetables are just as fascinating in their diversity—beans, corn, eggplant, kale, lettuce, peppers, potatoes, squash, and so much more. Seed companies and seed-saver and exchange organizations offer hundreds of heirlooms to tantalize gardeners for the rest of their lives.

PLANTING

In many regions of California, herbs and vegetables are grown year-round, but the keys to successful crops are the right soil, as well as timing, maintenance, and proper selection. Loam soil (40 percent sand, 40 percent silt, and 20 percent clay) is ideal because it percolates well by providing passages for water and air to move in and out of the root zone. At the same time there needs to be a balance between a well-drained soil and enough water-retentive capability to keep the root zones moist, but not soggy. Blending in 20 to 30 percent organic material such as compost, humus mulch, peat moss, or worm castings provides the perfect balance. For the majority of vegetables and herbs, prepare the soil to a depth of 2 to 3 feet by excavating the ground directly, terracing, building raised planting beds, or using containers. Turn the soil over to aerate it and break up any dirt clods. Add a commercial organic preplant fertilizer, a complete organic granular or liquid vegetable food or cottonseed meal; refer to Fertilizing. For specific amounts, follow the direction on the formulator's package. Then rake the soil level, and if planting in a regular or raised planting bed, create furrows between rows, especially where soils are clayey or heavy. For smaller gardens, plant seeds in 1- to 2-feet-square plots, rather than the more

HERBS AND VEGETABLES

space-consuming single file rows, but squash and melons need more room.

Continue to sow seeds or set out cool-season vegetable plants such as cabbage, spinach, broccoli, mustard, turnips, and beets, and English, sugar snap, and China peas for gardens that remain cool during the early summer months.

Swiss chard and eggplant seeds germinate pretty well indoors, but if there is no frost in your area, plant them directly in the ground. The same applies to tomatoes.

Gradually introduce indoor seedlings to outdoor life. Allow them about seven days in the shade and another seven days out in the sun, but bring them indoors at night. By the third week, they can be left outdoors through the night as their final "hardening off" phase before transplanting them in the garden. Read page 141 hints for planting seeds for more information.

Basil, fennel, and other annual herb seeds can be sown indoors four to six weeks before the last frost date in your neighborhood. Wait until two to three weeks before the last frost date if you want to sow fennel seeds directly in the garden.

Many perennial herbs and a few biennials such as parsley better tolerate chilly weather and can be planted outside during early spring. If spring is typically frost-free, plant herbs anytime. To encourage pollination, offer an herbal bee and butterfly buffet by including basil, borage, catnip, hyssop, lemon balm, mint, summer savory, and thyme.

After the last day of frost has come and gone, you can put in the warm-season herb and vegetable plants. Tomatoes, melons, corn, pumpkins, peppers, cucumbers, and eggplant can be planted by seed in the ground or transplanted from nursery-bought stock or seedlings grown indoors during winter. Sow corn in minimum blocks of four rows rather than single-file rows for better pollination, and continue successive plantings through early summer. Basil, dill, oregano, sage, thyme, and sweet marjoram are herbs that flourish in the warm spring and summer months. Towards the end of spring, plant more tropical vegetables such as squash and okra.

Squash, melons, and pumpkins do best when planted in raised hills with a grouping of three seeds or one or two plants, instead of rows. Mounding maintains soil warmth and provides a well-drained area for their roots. Make a 12-inch-diameter circle, and dig a trench 3 to 4 inches deep and as wide around it. Use the removed soil to make a slightly leveled mound in the center of the trench. Plant five to six seeds in the mound, and water the trench and mound until two or more true sets of leaves emerge. Thin out and leave the two largest plants. If you are transplanting, plant two seedlings in the center area and space 6 inches apart. For large pumpkin, melon, and squash plants, select the most vigorous seedling and allow it to remain while pulling the other out.

Plant the tallest growing crops on the north side of planting beds so they don't shade smaller plants. Pole beans, indeterminate tomatoes, and sweet corn should be north of eggplants and peppers. Follow a similar guideline for herbs, planting the taller African blue basil or angelica north of the shorter marjoram or oregano.

For water-wise herbs in a sunny place, plant dill, rosemary, and sage because they like dry spots once they have established.

Provide a trellis or a sturdy wood fence pegged with nails near the top to attach netting or string before planting climbing pole beans, cucumbers, or sugar snap or China peas. Another fun project is to set up three to eight bamboo or redwood poles (8 to 12 feet long) in a tepee fashion; near the top, tie them together with a sturdy nylon cord. Push the ends into the ground, making a $1^1/_2$- to 4-foot-diameter circle. Pole bush beans planted around the base will soon cover the structure and create a foliar tepee centerpiece in your garden. Corn stalks also make handy supports for pole beans or peas, but give the corn plants a head start and wait until they are at least 6 inches tall before planting the climbers.

Deciding between determinate or indeterminate tomatoes depends on what you want. For shorter plants that bear single crops over a period of four to six weeks, select determinate tomatoes. Indeterminate tomatoes continue to grow, flower, and bear fruit throughout the season. Determinate tomatoes adapt to small areas and make ideal container plants for hanging baskets and for larger pots. Indeterminate tomatoes require supporting poles or cages; if planted in containers, they must be at least 15 gallons. Since tomatoes grow adventitious roots, meaning roots that grow where roots don't normally grow, remove the lower leaves and bury the plant stems deeper than the soil level in their initial containers. New roots will grow along the buried stem. In our experience this transplanting technique develops a stronger plant. Depending on the mature height of a specific determinate tomato plant, it may or may not be necessary to provide supports by staking or caging, but indeterminate tomato varieties definitely need help. Before planting, pound in two 6- to 8-foot-long wooden or bamboo stakes 1 foot into the ground and spaced 8 inches apart. Plant the tomato between the two stakes. With plastic plant tape or strips of cloth, loosely tie the plant to the stakes by making a figure-eight pattern (the plant is in the middle of the figure eight). Continue to tie as the plant grows rather than waiting until they are already in their vigorous, sprawling mode.

Caging is another effective way to keep the fruit and foliage off the ground. Tomato cages are available at retail garden centers and agricultural suppliers, but you can also make your own out of concrete reinforcing wire mesh (for a 2-foot-diameter column, the circumference would be 6 feet, 3 inches). Drive two 6-foot stakes 1 foot into the ground and about $1^1/_2$ feet apart, on opposite sides of the cage, and tie the stakes to the cage to stabilize the whole unit. As the plant develops, tuck the branches into the cage.

Spring is a good time to divide herbs such as chives and mint. Use a shovel to slice through the center of the plant, or use two spading forks back to back to split the center. Replant the divisions at the same soil depth as they were originally, and water them with a transplanting solution three times, two weeks apart. Rooted runners of mints can also be cut and planted in another location. Just be careful where you plant mint because it tends to overstep its boundaries. It might be wiser to keep them in containers.

If you lack the space or enough sunny areas, there is still time to plant herbs and vegetables in containers. To make maintenance easier, mix in a water-retaining polymer and controlled-release fertilizer with the potting soil before watering and planting. Do not get carried away by adding too much polymer or fertilizer. Follow their directions because more is not better.

WATERING

Water is very important in all seasonal rhythms; it is the elixir that transports the nutrients from the root zone into the canopy of plants and prevents the foliage from wilting. California's average rainfall (10 inches or more) wets the soil by spring to a depth of 6 feet. If dry weather conditions prevail and the soil is not wet to this depth, supplemental watering becomes a necessity even before seeding.

How much to water and how often are two common questions; water deeply enough to wet the soil beyond the root zone. There needs to be sufficient water to replace the moisture transpired by the plant itself, as well as the amount of water that evaporates from the soil. Usually this means providing 2 inches of water per week for vegetable plants with shallow root systems that extend to a depth of 1 foot. Examples of shallow-rooted vegetables are cabbage, cauliflower, celery, lettuce, onion, radish, sweet corn, white potato, and most annual herbs. Asparagus, cantaloupe, carrots, cucumbers, eggplant, peas, pepper, pumpkin, summer squash, tomatoes, watermelon, and some drought-tolerant peren- nial herbs have root systems that extend deeper than 1 foot and need more water. When only the soil's surface is moist, most of the water evaporates, leaving salts to build up and raising the pH.

Clay soils hold more water than sandy ones. In a sandy loam soil, $3/4$ inch of water moves down to a depth of 1 foot in one hour, but the same depth of clay soil holds 2 to $2^1/2$ inches. Do not irrigate a clay soil as frequently as a sandy one. If you are having trouble determining the frequency and amount of water to apply to your plants and you are online, visit the Metropolitan Water District's Website at **www.mwdh2o.com** for the watering calculator. A tensiometer sold at retail nurseries also helps determine when it is time to water your plants.

The following watering methods are for herbs and vegetables in loam soils:

- If you use a sprinkler system, set empty soup cans under the sprinkler spray at different locations and monitor the time the sprinklers are on; when they are turned off, measure the water depth in the cans. To figure the amount of water applied when the sprinklers are on, take an average of the various depths.

- For furrow irrigation, create 5- to 6-inch-high raised beds spaced 32 to 40 inches apart from center to center. Level the tops of the beds, and spread them to 18-inch widths. Set the seed rows 3 inches from the bedding edges. Raised beds are also good for winter crops because they drain off excess winter rain. Furrow irrigation avoids wetting the foliage, a common cause of plant diseases, but more water is needed to moisten the soil to a depth of 2 feet, compared to sprinklers.

- Drip irrigation offers many advantages for the home grower. Water is delivered at a slow, water-conserving rate so that there is little waste and it is applied more accurately in the root zone. Unlike sprinklers, you can continue to putter in the garden while the drip system is on. Water efficiency, conservation, and time saved far outweigh the initial cost of a drip system and the maintenance of keeping the drip system plug-free.

- Soaker hoses are a variation of drip irrigation and are particularly useful for short 20- to 25-foot row plantings where the soil is level. They do not provide uniform irrigation for longer rows or on sloping soils; for such conditions, use the traditional drip system.

While the "inch of water per week" rule holds true as a general guideline for watering herbs and vegetables, adjustments are needed depending on the stage of growth, weather, and cultural conditions of the particular plant. Seeds need to be kept moist, but not soggy until germination. To prevent seeds from dislodging, spray with a mister or fogger. Young vegetable and herb seedlings recently transplanted outdoors have immature root systems and should not be allowed to dry out completely, particularly if there is no rainfall. Indoor seedlings also need to be watered whenever the surface soil feels dry. If seedlings have been transplanted outdoors in containers, allow them to dry slightly, about $1/2$ inch below the surface, before watering, and check them daily as the weather warms and the plants mature. Water most established herbs when the soil is dry down to a level of about 2 inches below the surface. Some herbs, such as dill, rosemary, and sage, are much more drought resistant and do not need to be watered as frequently as other herbs, such as mints. Vegetables that are budding and fruiting such as squash, cucumber, melons, peas, tomatoes, radishes, peppers, carrots, eggplant, and beets require an even amount of moisture throughout their growth, bud, and fruiting cycles. Herbs and vegetables planted in containers dry out much more quickly than those planted in the ground. Supplemental watering may need to be increased to two to three times a week, often daily if the weather is hot and dry.

FERTILIZING

We stress the importance of using organic fertilizers and soil builders in liquid or granular form that are byproducts of once-living organisms. The main reason is the impact organics have on the soil. Organic fertilizers feed the soil by supplying necessary organic matter and enhancing the soil structure. At the same time, they act as a storehouse for plant nutrients and encourage the proliferation of beneficial soil organisms. Plants take up the nutrients as they need them, at their natural rate, resulting in a higher resistance to attacks by insects and diseases. Many synthetic or chemical fertilizers are formulated to be fast-acting. Since plants can use

only a percentage of the chemical food at once, the rest is wasted. Besides suppressing beneficial soil organisms, chemical or synthetic foods often create harmful side effects by pushing tender, succulent growth that attract chewing and sucking insects. As a result, the plants weaken and become more susceptible to disease.

Without healthy soil, edible crops and all plants in general are not going to develop, mature, or produce well. After going through all the effort of adding organic matter and tilling it in before planting, why kill the soil with synthetic or chemical fertilizers? Instead mix in a complete organic, dry fertilizer. This encourages the development of new root growth without burning or damaging and provides nutrients at a slower, steadier rate for foliar growth. A complete organic vegetable food (4-5-3, 5-5-5, or 5-7-3) with nutrient-cycling bacteria and other beneficial soil organisms need be applied only once at planting, but for longer season vegetables such as corn, tomatoes, or perennial herbs, apply an additional dosage about halfway through the growing season. Follow the package directions for appropriate amounts and water in with a solution high in humic acid. If you apply a water-soluble organic fertilizer such as a liquid fish or kelp food (3-2-2), increase the feedings to once a month throughout the growth and bloom cycles, particularly for heavy feeders such as cabbage, celery, lettuce, onions, and tomatoes. Fish and kelp emulsions are also rich in micronutrients. Even if you fertilize twice with a granular food, it is often helpful to give vegetables an additional foliar feed with liquid fish or kelp food between the two applications of granular food for an extra boost. Medium and light feeders including asparagus, beans, carrots, corn, cucumber, sugar snap and China peas, eggplant, English peas, melons, peppers, pumpkin, okra, peppers, radish, squash, and Swiss chard should do fine with a water-soluble organic feeding about once every four to six weeks.

Organic fertilizers are most effective during spring, summer, and fall when the soil is warm and moist. Heat accelerates the decomposition process of organic materials, allowing nutrients to become available to the plants.

Organic preplant fertilizers (2-4-2) help ensure the successful transplanting or repotting of vegetables and herbs. Several brands contain mycorrhizae fungi that benefit root establishment, giving them a healthy head start. After there is a push of new growth and the roots are established, resume feeding with a complete vegetable organic fertilizer (4-5-3, 5-5-5, or 3-2-2).

Cottonseed meal (6-2-1) is another organic fertilizer that is recommended for acid-loving edibles such as potatoes, gotu kola, and stevia.

All members of the onion clan (bulbing onions, garlic, chives, leeks, and shallots) need monthly feedings of an organic, liquid fertilizer to push strong growth in spring.

Feed asparagus plants an organic, dry vegetable fertilizer in late spring.

Since watering is more frequent in container plantings, feed potted herbs and vegetables with a liquid organic food once or twice a month depending on the plant's feeding needs.

For indoor seedlings, add a water-soluble organic fertilizer after the first set of true leaves emerge once or twice a week at $1/4$ the dilution rate. For seedlings hardening outdoors, feed with a water-soluble organic fertilizer once a week at $1/2$ the normal dilution rate. Once transplanted outdoors, feed at the normal recommended dilution rate once every four to six weeks or apply a granular organic fertilizer.

A controlled-release chemical fertilizer for vegetables (14-14-14) is an acceptable option for convenience and if you do not have the time to use organic fertilizers, especially in containers. Controlled- or slow-release fertilizers are formulated to make the nutrients available gradually and add the advantage of applying it only once every three to four months.

Sidedressing is the process of spreading a band of dry fertilizer approximately 3 inches from the plants planted in rows with furrows on either side of their raised beds. About one month after planting, side-dress asparagus, broccoli, cabbage, cauliflower, and sweet potatoes. If there is no application recommendation for sidedressing on the organic formulator's package, reduce the normal recommendation by about half. Side-dress corn when the plants are about 6 inches tall.

MAINTAINING

If winter rains have eroded the soil in the planting bed rows, shore up the beds and shovel out the excess soil in the furrows.

Any crops that are ready to be replaced from last fall or early winter plantings should be dug up and made into compost.

Before the hot summer months, mulch the surface of the vegetable and herb gardens with 1 to 2 inches of compost, humus mulch, worm castings, or other comparable organic material to provide moisture retention, weed control, and temperature stability. Although many herbs tolerate poor soils, such as lavender and oregano, most flourish in well-amended, moderate to rich soils. Angelica, basil, chamomile, cilantro, dill, epazote, garlic chives, gotu kola, marjoram, mint, shiso, sweet woodruff, tarragon, and thyme are among the many herbs that are grateful for nutrient-rich soils and the protective cover of mulch during the warmer months.

Don't cover the ground with black or clear plastic (unless you are solarizing the soil, then use clear plastic) to keep the weeds down or to keep the soil moist. Mulch or "plastic-like" films made from cornstarch allow the soil to breathe while keeping out the weeds. Whenever weeds do come up, take them out with a hoe or hand-pull them while they are still young. For other weed controls, refer to Ground Cover Spring Planting.

Thinning seedlings is a ruthless, but necessary, maintenance chore to make enough room for the remaining plants. Seed-sown vegetables and herbs such as radishes, beets, Swiss chard, basil, and perilla (shiso) need room to properly develop. Instead of throwing away the excess seedlings, snip off their stems just below the soil's surface with sharp scissors and use them for microgreens in salads. They may be tiny, but their taste is mighty!

Patience is a definite virtue when it comes to asparagus, artichokes, and rhubarb. Wait until asparagus plants are two to three years old before harvesting the spears. Snap off the 8-inch shoots at soil level to avoid damaging the roots. Stop harvesting when the new stalks are the size of pencils and resume picking next year. The prized, succulent, white asparagus spears are harvested before the spears appear above the soil surface. Use an asparagus knife, a tool with a V-shaped blade at the end of a 12-inch shaft and a wooden handle on the opposite end to cut the spears. Slice them at an angle 6 to 8 inches underground; since they are never exposed to the sunlight, they remain white.

For artichokes and rhubarb, wait until their second spring before harvesting them so that they can expend all their energy toward developing strong root systems.

You'll be rewarded with larger harvests in the future. Select 8- to 15-inch tall rhubarb stems just after their leaves open, but before they flatten out. Once the plants are three years or older, take the stems for up to two months, but when they're only two years old, gather them for just two weeks. Instead of cutting the stems, gently pull or twist the leaves off. Yanking or cutting may damage the crown or cause rotting problems. Since their leaves and roots contain toxic levels of oxalic acid, cut off the entire green leaf blade and eat only the stems. Cut artichoke buds just before their scales begin to open up. When the top bud is cut, the lower ones will enlarge but they rarely develop as large as the top one.

Other vegetables are ready to harvest much sooner: Pick beets when their roots are 2 to 3 inches in diameter and pull up carrots when their broad shoulder tops are $1/2$ to $3/4$ inch across. As for green onions, harvest them whenever they are the size you like to use.

To extend the harvest of lettuce and other leafy crops, start clipping the "baby" outer leaves when the plants are about 6 inches high. If you leave about 1 inch at the leaf's base, it will regrow, allowing several cutting opportunities from each plant.

The ideal time for pea-picking is when their pods are a rich, deep green and the peas are small- to medium-sized. Pluck edible-podded peas from their sheltering vines when they are 2 to 3 inches long. To extend the harvest of all peas and beans (except dry peas and beans), gather them before they fully mature because if any pods start to develop dry seeds, the plant slows or even halts production. Don't forget to look for the pods at the bottom of the plant, so you won't miss any.

If bulbing onions are unreliable producers in your area, harvest them in spring while their tops are green and their bulbs are only slightly swollen. They may be small, but their taste is sweet. You can also snip onions, chives, and garlic greens for salads. Wait until summer to harvest garlic, shallots, and onions after their bulbs have swollen to size (refer to Summer Maintaining).

Off with the cabbage heads when they have grown to size, their leaves are still wrapped tightly around them, and they are firm to the touch! For care tips on cauliflower and Brussels sprouts, read Winter Maintaining.

Remove any damaged leaves when planting new vegetables and herbs, and pick off discolored or dead foliage from established plants. Don't forget to deadhead spent flowers unless you are collecting their seeds. Regular cleanups help prevent future insect and disease problems.

Most annual and perennial herbs need the tips of their branches pinched back when their branching stems grow out 4 to 6 inches. Timely clipping encourages more branching on the lower stems, creating a fuller, bushier appearance. Harvesting herbs regularly should be sufficient pruning, but with age, perennial herbs such as thyme, rosemary, and sage tend to get woody. Prune them back by about $1/3$ to fresh green wood, just above a leaf node or above another branch; this forces new growth and removes any dead branches. A fresh haircut provides a better shape and encourages fresh leaves to emerge.

Know an herb's growth habit when deciding when and how much to prune back. With some annuals like dill, coriander (for seeds), and cilantro (for leaves), the entire plant is harvested by cutting them to the ground at the end of the growing season. Parsley, angelica, and caraway are biennial and produce their leaves during the first year, but bloom and set seed the second year.

Perennials such as rosemary, sage, and thyme can tolerate as much as $1/4$ to $1/3$ of their foliage pruned back at once except during stressful times of heat or drought.

If you are growing tomatoes, pinch off the lowest two to three side branches to direct the energy towards improving and strengthening the upper portion of the plant. Pinching off encourages a more erect growth habit. Tomato plants may become so heavy that even stakes may not be able to support them. To limit the plant's heavy growth, remove developing suckers (those shoots where the leafstalks meet the stems) every week or two. Wait until the sucker develops a few leaves then pinch off the end of the shoot.

Clean up the dead leaves, and lop off the spent artichoke stalks at its base after they have finished bearing. Never twist or pull them out because you may damage or destroy developing shoots that increase the size of the plants. Once they mature (after the second or third year), the entire plant can be cut down at ground level in late spring and left on the dry side for two to four weeks. Resume watering after the dry period, and the plants may bear a fall crop. With age, it may be necessary to divide an overgrown clump and replant the rootstocks in early spring or late fall, just before the rainy season.

For better bulb formation, cut off flower buds when they appear on bulbing onions and garlic. Since it is not as critical to direct energy into bulb formation for leeks and shallots, their buds can be left alone.

If artichoke buds are allowed to open, they will become beautiful, thistlelike purple blossoms often used by florists in arrangements, but will stop the rest of the plant from forming more buds. For showy flowers, leave one plant alone during harvest season or allow a few of the side buds to bloom.

PROTECTING

If you are new to the practice of organic vegetable and herb gardening, and have traditionally used chemical pesticides and fertilizers as your first line of defense, you need to help build up the population of beneficial bacteria and fungi in the soil. Think of the soil as a living entity, teaming with fungi and bacteria microorganisms working as decomposers, as well as protozoa and beneficial nematodes that are preying on disease-causing bacteria, fungi, root-attacking nematodes, and other bad guys. By enhancing the beneficial microorganisms in soil, you are returning life into it. In addition to tilling in plenty of organic materials such as humus, worm castings, and compost, give your soil and plants a refreshing drink of compost tea.

The bad bacteria and fungi are anaerobic and thrive in reduced-oxygen con- ditions. By adding oxygenated compost tea, which is highly anaerobic, you are eliminating the majority of potential plant-disease-causing bacteria and plant-toxic products. Good bacteria helps consume the bad bacteria and produces inhibitors that work much like antibiotics. Many retail nurseries offer compost tea brewers, as well as "kitchens" where they brew this liquid plant elixir whenever you are ready to purchase it. If there is no service available or you would rather make your own, read page 163 for more information. Apply compost tea onto soil or foliage right after watering. Cover the surface with a light coating of compost tea using a watering can. One gallon of compost tea at a dilution rate of 2:1 should treat 50 to 200 square feet. A pressure sprayer puts out a fine mist and is able to cover as much as 300 to 700 square feet of soil per gallon of compost tea. When applying directly on plants, pressure-spray the bottoms and tops of leaves for maximum plant protection and benefit. Even seedlings can be treated as long as they have developed one set of true leaves. Apply full-strength compost tea every seven to fourteen days to infertile or heavy clay soils and to soils and plants with disease or insect infestations. As the soil improves, it will become looser with a more granular texture similar to coffee grounds and will better absorb and retain water than before. Continue treatment until the soil and plants show marked improvement. Thereafter, reduce the treatments to once a month. After six months to a year of regular application, there should be enough residual buildup of healthy soil microbes so that you can decrease the number of applications to the beginning of each growing season. Compost tea speeds the breakdown of toxins by increasing the population of beneficial microbes, helps suppress foliar diseases and insect infestations on plants and diseases in the soil, and increases the amount of nutrients available to your vegetables and herbs. These benefits are well worth the extra effort and time spent to replenish the soil.

Despite the best preventative and protective measures, damage from diseases and insects can still occur in the garden. Verticillium wilt, fusarium wilt, root knot nematode, and tobacco mosaic virus often attack vegetables such as tomatoes, squash, and melons and can persist in the soil for years. Vegetables with resistance to these diseases and to root knot nematode carry the letter V, F, N, or T after the variety names. Verticillium wilt occurs in cool, humid conditions and infects tomatoes, cabbages, eggplants, peppers, potatoes, radishes, and spinach. Mature leaves wilt while others develop a yellow patch, turn brown, and often dry up. Even when well-watered or fertilized, the growth remains stunted with little or no fruit. If you cut off the main stem near ground level, the center of the stem is brown instead of a healthy green. Control verticillium wilt by rotating plants that belong to the same susceptible families such as tomatoes and other nightshade relatives. Never plant them in the same spot each year. Solarize the soil when the weather is sunny and warm enough for four to six weeks, or distribute a 1-inch layer of worm castings and water it in with a product high in humic acid or mix in a granular concentrate of humic acid. Also apply compost tea at full strength and foliar-spray affected plants, on top and underneath the leaves. While never completely eradicated, these remedies keep the disease in check. Choose vegetable varieties that have a "V" after their names, or plant vegetables that are known to be verticillium-resistant such as asparagus, beans, carrots, celery, corn, lettuce, onions, and peas.

Fusarium wilt affects tomatoes, potatoes, peppers, eggplants, and other members of the nightshade family. The leaves may also yellow, wilt, and die, killing the entire plant. Often it is just one side of the plant that is initially affected before spreading to the rest of the plant. Cut the main stem, and look for dark chocolate-brown streaks running lengthwise through it. Potato tubers turn brown at the stem end and show brown spots inside the tubers when cut in half. Cankers develop at the base of pepper plants and eggplant foliage wilts from the bottom up before the plant collapses. Treatment is the same for both verticillium wilt and fusarium wilt. Also select vegetables that are identified with the letter "F" after their names. A double "FF" means that it is fusarium 1 and 2 resistant.

Root knot nematodes cause swelling or galls on the roots, stunting the host plants. Beans, beets, carrots, celery, cucumbers, peas, potatoes, pumpkins, radishes, and tomatoes are among many plants that are susceptible to these microscopic, thread-like worms. Their life cycle depends on warm temperatures, proliferating and doing the most damage during the warmest months of the year. Dig out and destroy the infected roots. Since nematodes multiply in weeds, cultivate the weeds out every two weeks, exposing the nematodes to the drying heat of the sun. Allow the ground to remain fallow for a season or two, and plant nematode-resistant sweet corn, cabbage, cauliflower, and chili peppers. Also add organic materials, humic acid concentrates, and compost tea to the soil. Since most French marigolds emit nematicidal chemicals, plant them to completely cover the areas of root knot nematode infestations as another natural control.

Mosaic virus symptoms are yellowing or mottled streaks in leaves, stunted growth, curling leaves, or a combination of these symptoms. Dig up an infected plant immediately and dispose of it. Tobacco mosaic virus commonly occurs on tomatoes in cool weather, causing malformed, "shoestring" leaves on young plants. On more mature plants, the leaves are mottled in shades of pale and dark green or bright yellow. Plants often have misshapen, brown-spotted fruits. When removing an infected plant, take out any tomato plants touching or near it. Wash tools used on the plant with a Physan20™ solution, and clean your hands and clothing thoroughly. Plant resistant tomato varieties labeled with the letter "T," wait a year before planting a susceptible crop in the same location (tomato, spinach, mustard), and do not let smokers handle susceptible plants without washing their hands beforehand because infected tobacco in cigarettes can spread the virus.

Mints and other herbs are also affected by viruses. Their leaves become spotted or streaked with yellow and curl up. Blast virus-spreading aphids and leafhoppers with a strong stream of water, or use an organic insecticide. Dig up any infected plants and throw them in the trash to avoid contaminating other plants.

Herbs such as thyme, Greek oregano, lavender, sage, winter savory, catmint, angelica, and rue, as well as other herbs and vegetables grown in water-logged soils, are prone to stem, root, and crown rot. Rotting tissues in the stem, root, or crown turn black and slimy, eventually killing the entire plant. Once rot sets in, dig up the plant and dispose of it in the trash. Never compost diseased plants. Solarize the soil, or allow it to dry out. Make sure there is better drainage in the affected area. Then dig in more organic material and apply compost tea to the soil. Review more about compost and compost tea under Spring Protecting.

Damping-off disease is a young seedling's worst nightmare, causing it to fall over and wilt. Make sure the soil drains well, give seedlings enough space between them for good air circulation, and add plenty of organic material to the soil if it is clayey. But do not add fresh, uncomposted material just before planting seeds. Also use sterile seeding mixes and containers when planting your own vegetables and herbs from seeds.

Powdery mildew is known by the light gray or white powdery substance covering the leaves. Several different kinds of fungi cause this problem in yarrow, lemon balm, rosemary, squash, pumpkins, cucumbers, peas, and cole crops. If caught early enough, simply wash off the plants and remove the affected foliage. Throw the leaves away to avoid spreading the spores, and spray the plants with compost tea or a lemon-myrtle-based oil organic fungicide. If the plants are too far gone, remove them. To prevent future outbreaks of powdery mildew, plant crops in more direct

sunlight, give plants enough space for good air circulation, water sufficiently, and avoid fast-release chemical fertilizers.

Catfacing commonly starts on the blossom end of tomato fruits with brown, rough-textured splotches often accompanied by deformed fruit with deep folds. It is caused by drought, temperatures above 85 degrees Fahrenheit or below 55 degrees. Other than providing even amounts of moisture and protecting the blossoms during extreme heat or cool weather, you can do little else except select tomato varieties that resist catfacing, such as 'Avalanche', 'Bonus', 'Floramerica', and 'Floradora'. Although catfaced tomatoes look ugly, they are still good to eat.

Blossom-end rot is another problem that appears most often on the blossom ends of tomatoes, melons, and squash. They turn brown and decay often before the fruit fully ripens. The problem is due to calcium deficiency, fluctuations in the soil moisture content, rapid changes in the ambient temperature, or a combination of some or all of the above. Even out the moisture availability, and apply a 10 percent calcium concentrate at a rate of 3 ounces per 2 gallons. If the blossom-rot has only affected part of the fruit, just cut away the brown or blackened portion before eating.

Sometimes flowers on your tomato plants don't set fruit and fall to the ground for no apparent reason. The culprit might be temperature related, since many tomatoes won't fruit if temperatures dip below 55 degrees Fahrenheit or rise above 85 degrees. If cool or hot conditions prevail in your area, plant cool-season or warm-season varieties with genetic characteristics that allow them to set fruit at lower or higher temperatures. 'Siberian' flowers and fruits in 38-degree weather, while 'Heatwave' and 'Sioux' are known to take the heat.

Watch out for aphids and whiteflies in the spring garden. Aphids are tiny pear-shaped sapsuckers and come in different colors, including black, white, green, or pink. They weaken plants and also transmit viral diseases that harm and kill herbs and vegetables. Whiteflies hide and feed on the undersides of leaves. When the plants are jiggled, they fly out in a white cloud of "plant dandruff." While aphids flourish in the cool weather and low-light conditions of spring and fall, whiteflies reproduce rapidly in sunny, warm conditions. If aphids or whiteflies set up housekeeping on your vegetables and herbs, spray with an organic garlic or Neem-oil-based insecticide or a horticultural oil (do not apply horticultural oil on plants with ciliated leaves) or wash them off with a strong stream of water. Continue treatment every few days until they are gone. Also release ladybugs and lacewings, predators of aphids and whiteflies. Another remedy for whiteflies is to set yellow sticky traps besides each plant. Sticky traps are available at retail nurseries or can be made with yellow cards smeared with petroleum jelly. Place the sticky traps or cards next to the plant, and shake the main stem. Whiteflies are attracted to yellow and will fly into the sticky cards.

For other insects such as crickets or beetles, use either a synthetic or natural pyrethrin, garlic extract, or Neem oil insecticidal spray. These are all safe to use on plants with edible parts. Picking them off by hand is another option. Since beans repel cucumber beetles, inter-plant beans with your cucumber plants.

Cabbage loopers are the larvae of a tan, white-spotted moth known as the cabbage moth. As their name suggests, the cabbage moth loves to lay its eggs on cabbage and other cole crops (broccoli, cauliflower, Brussels spouts). When the eggs hatch, the larvae feed greedily. Cover any vegetable or herb crop with a floating horticultural blanket as protection from loopers, other crawlers, creepers, and birds.

Even if an insecticide is organic and safe to use on vegetables and herbs, read the product label to make sure it is safe to use around bees. If it is harmful, spray at dusk.

Tomato hornworms are $1/2$- to 5-inch green larvae with diagonal stripes and single black horns on their behinds. They are perfect camouflage artists and are difficult to spot, but their damage is obvious: devouring tomato, pepper, egg-plant, and potato foliage; stripping stems bare; nibbling on fruit and leaving black-pepperlike droppings on the leaves. To make them more visible, sprinkle the plants with water; as they wriggle to shake off the water, pick and squish them. You can also spray with *Bacillus thuringiensis* (Bt), a bacteria that is safe to use on edibles but death to tomato hornworms and other larvae. Bt disrupts their digestive systems, so they literally starve to death.

Although the volatile fragrance of herb oils repels most insects, aphids and spider mites are the exception. Aphids are attracted to crowded planting conditions fueled by fast-growing, juicy, succulent growth typically caused by chemical or synthetic fertilizers. They are particularly fond of oregano, angelica, and basil. Their honeydew (sticky droppings) is a host for black, sooty molds and attracts ants. Spider mites proliferate in dry weather conditions, covering mints, oregano, basil, rosemary, sage, thyme, and other herbs with fine webs and causing speckled or dull foliage. Control both pests by spraying them with a strong stream of water or using a pyrethrum, garlic, or horticultural oil product. The best preventative defenses against pests on herbs are to provide good drainage, remove weak or infested growth, and pick off drying, dead, or infested foliage.

Keep the areas around your herbs and vegetables free and clear of weeds and plant debris because they are the favorite habitats and breeding grounds of many insects, such as beetles. Regular cleanups are necessary in any season.

French sorrel, basil, sage, or any herb or vegetable with soft growth are prime targets for slugs and snails. Control them with iron phosphate, or use decollate snails if it is allowed by your county. For more information on snail and slug control, read Annuals Spring Protecting.

For pocket gophers and rats, use manual traps or bait stations. Set a guillotine trap to eliminate insectivorous moles. If squirrels, rabbits, skunks, opossums, or raccoons are causing extensive damage to your herb and vegetable garden, use a live trap and relocate them. Check first with the California Department of Fish and Game to make sure live-trapping and releasing of specific wild animals is allowed. If not, hire a specialist licensed to remove wildlife. To discourage nibbling deer, use water-activated motion detectors, olfactory repellents, or set up a series of 6-foot stakes around the perimeter of the planting bed area and string monofilament line deer chest high around the stakes. The deer cannot see the line and are frightened away when the line touches them across the chest.

THE GOOD GUYS

Beneficial insects are effective as the weather warms and daylight hours lengthen. The following chart identifies beneficials and the insects they control.

BENEFICIAL	CONTROLS
Lacewings	mites, whiteflies, mealybugs, thrips, aphids, lerp psyllid, scale crawlers
12 Spotted Lady Beetles	aphids, scale crawlers, potato beetles, beetle larvae
Looper parasite	cabbage loopers
Mealybug Destroyer	mealybugs, scale, aphids, thrips, red spider mites
Encarsia formosa	green house whitefly, silver leaf whitefly
Big Eyed Bug	cabbage loopers, lygus bugs, mites, leafhoppers, boll worms, budworms
Ladybird Beetle	aphids, soft-bodied insects, scale
Spiny Soldier Bugs	caterpillars, beetle grubs, hornworms, cabbage loopers, webworms,
Scale Destroyer	hard scale, soft scale
Western Predatory Mite	avocado (Persea) mite
Beneficial Mites	mites, thrips
Beneficial Nematodes	root knot nematodes, thrips, fungus gnats, flea beetles

HINTS FOR PLANTING SEEDS

Proper sowing techniques make all the difference for successful germination. One of the most common errors is planting seeds too deep. As a general rule, the smaller the seed, the shallower the planting depth. Although seed packet recommendations are important to follow, remember their guidelines are based on sandy loam soils. If your soil is heavy or clayey, plant the seeds slightly higher than the package directions. Seeds are food storage embryos that provide the energy for the seedling to reach the soil's surface. Once the seedling breaks through the surface, it is able to manufacture food on its own through photosynthesis. When planted too far down or if the soil is heavy and clayey, the seed's food supply runs out before the seedling is able to reach the surface.

Till the soil so that it is loose, well-draining, and amended with organic materials. Moisten the soil before planting. For row planting, make a groove that is at the recommended depth, set in the seeds, cover them with loose soil, and gently tamp down so the seeds make direct contact with the soil. Do not push the seeds into the soil. For heavy, clayey soils that tend to crust over, dig a shallow planting trough for each row; fill in with a commercial organic potting soil, and sow the seeds directly into the potting medium. Keep the soil moist until the seedlings appear.

In addition to depth and spacing, follow the package directions for thinning plants to allow proper spacing between them and to meet the sunlight requirements. Also make sure the package date is for the current season. If the expiration date has passed, do not purchase the package.

When starting seeds indoor, put your pots in a planting tray to keep any excess water from staining your furniture, counter, floor, or window ledges. Plant several seeds in one pot, and thin out all of them except the most vigorous seedling. Instead of pulling out the excess seedlings, cut them at ground level to avoid damaging the roots of the remaining plant. When the seedlings are 2 to 3 inches tall, transplant them outdoors, but "harden" them off first by exposing them to outdoor conditions gradually. For the first week of hardening, set the seedlings in a shaded, protected area during the day and bring them back indoors at night. The second week, place them in a sunny location and return them indoors in the evening. By the third week, keep them outdoors day and night. At the end of the third week, the hardening-off process will be complete and they can be transplanted in the ground.

Dig a hole slightly larger than the seedling's container. Use a knife to loosen the soil around the edge of the pot. Turn the pot upside down while supporting the plant between your fingers and set the plant into its new home. Tamp the soil around it, and give the plant a light watering. Apply a transplant solution three times, two weeks apart (use any transplant solution containing indolebutyric acid or alpha naphthalene acetic acid).

SUMMER

When Sirius (the Dog Star in the constellation Canis Major) is in conjunction with the sun, the sultry dog days of summer remain for about 50 days. Summer's dog days provide chile pepper's heat, but a sun-ripened tomato is its heart.

PLANNING

It is important to remember that you should follow the rhythm of a plant's growth habits rather than calendar dates. The summer solstice marks the first day of summer and is the day with the most hours of daylight. Even though the calendar date tells you it is summer, the actual season embraces the changes in the seasonal weather pattern and can be a month or two before or after the actual calendar date. Observe and record the rhythms of change in your landscape rather than calendar dates, especially in your vegetable garden.

Summer might seem like a strange time to plan for a winter crop garden, but often areas that receive enough sun for warm-weather crops are inadequate for cool-weather ones. Take a midnight stroll with flashlight in hand through your garden during a full moon closest to June 21, the longest day of the year. We are not asking you to "dance with the devil in the pale moonlight," but do observe the portions of the garden that are bathed in moonlight. They will have the most winter sun.

Before selecting warm-season vegetables or cold-sensitive herbs to plant from seed, think about frost even though it is summer. If you have just moved and are not familiar with the average first-frost date in your area, contact your local University of California Cooperative Extension office. Most warm-season vegetables need to be planted so that they mature a minimum

two weeks before the first frost. Read the seed packet instructions regarding the length of time required for particular varieties to reach maturity, including days or weeks needed for germination. Then add ten more days to adjust for the possibility of a cool autumn. Subtract that total number from the date that is two weeks before the first frost. After doing the math, you will have the last planting date for warm-season vegetables. For example, if a warm-season plant needs 75 days from seed to maturity and the average first-frost date is November 15, then subtract 99 days (75 + 10 + 14 days) from November 15 and you will have your last planting date. Of course, if frost is not a typical event in your neighborhood, then just follow the recommended final planting date on the seed packet.

Consider purchasing a composter or building one yourself. You can put all your fallen leaves, cut-up twigs, pruned-off vegetable and herb stems, spent flowers and kitchen waste (except meat), pine needles, and barnyard manure to make compost and till it into your soil rather than buying bags of commercial amendments. To hasten the composting process, layer the compost pile like a lasagna, alternating layers of green waste (pesticide- and herbicide-free grass clippings, green leaves, fresh cuttings, coffee grinds, used tea leaves, and fruit and vegetable scraps) with brown waste (dried leaves, wood chips, wood ash, sawdust, ground-up branches and twigs, and shredded paper). Keep the compost pile as moist as a wrung-out sponge, and turn the pile once or twice a week to inhibit the growth of anaerobic, odor-causing bacteria. Composting in summer and early fall is especially efficient because heat accelerates the decomposition of organic materials. Avoid putting in any diseased or insect-infested plants or any plant that has been treated with chemicals. Do not add feces from animals because they can harbor disease. Bones, meat scraps, weeds with seedpods, and Bermuda grass are not suitable for composting because of seed germination, animal attractants, or because they do not break down readily.

As soon as one vegetable or annual herb stops producing crops, dig it up, amend the soil, and plant others, but do not plant the same crop or crops belonging to the same family in the identical space time after time. Crops belonging to the same plant family often share similar cultural conditions and suffer from the same diseases and pests. Since there are no chemical cures for many soil-borne diseases, rotating crops helps to slow down or halt the buildup of these diseases. In a severely affected area, it may be necessary to leave it fallow for a year or two. Crop rotation is easier in larger yards; if it is too impractical to rotate crops in a small garden, plant them in containers and replace or replenish the potting soil for each successive planting.

When it is too hot to work out in the yard, stay indoors and draw a map of your vegetable and herb garden, listing your current selections. This serves as a great reminder of what and where you are growing specific crops, enabling you to make better decisions about future plans. Try making a new map every time you change your seasonal plantings. Also categorize each crop according to its fertilizer needs and by its plant family. For example,

heavy feeders such as tomatoes belong to the nightshade family, and it would be beneficial to replace them with a crop that belongs to the legume family of beans, peas, or soybeans since legumes are soil builders. Even light feeders such as carrots or parsnips (both belong to the carrot family) are preferable to planting two heavy feeders in a row. If you must plant two heavy feeders in succession, make sure they do not belong to the same plant family. For instance, do not follow a planting of eggplant with peppers because both are heavy feeders and they belong to the same nightshade family. Choosing a soil builder in the fall or winter rotation cycle also allows you to plant heavy feeders such as summer squash or corn in summer.

After working the soil and properly feeding, watering, and caring for your vegetables and herbs, you should have a bumper crop by the end of summer. Keep enough for yourself, but share the bounty with neighbors, friends, and local food banks, soup kitchens, Meals on Wheels, and convalescent or retirement homes.

Summer's end offers an opportune time to reflect about which vegetables and herbs were the most successful, which were just so-so or worse, and which ones you want to plant again. Record any persistent maladies or pests and their remedies. Write these recollections down in your garden journal while they are fresh in your mind. When you begin to plant next summer's garden, you can review your past experiences and reap the rewards of lessons learned.

PLANTING

Coastal gardening offers pluses and minuses. While California's inland regions and the Central Valley experience typical summer temperatures in the 90-degree Fahrenheit range and above, San Francisco, Santa Cruz, Mendocino, Monterey, Eureka, and other coastal areas often face foggy days followed by brisk evenings in the 60- to 70-degree range. Salad greens like lettuce are normally cool-season crops, but they can grow in summer if you select a slow-to-bolt variety such as 'Forellenschluss' and start the seeds in a partially shaded area as early as possible in summer. Heat-resistant varieties grow successfully along the coast in full sun where temperatures rarely reach 90 degrees. If temperatures zoom up to 90 degrees or higher, lettuce seeds do not germinate. Sow only enough to eat in two to three weeks, and harvest their outer leaves regularly. The longer lettuce stays in the ground, the higher its chances to bolt or go to seed. The minuses of living in areas where summers remain cool and foggy are trying to grow crops that need lots of sunshine and heat, such as the icons of summer: tomatoes, corn, eggplants, peppers, and melons. In cool-summer climates, select varieties developed to tolerate lower temperatures and plant them in areas protected from sea breezes or blustery winds. 'San Francisco Fog' and 'Stupice' do very well in foggy, overcast, and cooler weather conditions. Heat-loving herbs and vegetables may not reach their peak potential, and they may fruit and bear later than the rest of California, but their homegrown taste will still be better than most supermarket offerings.

For areas that do have hotter summer temperatures, focus less on cool-season crops and concentrate more on sun-worshipping eggplants, peppers, tomatoes, beans, cucumbers, melons, okra, and squash plants. For later harvesting, sow them from seeds outdoors. Summer squash typically need sixty or more days to mature, but 'Papaya Pear Summer Squash' bear fruit in about forty-two days. Annual herbs such as basil, caraway, chervil, and dill can also be planted from seed for an outdoor culinary garden or placed in pots in full sun near your kitchen door. Refer to page 141 for more hints on planting seeds.

Sage and African blue basil are guaranteed to attract hummingbirds in your garden. Among the many different kinds of sage, try the pineapple sage (*Salvia rutilans*) because its pineapple scent is alluring to hummers and gardeners alike. The African blue basil with its panicles of heaven-scented lavender flowers will have bees, hummingbirds, and chefs competing for their bounty, especially during warm sunny days.

Take cuttings from herbs such as French tarragon, lavender, rosemary, and winter savory during the warm summer months. Snip off the newer growth in 3- to 5-inch lengths, remove all the leaves that would be below the soil surface, dip their cut ends in a rooting hormone, and plant in a flat of moistened potting medium. Set in the shade and keep the soil moist until the cuttings have rooted, in about three to four weeks. The cuttings can be planted directly in the garden or potted up.

Plant your herbs and vegetables in the late afternoon to allow them to fully hydrate before they are exposed to a full day of moisture loss.

Cool-season tomatoes need to be planted in late summer or early autumn while there is still enough soil warmth to get their roots sufficiently established, sustaining them through the shorter days and cooler temperatures in fall and winter. Early varieties such as 'Early Girl' do well, as do a host of others that originated from the more frigid realms of the world such as Alaska, Canada, Czechoslovakia, Hungary, and Russia. They all bear flowers and fruit in low temperatures, some as low as 38 to 45 degrees Fahrenheit ('Siberian' and

'Stupice'). For coastal conditions, consider planting cool-season tomatoes in spring or early summer for your summer-to-fall tomato crop. They may continue to bear through winter if coastal fogs and blustery winds stay away.

Plant chile peppers in early summer, and allow about eighty days for them to reach their full hot, spicy potential. If you enjoy the taste of chili peppers, but don't like their fire, try growing 'Fooled You', great-tasting chilis without the heat!

Sow cool-season bush bean, carrot, kale, mustard, and winter squash seeds, and transplant cruciferous vegetables such as broccoli, cabbage, and cauliflower from containers towards the end of summer or beginning of fall. For a continuous supply of winter crops, sow seeds or plants two more times about every two weeks.

WATERING

Adjust the frequency and amount of water depending on how hot or cool the days are during summer. As the plants grow larger, be aware that their watering needs increase. If there is less than 1 inch of rainfall per week (that figure pretty much applies to most of California in summer), keep providing supplemental water. Each vegetable plant should have about $1\frac{1}{2}$ gallons of water; tomatoes should receive $2\frac{1}{2}$ gallons.

Like most generalizations, variables such as heavy, clayey, or sandy soil (water drains out and plants dry out faster in sandy soils), dry winds, high or low humidity, hot or mild temperatures, full or partial sun, fast- or slow-growth rate, seedling or mature, shallow or deep-rooted plant, and ground or container plantings affect how frequently and how much water is necessary for your vegetables and herbs. Some plants may require triple the amount of recommended water and frequency of watering, while others may not need even the basic recommended amount of water. Monitor your plants closely during summer heat; if the plants look perky, hold off watering for a day or two. A tensiometer is a handy gadget to check soil moisture, but if you don't mind getting your finger dirty, just stick it in the soil next to the plant about 2 to 4 inches deep; if the soil feels dry to the touch, water.

As described on page 139, maladies like blossom end rot, which affect summer crops such as tomatoes, squash, and melons, are caused in part by erratic watering patterns. The soil is a reservoir for storing moisture, and the availability should remain steady rather than fluctuating from wet to dry.

For seeds, keep the soil moist with a mist sprayer as often as once a day until germination. After germination, water every two to four days depending on how quickly the soil dries out. For vegetables that are fruiting, provide adequate and regular watering once or twice a week, especially during any hot, dry spells.

Scientific studies indicate that the optimum time to water container plants is in the afternoon between noon and 6 p.m, particularly during a heat wave. It is no longer believed that beads of water magnify the sun's rays when watering in afternoon heat. Studies show that morning watering actually puts more stress on the plant and retards growth. If containers are watered in the afternoon, growth increases as much as 70 percent and produces more photosynthesis than pots watered in the morning. Apparently, container plants appreciate a cool afternoon shower just as much as we do on a hot, summer day.

Do not wet the leaves and blossoms of vegetables with ciliated (hairlike) leaves such as squash, melons, and tomatoes because they are prone to mildew and rot. Provide moisture around the plants, not on them.

It is almost impossible to overwater container plants. Depending on the humidity, heat, size of the pot, and the particular plant, it may be necessary to water once a day and sometimes twice a day. Watch over thirsty plants such as tomatoes, mints, stevia, angelica, gotu kola, and shiso. If they start to wilt during the heat of the day, water them more frequently. Perennial herbs, even drought-tolerant varieties such as sage, rosemary, and lavender, need enough water to keep them vigorous.

Towards the end of spring or beginning of summer, foliage on garlic, bulb onions, and shallots start to dry naturally. When this occurs, withhold water so that the dry outer layers can form tightly on the bulbs, keeping them fresh for storage.

FERTILIZING

During summer, apply a complete, dry vegetable fertilizer (4-5-3, 5-5-5, or 5-7-3) when first planting, but for heavy feeders such as corn, squash, or tomatoes, provide an additional feeding about midway through their growing season after they have set their fruits. Organic fertilizers that are water soluble or formulated as preplant foods, as well as chemical or synthetic controlled-release fertilizers, are other options. Increase the frequency of feedings if vegetable and herb foliage pale or if they do not produce fruits or flowers as they should. Refer to Spring Fertilizing for more information.

Nitrogen is not required in great quantities, but it is the primary element that pushes foliar growth. In the case of tomatoes, excess nitrogen makes their foliage grow too rapidly, resulting in little if any flowering. Choose organic forms of nitrogen, such as bloodmeal (13-0-0); they become available at a much slower rate compared to fast-acting mineral fertilizers such as sulfate of ammonia (21-0-0), which may quickly burn foliage. Read the application rates carefully to feed vegetables or herbs properly. When herbs are fed chemical fertilizers high in nitrogen, they quickly produce large leaves but with little flavor. It is best to use organic fertilizers that release nitrogen slowly for better tasting herbs and better vegetable production. Organic foods and products rich in humic acid increase the population of mycorrhizae fungi and other beneficial microbes, enabling nutrients to become more readily available to plant root systems.

If tomatoes are not setting fruits, due to temperature or moisture stress, spray the flowers with a blossom-setting product specifically formulated for tomatoes. There will be few if any seeds in the tomatoes as a result, but the fruits will be meatier.

Fertilize newly planted fall crops with a water-soluble organic food at the time of planting or wait until they have grown to about 4 inches high and side-dress with a granular organic or controlled-release vegetable fertilizer. Apply the amount and frequency according to the directions of the formulator.

After digging up a spent crop, work in more organic material such as compost, humus, or worm castings before you put in a successive crop. Organic materials not only improve soil texture, but also provide a low amount of fertilizer.

MAINTAINING

Cultivate the surface of the mulch so that it does not form a hardened crust. This allows water to percolate more evenly. Maintain a layer of 1 to 2 inches of mulch among herbs and vegetables to protect roots from high temperatures, to conserve water, and to keep weeds from growing. Stevia and other herbs with shallow feeder roots particularly need mulch to protect their roots from the heat of summer's sun.

Mints and oregano are notoriously aggressive plants once established. If they jump their boundaries and begin invading other plant territories, dig a 12-inch trench below soil level as a barrier. Be vigilant; keep cutting them back because they will tumble over their barriers and containers, spreading into places they should not be going.

Keep a watchful eye over your tomatoes, and continue to tie tomatoes to their stakes or make sure the branches are being properly supported within the wire cages.

Wait until onion, garlic, or shallot leaves start yellowing or until half the leaves have withered and fallen over before bending them to the ground (a process known as *lodging*). During lodging, the bulbs harden and cure for about three weeks before harvest. Harvest onion, garlic, and shallot bulbs when their foliage is crispy dry. Rather than cutting the dried tops of garlic, leave them on and braid groups of them together for easy storage.

Harvest cool-season vegetables such as broccoli, cabbage, carrots, and peas regularly if they are still producing. If you prefer to stretch out the harvest season of broccoli, such as 'Romanesco', just snap off the individual spears as needed. But once hot summer days kick in, cool-season vegetable plants quickly deteriorate and should be removed and placed in a compost pile. Cut off the spent pea vines at soil level instead of pulling them out. Peas and other legumes are nitrogen-fixing plants; that means their roots have nodules containing

excess nitrogen drawn from the air. As the roots decompose, nitrogen is released into the soil, becoming available for the next crop's use.

Cucumbers and squash are sweeter when picked small and will produce more for future harvests. Summer squash and zucchini are ripe for the plucking when their skin is easily nicked with a fingernail.

Look over your vegetables every day, and harvest when they have reached their peak size and flavor. Corn is fully ripe when the silk turns a chocolate brown. Pull back part of the sheath and squeeze a couple of kernels between your thumbnail and fingernail. When they squirt a milky instead of watery liquid, it is time for a corn feast. Pick eggplant when its skin is glossy and, when pressed, springs back with resiliency. If eggplants are plucked when they are still small and tender, peeling isn't necessary. Snip off 'Turkish Orange' eggplants while they are still green if you want to eat them. If you grow them for strictly ornamental value, leave them alone and let them turn into brilliant orange beauties. Okra should be harvested when the pods are 2 to 3 inches long. Pick bell peppers when they are green or red (they turn red if allowed to remain on the plant), and gather chili peppers towards late summer or early fall.

When is a melon ripe? Give it the sniff test. The fragrance of fresh, ripened fruit is a very good indicator, but if you do not trust your nose, here are some other tips. Cantaloupes are best when their greenish skin begins to turn a light sandy-beige. Gently tug at the stem; if it separates, it is ripe for picking. Watermelons are ready when their vine stems turn brown, the rinds lose their shiny sheen and become dull, and the portions that are closest to the ground change from pale to bright yellow.

We harvest our tomatoes a bit early, just when they turn their true color but are still pretty firm to the touch, because the resident birds peck at them when they are perfectly ripe. If you do not have bird problems, leave them on their vines until they are plump and true to color (they can be pink, orange, red, burgundy, green, yellow, and even white). For the highest sugar content in tomatoes, harvest them twenty-four to forty-eight hours after the last watering. Do not refrigerate them because they will lose their fresh taste and texture. Instead, set them on a counter away from the sun, with the blossom ends up. If you set them upside down, the weight tends to squash and rot the blossom end.

Herbs grown for their foliage, such as basil, angelica, mint, thyme, epazote, gotu kola, and perilla, are best harvested before their flower buds open, when their essential oils are at their peak. The exception is African blue basil. Its leaves continue to be aromatic and flavorful during the bloom cycle. Clip herbs mid- to late morning when the dew on the leaves has evaporated, but before the heat of the day. Forego harvesting during rainy weather. Do not cut more than 25 percent of the plant so that it can continue to thrive during the heat of the summer. Rinse the clipped herbs off in cool water, air-dry, store them in a plastic bag, and refrigerate until ready to use within the next day or two.

For herbs grown for their seeds (dill, mustard), collect the pods when their color changes from green to brown or gray, but before they disintegrate. To gather herb flowers, pick while still budded, just before they come into full bloom.

Stevia is at its sweetest when it is two years old. If it is able to survive winter in your area, harvest at that time. If not, treat it as an annual and cut the entire plant at its base just as it starts to bloom or just before the first frost in late fall. Hang the plant upside down in a warm, dry room with good air circulation. Plants should dry in two to four days. Loosen the leaves, and store them in an airtight jar.

Fresh basil loses its flavor when dried. To preserve its flavor, cut the leaves coarsely and set them in water-filled ice cube trays and freeze. Transfer the frozen cubes to a freezer plastic bag. Freeze other herbs the same way, or remove all the leaves from their stems and put them in a zip-lock bag or in a plastic container with a lid (after rinsing and air-drying them).

Do not dry herbs outdoors in the sun. Wash and set them on a screen indoors where there is good air circulation. Turn them around periodically to dry them evenly. Drying is complete in three to seven days. Herbs can also be dried in a microwave at the lowest power setting. Place them on a paper towel, cover with another sheet, and microwave in 1-minute intervals to properly dry. If they turn brown, they were "cooked" too long.

Harvest herbs whenever you are ready to use them throughout the growing season. This is the easiest way to maintain them, so clip away as much as you need, but follow a few guidelines. Consider an herb's growth habit before pruning back. Some annuals are harvested by cutting the entire herb down to the ground at the end of the growing season. Dill, coriander (for the seeds), and cilantro (for the leaves) are often gathered this way. Biennial plants such as parsley, angelica, and caraway bear leaves during the first year, but flower and produce seeds the next year. Do not prune if you want their seeds next year. Perennials can have $1/2$ their foliage cut back at once, except during stressful periods of heat and drought. Under those conditions, prune back by 1/4 if at all.

Regular pruning of herbs encourages vigorous growth, attractive shape, and sturdy plants. If you harvest herbs regularly, you are pruning. Simply pinching back 6-inch lengths of growing tips for drying and preserving encourages more branching. Woody herbs such as rosemary and rue should be cut back and their inner branches thinned out to keep the foliage dense and the growth compact. Prune the branches just above leaf nodes, or prune a branch down to the green part where you want to force new growth. Removing or deadheading spent flowers is also a great way to maintain healthy, attractive plants and to keep the flower factories blooming.

Indeterminate tomatoes are notorious for toppling over even when staked. Pinch out sucker growth between the main stem and branches; otherwise, the plant becomes too heavy. Suckers can be left alone if you have contained your tomatoes in sturdy, good-sized tomato cages.

For large pumpkins or melons, leave only one to three fruits per vine. If you are looking to super-size your pumpkins, cull off all but the one that seems to be the most vigorous.

Do not allow asparagus seedheads to develop in summer because the plant's energy should be directed into the maturing of the crown. Also, the asparagus that develop seedheads are female and, if allowed to germinate, will produce more female plants rather than the male plants that produce the edible spears.

Insects are attracted to rotting fruit and may overwinter, causing continuous problems through the following year. Remove any overripe or damaged vegetables, and throw them into the compost pile as long as the heat there is sufficient to "cook" the seeds. Toss them in the trash if they are damaged by insects or disease.

PROTECTING

Chewing, sucking, and rasping insects quickly get out of hand during warm summer months. While it is important to keep their populations in check, it is equally important to use insect controls and techniques that are safe for vegetables or any plants with edible parts. Wash foliage off early in the morning with a strong stream of water to blast off aphids, leafhoppers, and caterpillars. Apply organic controls such as a horticultural oil, garlic extract, or Neem oil. Do not use a horticultural-oil product on plants with ciliated leaves (tomatoes, squash) or during the heat of the day, especially in summer. Wait until late afternoon or early evening. For more details on insecticides appropriate for insects, read Spring Protecting.

Corn earworm is the larva of a greenish gray moth that destroys the kernels of corn. Control the infestation by dusting the silk with 5 percent carbaryl or spray with Bt as the silk emerges from the top of the corn ears. Black or brown insects on squash, gourds, or pumpkins are likely squash bugs. They are among the sucking insects. Use an organic garlic-based insecticide to spray the tops and bottoms of the leaves. Squish any egg masses you see.

Cotinis texana, commonly known as green fig beetles, are most active when summer fruits and vegetables are reaching maturity. They are 1- to 1 1/2-inch iridescent-green, buzz-bombing opportunists looking for any openings into fruiting vegetables, especially from bird damage. The female beetles lay their eggs below the ground, in compost, or in dung piles. After they hatch, the larvae feed on roots and decaying organic material.

To control them, net the adults, clean up dung piles, flood the soil and compost piles where the larvae live, and dispose of them when they rise to the surface.

Cutworms are the larvae of night-flying moths and deserve their moniker because they chew and cut off young seedlings at ground level. A few species even climb up plants. They destroy vegetable and herb starts in the blink of an eye. Turn or periodically flood the soil to expose and destroy them. Another safe control is to plant herbs or vegetables with a totally biodegradable plastic-like film (do not use regular plastic) made from corn starch. After preparing the soil, lay the film over the soil and cut slits for the plants. The film keeps the weeds out, protects plants from creepy crawlies, and warms the soil. After harvesting your crop, simply till in any remaining remnants of the corn starch film.

The problem with using Bt or any other larvae-destroying remedy is that butterflies seek out many herbs and some vegetables for nectar, shelter, egg-laying havens, and food stations for their larvae. Since butterflies have a particular fondness for dill, fennel, mint, rue, and creeping thyme, try not to use any larvacides on these herbs. The larvae of black and yellow swallowtail butterflies also feed on parsley, carrots, and parsnips. Having these fluttering beauties as regular visitors is one of life's great pleasures. Just plant enough of these crops to share with them.

Mints often develop orange, black, or purple rust spots on their leaves particularly during humid weather. Cut the plants back to 1 inch, and throw the infected leaves and stems in the trash. The new growth should not have the rust, but to avoid another outbreak, do not water from overhead and do increase air circulation by thinning out some of the nonproducing stems.

To control crown, root, stem, or blossom-end rot, as well as powdery mildew, refer to Spring Protecting.

PEST CONTROL EQUIPMENT

EQUIPMENT	USE FOR
Latex gloves and paper bags	hand and head protection
Goggles and long sleeve shirts	eye and arm protection
Aspirator	filtering air
Dry and liquid measurers	accurately measuring pesticides
Trigger sprayer	spraying small plants or small-target applications
Pump sprayer	spraying plants up to 8 feet tall
Tank sprayer	applying pesticides, liquid fertilizers, and misting
Hose-end sprayer	pesticides and liquid fertilizers
Backpack sprayer	pesticides
Trombone sprayer	shooting a stream 15 feet to 20 feet away
Drop spreader	dry fertilizers and granular larvae controls
Broadcast spreader	dry or granular fertilizers
Siphoning adapter	liquid fertilizers
Bait stations	protecting pets and children from poisonous baits
Wildlife traps	trapping and removing rodents

AUTUMN

The harvest moon is a special full moon. Near the autumnal equinox, the moon rises about sunset casting its light all night long. Farmers and gardeners alike can harvest their vegetable and herb crops under moonbeams.

PLANNING

Watch the weather; if cold weather arrives early, wait till spring to plant. Or begin starter plants in containers and grow them in a sunny location inside. If you have recently moved or haven't been keeping records of temperatures over the seasons, contact your local University of California Cooperative Extension office to find out the average first-frost date in your area.

For regions known for freezing periods in winter, decide what you want to do with frost-sensitive perennial herbs in containers. If you have room for them indoors where they will receive bright, indirect light, it would be nice to have fragrant herbs indoors and very convenient for culinary uses. You might also take cuttings and root the smaller versions of the parent indoors. The other choice is to dig them up, clear the bedding area, and plan for spring herbs or replace the herbs with cool-season vegetables.

If this is your first time planting vegetables and herbs, prepare the soil first. It often takes time to create perfectly textured and nutrient-rich soil. Since organic matter added to the soil decomposes quickly in warm weather, replenish the bedding areas with a fresh supply of humus, compost, or worm castings at least once a year. Refer to Spring Planning.

Fall is a great season to begin planting vegetables for winter or spring harvest, providing there are no early frosts in your area. In fact, vegetable gardening in the beginning of autumn presents a dilemma. Is it better to keep growing and harvesting the summer vegetables, or should you turn the beds over to the cool-season vegetables? If the summer vegetables are winding down their production or shriveling up, go ahead and dig them out, compost their sun-burned remains, and plant your fall or winter garden. Along the coast or other locales where summer vegetables may still be thriving and producing, continue to water and feed them for harvest or take them out by midautumn to get everything ready for your cool-season crops.

PLANTING

For autumn, plant only cool-season crops. Do not buy summer vegetable transplants because they will not have the necessary long days and warm nights to sustain them from late fall through winter.

Most of the winter or cool-season crops can be planted in the ground from seed in late summer or early fall. If you are pinched for time and don't need to plant so many single crops from seed, transplants are easy and more practical to put in around midautumn after the last Santa Ana or Chinook winds have blown away and cooler weather has settled in for the season. Brussels sprouts, cauliflower, cabbage, celery, lettuce, and parsley are available in 4-inch pots or six-pack cells, and potatoes and onions are for sale as sets at retail nurseries. Cole crops such as Brussels sprouts, cabbage, and cauliflower, as well as celery and carrots, dislike their roots disturbed, so think about seeding them instead.

Carrots germinate in soil temperatures ranging from 45 to 85 degrees Fahrenheit and can be planted just about anytime in most California locales. They can be sown from seed in a sandy loam soil directly in a raised planter bed or even a half-barrel. Since carrots have tiny seeds, mix them with some fine, commercial grade sand (not salt-laden beach sand) to make them easier to handle and sow evenly. A few seed companies offer carrot seeds in pelletized form, making it very easy to sow and to space so they do not have to be thinned out. Cover the seeds with $1/4$ inch of soil, and tamp it down so that the seeds are in firm contact with the soil. Thin the sprouts according to the seed packet's directions.

While the temperatures are still warm, do not pass the peas when it comes to early fall planting. Chinese pea pods (snow peas), snap peas, and English peas are the most common varieties and are a "snap" to grow. Put up a trellis for the tendrils to climb upon, and arrange their rows in a north-south direction, $1^1/2$ to 2 feet apart. Peas and other legumes germinate and produce much better when inoculated with a rhizobia (bacteria). Rhizobia form nodules on the roots of legumes, establishing a symbiotic (beneficial) relationship that enables legumes to take nitrogen from the air. Legume inoculants are sold at seed companies and retail nurseries in powder form. Sprinkle the inoculant into the hole or furrow, set the seeds 2 inches apart, cover with a 1-inch layer of soil along the coast and 2 inches inland, tamp the soil down, and water. Once inoculated, these plants do not need nitrogen fertilizer because the plants are able to manufacture their own supply. Although peas germinate from seed in temperatures ranging from 40 to 75 degrees Fahrenheit, they germinate much faster in warmer weather and can sprout in as quickly as six days.

Onions and garlic can be planted from seed (cloves in the case of garlic) or transplants during late summer through fall in mild climates. Where winters freeze, wait until spring. California days are too short to produce reliable crops of pungent-tasting, long-day onions, so those should be grown only for their greens, not their bulbs. There is a better chance of producing a good crop of mild-tasting bulbs from seed such as the short-day onions, 'Grano', and 'Granex'. Plant around the middle of autumn, and the bulbs will mature in early summer. See Winter Planting for medium-day length and day-neutral varieties and for additional information on bulbing onions, page 159.

Break garlic bulbs apart into single cloves, and plant them with their pointed ends up. Space 4 to 5 inches apart and cover with 3 inches of soil where the ground freezes and 1 to 2 inches in areas with mild winters. There are three different choices for garlic: softneck (the kind found at the grocery store, such as 'California Early', 'Italian Early', 'California Late', and 'Italian Late'); hardneck ('Korean Red', 'German Red', and 'Spanish Roja'); and elephant garlic (a large bulb that is really a leek, but used like a garlic). Because of its elephantine size, plant elephant garlic cloves 4 inches deep. Softneck and elephant garlic prefer spring planting in cold-winter climates, but hardneck varieties grow best where the ground freezes. If you live where winters are mild, store hardneck cloves in a plastic bag filled with potting mix until they sprout, then plant them outdoors.

For those who live in zones 10 and 11 where winters are mild, herbs can be planted year-round, but fall is one of the best times to plant perennial varieties. They then have plenty of time to acclimate before the stressful conditions of summer, and California's fall and winter rainy season should help get their roots established without too much supplemental watering. Unfortunately, for frost-prone locations, wait until spring.

If fall weather remains warm and mild, start annual herb seeds outdoors in pots and move them indoors after germination, or just bring them indoors when the weather turns cool. Some herb seeds, such as the biennial parsley, take a long time to germinate. According to folklore, parsley seeds travel to the devil and back nine times before they sprout. In reality, it takes twenty to forty days. Rather than your moistening parsley seeds every day for three to six weeks, our advice is to grow them from transplants. Give aggressive herbs such as mint or creeping thyme a separate area to themselves, or contain them in pots to prevent their taking over the rest of the garden.

Fall is also a good time to take cuttings of herbs so that they may overwinter indoors. French tarragon, stevia, rosemary, scented geraniums, and African blue basil propagate quite successfully from cuttings. Take a 3- to 5-inch length of new growth, and remove all the bottom leaves so they will not rot below the soil's surface. Dip the cut end in a rooting hormone, and plant the cuttings in a flat or pot filled with a commercial potting medium that has been moistened. Set the flat of cuttings under some shade until the cuttings have rooted (about three to four weeks). Keep the medium moist during the rooting process. After about a month, gently tug the cutting; if there is resistance, the cutting should have roots sufficient for you to transplant directly into the garden or into a larger pot. Add a root stimulator three times, two weeks apart, and set your rooted cuttings indoors where there is plenty of light, like on a sunny window ledge. Do the same for clumping herbs such as chives: divide and put them in pots.

WATERING

Keep all sown seeds moistened, whether they're planted indoors or outdoors. They usually need a misting about once a day, sometimes twice during hot, dry spells. Once the seedlings emerge, water whenever the soil surface feels dry.

Drip systems are one of the most efficient methods to irrigate new transplants or seedlings. Sprinkle their planting beds moist, but not soggy.

When and how to water carrots and other root crops is very important. To develop a deep and straight taproot, water daily until the seeds germinate. As soon as the sprouts emerge, delay watering intervals until the ground feels dry to a depth of 4 inches; then deep water just as the sprouts begins to wilt.

Many spring- and summer-planted herbs and vegetables remain viable until the days and evenings turn cool. Continue to water established herbs and vegetables, such as tomatoes and stevia, as long as they are still producing.

Don't be fooled by mild autumn days and brisk evenings. Seasonal Santa Ana and Chinook winds typically blast their way through California, drying everything in their paths. Vegetable and herb seedlings are particularly vulnerable to hot, dry conditions because of their immature root systems. Monitor them very closely and water them when the soil feels dry, before they wilt. Even established vegetables and drought-resistant herbs need enough supplemental water to compensate for dry, windy conditions and lack of rainfall and to prepare them for the cold winter months.

Water containerized herbs or vegetables when the soil surface is dry. Regular watering ensures that they will be able to survive the winter. For more watering tips, review Spring and Summer Watering.

FERTILIZING

Many established perennial herbs such as thyme, rosemary, sage, gotu kola, stevia, and mint, as well as biennials like angelica, begin to slow their growth during fall's slide into winter. Feed the herbs one last application of a liquid organic fertilizer at the beginning of autumn to better prepare them for the winter's cold. Also adding a product rich in humic acid in granular or liquid form helps build up the sugars in their stems and enables them to tolerate the colder winter temperatures.

Fertilize potted herbs and vegetables that are still growing and producing with a water-soluble food once a month until the growth slows or shuts down for the season.

For newly planted herbs and vegetables, use a preplant fertilizer (2-4-2), a granular organic fertilizer, or a controlled-release food and discontinue any additional feeding until early spring. Refer to Spring Fertilizing for additional information.

MAINTAINING

Weeds are very much a part of most California gardens even in autumn. Pull them up when you see them among your herbs and veggies. It should be very easy to tell the difference between your transplants from 4-inch pots or six-pack cells and emerging weeds, but more challenging to differentiate between a newly sprouted weed and an herb or vegetable seedling. If you sowed the seeds in rows, if the sprouts are coming up in rows, and if their growth resembles each other, chances are they are the crop seedlings. Just to be on the safe side, wait a bit longer for identifiable features unique to the crop, such as beets with reddish leaves or carrots with orange roots.

You won't have to weed and water as much if you maintain a 1- to 2-inch layer of mulch over your herbs and vegetables. Plus you won't have to worry as much about protecting them against hot or cold temperature fluctuations. Check to see whether the soil has become compacted around the plants. To promote better drainage for the upcoming rainy season, carefully loosen the soil by lightly tilling without damaging any of the root systems.

The end of fall should bring some of the cool-season crops to maturity. Cool-season tomatoes are ready to harvest when they turn color and their skins are slightly soft, but still resilient when pressed gently with the thumb. If freezing weather is predicted and the tomatoes have turned color, they can be harvested and ripened indoors. Store them on a counter, with their stem ends up. Avoid refrigeration because tomatoes lose their flavor and texture. For harvesting tips on summer crops that are still producing into fall; refer to Summer Maintaining. Refer to Winter Maintaining for harvesting winter crops.

Fill the open asparagus trench halfway up (about 6 inches) with a mixture of 50 percent organic material and 50 percent sandy loam soil, covering the asparagus crowns that were planted last winter. The second autumn, fill the trench all the way to the top with the same combination of organic material and sandy loam soil.

Carrots often have bitter-tasting green or red shoulders when they push up out of the soil. Mound soil or mulch around the base of carrots when their tops are 4 inches tall, and their shoulders will not turn color.

Harvest pumpkins and winter squash when their shells are hard. They will not ripen off the vine, so to make sure they are ripe, leave them on the vine until they have grown to size, they have stopped changing color, and their stems have turned brown. Leave a 2-inch stem on the fruit when cutting it off the vine, and store the fruit in a warm, dry area for a couple of weeks. Then move them to a cool (50 to 60 degrees Fahrenheit), dark place and set them so they are not touching one another. Pumpkins and winter squash store up to two months if kept under these conditions and the shells are not damaged.

If early freezes are predicted, spray frost-tender herbs and vegetables with an antitranspirant. It is safe to use on edibles, but since the protective coating adheres for several weeks, avoid spraying it on herbs or fruits of vegetables that you plan on harvesting soon. Set a cardboard box over smaller plants during the evenings, and remove the boxes during the warmth of the day. You can also cover larger plants with burlap or cotton sheets. Pound in two to four stakes around each plant, and lay the fabric over it. Again, remove the protective covering during daytime. Floating horticultural blankets made from polyester are available at retail nurseries and agriculture supply stores. They are lightweight enough to cover seedlings and small plants without damaging them. Make sure the edges are weighted with bricks or tucked

into the surrounding soil. If the herbs and vegetables are in convenient-sized containers, move them to a more protected location, such as under sheltering eaves. Never cover plants with plastic because plastic does not allow plants to breathe.

Bring frost-sensitive potted herbs indoors or place them in a more protected location.

Melons and pumpkins are still growing in the fall garden. Pinch the tips of the vines so that energy will be redirected into ripening the fruits that are already on the vine.

Pinch out the tips of newly planted herbs to force more branching and fuller growth. Do not prune established herbs in fall because many are preparing to go into dormancy, but do remove any dead growth.

Dig up any plants killed by fall frost or summer crops that are spent. They can be shredded and composted if they had no disease or insect problems. Otherwise, dispose of them in the trash.

PROTECTING

If you decide to take out all the summer vegetable and herbs at once, remember pests such as whiteflies and caterpillars do not stay put. They migrate, and so do larvae of moths and butterflies. "The worms crawl in, the worms crawl out..." and can journey from one plant to another, devastating plants, new and established. Before digging up all the plants and composting them, spray them first with the organic insecticide Bt. Wait several days for the "medicine" to take effect, and then dispose of them. A good, thorough cleanup in fall will make bug and disease spring-cleaning chores much easier.

Mites, aphids, grasshoppers, slugs, and snails are still preying on tomatoes, eggplants, peppers, basil, mints, and other vegetables and herbs. Organic controls are best to protect vegetables or any plant with edible parts from chewing, sucking, and rasping insects. Use the same insect controls and techniques under Spring and Summer Protecting. Hand-pick caterpillars or spray them with Bt, but remember butterflies also have a caterpillar stage. Read Summer Protecting for their favorite edibles while in the larvae stage. You may want to think twice about using Bt or hand-picking when it comes to swallowtail or other butterfly larvae. You can also keep insects and birds from attacking your vegetables by covering the plants with a floating horticultural blanket. Netting is another effective way to foil birds.

The rodent population is busily squirreling away food for the upcoming winter months. If they are damaging or destroying your vegetable and herb garden, live-trap opossums, squirrels, raccoons, skunks, and rabbits, and relocate them to a less urban area (contact the California Fish and Game Department for acceptable release sites, or seek the help of professional trappers). For additional information on controlling wildlife, read Spring and Summer Protecting.

Integrated Pest Management is a program developed by the University of California to help you manage pests—insects, diseases, rodents, and weeds. Access their information website at **www.ipm.ucdavis.edu**.

SEED-SAVING TIPS

Remember even heirloom plants may not yield seeds that bear true to form. If different heirloom varieties were planted close together, their flowers may have cross-pollinated and the resulting progeny may be a surprise. Keep heirlooms isolated from each other if you want to avoid cross-pollination. Hybrid cultivars either have either sterile seeds or, if they do germinate, will not mirror their parent's characteristics.

Wait until seedpods are dry before collecting their seeds. If you are not sure about the correct timing, wrap a piece of gauze, cheesecloth, or a paper bag around a ripening pod and tie a string around it. Check periodically and collect the bag when you see that the seeds have been released. For seeds inside fruits, allow the fruit to remain on the vine or stem longer than normal, but collect the seeds before the fruit rots. Remove pulpy seeds (tomatoes, melons) by soaking them in water and stirring occasionally. The pulp will rise to the surface and the seeds will sink in about two days. Rinse the seeds clean and lay them out on a paper towel to dry before storing them. To collect seeds from flowerheads, put the heads in a paper bag and shake out the seeds. Store collected seeds in a cool, dry place. Do not store them in plastic because of potential moisture damage.

WINTER

Cabbage, lettuce, parsley, and thyme, oh my! Their many shades of green provide a festive backdrop for baubles of cool-season red and yellow tomatoes. Make harvesting cool-season tomatoes the start of a new holiday tradition.

PLANNING

If you do not have a garden journal yet, buy one and start the New Year right. Get into the habit of recording the daily or weekly joys and challenges of your garden. Write down your thoughts about past, present, and future plans and plants for the edible landscape, as well as clippings and photo ideas. What about the herbs and vegetables you grew this past year? Did they meet your expectations?

Pile your garden catalogues and magazines beside a comfy chair to read whenever the weather is too rainy, cold, or blustery to work outdoors. Keep your garden journal or note pad in the same place to jot down ideas and must-have plant suggestions.

If you live where winter freezes are common, use this garden-quiet season to wander through your seed, bulb, and specialty plant catalogues; order the herbs and vegetables that interest you. Plant them in spring after the danger of frost has passed, or sow them indoors. Since many perennial herbs do not tolerate frost, it is best to plant them in containers that can be moved to more protected areas during cold weather or treat them as annuals under cold-weather conditions. Half the enjoyment of gardening with herbs is to experiment with new varieties to see which ones tolerate your unique climate and gardening needs.

Seaside communities are known for their frost-free winters, but remember the air is laden with salt spray and accumulates on plants and soil. Although gardens are more sheltered when the ocean breezes are obstructed by a house, fence, trees, or other sizable structures, many plants are salt-sensitive, including radish, celery, and green beans. Beets, kale, asparagus, spinach, and Swiss chard have a high salt tolerance.

Winter is the time when there might not be as much activity in our vegetable gardens below ground. Beneficial fungi and bacteria are still actively breaking down organic material, and the absorbing roots of cool-season vegetables are still expanding into new territories, but at a slower rate. As a result, plant your perennial herbs and cool-season veggies early in winter to get their roots established.

Do you know where there is enough sun for a winter vegetable and herb garden? It may not be the same as your summer garden. In summer, the sun is more directly overhead, but in winter the sun casts longer shadows. The difference in the angle of the sun can affect the amount of shade in your yard. Make an effort to look at your garden on December 21 at noon. This is the shortest day of the year, the day that casts the longest shadows. The best place to plant winter crops is wherever there is full sun at this date.

When selecting and planting vegetables, avoid repeatedly planting the same vegetable or any member of its family (cole crops such as cauliflowers belong to the cabbage family) in the same spot because they attract and share similar diseases and pests. Crop rotation is a much better way to plant vegetables.

If you do not have time to plant winter vegetables, dig up and prepare the soil for spring planting whenever there is an inviting day to putter in the garden.

While planning next year's vegetable patch, experiment more with heirloom varieties and save the seeds to produce future crops. If you are interested in sharing or acquiring more heirloom or rare seeds, trade with friends, neighbors, and members of your local garden club, or contact Seed Saver's Exchange at R.R. 3, P.O. Box 239 - D, Decorah, Iowa 52101.

Gather the supplies you need to plant seeds indoors: grow lights, peat pots, flats or other suitable containers, commercial organic potting soil, a misting spray bottle, water-soluble organic fertilizer, and organic fungicide and insecticide products. Read Spring and Summer Protecting for recommendations.

If you want to splurge, purchase a greenhouse, or start out small and buy a cold frame, which is available in retail nurseries, mail-order catalogues, or through the Internet. You could also build a cold frame from scrap lumber and old windows. As an added convenience, purchase an automatic opening device that will lift the lid at a certain temperature. During sunny days, temperatures can get so warm in the cold frame that the herbs or vegetables might cook. Cold frames are also handy when hardening off cabbage, broccoli, Brussels sprouts, and other seedlings   before planting them directly in the garden.

Before selecting herbs for outdoor containers or bedding areas, study their sizes. Herbs such as dill and fennel need more room than basil or sage, and ground-covering thyme and mint overrun their spaces unless contained in pots.

PLANTING

Many cool-season and warm-season vegetables and herbs can be started from seed indoors in the beginning of winter. These include broccoli, cauliflower, cabbage, Brussels sprouts, basil, dill, fennel, marjoram, sage, summer savory, and thyme. Depending on the variety, they take four to eight weeks before reaching transplant size for outdoor life. Tomatoes and chili peppers need about eight weeks before they can be transplanted outdoors. As long as you have the time to keep them moist until they germinate and provide enough light and warmth for them to develop, it is rewarding to transplant your own seedlings outdoors and watch them take off in the garden. Check the seed packets for the length of time between sowing and setting the plants outside. Then count back from that figure from your last-frost date to figure out the exact time to sow the seeds. Do not start too soon because the plants will become leggy and weak.

Use flats or peat pots, and fill them with a commercial, sterilized, organic potting soil. Heat pads (never use personal heat pads) or heating cables designed for germinating seeds keep the soil temperature at the recommended warmth (many germinate best at 70 degrees Fahrenheit). Once the plants have germinated, place the containers by a source of bright, indirect light or supply a grow light manufactured for indoor plants and hang it 7 to 10 inches above the containers. Leave the lights on fourteen to sixteen hours a day.

Artichokes, asparagus, and rhubarb are available as bare-root plants at retail garden centers in late winter or early spring. Choose crowns that are solid, rather than soft, and make sure the root systems are intact and evenly distributed. Also, the crown itself should be beige, not black. Since they should be planted within twenty-four hours of purchase, get their planting beds ready beforehand.

For asparagus, prepare a 12-foot-long trench 2 feet deep and 1 foot wide. Purchase the largest bare-root crown sections available; at the end of three years, each plant will produce six to twelve spears. Keep them moist before planting by soaking their roots in a bucket of water. Spread their roots, and space the crowns 1 foot apart. Backfill the trenches with 1 foot of sandy loam soil amended with 20 to 30 percent organic material (refer to page 307 on Soil Rhythms). Also blend an organic preplant or granular organic fertilizer into the soil mix, following the application directions on the package. Another fertilizer option is to use a controlled-release food. Again, follow the formulator's directions. This mixture provides excellent drainage while retaining sufficient moisture and food for the asparagus root system. Tamp down the soil, and water in with a root stimulator three times, two weeks apart. Make sure the asparagus crowns are at soil level. Asparagus require two to three years before bearing sizable crops, but will continue to produce for fifteen years or more if provided with excellent care.

Since mature artichoke and rhubarb plants become very large plants, select sites away from annual vegetables and herbs. Space them at least 3 to 4 feet apart, or plant them by themselves in large containers, such as half-barrels.

Cool-season vegetables such as beets, broccoli, Brussels sprouts, cabbage, carrots, cauliflower, celery, kale, kohlrabi, head lettuce, leaf lettuce, peas, potatoes, radishes, Swiss chard, and turnips can be planted where soils do not freeze.

Lettuce is very easy to grow from transplants or from seeds. If you plant from transplants, you will be able to harvest sooner, but seeds will yield more lettuce over an extended period. Their seeds are able to germinate from 35 to 75 degrees Fahrenheit, but sprout much faster at cooler temperatures. Although lettuce takes partial shade during spring, it requires full sun in winter. After preparing the soil and mixing in a preplant or controlled-release fertilizer, sow the seeds on a raised bed or in a wide furrow—about three seeds for every 2 square inches. Top the seed with $1/4$ inch soil. Read Spring Watering for more information about watering seeds and seedlings. If seeds do not germinate, check the pH of the soil. It may be too alkaline and could use a long, deep soaking to leach out the salts. Then start again with new seeds. Lettuce can also be grown in containers filled with a well-draining organic potting soil.

Medium-day-length onions, such as 'White Sweet Spanish' and 'Italian Red', perform well when seeded in early to late winter. But if there is a long, cool spring or one with alternating warm and cool periods, flowers will "bolt" up before forming good-sized, tasty bulbs. The secret is to sow their seeds in early winter in Northern California, but wait four to six weeks later in Southern California. Then transplant the seedlings outdoors when their lower stems are less than $1/4$- to $3/8$-inch diameter. If flower stems emerge, dig up the plants quickly and eat the bulbs before they shrivel up. Day-neutral onions like 'Buffalo' form bulbs anywhere and are not as dependent on daylight length.

Towards the end of winter, cool-season vegetables can still be planted along the coastal regions of California. Those who live farther inland or in the central valley where temperatures begin to warm quickly by harvest should harvest what is ready and wait until spring to plant the first summer crops.

If you decide not to put in a winter or early spring vegetable and herb garden, rejuvenate the soil by planting a legume cover crop such as soybeans. Plant legumes from seed about one month before the last-frost date, and till them back into the ground after they mature.

WATERING

Supplemental watering is not as vital because Mother Nature usually supplies winter rainfall. Be careful not to overwater, or root rot may result. Most established vegetables and herbs slow down or stop their growth rate, due to the cooler weather and fewer hours of less intense daylight. Adjust or turn off your irrigation clock.

Keep indoor and outdoor seeds and seedlings moist. Check them every day. It may not be necessary to water outdoor plantings at all during periods of normal rainfall. But water established and newly planted herbs and vegetables when the soil feels dry 1 to 4 inches below the surface. Shallow-rooted plants and seedlings need more moisture closer to the surface compared to more established ones. Monitor cool-season crops like celery closely when there is little or no rainfall because regular amounts of moisture encourage fast growth and sweet flavor. Read Spring Watering for more details.

To avoid mildew or rot, water seedlings during the sunny hours of the day, rather than late afternoon or early evening.

If the soil feels damp, do not water established herbs that remain indoors. Allow the soil to dry out slightly before watering, and don't let them sit in water-filled saucers.

FERTILIZING

For most of California, winter weather is still mild enough to keep cool-season herb and vegetables actively growing. If using a dry, organic fertilizer, water it in immediately to help move the nutrients into their roots. Start feeding seedlings as soon as they sprout one or two sets of true leaves. Maintain a regular feeding schedule, and select from the suggested fertilizers as outlined under Spring Fertilizing. Provide an extra boost of plant food if the cool-season herb or vegetable begins to yellow or its growth slows down.

Some minor adjustments may be necessary for particular cool-season crops. Six weeks after planting, feed celery with a water-soluble organic food every two weeks. Quick-growing vegetables such as radishes do not need supplemental fertilizer as long as you used a preplant fertilizer before planting. Continue to fertilize Brussels sprouts if they produce a crop in winter; they will continue to develop new sprouts throughout the cool season. Fertilize two-year-old and established asparagus plants twice with a granular organic fertilizer, once in late winter and again in late spring. Pinch off any new, growing tips of fava bean stems if they are bearing flowers but nothing else, and spray the foliage and around the base of the plants with a liquid organic food. You should see resulting beans in one to two weeks. Fertilize herbs that are still growing indoors, as well as seedlings. It is not necessary to feed herbs, particularly the perennial varieties, if they are not growing during winter.

MAINTAINING

Clean up garden debris by composting it or throwing it away. Inspect compost piles for large larvae, and get rid of them by picking, squishing, and throwing them away.

This is an excellent time to replenish the organic content of bare vegetable and herb beds. Apply a 1- to 2-inch layer of worm castings over the fallow soil area, and water it in with a solution high in humic acid.

Bring frost-sensitive potted herbs indoors or place them in a more protected location.

Once indoor seeds have germinated, give them plenty of bright, indirect light or put them under grow lights for at least fourteen to sixteen hours.

As soon as cauliflower heads begin to form, tie their leaves over them to protect them from sunlight. Without foliar scarves tucked around their heads, the curds turn green when exposed to sunlight. Although some cauliflowers are touted as "self-blanching" (their curds remain white because the leaves naturally curl over their heads), tie them anyway and the curds will be much whiter. Every few days, untie their "scarves" and check to see whether the heads are filling out. When they start filling out, check daily and harvest when the white buds are plump and their sections begin to loosen and separate on the outer edges. Do not wait until the cauliflower buds (actually the flowers) open because they will not be as tasty. After harvesting, remove the plants and compost them. If cauliflowers or other cruciferous vegetables never get big-headed and their leaves remain tiny, this may be the result of too much salt in the soil, inconsistent watering, lack of nutrients, or a dip in the temperature below 40 degrees Fahrenheit.

For better Brussels sprout production, cut off the bottom leaves, or twist them off in a downward direction, and pull off the sprouts toward the bottom, as well. The sprouts farther up the stalk will grow larger and faster as a result. When the remaining sprouts begin to grow, take off the rest of the leaves that are underneath them, leaving only the foliage at the very top of the stalk. Without as many leaves, more energy is diverted to sprout production and there is more room for sprouts to develop. Harvest from the bottom to the top as soon as they are big enough to eat.

Harvest broccoli when their buds are filled out, but still compact and tight. Unlike cauliflower, do not get rid of the plants after harvest. Leave them in the ground and fertilize them because they will continue to branch and generate side sprouts. You may get two to four more crops as a result.

Pick peas for sustained production. The more you pick, the more they will bear.

Rather than cutting the entire head at once, snip off outer lettuce leaves as needed to prolong the leafing period. Even after harvesting the whole head, it might be possible to grow new heads if the roots are left in the ground and they are watered and fed regularly.

It was common practice in the past to blanch celery by wrapping brown paper (or newspaper) around them and tying with string, leaving a few inches of leaf at the top. This process produced pale, tender stems, but much of the vitamin value was lost. Blanching is no longer necessary, but blanching might help if the celery stalks have become tough. Wrap them up three to four weeks before harvesting, and give them one more application of liquid fertilizer after they have been wrapped in paper.

If fava beans were planted last autumn without stakes, stake them now and tie them loosely with twine or plastic strips to protect them from being pushed down by wind or rain. Begin harvesting when the pods are 5 to 6 inches long.

Cabbage needs to feel as hard as a bowling ball before it is properly filled out. Once they are ready for the bowling alley, cut cabbages just below their heads. If you want "mini-me" heads, prune off the outer leaves of cabbage plants and leave their roots alone. Continue to feed and water them, and they will produce several smaller heads.

Do not prune perennial or newly planted annual herbs and vegetables during winter. Pruning stimulates tender plant growth, especially during a warm spell, and often results in frost damage during a cold spell. Remove only diseased or dead stems and branches.

Clip off any brown or yellowing leaves from potted herbs that are spending quality time indoors. Pinch them back periodically to prevent leggy growth and to encourage more branching for a fuller appearance.

PROTECTING

Although vegetables and herbs take less care in winter because pest problems are less prevalent, some pests persist. In mild-winter regions, snails and slugs are still active. They are particularly fond of celery and lettuce. Apply iron phosphate, an organic molluscicide that degrades into fertilizer and is safe around small pets and children.

Caterpillars are found munching their way through big-leaf crops like cabbage, cauliflower, collards, and broccoli, as well as herbs such as parsley. Pick them off by hand or spray them with Bt if the damage is extensive. Read more under Summer Protecting if there are concerns about butterfly larvae.

Indoor seedlings and frost-tender herbs brought inside are prone to aphids, whiteflies, and spider mites. Wash off with a stream of water, or take the plants outdoors and spray them with a garlic-based organic insecticide, or use horticultural oil (but do not spray oil on plants with ciliated leaves). Although the organic insecticides and horticultural oils are nontoxic, they may cause stains, so it is better to take them outside before treatment. Don't forget to bring them in after a couple of hours. See Spring Protecting for additional information on these pests.

Young seedlings may collapse or wilt suddenly. If there is sufficient moisture in the soil, the problem is probably a fungal disease known as damping off. Unless only one or two seedlings have been affected, it is better to start over. Plant your seeds in a commercial potting mix that is sterilized. Do not clump seeds too thickly, and thin the plants according to the directions on the packet. Make sure there is good air circulation by setting up a fan that provides air movement near them, but not directly on them. Monitor the watering very carefully. Make sure the potting medium is moist but not soggy. If there were just one or two affected seedlings, remove them quickly, increase air circulation, and allow the soil to dry out before watering. For the next few times, water from below.

Weeds can still appear outdoors when there are winter rains and warmer weather. Pull weeds by hand; then follow with a preemergent labeled for plants with edible parts. Do not apply a preemergent where you are planning to sow seeds.

For frost protection, read more under Autumn Protecting.

COMPOST TEA GUIDELINES

Start with mature compost (compost that has been turned several times so that weed seeds and pathogens have been "cooked" out) or worm castings. Then gather these supplies: two 5-gallon buckets, one aquarium pump large enough to run three air stones (also known as *bubblers*), three air stones, several feet of plastic air tubing, a gang valve to accommodate the air flow from the pump to the tubes attached to the bubblers, unsulfured organic molasses, a stirring stick, and a cheese cloth, tea towel, or nylon stocking for straining the tea.

Do not make compost tea without the aeration components because the beneficial organisms need to be aerated constantly. Without proper aeration, the aerobic (beneficial, oxygen-producing) microbes die and the anaerobic (harmful, oxygen-depleting organisms) microbes multiply. Brew for two to three days, and then use the tea immediately; you lose the greatest population of beneficial microbes if the tea is not used within twenty-four hours.

If the water in the mixture is chlorinated, allow the bubblers to aerate and evaporate any chlorine before making your tea. Fill the bucket halfway with compost (do not pack it in because it needs to aerate properly). Attach one length of tubing from the pump to the gang valve. Cut three more sections of tubing long enough to reach from the rim to the bottom of the bucket. Connect each onto a port on the gang valve, and push bubblers into the other ends. Hang the gang valve on the bucket lip, and bury the bubblers under the compost. Fill the bucket with water 3 inches from the rim, and start the pump.

Once the pump is activated, add 1 ounce of molasses and stir completely with the stick. The molasses is the food for the bacteria. Check the bubblers to make sure they are on the bottom and evenly spaced. Stir the tea a couple times a day, and check the bubblers to make sure they are properly positioned. After two to three days, turn off the equipment and allow the brew to settle for ten to twenty minutes. When properly aerated and mixed, the compost tea should smell earthy and sweet, never rotten. Then strain the mixture (use the cheese cloth, dish towel, or old nylon stocking) into a bucket and pour the mixture into your watering can or sprayer. Never put compost tea into a sprayer or watering can that has been used for pesticides or herbicides. Even minute amounts of these toxins damage or destroy the beneficial microbes. This will produce $2^1/_2$ gallons of tea and should be used within the hour if possible but definitely within twenty-four hours. The solids obtained from straining the tea can be put back on the compost pile or added directly onto the soil.

CHAPTER SIX

California Orchids

Gardeners approach orchids with a degree of uneasiness. And while orchids express themselves in very different forms and structures, these differences—however dramatic—are merely different looks for old familiar friends.

Orchids can generally be categorized into three groups according to bloom period: cool-season flowering orchids, warm-season flowering orchids, and continuously flowering orchids. After blooming, orchids generally enter a resting state for one to two months followed by several months of a vegetative growth period. Depending on environmental factors and the orchid variety, this entire process will take from eleven to fourteen months. Orchids can also be categorized into four groups according to their growing conditions—epiphytic (which thrive in rainforest canopies), terrestrial (which grow in soil), geophytic (which grow on rocks), and saprophytic (which grow on decaying organic material). Epiphytic and terrestrial orchids are the varieties most commonly available to California gardeners.

Understanding the rhythmic nature of orchids allows gardeners to solve the "orchid mystery" and successfully grow these beauties.

In Our Garden

My (Eric's) first memory of orchids is as a youth, growing up around my parents' garden center. As my familiarity with traditional floral shapes and configurations grew, I began to look beyond daisies and roses, searching for more unusual flowers to peak my curiosity. For a young gardener with a very short attention span, orchids fit that bill. Their strange, fat roots, variety of leaf shapes, and, of course, their elegant and extraterrestrial flower forms fascinated me.

As I grew older, I continued to find ways to include these extraordinary specimens in my day-to-day life. My wife, Stephanie, and I can hardly contain ourselves from purchasing a rare or unique orchid, even if our pocketbooks advise us against it. For centuries, horticultural enthusiasts have coveted orchids in much the same way we do. In prior decades, men and women have risked their lives in search of these curious plants. We do not go as far as risking our lives for them, but the passion for finding the unusual specimen still exists. Now, I am able to share my passion with my friends that shop at my garden center. There is a saying that we inevitably become our parents, however hard we may fight it. . . I suppose for me this is true, although the fight just wasn't in me.

CHINESE GROUND ORCHID

Bletilla striata

A perfect choice for California gardeners looking for a low-maintenance accent to shade gardens. Six to ten delicate magenta flowers are born atop wiry floral stalks. Corms naturalize readily—yet not invasively—in our native soils. Pleated, straplike foliage remains into autumn.

China, Taiwan, and Japan / Zones 6 to 11 / part shade / height 12 to 20 inches / width 12 to 24 inches / flowers early to midspring / soil / 20F to 85F

LADY'S SLIPPER ORCHID

Paphiopedilum insigne

The name refers to the slipperlike lip petal that all Paphs share. This readily hybridizing genus offers orchid enthusiasts a dizzying array of colors, shapes, patterns, and textures. A single flower can have a combination of colors, stripes, spots, veins, twisted wing petals, hairs, wavy margins, and warts!

China, India, SE Asia, S. Pacific / Zones 10 to 11 or indoors / full shade outdoors or bright indirect light indoors / height 4 to 16 inches / width 8 to 12 inches / flowers autumn or spring depending on type / medium grade orchid bark / solid-leaved plants 45F to 70F; mottled-leaved plants 55F to 80F

MOTH ORCHID

Phalaenopsis x hybrida

The genus name is Greek for "mothlike appearance." Nearly everyone has seen the familiar color combinations sporting white with a yellow lip, or white with a magenta lip. New hybrids merge colors and patterns that were once thought to be impossible. Their reblooming habit, low light needs, and large, long-lasting flowers make this orchid appealing to anyone.

Asia, New Guinea, and Australia / Zone 11 or indoors / full shade / height 4 to 12 inches / width 5 to 12 inches / flowers spring and summer / medium grade orchid bark / 65F to 78F

SPRING

Varying from year to year and place to place, spring's beginning occurs when the last remaining threat of frost succumbs to the lengthening day. Thus, spring comes earlier in southern California.

PLANNING

After the threat of frost subsides, epiphytic orchids that should be kept sheltered indoors in fall and winter should now be moved to a shady outdoor location, as long as nighttime temperatures do not drop below 50 degrees Fahrenheit. Areas such as lathe houses and simple shelving under the canopies of low-branching trees make perfect warm-season homes for these orchids. These areas should be swept clean and sterilized with a solution of 1 part bleach to 10 parts water in preparation for the move. Fungi and insects can lay dormant in the nooks and crannies of outdoor structures and should be treated before they have a chance to infect the arriving plant material.

PLANTING

After winter-blooming orchids such as Cymbidiums and Miltoniopsis finish their bloom cycles, it is time to consider repotting. In both cases, gardeners should repot their specimens when the pots are completely filled with pseudobulbs, or if it has been longer than two years since the growing medium was changed. Over time, bark and soil break down into finer particles. As this occurs, the orchid medium retains more and more water, increasing the risk of overwatering. To repot, gently remove the plant and swirl the root mass in a bucket of clean water, removing as much of the old potting mix and bark as possible. Fill the bottom of the new pot with orchid mix or $1/2$ medium-grade orchid bark and $1/2$ potting soil. Gently fan out the roots and lay them down on the mix. Center the plant and fill around the edges of the pot with more mix. To encourage the roots to grow out in the new medium, water deeply and then let it dry out before rewatering. For other planting medium suggestions, refer to page 170.

Very early spring is the time to begin planting the corms of *Bletilla*, the Chinese ground orchid. Corms are available in the bulb sections of most local garden centers. Pick an area that receives bright, dappled sun most of the day. A few hours of direct morning sun is also acceptable. Amend the area generously with compost. Cover the corms with 3 to 4 inches of soil and water thoroughly, then let them dry out to encourage root growth. To prevent the corms from rotting, ensure there is a period of drying out between each subsequent watering. Fertilize with a timed-release fertilizer (every six months) and a dry organic granular fertilizer (every six weeks). Blooms will emerge May through late June and will stop at the peak of summer heat.

WATERING

A simple top watering of bark-planted orchids does not provide enough moisture. Dry bark will shed such waterings, leaving the majority of the internal regions of the bark nuggets dry. The best method of watering epiphytic orchids planted in bark medium is the soaking approach. Fill a tub or sink with about 5 inches of water, place the potted orchids inside, and let the water saturate the bark for thirty to forty-five minutes. Remove inner containers from cachepots.

Root rot is by far the leading cause of an orchid's untimely demise; the frequency of watering is key in preventing this malady. Correct watering requires the gardener to continuously consider weather factors such as sun exposure, temperature, humidity, and wind. Understanding that potted orchids will dry out significantly faster outdoors than indoors is important when determining irrigation schedules. In addition to environmental factors, pot size and root-to-bark ratio will also affect the frequency at which a potted orchid will dry out. The best way to approach watering orchids is to saturate the growing medium and see how long it takes the medium to dry out. Dryness, when referring to potted orchids, should be determined by lifting the pot and feeling for water weight. A pot filled with bark that is saturated with water will weigh 50 to 100 percent more than one with dry bark.

Another method is to simply stick your finger into the medium to test for moisture. But it's best to test the lower regions of the pot by using the drainage holes as the point of entry. Often, the surface medium will be dry, but the lower medium will still be saturated. In these cases, irrigation should be withheld until further drying occurs. Moisture meters are inaccurate due to the large pockets of air that exist in orchid medium. Also keep in mind that, if outdoors, watering adjustments should be made due to changes in the weather.

FERTILIZING

Fertilize with a timed-release fertilizer early spring and early fall. Complement this with a half-strength liquid organic fertilizer twice a month. Additional fertilization with a half-strength high-phosphorous soluble orchid fertilizer should be made to warm-season flowering orchids (such as Oncidium, Phalaenopsis, Papiopedilum, Brassia, Beallara, Epidendrum, and Dendrobium) at this time (once a month for two months). This supplemental dose of phosphorous will increase bloom size and quantity.

MAINTAINING

An orchid that has filled its pot with pseudobulbs becomes cramped and eventually ceases to bloom. For this reason, spring is the time to divide fall/winter blooming orchids that have overgrown their pots. The most common of these orchids is the cymbidium, both the standard and mini varieties. The beginning of this process is identical to the changing of the growing medium process described in Spring Planting. Wait till the orchids have completed their bloom cycle to divide. Once the plant has been removed from the pot and the medium has been cleaned off the root system, cut out any back bulbs in the cluster of pseudobulbs. Back bulbs are old pseudobulbs that have lost their leaves and have either shrivelled or, if left long enough, died and turned completely brown. Green back bulbs can actually be planted and, given enough time, will bear new plantlets from their bases. After culling the back bulbs from the main plant, divide the orchid into clusters of three to four pseudobulbs. This division can be made carefully with a knife or a shovel (if the plant is monstrous, as they sometimes are), or simply by grabbing it and pulling it apart. A combination of two or more of these, cutting when necessary, but pulling apart firmly for the most part, is an effective way to divide. If cutting utensils are used, make sure they are cleaned and sterilized with rubbing alcohol between plants to prevent the spread of viruses and other diseases. After the clusters are separated, gently pull them apart to untangle the network of roots.

Once the threat of frost has subsided, it is time to begin moving frost-tender orchids from indoor windowsills to an outdoor location. The reason for this is to induce flowering and growth by increasing the differential in temperatures between day and night. These orchids fall into two general categories, those that prefer bright, dappled sunlight (where your hand casts a light shadow), and those that prefer a deeper shade (no shadow is cast). The first category consists of light-loving genera such as *Cattleya*, *Oncidium*, and *Maxillaria*. *Beallara*, *Phalaenopsis*, *Miltoniopsis*, *Phaius*, and *Paphiopedilum* species are among the orchids that prefer a cooler, densely shaded location in the garden. The ideal structure for frost-tender orchids is a lathe house, but if one is not available, a shady location underneath a tree can be the perfect spot.

PROTECTING

Root rot is one of the main concerns for orchid cultivators. Root rot is caused by fungi in the planting medium and can be transmitted via aerial spores or water. The symptoms of root rot include leaves hanging limply, as if in need of water. As the root mass dies back, the plant cannot absorb enough water to support the vegetative material. A common mistake that occurs with novices is to react to this symptom with additional irrigation or fertilizer. But this simply compounds the problem. The next symptom is the yellowing of the leaves caused by the reduction in nutrient uptake. Finally, the leaves begin to fall off (beginning with the lower leaves and traveling upward) and the plant eventually withers and dies. The best solution is to prevent it from occurring by correctly irrigating the orchids, maintaining periodic dryness between waterings. If the rot has already begun its course, then the proper action is to first dry the potting material out, then water in a liquid fungicide. After the fungicide has been applied, subsequent waterings should be made with a solution of auxin root hormone (such as IBA, or indolebutyric acid) to encourage new root production, still maintaining periods of dryness between waterings.

DIATOMITE PLANTING MEDIUM

New planting mixes are constantly being introduced. There are some ready-to-use orchid mixes that are 100% organic and highly absorbent. Some of these mixes are combined with diatomite, a sedimentary rock composed of the fossilized remains of microscopic algae impregnated with silica. Diatomite-based orchid mixes do not deteriorate or break down over time, are pH neutral, non-toxic, high in silica matter, and provide excellent air penetration.

SUMMER

The warmth of summer coerces buds to appear on several orchid genera. The rust-red blossoms of *Maxillaria tennuifolia* fill the air with the scent of coconuts, reminding us of a tropical paradise.

PLANNING

The heat of summer can wreak havoc on tropical orchids that have been moved from the shelter of indoors to outdoors. Although tropical orchids are generally native to areas that experience similar summertime temperatures, high levels of humidity (80 to 100 percent) prevent these species from desiccating. California summers come complete with dry Santa Ana winds and can desiccate an orchid collection quickly. Orchid cultivators must plan on increasing irrigation frequency according to rising temperatures, and improving humidity levels around their orchid collections. Humidity can be increased by using humidity trays (explained in detail in Summer Watering). Another, more costly and time-consuming way to increase humidity levels is to construct a microspray system in your outdoor orchid area on a timer to mist the specimens (45- to 60-minute intervals, 30-second duration, during daylight hours only).

PLANTING

The two major genera of orchids that bear keikis off their floral stalks are Phalaenopsis and Epidendrum (and some of their hybrids), although they can also occur on rare occasions with other genera. To propagate orchids by their keikis, simply cut the floral stalk just below the node where the keiki was born and repot in a small container with growing medium similar to the mother plant's. Another option for propagating keikis is to simply bend the floral stalk so that the keiki can be planted in a separate pot while still attached to the stalk. Once the root system of the keiki is established in the new pot, cut the floral stalk to release the new plant from its parent. In warmer regions, it is a good idea to use a mixture of both fine- and medium-grade orchid bark for the small plantlets to retain a little more moisture.

WATERING

Through eons of natural selection, orchids have evolved a protective translucent sheath called *vellum* that wraps around their roots; vellum provides protection from desiccation, yet still lets moisture, nutrients, and light (yes, epiphytic orchids also provide nutrients to the plant by photosynthesizing) to collect through the roots. Nevertheless, during the heat of summer, humidity is of primary concern when cultivating orchids. Shriveling pseudobulbs and leaves are a key indication that orchids are not being provided with the humidity they need. Most orchids available to enthusiasts in California are native to tropical rainforest regions like New Guinea, the Philippines, Southeast Asia, and South America. These environments offer significantly higher levels of humidity and rainfall throughout the year than California does.

To compensate for this, gardeners can create pockets of atmospheric moisture by using humidity trays under orchid collections. To create a humidity tray, simply find a large, water-holding, low-profile container such as a saucer. Make sure that your tray is large enough to extend at least a few inches away from the edge of the pots. Fill the saucer with coarse gravel, and place low bricks inside. This is meant to lift the bottoms of the orchid pots off the surface of the water. Fill the tray with water, stopping below the bottom of the pots to prevent the water from wicking up into the potting media and rotting the roots. Humidity trays such as these help create a continuous column of humidity around orchids. If a humidity tray is still not providing enough moisture (leaves and pseudobulbs are still a little wrinkled), mist the orchids down in the mornings and consider a larger tray (two to three more inches from the base of the pot).

FERTILIZING

Fertilize with a timed-release fertilizer in early spring and early fall. Complement this with a half-strength liquid organic fertilization twice a month. Supplement summer- blooming orchids such as Beallara, Maxillaria, Brassia, Phalaenopsis, Epidendrum, Cattleya, and Oncidium, with a half-strength soluble high-phosphorous orchid fertilizer once a month to increase bloom size and quantity. Fertilizing epiphytic orchids with liquid nutrient solutions should be done the same way they are watered, through soaking the entire pot in a tub of the solution for half an hour. This will ensure that the nutrients are absorbed into the bark medium and don't just run through the pot.

MAINTAINING

Once spring-flowering orchids have completed their bloom cycle, gardeners can repot them if the medium is over two years old, divide them or repot into a larger container if they are too crowded, or simply leave them be. Refer to Spring Planting for repotting instructions. After orchids bloom out, the gardener can then decide whether to leave the floral stalk on the plant, in hopes of producing a seedpod, a keiki, or a new floral shoot. If the floral stalk dies and turns brown all the way to the base (where it attaches to the parent plant), then it can be assumed that it has run its course and should therefore be removed. If, however, it remains green and turgid, then there is a chance of regeneration and could be left on the plant. On the other hand, leaving such structures on the plant to generate keikis, seedpods, or new floral shoots weakens the overall plant health as energy is focused on production other than general vegetative and root growth.

One spring-blooming orchid that needs specific care instruction happens to be the most commonly available to the public. The phalaenopsis orchid has a particular bloom habit that allows the orchid cultivator an opportunity to experience a rebloom off of an old floral stalk. Once the initial blooms have emerged and faded (which can take up to three months), all that is left is the green floral stalk that once supported the large mothlike blossoms. As time progresses, the bare stalk will begin to die back and turn brown, beginning at the tip. Eventually, if the specimen is healthy, the die-back will cease just above one of the floral nodes along the stalk, leaving the portion of the stalk below the node green and alive. Floral nodes are designated by small, slightly protruding scalelike leaf bases that occur about every $2^1/2$ inches along the floral stalk. The dead portion of the stalk can then be pruned away above the node, and new growth will begin forming at the node. At this time, one of two possibilities may occur. The first is that a new floral stalk will begin to emerge from the node and the orchid will rebloom from the old floral stalk. Keep in mind that the new stalk typically produces fewer blossoms than the original one did. The second possibility is that a new plantlet, called a *keiki*, will emerge from the floral node. The keiki will look like a miniature replica of the mother plant, with a set of two leaves and several aerial roots dangling below. This is an asexual clone of the mother plant and will retain the same characteristics.

PROTECTING

Increases in temperatures and day length and decreased humidity provide an ideal breeding ground for garden insect pests. The two most prevalent insect pests for orchids, both inside and outside, are aphids and mealybugs. The thick cuticles of orchid leaves protect them from the penetrating proboscises of piercing/sucking insects like aphids and mealybugs. But more sensitive areas of the plants, such as the floral stalks, pedicels (the tiny stemlike structures that attach the blossoms to the floral stalk), and leaf axils (where the leaves join the main stalk), are all prime targets for these prolific insects. To identify these infestations, daily observation is required, as the insect colonies will seemingly appear overnight. Similar to human ailments, early identification of an infestation will undoubtedly result in a quicker resolution to the problem. Organic sprays such as Neem oil and insecticidal soap can

be used as a control, as well as inorganic sprays such as imidacloprid. In all cases, apply one application every four days until the insect colony is eradicated. This usually takes two to three applications. Because mealybugs are soilborne insects, be sure to spray the base of the plant and the bark medium as well.

In addition to aphids and mealybugs, orchids are also susceptible to scale infestations. Scale infestations can be identified by the round protective shells that cover the colonies of tiny insects. The hard domes are usually grouped closely together along stem tissues, under leaves, or at leaf axils. Since scales have a protective dome that shields the colony from predators and insecticides, horticultural oil (parafinic oil similar to candle wax) or Neem oil (clarified extract from the seed of the neem tree) can be sprayed over the hard coverings to suffocate the colonies.

Orchids are susceptible to about twenty-five known plant viruses. Common viruses include the Tobacco Mosaic Virus (TMV) and the Cymbidium Mosaic Virus (CymMV). The symptoms of most orchid-infecting viruses are characteristically geometric discolorations of the leaf in either linear or circular concentric patterns. Unfortunately, as with other plants, there is no cure for these maladies. Eventually, the virus spreads to all regions of the leaves, inhibiting the plant's ability to photosynthesize and metabolize. The only course of action is to separate the infected orchid as soon as possible, as viruses can spread from plant to plant by contact. Regular observation and the use of sterile techniques when working on orchids will diminish the possibility of spreading a virus throughout the collection.

Odd-shaped pods dangle from the spent floral stalks of warm-season blooming orchids during autumn.

PLANNING

Along with the shortening of daylight hours comes a distinct drop in temperature, which can be detrimental to most orchids. Nighttime frost begins to threaten regions of California at different times, depending on elevation, latitude, and proximity to the Pacific Ocean. Inland areas and northern regions typically experience frost earlier in autumn, whereas coastal and southern regions usually experience theirs in late autumn. In any case, fall is the time to move cold-sensitive orchids from their outdoor lathe houses and shady spots to the protected environment of an indoor windowsill. In most areas, it is fine to leave out Cymbidiums, Epidendrums, and Bletilla corms throughout the entire year. If prolonged periods of evening frost are expected, cover cymbidiums with a frost cloth at night to prevent damage.

PLANTING

Orchids with high light requirements such as Cattleya, Oncidium, Beallara, and Maxillaria will prefer the sunnier east and west windowsills; they also like to be set back from a south-facing windowsill. Orchids that prefer shadier light intensity, such as Miltonia, Phalaenopsis, and Paphiopedilum, prefer cooler north- and east-facing windowsills. When choosing a location inside your house, especially in south- and west-facing windowsills, keep in mind that most orchids won't tolerate prolonged exposure to direct, unfiltered sunlight. The indicator that an orchid is receiving too much light is a pale scorching of the leaves that are facing the direction of the light. Conversely, the leaves of an orchid receiving too little light will appear a dark green. For all these orchids, use humidity trays beneath the pots to create envelopes of humidity as indoor atmospheric conditions are typically even more arid than outdoors.

Autumn is also the time to harvest seedpods that have developed on the floral stalks of spring- and summer-blooming orchids. Propagating orchids from seed is not a project that should be undertaken by anyone less than the most dedicated enthusiast. The tiny, almost microscopic seeds need a sterile, dark, and warm environment to have even a chance at germinating. Aerial fungal spores can infest the cleanest situation. Commercial orchid producers use glass bottles and agar (seaweed-based gelatin) medium mixed with other nutrients for their germination incubators. Germination can take up to four months, so patience is vital. If this germination period tests a gardener's patience, then the next three- to six-year waiting period from seedling to flowering specimen will be excruciating.

WATERING

Occasionally, a gardener may see a pattern of small dark spots appear on the leaves of their orchids. This is usually coupled with shriveled pseudobulbs or limp leaves and indicates that the orchid is getting irregular watering. If an orchid is left dry for prolonged periods, these spots begin to appear on the leaves. Although this condition is not fatal, if the irrigation schedule is not corrected, the specimen becomes increasingly stressed, thus becoming more susceptible to insect and disease infestation. Upon correction of the irrigation schedule, the symptoms on the old leaves will remain, but the new leaves will appear green, healthy, and spot-free.

FERTILIZING

Dropping temperatures (even in an indoor windowsill location) and shorter days signal spring- and summer-blooming orchids to slow their metabolism. For these orchids, the growing and flowering season is over and many of these varieties enter a state of dormancy, growing very little and occasionally even dropping one or two leaves. Even though growth is slowed, nutrients should still be made available to prevent any possibility of deficiency, so fertilize with a timed-release fertilizer in early autumn. Complement this with a half-strength liquid organic fertilizer twice a month to feed biological activity in the medium. For winter-blooming orchids like Cymbidiums and Miltoniopsis, a half-strength application of soluble high-phosphorous fertilizer can be applied once a month for two months, in preparation for their blooming season.

MAINTAINING

Maintenance for orchids is actually fairly minimal, especially for indoor situations. Orchid cultivators should keep dust off the leaves of indoor orchids, as the dust can limit photosynthesis. Plain water is the best cleaner. For a shinier finish, try a mixture of half water, half milk.

For terrestrial orchids outdoors, such as *Bletilla striata*, mulch the ground above the corms with shredded redwood or cedar mulch in areas that experience prolonged frost in the cool seasons to protect the corms from cold damage. Prolonged frost is defined as 400 or more chill hours (hours below 48 degrees Fahrenheit) in a year.

PROTECTING

Gardeners would be wise to keep in mind that household environments shelter garden pests from natural predators and swings in temperature and moisture. For those insects that pose a threat to orchids (and to houseplants, for that matter), the protected environment of a house or apartment is an ideal breeding ground. Daily monitoring of your plants will result in early detection of dastardly parasites such as mealybugs, aphids, scales, and spider mites so that you can deal with them swiftly and easily.

Orchids that exhibit monopodial growth habits (growing upward along one axis) such as phalaenopsis and vanda, may begin to exhibit rotting at the apex of their growth. This is called *crown rot*. Too much moisture left stagnant in the crown of the plant (where the new leaves are born) can harbor fungus and bacteria, which will quickly rot out a plant from the top down. To prevent this, refrain from top watering your Phals. Instead, soak them in a sink. When misting them, if some water collects in the crown, simply give it a swift blow of air to disperse the water, or wick the excess moisture with a soft cloth or paper towel.

WINTER

The floral stalks of cymbidiums rocket skyward, opening in fantastic sprays of color. Their grand display brightens up the California garden when other plants are resting and reminds orchid cultivators that winter is upon them.

PLANNING

Often, a blooming orchid plant will appear top-heavy because of the giant sprays of enormous flowers that can erupt from only a handful of leaves, stems, and pseudobulbs. These disproportionate stalks of flowers often need support to lift them high above the parent plant for all to see. In their native habitats, many species' flower stalks are actually designed to hang below the plant, as it clings to the underside of a branch. Orchid cultivators should always have devices available for floral stalk support. Manufactured decorative spirals can be purchased at garden establishments to help support smaller indoor varieties. Larger specimens, such as the winter-blooming Cymbidium orchids, require longer, thicker supports, such as bamboo stakes. Cymbidium cultivators should have many of these handy during winter, as a sizeable, healthy, mature Cymbidium can produce ten to fifteen floral spikes, each laden with five to nine blossoms!

For orchid enthusiasts, lengthening the duration of an orchid bloom is top priority. Two key factors cut time off a bloom cycle: temperature and light. When buds swell and open, move orchids to a cooler, shadier location to increase the duration of the bloom.

PLANTING

Winter is a time of rest for spring- and summer-blooming orchids. Plant metabolism slows down, and these orchids tend to fall into a state of dormancy or hibernation. Some orchids can actually begin losing leaves at this time (this is normal for certain Dendrobium species, so gardeners should not be alarmed). But most just stop growing and enter a stasis period until the weather warms again. This is an ideal time to repot or divide warm-weather orchids. When an orchid plant becomes too tight for its pot, bloom production eventually decreases. Repotting into a larger container stimulates new shoot production and will increase bloom production in the second or third year after repotting. Refer to Spring Planting for repotting instructions. Winter and early spring flowering orchids are in or near their bloom cycle and should not be repotted until the cycle has been completed.

WATERING

Watering practices for indoor orchids should remain the same as with previous seasons, adjusting for slight temperature and humidity variances. Outdoor genera such as Bletilla and Cymbidium orchids, on the other hand, need adjustments during the wet season. Increased precipitation maximizes the chances of root rot (or corm rot for Bletilla), so irrigation of these orchids should stop in times of rainfall. California can also experience bouts of summerlike heat during the cool season, so adjusting to these rare, but entirely possible, climactic aberrations with additional irrigation is also important.

ORCHIDS

FERTILIZING

Continue fertilizing all orchids with a liquid organic fertilizer twice a month. Fertilize winter and early spring bloomers (Bletilla, Cymbidium, Miltoniopsis, and Paphiopedilum) with a half-strength soluble high-phosphorous orchid fertilizer to increase bloom size and production. Since epiphytic orchids absorb nutrients through their leaves and their aerial roots (which are often creeping outside the potting medium), orchid cultivators occasionally foliar feed with a liquid fertilizer such as seaweed extract, a great supplement of micronutrients and natural growth hormones. To see results, you can do this as often as once a month or as little as once a season.

MAINTAINING

If you have brought orchids indoors during winter, do not take them outdoors on a warm, sunny winter's day and leave them. After several weeks of adjusting to the lower indoor light conditions and higher indoor temperatures, it's too much of a shock. Wait until spring to take orchids outside again.

Cattleya, Paphiopedilum, and Phalaenopsis orchids prefer evening temperatures 15 to 20 degrees Fahrenheit lower than daytime temperatures. Move them at night to a cooler part of the house if they have been brought indoors for winter, to encourage the development of flowering spikes.

While they're indoors, give orchids a quarter-turn each time they are watered for even growth and balanced light exposure. Stake any new growth and flowering spikes to prevent the spikes from breaking off and to display the flowers properly.

If it is not practical to move all orchids indoors when temperatures remain between 30 to 40 degrees Fahrenheit or lower (Vanda and Miltoniopsis orchids are particularly cold sensitive), then protect them at night by covering them with a cotton cloth (never plastic) or moving them to a more sheltered area away from cold winds.

PROTECTING

An excess of water encourages fungal pathogens such as Phytophthora and Pythium, which cause root rot. In addition, excessive watering can cause bark and soil media to break down at a much faster rate than normal, causing the medium to hold more moisture, compounding the problem. This is especially a concern for orchids left permanently outdoors in areas that receive heavy rainfall during winter. Moving such potted orchids under eaves or patio covers during particularly wet times will prevent root rot during winter. Terrestrial orchids, such as Bletilla, are generally planted in flower beds and should be left in the ground. These orchids are adapted to more saturated soil conditions and are usually unaffected by winter precipitation.

In most areas of California, precipitation means onslaught by regiments of militant invertebrates—slugs and snails, to be precise. What these slimy soldiers lack in backbone, they clearly make up for in appetite. While the large garden snails rasp away at the succulent orchid leaves and pseudobulbs, smaller slugs creep their way into bark-filled pots to feed on unsuspecting roots. Prevent slugs from crawling into drainage holes by placing mesh screens in the bottom of pots. Since copper naturally holds a minute electrical charge, copper tape can be used around the circumference of a pot. When slugs and snails attempt to cross the tape, they receive a tiny jolt of electricity that makes them recoil. Use poison-free snail baits containing iron phosphate to kill the snails.

CHAPTER SEVEN

California Perennials

Unlike annuals, which complete their reproductive cycles in one season, the root systems of perennials remain viable. Whether woody-stemmed or herbaceous, perennials might die down completely at the onset of cold weather but they send up new shoots once the weather warms. Perennials give color and texture to gardens in shady nooks, sunny slopes, and meadows and brighten pond and rock landscapes. Nor should we forget how perennials provide the "sigh-factor" in casual cottage landscapes. Without Canterbury bells, delphiniums, foxgloves, coneflowers, daisies, heliotrope, and wandering geraniums, there would be no need for white picket fences.

Perennials ease the transition from one space to another. Because of their more limited longevity, nestle perennial plantings as color, texture, and size accents in front of more permanent shrubs and trees.

Choosing perennials are limited only by one's imagination. From the ornate to the starkly minimal, from the floriferous to the ever-green, perennials provide the "spice" in a garden.

Technically speaking, perennials are flowering or foliage plants with lifespans of two or more years, and they are herbaceous because they lack the woody stems and branches characteristic of shrubs and trees. One of my (Bruce's) favorite quotes is that "there are no absolutes in gardening." This is particularly true of perennials: Some last a few years and others survive for decades. Some have top growth that shrivels and dies every winter, but the roots survive and send up new shoots each spring.

The most important thing to consider before planting perennials is to determine their compatibility with each other and with the site, especially with regard to light, soil, and water needs. Use perennials to add color and texture to mass planting displays in expansive meadow and woodland areas, to add structural focal points in beds and borders, to highlight and accent pond or rock landscapes, to supply food sources for wildlife, and to provide foliar and floral clippings for fresh flower arrangements. Weave in an abundance of perennials as the more permanent threads in your garden tapestry.

LENTEN ROSE
Helleborus × hybrida

By March, our Lenten roses bear an astonishing array of pastel-colored, nodding flowers. Some cup-shaped blossoms have interior petals painted in a light green while the exterior is tinged in lavender. Others come in hues of pink or white speckled with purple.

Greece / Zones 6 to 11 / part shade to shade / height 12 inches / width 12 to 18 inches / flowers spring

MADEIRA GERANIUM
Geranium maderense

One of our favorite true *Geranium* plants has deeply divided, snowflake-shaped, overlapping leaves. A biennial, its spectacular clusters of magenta-eyed, lavender-pink blossoms appear the second year. Lower leafstalks serve as a support; if the lower foliage is removed, the plant may collapse under the weight of its top-heavy canopy. This native of Madeira gives lots of pizzazz.

S. Europe / Zones 10 to 11 / full sun / height 24 to 48 inches / width 24 to 48 inches / flowers summer

PEONY
Paeonia species

Peony is a versatile and long-lived perennial, often flourishing for over forty years. Its foliage consists of distinctive, deeply cut lobes resembling bright green fern fronds. Even peony fragrances are as diverse as their color and form. *P. lactiflor* cultivars, commonly called Chinese or French peonies, are pleasingly fragrant, particularly the pinks and whites. Often described as thornless roses with flowers twice as large, few other perennials compete with the hardiness, beauty, and fragrance of a peony.

China, Japan, and California / Zones 4 to 10, depending on species / part shade / height 1 to 5 feet / width 1 to 3 feet / flowers spring to autumn, depending on species

Each year the sun crosses the equator on its way northward to the Tropic of Cancer. It is the beginning of spring, and the flowers of peony fulfill its promise of renewal.

PLANNING

Grow perennials in an area of the garden that can be completely renovated from time to time. Renovation is an important consideration when growing perennials because at some point, they must be replaced; they lose their momentum and no longer generate new growth. Intersperse compatible, more permanent shrubs, like pink Indian hawthorn or Wheeler's dwarf pittosporum, in a perennial garden to make renovation periods less obvious.

Spring is an excellent season to review your garden design and select perennials that are a little bit different—touches of pizzazz. Madeira geraniums with burly trunks several feet tall covered in a canopy of 1-foot-wide leaves resembling green snowflakes and lavender-pink flowers are bold statements for large, sunny spaces. To highlight shaded nooks and crannies, *Trifolium repens* 'Dark Dancer' provides dark burgundy, clover-like foliage with chartreuse edging and grows only 4 inches tall.

For a perennial border design, start with tall or long-lived specimens such as delphinium, foxglove, and coneflowers, and plant them in the back. Then use medium-sized plants such as daylilies, lily of the Nile, columbine, and Marguerite daisies to provide support for the taller neighbors and fillers for the middle portion of your planting bed. Incorporate more compact plants or ground-huggers towards the front of the border or as fillers for blank spaces; try 'Dark Dancer', coral bells, ivy geraniums, candytuft, or impatiens. An accent container with a single spectacular tree peony or a stand of shaded hostas or Lenten roses also add sparkle.

If you are planning on building raised beds, gather the supplies you need, including wood for the framing, lag screws, organic potting soil, and amendments. Refer to Herbs and Vegetables Spring Planning for recommended sites and ideal plant-bed dimensions.

Look over your existing perennials. If some are still struggling after three years, dig them up, move them to a new location, or give them to a friend who might have better luck. With such a wide world of perennials to choose from, spend your time on plants that will flourish for you. When selecting plants, learn about their mature height and width, temperature and water tolerances, as well as light and soil needs.

Keep a journal and record what perennials are blooming and the length of blooming time; make note of any bare areas that need filling in or areas that require a bit more color or interesting foliage. Also jot down the plants that survived this last year and those that didn't. The list will define some of the limits for perennial culture in your neighborhood, such as soil quality, cold tolerance, sunlight demand, and watering frequencies.

In southern California, plant perennials where they are protected from the hot and dry Santa Ana winds. In northern California, similar winds blow hot and fast from Oregon's Cascade mountain range. If possible, plant them on the lee side of permanent shrubs.

The vast majority of perennials prefer sandy loam soils with 20 to 30 percent moisture-holding organic content. Sandy loam soils allow for air movement in and out of the soil and percolation through the root zone.

Soil should also have a slightly acidic pH (6.5 to 6.8) to maintain nutrient availability. Use a pH test kit, and if the level is above 7 or below 6, adjust the pH to levels between 6.5 and 6.8. (See page 307.)

PLANTING

If the soil lacks organic material, evenly spread 2 to 3 cubic yards of amendments over an area 20 by 50 feet, and then till all the ingredients into the soil. Rake the amended soil smooth, removing all large rocks and solid clods of earth. Soak the soil thoroughly to collapse any air pockets. The bed is now ready for planting your perennials. Individual perennial plants that grow 3 feet tall and as wide, such as Marguerite daisies or peonies, might warrant their own watering basins. Refer to Trees Spring Planting for tips on building watering basins.

Set out perennial starter plants after the last projected freeze day in your area. Although a few perennials live for many years, most are not considered permanent plants. They should be grown, enjoyed, and replaced in kind or with perennials that have similar growing requirements. The process is exciting because there are always new varieties arriving at your local garden center.

Once a perennial is selected and planted, pour a solution of root stimulator (indolebu-

tyric acid or alpha naphthalene acetic acid) to stimulate new roots and to help reduce transplant shock. Follow up with two additional applications, one week apart.

If there are perennials in your garden such as Madeira geraniums, you can expect a multitude of seedlings to germinate from the dispersal of seeds during mid- and late summer of the past year. When the seedlings develop two sets of true leaves, dig them up carefully and replant them in full sun, at intervals of 1 to 2 feet. If the seed dispersion resulted in many seedlings sprouting up in a small area of your perennial garden, cull the seedlings to permit the remaining plants to grow and bloom to their potential. Share some of the culled seedlings with family, friends, and neighbors.

Plant tree peonies so that the graft union is 4 to 6 inches below the surface to protect the grafted portion from snapping off and to encourage better root development. Locate it in a wind-protected spot with morning sun. For areas along the coast, full sun should be fine. Farther inland, tree peonies need to be planted in containers and moved to protect them from intense, summer heat.

The general rule of thumb for dividing perennials is: divide spring-bloomers in autumn and summer- or fall-bloomers in spring. For areas where winter freezes are common, divide any perennials in spring after the last frost date. Where winters are mild, divide in fall or spring. For spring-flowering perennials, wait until after their blooms are spent before dividing. Water the parent plant thoroughly twenty-four hours before dividing it. Just before digging, cut off about a third of the growth if the plants are taller than 6 inches. After digging it up, wash off any soil still clinging to the root and separate with a sharp shovel or knife. Replant the divisions in new areas or pots.

Perennials that root from stem cuttings typically have hollow stems, such as campanula, chrysanthemum, and phlox. Cut new shoots approximately 4 inches long from their base with a sharp knife. Wash the cuttings to remove any dirt, and snip off the bottom leaves (do not yank by hand because that damages the stems). Fill 1-gallon-sized pots with a sterile, well-draining potting medium and moisten, but do not oversaturate. Poke 2-inch holes with a chopstick, pencil, or narrow dibble. Cut out the bottoms of clean 2-liter plastic soda bottles. Dip the cut ends in a rooting hormone, place them in the holes, and tamp the soil firmly around each plant. Water lightly again, and cover with the plastic bottle for an instant greenhouse (keep the cap off for better air circulation). If you prefer to plant your cuttings in flats, use a plastic bag to cover them. Place in a protected spot away from direct sunlight, such as the shaded canopy of a tree. Gently tug at the cuttings after a couple of weeks. When there is resistance and new growth has emerged, separate the cuttings and use them individually to fill in any blank spaces throughout your garden.

Other perennials root successfully from tip cuttings—such as asters, dianthus, and penstemons. Cut 4-inch sections from the tips of new growth, and follow the same guidelines as for stem cuttings.

WATERING

Most perennials have rather dense and surface-oriented root systems, so it is necessary to monitor the soil moisture content on a regular basis.

Initial waterings of newly planted or transplanted perennials should be very thorough. Apply enough water to wet the soil to a depth of 8 to 10 inches; that will settle the soil and collapse any air spaces around the plant's roots. Follow this initial watering with an application of a root stimulator. Several formulators use the plant growth regulator indolebutyric acid or naphthalene acetic acid (or both) as the active ingredient in their root stimulators. Both ingredients effectively develop new roots, as well as protect existing ones.

The routine for watering perennials growing in containers is not too complicated. If the early-spring, late-winter rains have subsided, most perennial plants will start growing again; as leaf surfaces expand, transpiration increases and soils dry rapidly. It is nearly impossible to overwater plants growing in containers that have drainage. The water that you put on the surface of the soil should gravitate through the root zone and out the drainage hole. There should be no standing water in the container. The only time that there seems to be a problem with overwatering is when the container is resting in a saucer and the water accumulating in the saucer siphons back into the potting soil, causing the roots to rot. Avoid this problem by resting the bottom of the container on two bricks placed in the center of the saucer.

For perennials with separate watering basins, mulch the surface of the ground a little beyond the plant's drip line (the limits of the outer foliage). The mulch will help stabilize the soil moisture.

Plants that are newly divided or are being rooted as stem or tip cuttings need to be kept moist, but not waterlogged. Do not allow the medium to dry out. If the surface half-inch feels dry to the touch, water again. Until the plants have a firm foothold in the medium, moisten with a spray mister to keep the plants stable.

PERENNIALS

FERTILIZING

After the last frost in early spring, apply a dry organic fertilizer in a band just inside the berm of the watering basin and thoroughly water it in. Repeat the application in late spring. By feeding the soil, the nutrients become available to soil microorganisms at a slow rate and as the plant needs it, which make for a healthy soil. Healthy soil in turn develops healthy perennials. In addition, water in a solution high in humic acid. If you prefer liquid organic fertilizers, make the applications in early, mid- and late spring.

The following are a few perennials that benefit from a supplemental feeding of special nutrients from natural sources:

- Gypsum (Australian fuchsia, lupine)
- Bloodmeal (hostas, coleus, leopard plant, coral bells, Lenten rose)
- Bonemeal (coral bells, Lenten rose)

Perennials prefer a soil pH from 6.5 to 6.8. Periodically, monitor the pH level of your soil; if the pH is too high (7.5 or above), begin the process of lowering it by increasing the organic content, such as humus mulch or worm castings, dissolving and leaching the salts, and adding soil sulfur, 1 pound per 100 square feet. Apply cottonseed meal to further acidify the soil, but follow the directions on the package for recommended applications rates. Some perennials, including hostas, peonies, butcher's brooms, and Lenten roses, tolerate slightly alkaline soils.

For perennials in containers, use a liquid or dry organic fertilizer at the same frequency as their counterparts planted in the ground. Another option is to use a controlled-release fertilizer. Depending on the formulator, the fertilizer should last three to six months.

MAINTAINING

Dry, clayey soils usually have a crusty layer at the surface. This layer makes it difficult for water to infiltrate into the root zone. Maintain a 2-inch layer of mulch to retain moisture; that in turn keeps the soil from crusting. Keep the mulch 2 to 4 inches away from the main stem or base of the plant. In areas where there is no mulch, cultivate the top 2 inches of the soil around the base of perennial plants to break up the crusty soil.

Some tall or sprawling perennials need extra help against wind and sudden downpours. Stake peonies, foxgloves, and delphiniums early in the season so that their mature growth will eventually camouflage the stakes.

Pull up any weeds that begin invading your perennial beds. Use a systemic herbicide on stoloniferous weeds such as Bermuda grass, but be very careful when applying it so that it is not sprayed on the perennial plants. Wait until the air is calm to avoid any drift from spraying, and use a piece of cardboard to shield the perennial plant from the systemic application.

One of the major summer chores is deadheading perennial flowers as they fade. This not only keeps the garden looking tidier, but encourages plants to increase their bloom production and diverts energy back into the plants, rather than into seed production. When there are extensive stands of plants such as geraniums, coral bells, or Marguerite daisies, it may be simpler to shear them off instead of clipping each flower off by hand.

Be selective about shearing; it encourages a flush of the new growth on the outside perimeter of the plant. This new flush of growth shades the interior of plants and makes the interior branches less and less viable. It is preferable to thin out any dead or dried branches in the interior, thereby lacing the plant so that more sunlight can reach its interior and develop new growth. There is a similar technique for older perennials known as "heading back." With age, many perennials become woody, so it is important to selectively prune out the old sparsely leafed branches, dead or diseased wood, and twigs that crowd the center of the plant.

Marguerite, Felicia, and euryops daisies live for several years before they become woody with skimpy growth and low flower production. When the daisy has grown to 3 feet high and 4 feet in diameter, stimulate new growth by pruning it back 60 to 80 percent in late winter or early spring, before spring growth begins. By mid- or late spring, the plant should be pushing out new foliage and abundant flower buds.

In early and midautumn, continue the summer routine of deadheading perennials, such as those in the daisy family. Before winter sets in, they usually experience a flush of growth and a few flowers. Prune out any dead, diseased, or interfering branches on the Marguerite, Felicia, and euryops daisies so that they should be headed back 60 to 80 percent in late winter or early spring before they begin to regrow.

If you want exhibition-sized chrysanthemum flowers, select one to three vigorous stems and remove any side branches. Take off all flower buds except the terminal flowering bud. For a fuller plant and a multitude of flowers, pinch back the outer stems by about 2 inches every month until midsummer.

PROTECTING

Since the majority of perennial plants are herbaceous, they make luscious targets for chewing, sucking, and rasping insects such as aphids, thrips, and leaf hoppers. Save time, expense, and frustration over the long term by controlling the insect population early. Use the organic pest formula on page 203, Neem oil, or a pyrethrum-based pesticide. Apply once or twice a week until their populations are gone. If perennials are growing in an area where there are no plants with edible parts, a systemic insect control with imidacloprid as its active ingredient is available. Since imidacloprid remains in the plant's system for one year, it is an effective and convenient control. Adhere closely to the formulator's directions.

Spring's typically cool and damp weather is the perfect environment for those slimy snails and slugs to munch on hostas, coral bells, leopard plants, and peonies. To stop them dead in their trails, use a molluscicide with iron phosphate as its active ingredient. Iron phosphate is a natural control. It can be used in areas near plants with edible parts and is safe around pets and small children. Another advantage is that eventually iron phosphate degrades into fertilizer.

To protect perennials from parasitic fungi such as mildew, follow the recommended formula on page 203 or use Neem oil once or twice a week until the fungi are eradicated. Chemical products with azadirachtin as the active ingredient are also used to control fungi. These controls, whether organic or chemical, should not be applied if there is rain predicted within seventy-two hours of spraying.

SUMMER

Blooming perennials, such as Marguerite daisies, heliotropes, purple coneflowers, and coral bells, brighten up the dog days of summer. They help us shake off summer's doldrums and renew our wilted spirits.

PLANNING

Most perennials develop root systems that obtain their nutrients and moisture in the top 12 inches of the soil. It is usually sufficient to prepare the soil to a depth of 8 to 10 inches, especially when planting purple coneflower, heliotrope, and butcher's broom.

Local nursery and garden plant sales are great places to look for colorful perennials that are "in the zone" for your garden. Spring color is past, and the bold hues of summer are at the forefront. If your summer perennial bed is in an area that receives dappled sunlight and you select perennials such as coral bells, leopard plants, and hostas, they should be clustered in drifts as they are in nature. For shady refuge, foxglove is still available. In sites with full sun, choose perennial baby's breath, candytuft, Marguerite daisies, geraniums, columbines, and daylilies.

When it is too hot to be outdoors, spend the time catching up on your garden journal entries. Include not only what you have planted, but where you purchased them. Include the grower, too, if possible. Often, cultivars and varieties come and go; if there is one that becomes a special favorite, it is easier to trace if you have a record of where it was purchased and the name of the grower. Also remember to include blooming periods and any pertinent weather information.

Spend time at your local arboretum or public garden with a pad and pen in hand. Write down any plants that look particularly good during periods of heat and humidity, as well as overcast days.

Spend balmy evenings at dusk chatting with your neighbors to find out what perennials they are enjoying in their gardens. This is also a good opportunity to be truly neighborly by offering to babysit their plants while they are on vacation.

Think outside the box when it comes to perennials. While beds and borders are wonderful areas to show off perennials, rock gardens and sites around water features are also places to plant perennials. Geraniums spilling over rocks or giant leopard plants looming over a shaded pond add exciting spots of color or foliar and textural contrast to their surroundings.

PLANTING

Planting perennials in summer should be done early in the morning rather than at midday or afternoon in order to avoid rapid moisture loss, which in many cases results in transplant shock (wilting) and possibly the death of the plant. Applying a root stimulator is generally a good idea because it helps jumpstart most newly installed plants. Follow up with two more applications of root stimulator, one week apart.

If you must plant perennials during a heat wave, spray the foliage with an antitranspirant to keep the foliage moist and supple.

When perennials become overcrowded, divide them, pot them, and transplant them to another part of the garden. You can also give some to your neighbors and friends. Follow the propagation tips under Spring Planting.

WATERING

The most efficient time to water is late afternoon or in the early morning, allowing enough time for the root system to absorb the moisture and begin moving it into the canopy of the plant.

It is better to water deeply and infrequently than to spritz shallow, frequent amounts. Frequent, shallow spritzings encourage the development of shallow roots, making them less tolerant of drought and dry heat. A drip irrigation system is one of the most efficient watering methods because it delivers water at a slow rate, avoiding evaporation and water runoff. If there are just a few plants to water, hand watering with a hose works very well. Whether using an automatic drip irrigation system or hand watering, make sure there is enough water percolating to a depth of about 8 inches. Determine this by shoveling down or using a tensiometer or soil probe.

For summer container gardening, recent studies indicate that the optimum watering time is in the afternoon between noon and 6 p.m. It was formerly believed that watering in the heat of the afternoon burned plant foliage because beads of water magnified the sun's rays. Now studies show that morning watering actually puts more stress on plants and retards growth. If containers are watered in the afternoon, growth increases as much as 70 percent and plants produce more photosynthesis than pots watered in the morning. Afternoon watering allows over sixteen hours for water to move from the soil in the container into the plant's canopy. Afternoon watering is like giving your container plants a cool, refreshing shower on a hot, summer day.

Water newly planted perennials and recent cuttings or divisions more frequently than established perennials. Read more under Spring Watering.

Some perennials are thirstier in summer, especially hostas and heliotropes, whereas some tolerate drought better, like purple coneflowers.

Keep an eye on the local weather pattern, and if a high-pressure cell is projected over your region, expect hot dry weather and adjust your irrigation clock to water more frequently. As with all plants, don't irrigate perennials by the clock or calendar, but by observation. Look for cirrus cloud formations, dry winds, drooping flowers, folding or wilting leaves, and cracked soil surfaces. Buy a tensiometer at retail garden centers or agricultural supply stores if you have problems determining when to water and when to hold off.

Visit helpful websites, such as **www.mwdh2o.com/** (Metropolitan Water District's Watering Calculator), **www.cimis.water.ca.gov/cimis/welcome.jsp** (California Irrigation Management Information System), for watering advice, and **www.nws.noaa.gov/** (the National Oceanic and Atmospheric Administration's weather page) for predicted weather conditions.

FERTILIZING

For established perennials that have completed their growth and bloom cycles, feed one last time at summer's end with a complete, dry organic fertilizer. In addition, water in a solution high in humic acid. If you did not use a controlled-release fertilizer in your containers last spring and prefer liquid organic fertilizers, apply again in late summer. Read Spring Fertilizing for application hints.

Perennials that have just been planted should be fed with a dry or liquid organic fertilizer.

MAINTAINING

Before you renovate an entire perennial bed, hoe out, hand pull, or spot kill weeds using a systemic herbicide, before they reseed themselves. After replanting, apply a pre-emergent herbicide and mulch with 2 inches of compost, humus, or comparable organic material to eliminate the next generation of weeds. Continue to remove weeds around established perennials.

Make sure the stakes and supports are still firmly in place among the perennials. Reattach the ties if they have become undone. Use Velcro or soft plastic plant ties.

During summer, replenish the mulch around perennials so that the layer remains at 2 inches.

Consider replacing perennials in late summer or early fall when they become less vigorous, off-color, and woody, or when they don't respond with new growth after being fertilized and pruned back in spring and early summer.

Perennials such as Transvaal daisies and lupines should be left alone until their foliage collapses. As their foliage is declining, nutrients for next season's growth are being stored in the plant's root system.

If you are growing pincushion or daisy chrysanthemums for the holidays, pinch the stems back 1 to 2 inches to force additional branching at a lower level. The mum plant will then stay more compact, and there will be many more flowers.

When summer-blooming perennials, such as heliotrope and phlox, are becoming leggy, head back their stems to shape the plant and to encourage denser growth and continued flowering.

Do not remove any of the brown stems or foliage around the base of Madeira geranium. Without the support of the dried stems and foliage, the top-heavy plant would collapse.

Continue to deadhead spent flowers on summer-flowering perennials so that more of the plant's energy is directed toward reblooming and increased plant growth (rather than the production of seeds). Lacing and thinning are the same procedures—the selective removal of interior branches.

PROTECTING

As summer progresses, rabbits, raccoons, skunks, squirrels, opossums, and other furry creatures may visit your garden and forage for food. Unless they are causing a great deal of damage, let them be part of the circle of life in your garden. If they are damaging your perennials, deter them with olfactory (scent) repellents or live-trap and relocate the critters to a more wilderness-friendly area. Check with your County Department of Agriculture or the California Department of Fish and Game to find out whether live-trapping and releasing is allowed in your area.

For pocket gophers, use manual traps or poisonous bait in a bait station; for burrowing moles, use guillotine traps. Control rats and mice with manual traps or bait stations.

To keep deer out of your garden, use motion-activated sprinklers or olfactory repellents; for small areas, set up a perimeter of 6-foot stakes and string monofilament line around the stakes, deer chest high. Deer cannot see the line when they bump into it, and this frightens them.

Diseases such as powdery mildew are always present in outdoor perennial gardens. The spore of the fungus that we call powdery mildew is windblown and moves from plant to plant at the whim of the air currents. One of the safest methods to control this malady is to wash off (syringe) the foliage in the early morning with a stream of water, letting the foliage dry during the day. If washing is ineffective, the next step is to apply a botanical (naturally derived) fungus control such as Neem oil or the pest formula on page 203.

Since it is difficult to differentiate a butterfly caterpillar from a moth or other larvae, you may have to accept the damage they do to your perennials. *Bacillus thuringiensis* (Bt) is an effective, organic larvacide; try that if the plants are being destroyed. Some gardeners prefer to remove caterpillars and place them in more wilderness-friendly areas, but the choice is yours.

Continue to spray with the pest formula on page 203 to control thrips, mealybugs, and aphids. If the infestation persists, use a synthetic pyrethroid or a product containing imidacloprid. Read the label carefully for directions and whether or not it controls a particular insect.

Spider mites leave tiny webs on the undersides of leaves, and the topsides have a silvery sheen. Use the pest formula on page 203, but if they persist after several applications, consider a miticide specifically for mite control. Most insecticides do not kill mites, because they are not insects.

NATURAL SOURCES OF PLANT NUTRIENTS

Nutrient	Source	Comment
Calcium	rock phosphate	for acid soils
	gypsum (.20 Ca)	also provides .16 S
Nitrogen	alfalfa (2-.5-2)	also provides Fe, Mg, P, K, S
	bonemeal (3-15-0)	also provides P
	cottonseed meal (6-2-1)	slow release
	bloodmeal (13-0-0)	moderately fast release
	fish emulsion	for foliar and root feeding
	fish meal	for foliar and root feeding
Phosphorus	steamed bonemeal	quick release
	rock phosphate (0-3-0)	slow release
Potassium	green sand (0-0-3)	also provides micronutrients
	kelp meal (1-.01-2)	also provides K and micronutrients
	wood ash (0-0-8)	don't over use
	sulphate of potash-magnesia	quick release
	sul-po-mag (0-0-22)	also S, Mg
Magnesium	dolomite lime	also S
	epsom salt	also S

AUTUMN

Autumn's shadow lengthens, triggering most perennial flowers to fade away, but the chrysanthemum is just beginning to show its brilliant fall colors. Their yellows, golds, oranges, rusts, and reds shout "Pick me! Pick me!"

PLANNING

Take a stroll through your neighborhood, and list the perennials that capture your fancy. Make notes of perennials that are blooming and those that are not. Shasta daisies, coreopsis, delphiniums, yarrows, heliotropes, coral bells, fan columbines, Lenten roses, Madeira geraniums, Marguerite daisies, and peonies bloom in spring, and some extend their flowering period through summer and even fall. Others, such as butcher's broom, hosta, and leopard plant, are foliar shade lovers. Still others love the warm rays of summer and the fall sun, such as heliotropes, geraniums, purple coneflowers, and chrysanthemums.

If perennials with different growing needs are planted in the same areas, think about regrouping them so that they are more compatible. Cluster the thirstier ones, separating them from the more drought-tolerant plants. Perhaps plant more water-needy perennials closer to the house to allow more careful monitoring and put the water-conserving varieties towards the outer perimeters of your property.

Consider replacing annuals with perennials to fill in the spaces among shrubs and under trees. Butcher's broom grows under established trees where nothing else will grow. Hostas also provide a lush carpet of foliage under trees. Geraniums, chrysanthemums, and marguerite daisies brighten areas between evergreen shrubs and don't need replacing every few months.

PLANTING

Planting or propagating in autumn gives perennials a head start over those planted later in spring, particularly if you live in a frost-free area. For regions where winter freezes are common, delay planting until spring except for herbaceous peonies from tubers. Plant in late autumn, burying the tubers 2 to 4 inches deep, 2 to 3 feet apart in soil rich with organic amendments. Unfortunately, most peonies do not do well in climates with mild winters. For those regions, try planting grafted tree peonies in spring. Also read Spring Planting.

Through hybridization and meticulous selection, chrysanthemums are now available year-round, but you will have the widest selection in fall. To plant in the ground, dig a hole as deep as the original container and backfill with rich, organically amended soil. Plant at the same level as the mum was in the original pot so that the clump can expand as it matures. Mums are also colorful fall accents in container planting. Use a well-draining, organic potting soil and apply a root stimulator three times, one week apart.

Peonies do not need dividing for several years. When they must be divided, do so in early autumn and make sure there are three to five eyes or buds for each division. More than likely, they will not bloom profusely for the next year or two. Read how to divide perennials under Spring Planting.

Plant divisions about 2 inches deep in well-draining, richly amended soil.

Slow-growing butcher's brooms make wonderful holiday container plants. The cut foliage can be used in flower arrangements, remaining fresh for weeks after the flowers have been thrown away. Parts of the plant's crown can be divided. Use a 10-inch pruning saw or a serrated knife to remove about an 8-inch part of the crown. Set that part aside in a cool, dry location for a day to let the wound callus; then dip the root mass in a solution of rooting hormone and plant it in a 1- to 5-gallon container, using an organic potting soil. Place the container in a well-lit, warm, protected area; as soon as new growth appears, apply a complete dry organic plant food.

Collect ripe seeds from the spent flowers and semihardwood cuttings from last summer's growth. Root them in a cold frame or hothouse. A simple method to propagate seeds is to fill a zip-lock plastic bag with about a third vermiculite or perlite; moisten it so that it is wet, but not soggy. Then put in your seeds, zip up the baggy, and place it on a windowsill where it will receive filtered light. If too much moisture beads inside the bag, open the bag periodically to air it out. The germinated seedlings can be planted in peat pots or outdoors after the danger of frost, when they are about 2 inches tall. Divide established perennials by digging out the entire clump with a shovel. Lay the plant on its side, and use a hatchet or pruning saw to divide the clump. Then replant, maintaining the same soil elevation as the original rootball. Soak thoroughly, and apply a root stimulator three times, one week apart.

WATERING

Like most plants that evolved in arid regions, the Madeira geranium protects itself by tolerating dry conditions for a while, but then completely collapses. If it is not irrigated within hours of collapsing, it perishes. Allow the plant to dry out a bit between waterings, but not to the point of total collapse. Although it may recover if watered immediately, successive periods of total wilt will progressively weaken and possibly kill it.

Here is the yin and yang of watering in autumn. As the weather cools and many perennial plants begin to slow their growth rate or enter dormancy, the frequency and amount of water should be reduced. It is important not to overwater during the cooler seasons. The big "but" here is when California experiences dry winds that are typical at some time in fall. Supplemental water becomes necessary for perennials that remain evergreen, as well as those that are still growing and blooming, such as chrysanthemums. Even plants that are dormant in winter need enough moisture to withstand the stress of frost. New divisions or recently transplanted perennials should be watered as often as twice a week if there is no rainfall and possibly every day during periods of Santa Ana or Chinook winds. The same watering frequency applies to containers—twice a week or even daily, depending on weather conditions.

Once cool weather settles in for the season, adjust the irrigation clock to accommodate cooler weather, fewer daylight hours, and the slowdown in plant growth rate. Water perennials just enough to prevent the soil from drying out completely. A quick way to check the soil moisture content is to use a soil probe or trowel and dig down about 8 inches or the depth of the rootball. Take a handful of the dirt from that depth and squeeze; if it holds its form, wait a day or two before watering again, but if it breaks apart, it is time to water. If it holds its form and leaves moisture in your hand, the soil is overly saturated and needs to dry out a bit before watering again. Do not water plants that are dormant.

FERTILIZING

Stop fertilizing all perennials unless you live where winters are mild and frost-free. Fertilize with an organic dry fertilizer one more time so that the beneficial microorganisms have a food source during winter and so the plants can still use the nutrients as their roots need them. For regions that experience winter freezes, it is not necessary to fertilize. Container perennials can also be fed one more time with a dry organic fertilizer.

MAINTAINING

Add more organic material to the layer of mulch so that it remains about 2 inches thick. In areas where frost or freezing weather prevails, increase the mulch to 4 inches, especially over grafted peonies and the crowns of leopard plants.

Continue to stake perennials that are still growing and blooming, such as chrysanthemums. Pull up any stakes and supports that are no longer being used, rinse them off, and store them.

To protect plants that are still blooming from a damaging early frost, cover them with a cotton sheet or spray them with an antitranspirant.

Move pots of frost-tender perennials to more protected areas. If possible, move them back out during the warmer days and return them to a more protected location during the colder evenings.

Clear out any fallen leaves, flowers, and other debris. Put them in the compost pile if there are no signs of disease or insect

infestations. Also add old potting soil to the compost pile if there were no disease or insect problems.

Cut chrysanthemums back to just a few inches above the soil after their bloom cycle is over. They will rebound in spring as energetic and floriferous as ever. Any perennials that rebloomed in fall should also be pruned back after their flowers are spent.

To encourage dormancy, cut back the stems of herbaceous peonies below the ground and defoliate tree peonies in early autumn.

Along with daylilies and lilies of the Nile, bird of paradise features its most prominent and colorful flowers in spring and autumn. The emergence of new flower spikes from the plant's center is a good reminder to prune out any spent flowers that dried during summer; also prune out old leaves that have dried margins or are bending towards the ground.

Head back errant growth to shape the plant. For example, Marguerite daisies occasionally develop rapid stem growths disproportionate to the rest of the plant; it is a simple matter to prune off the errant stems.

Do not shear or hedge perennials such as Marguerite, Felicia, and euryops daisies. Shearing creates a dense layer of twigs, flowers, and foliage on the outer surface of these perennials, which blocks sunlight from entering the plant's interior. The plant eventually becomes woodier and woodier, losing its vitality. Lacing out the interior by removing the woody, nonproducing branches in the middle is a better way to prune it.

Continue to snip off dead flowers among your perennials to develop root growth rather than seed production.

Prune back any perennials that are infested with insects or disease, and dispose of the cuttings in the trash, not the compost pile.

PROTECTING

Snails, aphids, and root rot are problems for shade-loving perennials in autumn. Control snails and slugs in your perennial beds by applying iron phosphate to the soil surface near and under the plants or, if your county permits, distribute decollate (killer) snails to prey on the brown garden snails. During periods of hot, dry weather, snails and slugs slime their way out from cool, humid, protected areas in search of succulent foliage on perennial plants like hostas, leopard plants, the tender shamrocklike foliage of 'Dark Dancer', and coral bells. Control aphids by eliminating the ant population and introducing beneficial predacious convergent lady beetles onto the infested plant. It is also helpful to apply the pest formula on page 203 and to wash off the aphids with a stream of water on a daily basis until the infestation is eliminated. Refer to Spring Protecting.

If plants begin to shrivel and fall over, chances are that root rot or water molds (*Phytophthora, Pythium, Rhizoctonia*) are the cause. These molds love cool-weather conditions and waterlogged soils. Remove infected plants immediately and throw them in the trash. Allow the soil to dry out; then begin treating it with compost tea, humic acid, and worm castings. All three increase the population of aerobic beneficial microorganisms (oxygen-consuming good guys) and decrease the anaerobic microorganisms (the bad guys that thrive in oxygen-deprived soils such as water molds). In time, the beneficial microbial activity in the soil will aerate it, increase soil porosity, and leach out salts. For additional information, read Soil Rhythms on page 307 and Herbs and Vegetables Spring Protecting.

WATER DANCE

Plants should not be watered by the clock or the calendar, but by keeping in touch with the rhythms of Nature and your garden. The following rhythms are "time to water indicators":

- Rising barometric pressures indicate fair weather and no rain.
- Cirrus cloud formations lack moisture and appear when there is no short-term rain predicted.
- Dry winds accelerate evapotranspiration.
- Drooping flowers bow their heads for more water.
- Falling petals are a predictor of wilting flowers.
- Invading ants escape from their airless underground dwellings.
- Folding leaves pray for water as they wilt.
- Wilting foliage indicate that it might be too late to save the plant.
- Cracking soil surfaces indicated desiccated expansive soils.
- Drying vernal pools summer has arrived.
- Frenetic mud wasps look hurriedly for water to form the mud nests.
- Tensiometer readings tell the tale, wet or dry.

WINTER

While most flowers are long forgotten during winter's slumber, the Lenten rose begins to bloom and nod, knowing full well that its beauty astonishes all who see it.

PLANNING

Winter is an excellent time to sit down, relax, spread out your gardening catalogues and garden diary, and think about perennial selections for spring planting. For additional ideas, read California gardening books and magazines, or visit your local garden center, arboretum, or botanical gardens. Also contact the University of California Cooperative Extension's Master Gardeners program. Master Gardeners are knowledgeable volunteers who help answer your gardening questions and concerns. (If you want to become a master gardener, call your local University of California Cooperative Extension office.)

Ordering perennials by mail order is usually more expensive and the plants may be smaller than at retail nurseries. The primary advantage is that mail-order companies offer rare or unique plants that may be difficult to find locally. Before you order, however, make sure that the must-have plant belongs in the same climate zone as your garden. Do not rely just on the mail-order company's description. Look the plant up in a garden reference book to confirm that the cold-hardiness and heat zones are appropriate.

Purchasing perennials at your local retail garden center allows you to "look before you buy." You can inspect them carefully for insect infestation, disease, or rootbound problems. The prices are generally better, and the plants are larger and well suited to your climate conditions.

While visions of dreamy perennials dance in your imagination, think about certain problem areas that might be resolved with the right perennial. If you need a perennial that resists drought and grows under a tree where nothing else will grow, select butcher's broom. For a shady area that's frosty in winter, choose "lotsa" hostas. Be careful about planting perennials such as columbine, peonies, chrysanthemums, geraniums, hostas, and daylilies near black walnut trees because those plants are very sensitive to the juglone toxin released by the walnut tree's roots.

When planning your perennial garden, consider incorporating Canterbury bells, delphiniums, and foxgloves in a triangular pattern.

One of the most beautiful perennials to bloom in late winter or early spring is the Lenten rose. Its colors and markings are astonishingly variable, and the nodding flowers are perfect beside a shaded wall or along a walkway with dappled light. Ask your retail nursery when the Lenten roses will be arriving, and purchase them while they are still flowering so that you can select the cultivars and varieties that suit your color palette.

PLANTING

It is still possible to plant perennials in areas where winters are mild as long as the soil is not too wet, especially if the texture of the soil is clayey and dense, and does not allow for percolation. Waterlogged soils promote an environment ideal for water molds and other fungi that invade the root systems of plants and destroy their ability to absorb water and nutrients. When winter rains oversaturate the soil or when freezes occur, wait until spring before planting tender perennials.

People with green thumbs who cannot keep their hands out of the dirt can start purple coneflowers, coreopsis, and other perennials from seeds indoors. Check the package for the number of days required from the time the seed is sown to the time it can be transplanted outdoors. Then do the math and count back from the last average frost date in your neighborhood to the number of days the plants must have to germinate and develop. If you have just moved to your home and do not know the last frost date, contact your local University of California Cooperative Extension office for the information. Refer to page 141 for seed-starting hints.

Even in inclement weather, you can plant perennials such as coral bells, hostas, Lenten roses, and peonies in containers. They can easily be moved indoors or under sheltering eaves for protection.

If the soil isn't soggy, prepare a new perennial bed during a pleasant winter day by digging up the soil 8 to 10 inches; then spread 2 inches of organic matter such as humus, compost, or worm castings, on the surface, and till it in. California often experiences winter drought. During those periods, add humic acid and compost tea to keep the soil moist and porous. By late winter or early spring, the bedding area will be ready to plant.

WATERING

The rainy season in California extends from November to the middle of March. During this period there is little need to water your perennial garden unless there is a hot, dry spell. Adjust your irrigation clock to accommodate the change in the weather pattern.

Late winter is a good time to record the following information in your garden journal:

- Locate the wrench to close the water meter and irrigation clock.
- Make a list of which clock station is wired to which clock.
- Locate all valve manifolds.
- Make a list of all anti-siphon valves, their location, and their sizes.
- Note the wire color that goes to each valve.
- Write down the location and size of the water meter and all the hose bibs.
- Note the morning, midday, and evening working water pressure.
- Note the manufacturer and description of all irrigation equipment.
- Purchase a parts-and-maintenance manual from the manufacturer of the equipment.

To test the condition of your irrigation system:

- Open each valve separately using the bleeder valves.
- Note, remove, clear, reinstall, and adjust all the clogged irrigation heads.

Continue to water container plants, and don't allow seedlings, divisions, or newly rooted cuttings, to dry out.

Monitor plants that do not get rainfall because they are planted under eaves. Make sure they receive adequate, supplemental moisture.

FERTILIZING

No fertilizing is necessary during winter except on seedlings. Fertilize seedlings with a water-soluble organic fertilizer diluted to $1/4$ the normal rate, feeding them after two sets of true leaves have emerged; feed them once every two weeks. Increase the dilution rate to $1/2$ the normal rate during their hardening-off period outdoors (refer to Spring Planting for more details about hardening off seedlings), and continue to feed them every two weeks. After they have been transplanted outdoors, feed the seedlings every two weeks at the full, recommended dilution rate.

MAINTAINING

Rebuild the watering basins around individual perennial plants, and remulch the surface of the watering basin with compost, humus mulch, worm castings, or a comparable organic topdressing.

Replenish mulch to a layer of 2 inches where necessary and 4 inches over plants that need protection from winter freezes.

When weather permits, continue picking up and disposing of plant debris.

Look for pockets in the garden that have poor drainage. Mark the areas with stakes; then take remedial steps to improve drainage now or in spring. Cut a drainage trench to a lower elevation. It may also be necessary to regrade the land if the problem is extensive. Perforated drain lines may help alleviate drainage problems, as well.

Protect tender perennials from damaging frost by covering them with a cotton sheet or floating horticultural blanket or by spraying the foliage with an antitranspirant the afternoon before freezing weather is predicted.

Apply a pre-emergent weed control in midwinter before seeds germinate. Your back will thank you in spring.

Marguerite, Felicia, and euryops daisies should be pruned back 60 to 80 percent in late winter or early spring before they begin to regrow. In late winter or just after the last frost, whichever comes last, prune back leggy perennials by as much as 60 to 80 percent. Remove any dead, interfering, diseased, or injured branches.

PROTECTING

For overwintering insects, such as soft brown scale, aphids, and thrips, apply horticultural oil when the weather predictions are no rain for seventy-two hours.

For wildlife controls, read Summer Protecting.

Water molds and root rots may continue to be problems during winter rains. Refer to Autumn Protecting for appropriate controls.

CHAPTER EIGHT

California Roses

Everything is coming up roses. And so it is, because somewhere in the world, at all times, sunshine is bathing the world's most popular flower. Over a hundred species and thousands of hybrids are found in gardens, in arboretums, and in their natural habitats. But it is California's upper San Joaquin Valley that is the "Rose Growing Capital of the World." Its rose ranches and research facilities produce millions of roses, on hundreds of acres, which find their way into rose gardens across the world.

For years, we resisted reestablishing our rose garden because of the long-term commitment needed to grow beautiful roses, and also because of the chemical pest controls once considered necessary for maintaining quality roses. With the greater recognition and use of natural controls, however, rose culture has become much less difficult. The secret to our rose garden is that we have learned to look at rose care from the rose's point of view and its unique seasonal rhythms. The "rosy" thumb suggestions we share are from our own trial-and-error experiences; hopefully, they will make your rose garden as fun and rewarding as ours has been.

It is physically and psychologically impossible to pass a rosebush without tenderly cupping one of its beckoning blossoms in hand and inhaling its fragrance. When its perfume matches its beauty, then the blending of these two traits creates an alchemy that transports us to a world of magical wonder. Although there is a common belief that most modern roses have little or no scent, Dr. James A. Gamble discovered in 1956 that of the 3,900 varieties of roses he tested, 20 percent were very fragrant, 25 percent were not fragrant at all, and 55 percent had some degree of scent. To encourage the hybridization of more fragrant roses, Dr. Gamble established the James Alexander Gamble Fragrance Medal under the auspices of the American Rose Society with the stipulation that the winning selection must also have an ARS rating of at least 7.5 on a 1 to 10 scale. With such lofty standards, only a few roses have received this medal since its inception in 1961, and 10 of them have been hybrid teas.

'**Angel Face**' won its AARS crown in 1969, but it took another 33 years before this heaven-sent beauty received the Gamble tribute for fragrance. Perhaps its gorgeous buds with petals painted in deep mauve-lavender tints so captivated rosarians that its intense, sweet lemony fragrance was considered secondary. Garbed in coppery green leaves, buds open slowly to reveal fully double, $3^1/2$- to 4-inch flowers fringed with a touch of ruby blush. 'Angel Face' is a bloom machine that flowers close to the ground; we use it as a colorful border plant.

We were visiting our son and daughter-in-law in San Francisco during the tragic events of 9/11. Like many, our return reservations were canceled and car rentals were non-existent. So we embarked on a long journey home by train. As we made small talk with a fellow traveler, she shyly mentioned that her late husband had arranged for a particular rose to be her namesake. Our fleeting time with Katherine Loker was made more special because now the '**Katherine Loker**' rose is our favorite yellow floribunda. Hybridized by the great rose grower, Jack E. Christensen, it produces rich, yellow flowers singly and in small sprays. Stately buds slowly open into creamy, butter-churned-yellow blossoms with impeccably formed petals.

One favorite miniature in our garden is '**Gourmet Popcorn**'; though designated as a miniature, it acts more like a bushy shrub. The rounded plant is smothered with so many cascading buds they seem to pop open before our eyes into fragrant white blooms. Dark green, disease-resistant leaves accompany abundant sprays of yellow-eyed, puffy flowers. Sprays of 'Gourmet Popcorn' make excellent fillers in our flower arrangement; they last longer than traditional filler such as baby's breath and add a delicate fragrance.

The nineteenth century author and poet, George Eliot, (pseudonym of Marian Evans Cross), echoed our sentiment when she said, "It will never rain roses. When we want to have more roses, we must plant more ..." In that spirit, we offer the following list of our personal favorites.

Cultivar	Type	Bloom Colors	Hybridizer
Angel Face	F	mau / lav	H. Swim / O. Weeks
Barbra Streisand	HT	lav	T. Carruth
Black Baccara	HT	blk / drk rd	House of Meilland
Blaze (improved)	Cl	rd	JP
Bonica	S	pk	Hse of M
Candelabra	Gr	cor / or	Dr. K. Zary
Carefree Beauty	S	rs / pk	G. Buck
Cherry Parfait	Gr	wh / rd	House of Meilland
Double Delight	HT	wh / red	H. Swim / A. Ellis
Fame!	F	pink	Dr. K. Zary
Fourth of July	Cl	rd / wh	T. Carruth
Gemini	HT	wh / coral pink	Dr. K. Zary
Green Ice	Min	pk, wh, grn	R. Moore
Gourmet Popcorn	Min	wh	L. Desamero
Graham Thomas	S	yel	D. Austin
Hot Cocoa	F	choc /or	T. Carruth
Iceberg	F	wh	R. Kordes
Joseph's Coat	Cl	rd / yel / or / pk	H. Swim / Armstrong
Katherine Loker	F	yel	J. Christensen
Magic Carousel	Min	rd /wh	R. Moore
Moonstone	HT	wh	T. Carruth
Mr. Lincoln	HT	red	H. Swim / O. Weeks
Purple Simplicity	S	pur	Dr. K. Zary
Purple Tiger	F	pur / wh	J. Christensen
Queen Elizabeth	Gr	pk	Dr. Lammerts
St. Patrick	HT	grn / yel	F. Strickland
The Fairy	Pol	pnk	A. Bentall
The Squire	S	rd	D.Austin
Trumpeter	F	rd / or	S. MacGredy
Yves Piaget	S	pk	House of Meilland
Zephirine Drouhin	Cl	pnk	Bizot

HT	Hybrid Tea	Cl	Climber	F	Floribunda	S	Shrub
F	Floribunda	Hdg	Hedge Rose	Min	Miniature	Gr	Grandiflora

Rose expert John Bagnasco has created two formulas for the *Garden Compass*™ program that really work in our garden. The rose food formula should be applied just before bud break, in late winter or early spring, along the inside perimeter of the watering basin.

ROSE FOOD FORMULA

* Step one:

1 cup dry organic rose fertilizer (5-7-2, 4-6-2, or 5-6-3)

2 cups worm castings (make sure it is 100 percent worm castings, preferably with kelp)

4 tbsp. controlled-release plant food (13-13-13, 10-10-10, or 14-14-14)

1 tbsp. chelated iron

Mix the above ingredients into the soil around each established rosebush. Use half this amount for new roses or miniatures (apply in late winter or early spring).

(New bare-root roses should have a pre-plant fertilizer (2-4-2) mixed into their soil. Some come in a handy ready-to-use packet that you can just plop directly into each hole at planting time without all the hassle of mixing loose ingredients into soil.)

* Step two:

In a plastic watering can, mix the following ingredients in 1 gallon of water:

2 tbsp. organic liquid fertilizer (3-3-3, 4-3-3, 7-9-5, or 12-12-6)

2 tbsp. water-soluble humic acid concentrate

Use this solution to water in the dry ingredients around each rose. One gallon of solution will take care of one or two roses.

* Step three:

Use an organic liquid fertilizer (3-3-3; 4-3-3, 7-9-5, or 12-12-6) at least once a month, but ideally every two weeks.

* Step four:

Repeat steps one and two in early summer and early autumn for quality blooms through the entire growing season. Discontinue the controlled-release fertilizer in Step One after two to three years because the soil should be healthy enough to do without it.

ROSE PEST CONTROL FORMULA

This is an organic, safe, effective recipe for controlling insects and diseases.

1 ounce garlic and stipitata pepper-based insecticide

1 ounce lemon myrtle-based fungicide

1 ounce horticultural oil or canola oil

1 tablespoon white vinegar

Mix the ingredients into 1 gallon of water, and spray the mixture on the plants. **Caution:** this formula should be applied in the late afternoon or evening since spraying with the horticultural oil might result in leaf burn. If you are not spraying for rust, eliminate the oil. **Note:** There are garden products containing concentrations of d'limonene (orange oil) or clove oil. Adding 1 tablespoon of either d'limonene or clove oil per gallon to your rose pest formula will kill ants on contact (there is no residual effect). Although all the ingredients are food-grade safe, do not use this formula indoors because it does stain. For indoor plants, take them outdoors before spraying. Spray once a week until the insect infestation or disease is under control. In cases where insect infestation is persistent, double the organic insecticide proportion of the recipe and spray twice a week. For persistent disease problems, double the organic fungicide proportion and increase the application to twice a week.

Roses, no matter how old, become young again and bear their brilliant flowers during spring. They are the perfect metaphor for spring's promise of rejuvenation.

PLANNING

As in life, growing roses is an artful exercise, not an exact science, but roses dance to certain recognizable rhythms. Make notes about any new roses planted this year, when each rose bloomed, their pruning times, the last frost date, the effectiveness or ineffectiveness of any new rose product tried, and the amount of rainfall and average temperatures. Over two or three years, you will accumulate a great deal of information that will help clarify the mystique of rose culture. Doing the right things at the right time will make your rose gardening much easier.

Join a local rose society. Many of them are affiliated with the American Rose Society, and they will gladly share their expertise, as well as recommend the roses that do best in your neighborhood.

Websites are another fantastic source of information. The American Rose Society at **www.ars.org** has a list of roses rated 8.0 and above and additional information about selecting and growing roses. The All-America Rose selections awards at **www.rose.org** provides a list of winners that you might like to try since they have been tested in many different parts of the country and usually resist diseases.

Visit local botanical gardens and arboretums, and note in your journal your favorite roses. Find out whether there are any All-America Rose Selections test gardens nearby. Many test and grow the AARS winners, as well as other roses.

Garden Valley Ranch in Petaluma, the Flower Fields in Carlsbad, and Rose Hills Memorial Park in Whittier are among the AARS test gardens. There are also AARS-accredited public rose gardens throughout California.

Assemble all the tools necessary to prune your roses and keep them sharp and clean. Before puttering among your rosebushes, put on a long-sleeved shirt, long pants, and thorn-proof gloves to protect yourself against any "thorny" problems. When you venture outdoors, don't forget the sunscreen, special waterproof garden clogs or boots, and a comfortable, wide-brim hat with a chin strap.

Roses do best in spots that receive at least six hours of full sun each day. When there is a choice between morning or afternoon sun, select morning sun because it allows enough time for the roses to dry out before evening settles.

Plant roses on the south side of a wall or building to make sure there is sun year-round. Set taller roses for the back or center of a rose bed, and use the miniature or polyantha roses towards the front where they can be easily appreciated.

PLANTING

Remove mail-order and locally purchased roses from their packaging as soon as possible. Due to weather or our own busy schedule, it is sometimes inconvenient to plant the bare-root rosebush immediately.

Store it in a cool, dark place; if the roots are on the dry side, sprinkle with water every day for up to two weeks. Never set or store a new rose in direct sun. Roses can also be temporarily "heeled" in a shady, protected location outdoors. Set them in at a 45-degree angle in a 12-inch trench, allowing their roots to be covered with soil. Cover up to one-third of the cane to protect them from sunlight and moisture loss, and to discourage new growth. If you know that several weeks will pass before you get to them, plant the roses in 3- to 5-gallon black plastic pots. Always keep roses well hydrated before planting. Where temperatures dip below freezing, bring them indoors during the evenings and set them back outdoors in the warmer daytime temperatures.

Before planting, soak the roots of bare-root roses for up to twelve hours in a mixture of lukewarm water and a plant growth regulator (with alpha-naphthalene acetic acid or indolebutyric acid), or use Mother Nature's own source, the willow. Cut a hefty handful of willow (*Salix*) twigs from a shrub or tree, and clip them into 2- to 3-inch pieces. Fill a plastic container with a few inches of tepid water, and soak the clippings for one to two days. Then set bare-root roses in the solution. For each use, make a fresh brew. Willows contain high levels of indolebutyric acid (IBA), but the effectiveness varies by the number of twigs, the level of IBA in the twigs at the time of harvesting, and the amount of soaking. Make sure the rose roots are soaking right up to where they meet the canes. Cut off any damaged roots or stems.

Container-grown roses transition better into the garden if they are given a thorough drink of water for a couple of days before planting. Place them in a shaded spot protected from the sun and wind, perhaps the north or east side of your house. Use clippers to remove any damaged stems, and remove any blooming flowers so that all the plant's energy can be directed to the development of new roots, foliage, and stems.

Even though $20 seems to be a lot of money to spend on a rose, it is still far cheaper than buying a dozen cut roses that last only a week. If you plant the rosebush correctly and provide the required soil, fertilizer, and water, your $20-plant will reward you with a lifetime of blooms. To make planting day as stress-free as possible, follow these tips:

- Dig a hole 2 feet deep and 2 feet wide. Loosen the soil in the hole, around the sides and on the bottom, by roughening it up with a trowel. Amend the soil removed from the hole with such organic material as worm castings, peat moss, compost, or humus. The ratio should be 1 part organic material to 2 parts soil to make sure the soil is nice and loose for roots to grow well. Mix in a preplant fertilizer (2-4-2) with the amended backfill, or add a biodegradable packet of preplant fertilizer to the bottom of the planting hole. For a large rose bed, make the digging easier on your back by soaking the area thoroughly a couple of times to soften the soil if there has been no recent rainfall.
- Plant during a cool, overcast day or in the early morning.
- For bare-root roses, create a cone-shaped mound of amended backfill soil at the bottom of the planting pit and spread the roots over the mound. Plant the rose so that bud union (the juncture where the desirable flowering variety joins the rootstock, often a large, knobby area from which the canes grow) is slightly above the

finished soil level (about 1 inch) in most mild climates. Where winter freezes are common, plant the rose so that the bud union is just at the soil surface for frost protection. The same applies to potted roses. If they have bud unions, plant them above the soil surface in areas with mild winters and level to the soil surface where winters are cold. Plant own-root roses so that the juncture where the stems emerge from the roots is just below the soil surface. Add the soil mixture, and gently tamp around the roots.

- To collapse air pockets, water while you are filling in the soil. Continue to add more soil until the hole is filled; then apply a root stimulator or use the soaking water that your rose was sitting in if you are planting only one or two roses. If you are planting several roses, mix a larger batch of water-soluble root stimulator.

- Build a watering basin, 1 foot larger in diameter than the average diameter of the rosebush (18 to 36 inches), and create a 3- to 6-inch-high berm around its outer edge. Generally, roses have shallow, fibrous root systems that extend outward beyond the drip line of its canopy. Basins encourage deeper root growth. The deeper the roots, the less often you will have to water.

- With a hose or watering can, give the newly planted rose a slow, thorough soaking. If the rose settles too deep after this initial watering, gently tug the main stem up to the proper level or you may have to remove the plant and add more backfill to the soil.

When a climber or rambler is selected, make sure the support is in place before you plant; otherwise, you might damage its root system when you shove the support into the ground. Plant the rose about 12 inches from its support so that the roots have enough room to expand, the plant has good air circulation, and it is close enough to tie back the canes. Start training your climbers or ramblers early, and gently tie the canes so that they grow upward while they are young. Choose ties strong enough to hold the canes steadfast but supple enough not to damage or girdle the canes (plastic or cloth strips are available at nurseries and agricultural supply stores). Once the canes are a bit hardened but still flexible, train them to horizontal supports for the most floral production.

Spring or early summer is another good time to root rose cuttings and pot them, especially for single-blooming plants. Read Autumn Planting for cutting and layering propagation guidelines.

WATERING

Unless Mother Nature has provided sufficient rainfall, give roses enough water so that their foliage, stems, and buds grow lush and healthy. Roses prefer moist soil to a depth of about 12 inches.

How much water does a rose need? If your rose is growing in a container, water it every two or three days during the growing season. Roses planted in sandy loam soil should have 1 to $1^1/2$ inches of water per week during cooler weather, but as much as 3 inches per week when the weather warms up. Roses are particularly thirsty once they begin their growth cycle. When in doubt, use a tensiometer or shovel just outside the root zone down to a depth of 12 inches. If the soil is beginning to dry at that level, water again.

The type of irrigation system is not as critical for the central, inland, and desert regions where there is plenty of dry heat and sun. Along the coast or areas with high humidity, it is best to use drip irrigation, soaker hoses, or in-ground watering systems to avoid splashing their foliage and to keep moisture at ground level. Fungal diseases proliferate much more rapidly during humid conditions. Also, water early in the morning so that the plant's foliage, stalks, and stems have enough time to dry out before evening.

Once roses are fully leafed out with lots of buds and blooms, they may need soil moisture down to a depth of 15 inches. Check to see how long it takes for water to penetrate down to that level.

A water wand attached to the end of a hose works well if you have only a few rose plants. Both types of irrigation allow the water to penetrate the soil slowly around the base of the plant without splashing. But the avid rose collector should install a drip or in-ground system. Less time spent watering means more time "to stop and smell the roses."

Newly planted roses should be watered deeply after planting and fertilizing. If there is little or no spring rainfall, provide supplemental watering to wet the soil about 12 inches deep.

FERTILIZING

Fertilize in late winter or early spring, just before the buds break. There are a host of rose fertilizers to choose from, but we recommend organic—which means it is healthy not only for the plant, but for the soil, as well. Refer to page 203 for the formula that works for us. An excellent recipe for those who are committed to organic gardening, the formula can also be effectively used for roses and for all your plants. Follow every two to three weeks with a water-soluble organic fertilizer appropriate for roses. For newly planted roses or miniature roses, cut the recommended amounts to half. Mark the fertilizing dates on your calendar so you won't miss any feedings.

For those who prefer to use a chemical or synthetic rose fertilizer, choose a controlled-release type (timed release) because the nutrients become available slowly, similar to organic foods. This is particularly important for new roses, as well as established roses that are just emerging from dormancy. In both cases, a controlled-release food is much less likely to damage the tender roots. Another advantage is that the application rate is usually every three to six months. You may still wish to apply an organic water-soluble fertilizer to spray on the foliage for an extra boost after the first flush of blossoms fade. A hose-end sprayer is a convenient applicator, but if you just have a couple of roses, use a watering can.

For container roses, apply a water-soluble organic fertilizer every seven to ten days or add a dry, organic food every two weeks to keep them blooming. Another convenient option is to feed them with a controlled-release fertilizer designated for roses. Follow the recommended application rates of the formulator.

MAINTAINING

After pruning, pick up the plant debris. They offer shelter and breeding grounds for pests, and diseased debris can spread to your other roses. If there was extensive disease or insect problems, throw the clippings and foliage in the trash rather than the compost pile. Since most rose clipping are a bit too woody and thorny to use in a composter, a shredder is more practical.

For clayey soils, apply 2 cups of gypsum ($CaSO4$) over the surface of the watering basin and water it in thoroughly. Gypsum loosens the soil surface and creates better infiltration through the soil surface, which helps leach out salts. Soil aggregates form, creating spaces so that water and air can move freely into the root zone (the process is known as *flocculation*). A reapplication of gypsum is necessary every three to five months because the results are temporary. Continue to add the recommended organic materials into your soil, and in time, it should no longer be necessary to apply gypsum. Read page 307 under Soil Rhythms for more information.

Apply 2 inches of compost, humus mulch, or comparable organic material over the ground in the watering basin, from the root flare to the drip line, to stabilize soil temperature, retain soil moisture, and control weeds. Keep the mulch 2 to 4 inches away from the base of the plant so that moisture does not accumulate.

Where freezing winters prevail, maintain the insulating 4- to 6-inch layer of mulch through the last frost date in spring, then reduce the mulch to a depth of 2 inches. Do this gradually over a week or two, and rake the excess into other beds.

It is important to check your climbers and ramblers every seven to twelve days during spring because they sprawl quickly and need to be tied for support.

Pull out any weeds while they are still young if they happen to pop through the mulch surrounding your roses. For Bermuda grass or other weeds that spread by stolons, use a systemic weed control. Set a piece of cardboard around the weeds before spraying to prevent the systemic from getting on your roses. Another method is to put on a pair of plastic gloves and slip on some cotton gloves over them, then wet the glove fingers with the systemic and apply it directly to the weeds. Wash the gloves thoroughly after use, or throw them away. Dipping a paintbrush into the systemic solution and "painting" the weed also works.

General pruning guidelines:

- In regions where winter and spring freezes are typical, prune roses after the last day of frost, but for those who live in mild winter and spring locales, prune soon after the New Year or in early spring. Use sharp, sterile cutting tools. Hand pruners are best for 3/4-inch canes, but for larger canes up to 1 3/4 inches, cut with loppers. For anything larger, use a saw.

- Eliminate any plant part that is damaged, diseased, dead, or spindly, and cut out canes that are rubbing against other canes or canes that are growing inward (toward the center of the plant) rather than outward.

- Suckers are not a problem with own-root and many shrub roses, but hybrid teas and floribundas and other varieties that have been grafted onto hardy rootstock generate suckers. Remove all sucker growth that appears on or below the bud union or from the ground because they are part of the rootstock and not the hybrid variety that has been grafted onto the rootstock. Suckers typically have a different color with a smoother surface or a lankier habit. If allowed to remain, they will eventually take over the less vigorous grafted hybrid.

- Since water accumulates around level cuts, increasing the likelihood of decay, try to make the cuts at a 45-degree angle.

- Bud eyes are usually nestled just above branches or leaves; at the beginning of spring, they are rather small and brown or red. Not to be confused with thorns, bud eyes are where new growth emerges, with some buds facing outward, to the side, or inward. In most cases, cut $1/4$ inch above an outward-facing bud eye to encourage fresh growth away from the center of the rosebush. If your rosebush is looking rather skimpy and thin, and needs denser growth, prune stems back to just above an inside eye, the bud that is pointing toward the bush's center. Do not cut too close or too far away from the bud eye; it may not grow well or may appear unsightly.

- After cutting out damaged, dead, and interfering branches, prune off thin, twiggy growth. Leave a branch alone if you're not sure about clipping it. You can always cut it later, but once cut, there is no going back if you have second thoughts.

- Cut back any lanky or disproportionate stems to the rest of the rosebush. Shortening them will keep the plant neater and more compact, and encourage new growth.

- For most roses (there are exceptions, such as climbers and ramblers), prune to create a vase shape, spacing the flowering canes evenly on all sides of the bush and keeping the center of the plant open.

Specialized pruning tips for certain types of roses:

- Areas prone to winter and early spring frosts should prune after the last day of frost, but in frost-free locales, pruning chores can done in late winter or early spring.

- Climbers or ramblers look their best when their older stems are allowed to form the "bones" or framework that gives them their distinctive look. If the mature canes are producing only sparse growth, lop them off at the base in early spring to quickly develop replacement canes, but most ramblers and some climbers bloom only on last year's wood. For most cases, prune back flowering branches that are growing from the main canes after their bloom cycle is completed (usually in summer). Stimulate nonbranching canes to produce more branching and flowering stems by pruning off the top couple of inches. Ramblers and climbers typically develop a plethora of stems and canes, but wait until climbers and ramblers are four years old before pruning heavily.

- Prune floribundas at least once a year to prevent twiggy growth. Don't get too scissor-happy because old stems are the first to bear in spring; if you want them to show off, be conservative when pruning. After bloom, remove the oldest canes, leaving six to eight of the younger, more vigorous ones; keep them 20 to 30 inches tall. The young stems develop flowers later in the season. Give floribundas a rounded shape to encourage flower coverage all over the plants.

- Grandifloras are generally larger plants than hybrid teas or floribundas, so clip off any dense, interfering interior growth but allow four to five flowering canes to remain and keep them 36 inches high.

- Since ground-cover roses are meant to sprawl, pruning slows their development. Just remove dead wood and any lanky or obstinate stems that are growing vertically.

- Many hybrid teas are bred for their elegant, long cutting stems, but harvesting too many can make them look bedraggled. Be careful not to cut too many stems while they are in full bloom. Leave more greenery to keep the bush stronger. Cut flowers only from plants that are older than one year, and make the cut just above a five-leaflet leaf facing towards the outside of the plant. Follow the general pruning guidelines outlined above, and once a year, prune back all but three to five of the healthiest, sturdiest canes that are 12 to 18 inches tall. The remaining canes should be evenly spaced and the center of the plant somewhat open, similar to a vase shape.

- If miniature rose plants are 4 feet tall and need a smaller presence in your garden, cut their lengths back like hybrid teas to a height of 10 to 16 inches. That will keep them within bounds. Otherwise, simply snip off any old stems that are no longer producing very well, and prune for shape.
- There are a wide variety of old garden roses (OGRs), but generally keep the clippers in your pocket except for aesthetic trims and for shape. Many OGRs bloom only once a year and often wait until early summer before they are ready to show. Wait until after their bloom cycle before pruning, except for dead, interfering, or diseased canes. These can be removed anytime, especially in late winter or early spring before their buds break.
- Reduce polyanthas to six to eight healthy canes (remove the oldest ones) that are 20 to 28 inches long.
- Shrub roses are a mixed group, from bold modern English roses to hardy landscape roses, making generalizations difficult. Most appreciate a yearly trim. Cut back tough shoots emerging at ground level by a third; remaining branches coming off these shoots can be shortened to approximately a foot. To avoid thickets, keep

after the twiggy growth and make sure the plants are thinned out regularly.

- When roses are used as hedges, take off one-third to one-half their growth with hedge clippers. For better bloom production, give each plant a slightly domed shape rather than a flat crewcut, whenever possible.
- Tree roses look their best when pruned in a symmetrical, rounded shape. Also be vigilant about clipping off any suckers along the main stem.

Timing and technique is everything when it comes to showing off roses at a rose show. To make sure your roses are ready, prune the rosebushes four to six weeks before the date of the show; encourage exhibition-sized blossoms in hybrid teas and grandifloras by disbudding. For a truly bodacious, exhibition-quality rose, look for a stem with a large flower bud and cut off the buds that are forming along any of its side stems. The remaining bloom will be bigger, and often the color is more intense. Since displaying a side bud usually disqualifies you from a rose show, disbud and encourage that one bud to flowering perfection. Do not disbud roses that are meant to grow in clusters, such as floribundas or polyanthas (except remove the center bud of a floribunda if you want the surrounding flowers to open at the same time, creating an instant bouquet).

PROTECTING

Without healthy soil as the main "ground rule" for gardening, plants cannot develop to their maximum potential. Read under Herbs and Vegetables Spring Protecting for guidelines on creating a soil alive with beneficial microbes and mycorrhizal fungi. Roses, like any other plant, need good soil to flourish properly.

ROSES

In addition to creating a healthy soil, here are a few preventative ideas to minimize or eliminate disease and insect problems before they start:

- Select roses resistant to diseases that are common in your area. For example, if you live where summers are dry or overcast, go to your knowledgeable neighborhood nursery and ask for the selections that resist mildew or rust.

- Purchase big eyed bugs, lady beetles (ladybugs), lace wings, and predatory mites from your local nursery or mail-order insectary. They prey on rose pests and provide a natural system of checks and balances in your garden. Since many of them love to feed on aphids and other honeydew-secreting insects, get rid of the ants before releasing the beneficial insects. Ants harvest honeydew and will protect this food source by attacking the beneficial insects. Also, follow the retailer's directions when releasing beneficial insects. Some, such as lady beetles, should be released in the evening when they are less active so that they linger in your garden as long as possible. Others need warm weather to become mobile.

- Add worm castings to your planting soil, and apply a 2-inch layer of worm castings as a mulch over the rosebushes. To make it more readily available to your roses, add a water-soluble product containing concentrated humic acid. There are also granular products with humic acid that can be mixed and watered into the soil. humic acid are like sparkplugs, activating the beneficial microbial and fungal activity in the soil. Research studies have shown that worm castings dramatically increase the chitinase level in plants, which can dissolve the chitin exoskeletons of many insects. With elevated levels of chitinase, plants taste like sour milk to aphids, scales, beetles, and other insects, and they move on to more palatable plants that have not been treated with worm castings.

Even under the best of circumstances, insects and diseases will try to get the upper hand, especially when it comes to one of their favorite targets, the tender new foliage and young buds of roses. Some rose growers spray with chemical fungicides and insecticides every seven to ten days to keep insects and diseases at bay, but for healthy soil and sound environmental practices, we recommend organic solutions whenever possible. Refer to page 203 for an organic pest and disease control formula that is safe and effective. It can be used against aphids, scales, whiteflies, and spider mites, as well as diseases such as powdery or downy mildew and rust. Since they are food-grade safe ingredients, the formula can be used as a preventative or whenever the problem develops. Treat every seven days until the infestation or disease is gone. Increasing treatment to every few days for persistent problems will not harm the plants.

Aphids are tiny, pear-shaped sap-suckers and come in different colors, including black, white, green, or pink. They weaken roses, causing their leaves to curl up and distort, and they also transmit harmful, often fatal, viral diseases. Aphids also secrete copious amounts of honeydew, which blackens leaves with a sooty mold. Although ants do not harm roses, they do farm aphids for their honeydew and are a nuisance when you are trying to prune or harvest the flowers. Wash them off with a strong stream of water, and spray with the organic formula on page 203 (adding the d'limonene, as listed, to kill the ants on contact). You could also use Neem oil (wait till late afternoon or early evening). Continue treatment once a week or more, until they are gone.

Young larvae of the sawfly nosh until only skeletonized leaves are left, while the mature larvae chew large holes before moving on to the next leaf. Known as the rose slug, they are black or pale green and resemble caterpillars. Wash them off with a strong stream of water, or pick and destroy. Since they are the larvae of a wasp and not a butterfly or moth, Bt (*Bacillus thuringiensis*) is ineffective. If the problem is severe, use a product that contains imidacloprid. A systemic, imidacloprid is applied around the plant once a year. The caveat is it cannot be applied near plants with edible parts or if you plan on harvesting rose hips for teas, syrups, jams, or other delectable recipes.

Scale is another sap-sucking insect that gathers in colonies on stems and leaves. For most of their lives, scale have no legs and live immobile under tiny, armored limpetlike shells. When the pest is in its crawling stage, spray with horticultural oil and release parasitic wasps. If the infestation is minimal, dab a cotton swab in isopropyl alcohol and apply directly.

When canes begin to wilt or die, look for any visible entry holes with frass resembling sawdust around the holes. The culprit is a tiny, wormlike larva that is partial to young canes or newly cut ones. Cut out and destroy the affected canes. If they persist, use a chemical product that has imidacloprid as its active ingredient. Most products containing imidacloprid are soil drenches and can be limited to applications directly around the affected plant.

Beetles such as the Fuller rose beetle and the Hoplia beetle can be handpicked and disposed of in a bucket of soapy water. Squishing is not recommended because it often releases pheromones attracting more beetles. The Fuller rose beetle is brown, flightless, and about $3/8$-inch long. It feeds at night and leaves foliage notched or ragged. Hoplia beetles are $1/4$ inch and nosh on petals of open flowers. Prevalent in the Central Valley from Sacramento to Bakersfield, they are partial to pale roses.

Even if an insecticide is organic and is not harmful to people or animals, read the product label to make sure it is safe to use around bees. Neem oil derived from the Neem tree in India and insecticides with pyrethrum or its variants are harmful to bees. Variants of pyrethrum include pyrethrin, permethrin, cyfulthrin, deltamethrin, and bifenthrin. Spray these products at dusk when bees are no longer active.

Powdery mildew is a fungus recognized by its light gray or white powdery substance covering leaves. It thrives in dry weather, when daytime temperatures are warm and dry and the evening temperatures are cool and humid. If caught early enough, simply wash powdery mildew off the plants and remove the affected foliage. Throw the leaves away to avoid spreading the spores, and spray the plants with the organic formula on page 203, or use compost tea as outlined on page 142. Downey mildew appears in cool, humid weather; it causes purple blotches on leaf surfaces and turns the edges yellow. Use the same remedies recommended for powdery mildew. Spray once a week or more, until the problem is remedied.

If rose leaves develop rust-colored pustules on the undersides and yellow spots on the tops, the problem is rust. It flourishes in warm, humid weather. Follow the same recommendations to control powdery and downy mildew.

Blackspot is not as common a problem as in other areas of the United States, but occasionally it does crop up. When it does, small black spots appear on the leaves. Remove and throw away any diseased leaves, and prune to facilitate better air circulation. As with the previous fungal problems, apply the suggested remedies.

Rose mosaic virus causes yellow or brown rings or yellow splotches on leaves, while the uninfected portions remain green. New foliage appears puckered or curly, and flower buds are deformed. Usually the virus is transmitted in commercial growing fields when an infected plant is grafted or budded onto a healthy one and can be spread by the home gardener by pruners used on infected roses. Commercial growers are trying to make sure that budwoods are grafted onto healthy rootstock. Some growers are also sidestepping the problem by developing own-root roses that are healthy from the roots up. Since the virus spreads through the entire plant, it is best to dig up the infected plant and dispose of it. Wash pruners used on the diseased plant with a disinfectant solution, and clean your hands and clothing thoroughly. Spray the affected soil with compost tea; add worm castings, and water in with a concentrated solution of humic acid. Allow the area to remain fallow for a couple of seasons and notify the retailer where you purchased the infected plant.

If you are unable to apply the organic remedies in a timely manner and the disease or insect infestation is widespread, choose a water-soluble synthetic or chemical product that is formulated for roses. One of the best triple controls contains a fertilizer, insecticide, and fungicide. Since it is applied as a soil drench directly around the affected plants, it won't have such a negative impact on your efforts to main-tain a healthy soil in the rest of your garden. And it has to be applied only every six weeks, depending on the manufacturer. Whenever possible, choose the less-toxic treatment, but there are times a chemical control is necessary and practical.

Slugs and snails become quite active in spring. Control them with iron phosphate, or use decollate snails, if allowed by your county. For more information on snail and slug control, read Spring Protecting.

For pocket gophers and rats, use manual traps or bait stations. Set a guillotine trap to eliminate insectivorous moles. If squir-rels and rabbits are causing extensive damage to your roses, use olfactory repel-lents, wire baskets around your rose plants, or live traps. Check first with the California Department of Fish and Game to make sure live-trapping and releasing of specific wild animals is allowed. If not, hire a specialist licensed to remove wildlife. To discourage nibbling deer, use water-acti-vated motion detectors, use olfactory predatory urine repellants, or set up a series of 6-foot stakes around the perimeter of the planting bed area and string monofilament line chest high around the stakes. The deer cannot see the line, and they are fright-ened away when the line touches them across the chest. If deer are hungry enough, however, a 6-foot-high fence may be the only permanent solution.

A common deterrent against cats using rose beds for kitty litter is to scatter cut sections of thorny rose stems around the ground. As cat lovers, we think this is awfully mean and prefer to use olfactory repellents. Some gardeners have success with jars of water, mirrors, and other reflec-tive materials interspersed amongst the roses. The rationale is that cats do not like to see their own reflections.

SUMMER

Early in the afternoon, when the air is still and the temperature is at its zenith, fragrant roses release their heaviest perfumes, enticing pollinators to linger in their flowers while refreshing our summer spirits.

PLANNING

Early summer brings forth a continuing burst of lush growth and blossoms. Often the flowers may not be as large or as profuse as the spring show, but what they lack in size and quantity is compensated by their perfume. By the end of summer or early fall, do not be alarmed if your roses take a short nap. They are just recharging their batteries to prepare for another floriferous display in autumn.

On a hot summer day, take a break from rose chores and make yourself a tall, frosty glass of tea or lemonade before writing down your thoughts about how your roses are faring so far—the good, the bad, and the ugly. Include any ideas about what new roses you might like to try next year as well as the difficult decision about taking out some that are not thriving, or perhaps moving them to a different location. Jot down any persistent problems, and contact a consulting rose expert or knowledgeable nursery salesperson for advice. Visit local public rose gardens and arboretums to see which roses are looking their best in summer's heat and which are not.

When it comes to roses, what you see is what you get. If you find a bare-root rose on special or your grocery store features a sale, pass on it. It is always best to purchase high-quality roses from a reputable retailer.

When making vacation plans, find out whether any notable rose gardens can be included in your itinerary. Some specialize in certain roses, such as old garden roses, while others offer a wide variety and many include the latest award winners. Getting up close and personal with roses—their fragrance, color, form, and growth habit—is more meaningful than reading descriptions and looking at photos in catalogues. Visit the All-America Rose Selections website at **www.rose.org** for a list of accredited public rose gardens around the United States.

Ask a neighbor or friend to watch over your roses and other plants while you are away. If you have an automatic irrigation system and it rains while you are gone, ask your friend to turn the timer off. To combat any disease or pests that might crop up during your vacation, ask a rose-knowledgeable friend to look them over as a precaution.

Gather a bouquet of roses, and share them with others. Cut them in the early morning, when the moisture levels in the stems are at their highest. Give their stems a fresh cut underwater at an angle before arranging them in a vase. Standing on their angled tiptoes allows them to uptake water more efficiently; if you add a packet of floral preservative, the flowers will last even longer.

PLANTING

Retail nurseries still offer container roses. Be discriminating in your selection; evaluate the overall health of the plant. If it appears healthy with no broken stems or insect or disease damage, it is still fine to plant. Make sure you plant on a cool, overcast day. Listen to the weather report. If a prolonged heat wave is predicted, keep them in their containers and water frequently. Refer to Spring Planting for techniques. After transplanting, spray with an antitranspirant to protect the foliage from wilting.

Transplant potted roses into containers suitable for patios, decks, or any other area that receives full sun; they make beautiful color accents. Make sure the container has drainage holes and is at least one size up from its original pot. If the roots are in a tight mass, "fruff" up some of the outer roots to loosen them. Plant it in a well-draining organic potting soil, and place at the same level or slightly above the level it had been in its original pot. Container plants have to be watered as often as once or twice a day during summer because they dry out so rapidly compared to in-ground plants. Save water and time by mixing in a water-retentive polymer with the potting soil. Polymers allow you to water much less frequently and continue to work for several years. Follow the quantity recommendations carefully. If you add too much, the soil medium will literally "bubble over" and you may have to start over again.

The word *miniature* in "miniature roses" refers to the size of their petite blossoms and not necessarily to plant height. Depending on the variety or cultivar, they can reach 4 feet high or more. If you prefer to keep their size mini, as well as their flowers, plant them in containers or keep them clipped back to control their growth.

WATERING

The sole purpose of watering your roses, other than washing off dust or aphids, is to replenish the water lost by the plant through transpiration or lost from the ground by evaporation. Water deeply two or three times a week if the weather is hot and dry and the soil texture is sandy loam. Roses require an inch or more of water per week to percolate down 12 to 15 inches in sandy loam soil. As summer temperatures climb, use a tensiometer or carefully dig into the soil with a trowel to determine the moisture depth. When the soil is dry at that depth, water the roses again. Deep and regular watering is essential for roses during their growth and bloom cycles. This will also encourage the development of deeper roots rather than shallow, surface roots that demand more frequent watering. Read page 206 under Spring Watering for more information on water needs.

If you have an automatic irrigation system, check it over to make sure it is functioning properly, especially before going on a vacation. Determine beforehand how long the timers need to be on in order for the water to reach a depth of 12 to 15 inches for your roses and adjust accordingly.

Water potted roses as often as every day during summer, but if you added polymers to the potting mix, their watering needs will probably be cut by 50 percent.

To help prevent the proliferation of disease, avoid watering your roses overhead or splattering water from the base of the plants onto the foliage. If possible, water them early in the morning so that they will have enough time to dry off before evening.

FERTILIZING

Early summer is the second time to apply the fertilizer as outlined on page 203.

Continue with a follow-up feeding every two to four weeks with a liquid organic fertilizer. For roses that bloom just once a year, it is not necessary to follow up with a liquid organic fertilizer. Continue to mark the fertilizing dates on your calendar to keep up the feeding schedule.

For gardeners who prefer chemical or synthetic fertilizers, select a controlled-release dry food formulated for roses, follow the application directions on the label, and water it in thoroughly. Depending on the formulator, application rates are usually once every three to six months. If the rose plant was fed with a controlled release fertilizer near the beginning of spring, the next application should be somewhere between early summer to early autumn. Chemical or synthetic water-soluble fertilizers are another alternative and can be sprayed over the entire plant. As with watering, try to do this during the early morning hours so that the plants have sufficient time to dry out before the cooler, more humid evenings. If a rose is growing well but not blooming, it might need more sunlight; if there is abundant foliar growth, but no flowers, the problem might be too much nitrogen. Change the fertilizer to a low-nitrogen formulation.

Refer to Spring Fertilizing for information on feeding container roses.

Let the newly transplanted roses get used to their new home and wait about two weeks before feeding them.

MAINTAINING

Maintain a 2-inch layer of compost, humus mulch, worm castings, or comparable organic material over the rose beds or in the individual watering basins, 2 to 4 inches from the base of the plant out to the drip line. This organic blanket stabilizes soil temperature and soil moisture and helps control weeds. Read Spring Protecting about using worm castings for mulch and pest control.

Continue attaching the climbers and ramblers to their supports. Tie them securely, but loosely enough to avoid damaging the stems. Monitor their growth every 2 to 4 weeks, and train the growth horizontally or in a fan shape to increase bloom production.

Keep weeds under control by pulling them out whenever they pop up. Don't wait until they get established because they are much more difficult to control. For weeds that spread via runners, read page 208 under Spring Maintaining.

When it comes to flowers, "deadhead" does not mean you are a follower of the Grateful Dead. It really refers to cutting off spent flowers. With deadheading, the energy normally expended into forming seedpods is diverted back into the plant itself, encouraging reblooming. Of course, snipping roses while their flowers are still fresh and beautiful provides the same benefits as deadheading.

Many old-fashioned shrub roses such as rugosas are notable for their extraordinary large, vibrant-colored hips (seedpods) in autumn and winter. If the plants are healthy and growing vigorously, allow the spent flowers to develop the hips.

Towards the end of summer or early fall, flower production begins to decrease in order to gather strength for their autumn show. Help your hybrid teas, grandifloras, floribundas, and other repeat bloomers by giving them a light trim to stimulate autumn blossoms. Prune off spindly or lanky growth back to a plump leaf bud or eye. How far back should you cut a flowering stem? Generally, cut back blossoming stems by about one-third unless they are on older or larger bushes. Then they can be pruned off by as much as half.

Not all leaflets are created equal on a rosebush. The strongest, most viable are those with five leaflets. The point to prune off the spent flower is $1/4$ inch above such a leaf, preferably one growing away from the center axis of the rose plant. New growth will emerge at the point where the cut is made above a five-leaflet leaf.

Prune out any dead, diseased, or interfering wood wherever it appears. Remove errant branches that disrupt the vase-shaped symmetry of your hybrid tea rose plants. Take out sucker growth emanating from below the graft or bud union of rosebushes any time they emerge. Brush the wound with a product that inhibits regrowth because sucker growth from the rootstock is more vigorous than the grafted rose and will bear less attractive flowers.

Many old garden roses bloom only once a year in the summer. Cut their main canes back lightly to maintain their shrublike shape after they have completed their bloom cycle. When they are about five years old, begin pruning off about 25 percent of their oldest canes all the way down to the ground each year after they bloom.

If your rambler blooms only once a year, wait until it finishes flowering before pruning because it bears on year-old wood. Many rose aficionados prune them down to the ground after they bloom, but water and fertilize them afterwards. A less drastic approach is to prune out old gray wood, twiggy stems, and canes that bloomed this year, as well as any dead or diseased wood. If size control is not a problem, ramblers and large-flowered climbers look magnificent sprawling over the support of a roof, mature tree, or other sturdy structure. Allow them to grow without being pruned,

or cut off the interior dead canes after the bloom cycle. Remove spent flowers back to a five-leaflet cluster for repeat-blooming ramblers and climbers. Climbers that flower only once a year need to be clipped lightly after blooming. Remove only the nonproducing, old woody, or spindly canes. Leave as many of the younger canes and the new ones that grew this year as possible because two- to three-year-old canes are the best producers. Damaged wood can be cut out at any time, but wait until climbers and ramblers are four years old before giving them their annual pruning.

Lightly shear miniature roses for shape, but once a year try to give them a proper pruning by cutting off the flowers back to and just above an outward-facing five-leaflet leaf.

Remove and dispose of any foliage that is yellowed or diseased on the rosebushes or any that have fallen on the ground. Good "grounds-keeping" is basic to preventing disease and insect damage.

For additional pruning guidelines, read Spring Maintaining.

PROTECTING

Many beneficial insect controls for rose protection can be purchased through insectaries or your local garden center. To control aphids, release predator lacewings or lady beetles. Since ants harvest the honeydew from aphids and farm aphid populations, use ant baits, d'limonene (orange citrus oil), or clove oil to keep ants at bay. Other beneficial insects include *Encarsia formosa*, wasps that prey on greenhouse whiteflies; green lacewings and predatory mites, which consume thrips (predatory mites also feast on two-spotted mites and fungus gnats). Instruction sheets are enclosed with the beneficial insects detailing the best times and conditions to release them.

Spider mites proliferate in dry weather conditions, leaving a silvery sheen or stippling on all portions of leaves. They are very difficult to see with the naked eye, but you can spot their telltale fine, white webbing on the undersides of leaves. Control mites by spraying them with a strong stream of water, horticultural oil, or miticide. Most insecticides are ineffective against mites because they are spiders, not insects.

Thrips, small yellow or brown insects, are most common during the warm summer months. They cause deformed leaves, and buds and flowers are riddled with mottled brown spots. Spray with the organic pest formula on page 203, or use Neem oil or a pyrethrum-based spray.

Rose midges are the larvae of tiny flies that appear in mid- to late summer. These white maggots feed at the base of buds and at stem tips. Eventually the buds shrivel and turn black before they can open up. Clip off and dispose of the infested parts, and treat the remaining plant with the organic pest formula on page 203.

If there is stunted growth, lift up the rosebush to check for signs of swelling or galls on the roots. The culprits might be nematodes, microscopic worms that enter through the root system, stunting the growth of the host plant. Since their life cycle depends on warm temperatures, they proliferate and do the most damage during the warmest months of the year. Dig out and throw away the infested plant, roots and all. Also, continue to clear out any weeds because nematodes breed in them. Allow the ground to remain fallow for a season or two and add generous amounts of organic materials, humic acid concentrates, and compost tea to the soil to increase the beneficial microorganisms in the soil. Refer to pages 136, 142, and 163 for application rates of compost tea. Since most French marigolds emit nematicidal chemicals, plant them to completely cover the affected area of nematode infestation as another natural control.

Bacillus thuringiensis (Bt) is an organic control that stops caterpillars dead in their tracks by disrupting their digestive systems and causing them to starve. If they are not creating too much damage, think twice before destroying them because it is often difficult to differentiate between a butterfly caterpillar and the larvae of other flutterers.

If rust, powdery mildew, blackspot, or insect infestations continue to persist despite your best efforts at organic controls or if you lack the time to apply the natural remedies, use a rose product formulated with a systemic fungicide, insecticide, and fertilizer. Do not use if plants with edible parts are nearby. Apply every six weeks during the growing season.

Control rabbits and other critters with live traps available at garden centers and agricultural supply stores. Trap and relocate the local wildlife only if they are causing extensive damage to your roses and other plants or if their tunnels are compromising your slopes. For additional information on controlling wildlife, read under Spring Protecting.

AUTUMN

After a brief late-summer or early-autumn nap, burgeoning rose buds get ready for a burst of festive fall color. It is their last trumpet call before gradually declining and preparing for cold weather.

PLANNING

Autumn is the time to select and preorder new roses from your local garden center, online, or by mail. One of the best ways of selecting roses is to choose varieties that have already been scrutinized by experts. The annual AARS winners are chosen from thousands of offerings, tested in a variety of gardens throughout the United States and Canada for at least two years. Although not all of the winners are suitable for every region in California, they are usually exciting new introductions and most resist diseases.

If fragrance is important to you, the James Alexander Gamble Fragrance Award has crowned only a few since it began in 1961, including 'Crimson Glory', 'Tiffany', 'Chrysler Imperial', 'Sutter's Gold', 'Granada', 'Fragrant Cloud', 'Papa Meilland', 'Sunsprite', 'Double Delight', 'Fragrant Hour', 'Angel Face', 'Secret', and 'Mister Lincoln'. Determine the fragrance that suits your scent palate: citrus, spice, fruit. There are myriad fragrances, just as there are perfumes, and there are bound to be many that appeal to your senses.

Also leaf through rose catalogues published by rose growers, talk to members of your local rose society, visit public rose gardens, and attend rose shows. Spring, summer, and fall are the most popular seasons for rose shows. No matter what time of year, they offer an amazing display of cultivars and species—old and new—as well as society members willing to give advice and answer your questions.

Find out your hardiness zone, and select roses appropriate to it. Other criteria include the type of rosebush (hybrid tea, floribunda, grandiflora, miniature, old garden rose, etc.), flower colors (solid, bicolor, blend, striped), petal count (single have five to twelve petals in a single row, semidouble have eighteen to twenty petals in two to three rows, double have seventeen to twenty-five petals, full have twenty-six to forty petals, and very full have up to a hundred petals), and single or repeat bloomers.

Test the soil pH in fall, before the rainy season arrives, because the soil alkalinity (pH) is usually at its highest concentration. Refer to Winter Planning for remedies to lower or raise soil pH.

PLANTING

Where winter freezes are common, do not plant roses again until spring. During cool, crisp days, prepare your soil for future rose plantings by acidifying the soil if it is alkaline. Leach out accumulated salts by watering the area thoroughly, and amend the soil by adding organic materials. Increase beneficial microorganisms by adding compost tea, which produces humic acid concentrates. Soil porosity can also be improved by double digging, meaning dig up the soil to the depth of a shovel and dig again. For mild-winter locales, roses can still be planted from containers in early to midautumn. Refer to Spring Planting for planting guidelines.

Early autumn is also an excellent time to harvest cuttings from species roses and their cultivars, hybrids, ramblers, climbers, and miniature roses. Hybrid teas and floribundas are not as easy to propagate from cuttings and may require a longer time to root. Depending on the rose, successful rooting may take as little as a few weeks or as long as several months. Keep in mind it is illegal to propagate patented roses until the patent expires (twenty years from the introduction date) without paying a royalty to the patent holder. Select stems that are free of insects and disease and that have recently flowered or have hips (seedpods) beginning to form. Remove the flower heads or hips down to the first set of five- or seven-leaflet leaves, and make the first cut. Make the second cut at a 45-degree angle four to five leaf sets down from the first cut (6 to 9 inches).

Miniature rose cuttings need be only 2 to 4 inches long and planted 1 to 2 inches deep. Recently flowering stem cuttings (new wood) that have a diameter about the size of a standard pencil are ideal. Take about six cuttings so there's a better chance for one or more of the cuttings to root successfully. To avoid tearing the protective outside layer of the cutting, snip, do not yank off, the leaves. Some prefer to keep at least two leaf sets on the top portion of the cutting, but others believe removing all the foliage reduces transpiration from the leaflets and encourages new roots to develop without having to divert energy to vegetative growth. Whatever your preference, do not allow the cuttings to dry out or expose them to extreme heat or cold. Dip the bottom of the cutting into a rooting hormone.

A 2-gallon black plastic nursery pot or something similar is a fine starter container. Fill with an organic, well-draining, sterile potting mix. Water sufficiently to moisten the planting medium, but do not make it soggy. Use a narrow dibble, pencil, or stick to open six 1-inch-diameter holes at a 3- to 4-inch depth in the rooting medium. Place the lower half of the cutting into the hole, making sure no leaves remain on the lower half; then tamp down the planting mix around the cutting. Place the cuttings in a protected area with filtered, light shade, such as under a tree.

Create a mini-greenhouse by cutting the bottom out of a 2-liter soda bottle and placing the bottle securely over the cuttings. Put the cap back without tightening it. After a couple of hours, check to see whether there is some condensate on the surface of the bottle; if there's not, add a bit more water. Replace the bottle cap. Remove it after seven days to provide more air circulation.

Sealable, large-sized baggies filled with about one-third moistened potting mix are also convenient mini-greenhouses for rose cuttings. Shape the baggie-filled medium into a ball, and make a 2-inch-deep hole with a pencil or stick. After inserting the cutting, seal the top of the bag. To avoid mildew or other fungal problems, air it out periodically if excess moisture accumulates on the surface of the bag. Baggies offer the additional advantage of allowing you to see when roots develop. You'll also know rooting occurs when the bud starts to swell on the upper half of the cutting or if there is resistance when you give the cutting a gentle tug. Continue to keep the rooting medium moist, but not waterlogged.

Once the rooted cuttings can no longer be contained in their soda bottle or baggy, harden them off by removing the bottle cover or by opening the baggie. Continue to keep them moist, but not soggy. Transplant each plant into individual containers when its roots are well established. The plants can also be placed directly into the garden in early spring. Apply a plant growth regulator containing indolebutyric acid (IBA) or alpha naphthalene acetic acid three times, two weeks apart, after you move the plants into pots or the ground. These own-root roses will not develop suckers. They are replicates of the parent plant and, in three to four years, will reach a respectable size.

Seeds extracted from rose hips is another method of propagation recommended for species roses such as *Rosa rugosa*. When the flower petals fall off, reddish-orange hips develop, most often during fall and winter. Harvest after they have changed their color from green to red or orange. Open the hips with a knife or your fingers, and take out the seeds. Drop them in 1 cup of water (some prefer to add 1 teaspoon of bleach), and keep only the seeds that sink; the floaters are sterile. Wrap the seeds in a moistened paper towel or peat moss, and place them in a sealable baggie. Label each baggie with the rose species or variety, and store the baggie in the vegetable crisper set at 40 degrees Fahrenheit (never the freezer) for forty-five to sixty days. This process of cold storage is known as *stratification*.

At the end of this period, remove the seeds from the refrigerator and sow them into a moistened sterile potting mix in a seed tray or individual peat pots. Space them 1 inch apart and cover with $1/2$ inch of potting mix. Spray with a mister to keep the medium moist, and set them out under the protected canopy of a shaded tree. If the weather is too cold, place them indoors under grow lights. If you propagate indoors, keep the lights on for sixteen hours; germination should occur in two to four weeks. After two or more sets of rose leaves emerge, transplant them into 3- to 4-inch plastic pots (use a transplant solution three times two weeks apart following the application rate of the formulator). Keep them under grow lights or in their same location outdoors, and apply a water-soluble organic fertilizer at 25 percent the normal dilution rate once or twice a week. Continue to water the seedlings whenever the soil surface feels dry to the touch. They may need to be transplanted into large containers when they become rootbound. Keep them in containers or transplant directly into the ground after one to two years.

Pegging or layering is a propagation technique easily used for climbing or rambling roses. Select a long, pencil-thin rose cane; bend without snapping it. Clip off the foliage from the part that will be buried in the ground. Slice a small knick at the elbow of the bent cane, and insert a toothpick or stick to keep the wound open. Dip that elbow in a rooting hormone; then bury it 8 to 12 inches under the ground. Cover and brace it with a wire hoop. You can also fashion a wire coat hanger into a bobby pin to hold the plant in place underground. Tamp the soil around it, making sure there is enough leafy portion of the plant stem sticking out of the ground. Water regularly until new roots form, in four to six weeks. The portion of the plant that is sticking out of the ground will continue to grow as its roots form. Once rooted, they can be cut off from the mother plant. Wait a few days to make sure the plant is doing well before transplanting it to another location or into a container. Use a transplant solution as recommended for cuttings.

AUTUMN

WATERING

If there is little or no rainfall in autumn, supplement the water to keep the soil moist. Dry, hot winds known as the Santa Anas or the Chinooks can also be devastating to roses. Pay attention to weather reports, and if possible, give roses a thorough, deep watering twenty-four hours before any predicted heat wave or dry winds.

In most regions of California, repeat-blooming roses flower very well during the cooler months of fall. To keep them flowering and healthy, water regularly, preferably in the early morning to allow enough time for them to dry before nightfall. As temperatures begin to dip, it may not be necessary to water as frequently. Check the moisture level in the soil with a tensiometer; trowel or shovel down 12 to 24 inches if you are unsure when to water. Read Spring Watering for more information.

Continue to monitor container roses because they dry out much more rapidly than those planted in the ground. Also, keep cuttings and seedlings moist. They may have to be watered as often as every day. Use the finger test; if the surface feels dry to the touch, give them additional water, but do not get them too soggy.

FERTILIZING

To increase the basal cane breaks, apply magnesium sulfate ($1/2$ cup per plant) two times a year, once in late winter (when roses are still dormant) and once in early autumn. For miniature and polyantha roses, it's best to start with $1/4$ cup per plant. Basal breaks are new growth that emerge from the graft site or bud union and eventually become strong new stems or canes. They are the lifeblood of roses, keeping them forever young. For rose-bushes older than five years, increase the

magnesium sulfate to 1 cup per plant (keep climbers and ramblers at $1/2$ cup).

Mark your rose fertilizer schedule on the calendar so that the feedings are made on time. Feeding roses planted in the ground and in containers, as recommended on page 203, in early autumn is for regions with mild winters. For those areas with winter freezes, withhold fertilizing until early spring, except for the application of magnesium sulfate for basal break development and a supplemental feeding of $1/2$ cup kelp meal to prepare them for winter. Kelp meal increases the plant's sugar content, which in turns increases its tolerance to cold.

Generally, a slowdown in fertilizing and watering during autumn encourages roses to go dormant in midwinter.

After seedling roses have developed two sets of true leaves or have grown to 4 to 6 inches tall, begin fertilizing them once a week with an organic liquid fertilizer diluted to $1/4$ strength. When new growth appears, feed cuttings and transplanted layered plants at the same dilution and application rates as seedlings.

MAINTAINING

Just like us, roses hate wet feet, especially during the rainy season. After adding all the organic amendments and applying products high in humic acid, as well as compost tea, if the soil is still too clayey, apply 2 cups of gypsum ($CaSO4$) over the surface of the watering basin and water it in thoroughly. Gypsum not only loosens the soil, but it improves percolation, which in turn helps leach out salts. Reapply gypsum every three to five months because the results are temporary. Continue to add the recommended organic materials into your soil; in time, it should no longer be necessary to apply gypsum. Read page 307 under Soil Rhythms for more information.

Replenish mulch to maintain a 2-inch layer over your rose plants or remove the old mulch and replace with a fresh supply. This is recommended if insect infestations or disease problems were particularly severe during the previous seasons. Old mulch often provides a comfortable haven for pests and diseases. Spread the blanket of mulch evenly around each rose, but keep the mulch 2 to 4 inches away from its base.

Continue to tie the new growth of climbers or ramblers securely to their supports.

Good "grounds-keeping" practices such as raking, picking up and removing fallen rose foliage, and weeding curtails overwintering diseases and insects.

Many old-fashioned and species roses like rugosas bear gorgeous hips that turn brilliant red or blazing orange in autumn and winter. They add color in the garden and elegance to arrangements, bear seeds for future rose progeny, and provide a food source for wildlife, as well as for us. If used as an edible, never treat the rosebush with a pesticide or insecticide that prohibits use for food crops. Harvest hips when they have turned color and are slightly soft. Slice off the blossom and stem ends, cut them in half, remove the hairs and seeds, and rinse thoroughly. Spread them in single layers in a dehydrator or in the oven heated at its lowest setting. Store them in glass jars in a cool, dark place, and steep them for teas or to make syrups, jams, and sauces. To retain their high levels of vitamin C, do not use aluminum utensils or pans when preparing rose hips.

Remove spent flowers unless you collect petals and hips for potpourris, seeds, or recipes. Continue to prune off any diseased, damaged, dead, spindly, and interfering canes or stems. Use a sealant for pruned roses if there have been problems with borers; otherwise, allow the cut ends to callus over naturally. Whenever suckers appear growing from the roots, or stems are emerging at or below the bud union, prune them off immediately.

Stop deadheading by midautumn if you live where winter freezes are common; removing spent flowers encourages the rosebushes to continue their growth rather than go dormant.

PROTECTING

Despite the cooler weather, insects and diseases continue to be a problem as long as there are rose flowers and leaves to attack. Be on the alert for aphids, whiteflies, mites, and pest larvae such as the rose slug. Rust, mildew, blackspot, and other fungal or viral problems may still persist, as well. Refer to Spring and Summer Protecting for control recommendations.

WINTER

Winter is bare-root rose season at retail nurseries and mail-order companies. There will be hundreds, if not thousands, of varieties to tempt you because every cluster of dormant sticks promises more roses.

PLANNING

Retail nurseries and mail-order companies have a full inventory of bare-root roses by late to midwinter. This is the time of year to make your selections. Gather your rose catalogues and review the dog-eared pages you carefully turned down, or go over your journal notes to glean the names of all the roses you jotted down as possible additions to the garden.

If particular roses are susceptible to the same problems year after year, it may be time to replace them. Recent evidence indicates roots of original rose-bushes may exude toxic substances that are not tolerated by replacement roses. To counteract this potentially harmful effect, allow the planting holes to remain fallow for several months and begin adding more organic material. Also treat the soil with compost tea, humic acid, and worm castings to increase populations of beneficial microorganisms and provide a healthy environment for the replacement roses. Refer to Spring Protecting for additional information on healthy soils.

Use a pH testing kit available at retail nurseries and agriculture supply stores to test your soil, especially if you are planning a new rose bed or if you have not tested the soil in the past few years. The soil pH range from 6.0 to 6.8 provides the best nutrient availability for your rose plants. If the soil pH registers above or below that range, roses are unable to absorb nutrients efficiently, resulting in yellowing and diseased leaves. A reading of 8.0 pH means the primary element of nitrogen is completely unavailable to their roots. Dig in soil sulfur to acidify highly alkaline soils and dolomitic limestone to neutralize overly acidic soils below 5.6 pH. For additional information, refer to page 307 on Soil Rhythms. Soil samples can also be sent to a soil-testing lab; let them know that you want to grow roses. Contact your local University of California Cooperative Extension office for a referral.

If you are new to the world of roses, congratulations! A life filled with excitement and incredible beauty awaits you. Visit the American Rose Society's website at **www.ars.org**, join a local rose society, go to your neighborhood retail nursery, or contact your local Extension office. They are rich sources of information on what roses are tried and true for your area, as well as the most current and intriguing introductions. When you are just starting out, it is probably wise to plant the varieties that are fairly trouble-free in your area, but if you see a rose that captures your heart, follow its path and see where it leads. Roses have the undeserved reputation of being too difficult, but like any other plant, once roses are planted and maintained properly, they flourish year after year, providing exquisite bouquets.

Know the type of rose before you plant it. The following are a few of the most common classifications, as well as how far apart they should be spaced:

- Hybrid teas are erect growers with single, often large-headed, flowers typically used in florist arrangements. They are borne on long stems and make beautiful vase arrangements. Space them 3 to 4 feet apart.
- Floribundas bear daintier flowers in clusters, but if you remove the center bud, the surrounding buds will open, creating an instant bouquet. Since they tend to be smaller bushes compared to hybrid teas, they can be planted $2^1/2$ to 3 feet apart.
- Grandifloras have a combination of characteristics. They are taller than hybrid teas or floribundas and bear blossoms that resemble hybrid tea flowers on long, elegant stems, but they are borne in clusters. Plant these giants at least 4 feet apart.
- Climbers and ramblers are known for their long arching canes often seen spreading and sprawling over fences, walls, and trellises. Generally, climbers have larger flowers with canes in the 8- to 20-foot range, while ramblers have smaller flowers, grow to 30 feet or more, and usually bloom only once. Both types should be supported with ties.
- Miniatures do not necessarily refer to their height. They often stand 4 feet tall, but the blossoms are tiny versions of their larger flowered relatives. Depending on their mature size, plant them 1 to 3 feet apart.
- Old garden roses, such as Bourbons, Centifolias, Damasks, Chinas, Gallicas, Moss, Noisettes, Teas, Musk, and Rugosa, are also popular because of their romantic, old-fashioned look. Many of them are known for their intense fragrances, but you should find out whether they bloom more than once a year because many do not. Consider whether repeat blooming is important to you. Give them 4 to 6 feet or more to stretch out.
- Polyantha roses were predecessors to the modern floribunda and remain popular today because of their strong, 3-foot-tall growth and clusters of tiny, delicate flowers. They are an ideal border plant and can be spaced $2^1/2$ to 3 feet apart.
- Shrub roses, often known as landscape roses, come in a variety of shapes, sizes, and forms, but all are relatively easy-growing, vigorous, and hardy. David Austin and House of Meilland are among the growers producing many of these summer and winter-hardy varieties. Some shrub roses can also be displayed as hedges or pruned as borders. Depending on their mature size, plant them 4 to 6 feet apart or more.

Select field-grown bare-root roses using the American Nursery Standards. A #1 rose has the highest grade and is especially recommended for beginners. Whether it is a hybrid tea, tea, rugosa hybrid, hybrid perpetual, grandiflora, floribunda, moss, or climber, it has at least three canes with minimum diameters of $5/16$ inch and up and branches no higher than 3 inches above the bud union. In order for polyanthas (for example, 'The Fairy') to be considered #1, they must have four or more canes and are usually not graded below #1. Shrub and landscape roses have at least $1/4$-inch diameter canes and follow the same specifications for the #1 rose grade. A #$1^1/2$ rose has two strong canes with the same minimum diameters and branches no higher than three inches above the bud union. Bargain roses are #2 and should be planted only if you have the nurturing gene.

Mail-order companies offer a large, varied supply of standard-grade roses and some have hard-to-find roses grown as stentlings and started eye roses. Stentling roses are grafted plants that have been greenhouse grown for about three months. The delicate, slender cane is available in 2- to 4-inch pots for shipping. Usually available through mail order, they need to be repotted individually in 2- to 3-gallon-sized containers and grown for an additional four to six months before planting directly in the garden. Started eye rosebushes are field grown and have at least two canes that are pruned 4 to 8 inches before being shipped bare root. Try these as you become a more experienced rose gardener.

Own-root roses are becoming quite popular among growers because, as their name suggests, they are grown on their own roots rather than grafted or budded and tend to be more resilient under adverse conditions. As long as their roots remain alive, own-root roses will come back true to type even after a harsh winter. Generally, own-root rose plants develop sturdy roots and strong growth, and don't develop suckers. Grafted roses, on the other hand, may die back to the bud union. By spring, the rootstock may be the only viable part and will send out its own suckered canes and inferior flowers. It is possible to graft another rose onto the rootstock, but for most gardeners it is simpler to replace the entire plant.

Design your rose garden on scaled graph paper ($1/8$- or $1/4$-inch grid) available at any art supply or blueprint company. Decide whether you want to keep your roses in a separate area for ease of maintenance, irrigation, and pruning or intersperse them with annuals and perennials.

Choose rose companion plants carefully, and make sure they have similar growing requirements. Annual low-growing borders of dusty miller, angelonia, or nemesia are perfect complements to a bed of pink roses. Good companions for statuesque grandifloras or English roses are fragrant salvias and African blue basil, or ethereal pink guara and perennial baby's breath. Low-growing miniature, polyantha, and shrub roses are lovely when massed together to border taller growing roses or line pathways. Ground-cover roses provide a floriferous carpet for evergreen perennials. Since bulbs have different maintenance needs, it is best to plant them away from roses.

Color is another factor to consider when making your decisions. Pastels recede and give the illusion of depth, and bright colors advance, giving the illusion of closeness. Select climbing roses as contrasting color accents by planting more muted shades against a dark backdrop and bolder hues against a light background.

Make a list of supplies: thorn-proof gloves, a good pair of bypass shears, loppers, hand clippers, a backpack or other convenient sprayer, and any other tool that will make your life among roses easier.

PLANTING

The time to transplant rosebushes is when they are dormant in winter or early spring. For many areas of California, roses are still blooming and flourishing during winter. If this is true in your garden, enjoy your winter roses for the holidays and prune them back after the New Year. Whether the plants have been "forced" into dormancy or became dormant naturally, move them when the soil is relatively dry and the temperature above freezing. Prepare the new planting hole before you dig up the rosebush. If you haven't done so already, cut the canes back to 3 to 4 feet high, and then move the rose into its new home. Read about soil needs under Spring Planting.

To prepare a new rose bed, till the soil and amend it as outlined under Spring Planting. Planting of bare-root roses begins in late winter or early spring.

Plant the taller growing roses on the north side of the garden and the lowest growing varieties on the south side to provide the most sun exposure as the sun moves from east to west.

If space is limited or you need more time to decide where you want to permanently plant your rose in the garden, pot them in 5- to 15-gallon-sized containers. Use a well-draining, organic potting mix, and plant your rose with the bud union at or slightly above the soil level. Read Spring Planting for more planting hints.

WATERING

Before winter rainstorms arrive, make sure that the surface drainage will flow from your rose garden to a lower elevation. Roses typically have shallow root systems; 95 percent or more of a rosebush's root system can be found in the top 12 inches of the soil. This is why it is important to rebuild watering basins for roses. The berm that forms the basin should be 4 to 6 inches high and have a diameter 10 to 20 percent wider than the canopy of the rose plant. The soil surface in the basin should pitch away from the root flare, not toward it. Read Spring Planting for details about building a watering basin and berm.

Roses do not like their feet wet, particularly in clayey soils that are oversaturated with moisture. If there is standing water in the basins due to heavy rainfall, open up the berms to release the accumulated water. Also, cultivate the blanket of mulch and break it up to allow air into the soil surface.

The yin and yang of California winters is that there may be little or no rainfall. During periods of drought, supplemental watering is necessary, particularly if the roses are still blooming. Water regularly and deeply to a depth of 12 to 15 inches. Use a tensiometer or soil probe if you are unsure when to water. For roses that have been pruned back and are dormant, water once or twice a month, just enough to keep the root zone moist. Follow the same recommendations for potted roses, except container plants dry out faster than in-ground plantings and need more frequent watering. Keep their soil moist, but don't let them sit in saucers of water. Read Spring Watering for additional guidelines.

Rooted cuttings, layered plants, and seedlings also need to be kept moist, but not waterlogged. If they are outdoors during heavy rainfall, move them under eaves or indoors for temporary protection. During periods with little or no rainfall, keep them moist with supplemental watering.

FERTILIZING

To increase the basal cane breaks, apply magnesium sulfate ($1/2$ cup per plant) twice a year, once in late winter (when roses are still dormant) and once in early autumn.

Do not fertilize established roses during winter. The same is true for potted roses, unless they are miniature roses that are on a sunny ledge indoors. Feed the indoor plants an organic water-soluble food at half the normal dilution rate.

If seedlings, rooted cuttings, and transplanted layered roses are still leafing, keep them in an area protected from frost and continue to fertilize every one to two weeks (depending on their rate of growth) with an organic water-soluble fertilizer at $1/4$ the normal dilution rate. Do not feed if they are dormant.

MAINTAINING

To protect roses from freezing temperatures, insulate their bud unions by mounding about 6 inches of organic material such as humus, compost, worm castings, or soil (if it is a sandy loam soil and not clay). For own-root roses, apply a 2- to 4-inch layer of mulch. Also protect frost-tender roses by spraying them with an antitranspirant.

During periods of frost, bring the cuttings, seedlings, and layered plants that are in pots indoors where there is bright, indirect light or keep them outdoors in a protected area under filtered light. During freezing temperatures, cover them with a cotton sheet at night and remove the sheet during the warmer daylight hours, or spray them with an antitranspirant.

Often hybrid teas, grandifloras, and other grafted roses become woody and less productive with increased age. Rub their bud unions with coarse steel wool to encourage more basal break development. The wood surrounding an old bud union is rough and should flake off easily. Don't rub too hard because it may injure the latent buds, but apply just enough pressure to loosen the dry protective covering. This method can be done during early winter where there is no danger of frost or during spring after the last day of frost.

Apply a granular preemergent weed control to stop the next generation of weeds because it will save hours of back-breaking weed pulling in spring.

Clear all debris and dispose of it in the trash. If the debris is free of severe insect infestations or disease, the thorny branches and stems can be ground up and used as compost. They are too woody and would not decompose readily if placed directly in the compost pile.

If your garden is in a frost-free zone, along the coast, or in a protected location, and your roses have not gone dormant, prune them back in late winter because they need time to rejuvenate. Make your cuts at an angle to avoid water settling on the cut portion. For areas where roses enter dormancy naturally due to cold temperatures, wait until early spring. Read Spring Maintaining for pruning tips.

Remove any dead, diseased, damaged, and interfering wood (branches and twigs that rest upon each other, grow towards the center of the plant, or grow sideways). Dead wood has no new growth and is dull gray or brown. Its pith or innermost part of the stem is dark and dried out whereas the pith in healthy wood is creamy white. Cut back to live wood, but if in doubt, wait until new buds form in spring. Damaged wood should be cut just below the affected portion and at the point of green, active growth. If the wood is diseased, dip your shears in a commercial sterilizing mixture for tools such as Physan20™. A bleach mixture might rust your tools.

Cut off any spindly canes that are less than the diameter of a pencil on mature rosebushes. Grafted roses often develop suckers that come up at ground level, above or at the bud union. Remove all rootstock suckers because they are more aggressive, bear inferior flowers, and will eventually take over the less vigorous grafted rose.

How far should you prune a rose? Ideally, the remaining canes and their stems need to be pruned to allow optimum growth, ample light, and good air circulation. Details about technique and timing are covered under Spring and Summer Maintaining depending on the rose classification.

After pruning, remove any remaining foliage. Snip the petioles and peduncles near their bases rather than yanking them off because it may scar the stems.

PROTECTING

Apply dormant spray, such as a horticultural oil, to kill any overwintering insects and their eggs. Follow the directions on the product label regarding temperature guidelines, and do not apply if rain is predicted within seventy-two hours after application.

If borers have been a problem, use a rose-pruning sealant immediately after pruning to prevent them from entering the cut ends.

To protect your roses from browsing deer and rabbits or tunneling moles and gophers, refer to Spring Protecting.

PRUNING TOOLS

PRUNING TOOL	BRANCH DIAMETER	BLADE TYPE	USE
Hand pruner	$3/4$ in.	bypass	for general pruning
Hand pruner	$1/2$ in.	bypass	for thinning
Hand pruner	$1/2$ in.	bypass	for cut and hold (flowers & fruit)
Loppers	$1^1/2$ in.	bypass	for heading back leaders
Hedge clippers	$1/2$ in.	bypass	for shearing hedges & ground covers
Knob cutter	1 in.	pinch	for close cutting bonsai pruning
Telescoping Pole pruner	$1^1/2$ in.	bypass	for pruning branches from the ground
Telescoping Pole pruner	$1/2$ in.	bypass	cut and hold / fruit harvesting
Pruning saw	2 in.	pull	for removing branches
Chain saw	4 in.	gas/electric	for removing scaffolds

See pages 55, 261, 293, 298, 302, 306, and 309 for more pruning information.

CHAPTER NINE

California Shrubs

By definition a shrub is a woody plant smaller than a tree; yet, a shrub is so much more. Shrubs manufacture life-sustaining oxygen, mitigate nuisance noise, define spaces and boundaries, and surprise us with their individuality.

Like other plants, shrubs serve as touchstones to places traveled, events experienced, and friendships gathered. For us (Bruce and Sharon), rows of Italian cypress bring to mind southern France, while camellias conjure up images of Japan's ancient gardens. And holiday decorations would not be complete without clippings from Bruce's parents' variegated English holly. In our own front yard, we have three rose of Sharon shrubs planted together, the most precious one from a cutting from a dear friend—a floral metaphor for our friendship.

To draw eyes skyward, intermix taller, bolder varieties toward the back of groupings. To spotlight more earthbound visions, cluster smaller, subtler plants toward the front or along walkways. Use shrubs as a gifted conductor would use his orchestra—to create a composition of undulating rhythms, modulating diminuendo tones, and accentuating fortissimo notes—a symphony for your garden.

There is a shrub for every purpose—whether the landscape calls for evergreen or deciduous, berry- or flower-bearing, screening or showcasing. Shrubs offer different leaf shapes, textures, sizes, and colors to soften or camouflage, to brighten or shade, or to add flowers or greenery to a garden. Most importantly, they serve as artful bridges between our sentinel trees, smaller perennials and annuals, and ground-hugging lawns.

Fuchsias are outrageously flamboyant when their pastel-green, teardrop-shaped buds explode into a floral extravaganza from late spring through fall. Suspended from recurved sepals, ruffled corollas dressed in jewel-drenched tones of red, purple, pink, or white as well as hues of salmon, magenta and cerise engulf long, drooping stamens. Satsuki azaleas are shade-loving, slow-growing, evergreen shrubs with small, hunter-green foliage. During May, they flower in a rainbow of color combinations blanketing dense, twiggy branches.

Whether it glitters as an extrovert flowering performer or peeks shyly from under the protective shade of more forceful plants, there is a shrub for every need and every site.

BURFORD HOLLY
Ilex cornuta 'Burfordii'

Green holly is perfect for holiday floral designs. 'Burfordii' is one of the glossiest with dark-green, stiff, and almost spineless leaves. It's a prolific producer of large, Christmas-red berries. Once established, Burford holly is low-maintenance, provides fruit and nectar for birds and bees, provides holiday greenery, and makes a wonderful accent or evergreen hedge.

Asia / Zones 7 to 11 / full sun, part shade / height 15 to 20 feet / width 6 to 10 feet / berries autumn to winter

ROSE OF SHARON
Hibiscus syriacus

I am partial to rose of Sharon, not only because my parents chose it as my namesake, but also because a dear friend gave me several cuttings. My pink- and lavender-blossomed rose of Sharon plants occupy a special place because they came from the garden of my beloved friend. Rose of Sharon survives hardships and continues to flower year after year, much like true friendship.

Asia / Zones 7 to 11 / full sun / height 6 to 10 feet / width 3 to 6 feet / flowers summer

SKY FLOWER
Duranta repens

In our garden, we have sky flower 'Sapphire Showers'™. It bears bodacious clusters of deep sapphire-blue to royal-purple flowers and gives off a light fragrance similar to candy. The ruffled flowers display a picotee look with their white-edged petals. 'Sapphire Showers'™ is candy for the eyes and the nose in containers, but keep it pruned when it's planted in the ground.

Subtropical Americas / Zones 10 to 11 / full sun, part shade / height 8 to 15 feet / width 8 to 15 feet / flowers summer to autumn

SPRING

The rhythms of spring begin in California as the rainy season ends. Camellias, budding and blooming since autumn, shed spent flowers and begin to grow, while azaleas await warmer days to display their color.

PLANNING

Consider designing new planting areas or renewing older areas of your garden with shrubs that require similar growing conditions, such as drought-tolerant plants from Australia and southern Europe or shade-loving plants from Japan. Most regions in California are subject to prolonged periods without rain, so it makes sense to select plants, such as the rose of Sharon, the Australian fuchsia and the gumi, and cluster them in drifts, much like a paisley print. Once these shrubs are established, they require little or no care. If you continue with drought-tolerant plants, all having the same growing requirements, the garden will ultimately become a self-sustaining landscape.

Excavate the planting pits for new shrubs as soon as the weeds have been removed and the soil has warmed (55 degrees Fahrenheit) and is no longer muddy. There are many recipes for blending backfill materials. One calls for 1 part sharp sand, 1 part excavated soil, and 1 part organic planting mix, such as compost, worm castings, or humus mulch for the backfill. Spring is the best time of the year to plant; the soils are pliable and warming, which encourages root growth. Plus the daylight hours are lengthening, which will give new plantings an entire growing season to establish themselves.

PLANTING

Prepare new shrub planting areas by first testing the soil to determine whether the soil is acidic, neutral, or alkaline. If the pH results fall between 6.5 and 6.8, the soil will not hinder the absorption of nutrients for 95 percent of all shrubs.

Encourage rapid lateral root growth of newly planted shrubs by increasing the width of the planting pit to three or four times the breadth of the bare rootball; if there is a mass planting, excavate a trench two to three times the width of the rootball. The planting pit or trench need not be any deeper than the height of the rootball, and the inside surfaces should be scratched with a cultivator to encourage new roots to begin growing into the native soil. The cultivator roughens the inside surfaces of the planting hole to prevent "glazing" of the side surfaces.

If the right plants are selected for the right locations, they should thrive with only a minimum of care. Knowledge about the origin, soil pH requirements, soil texture, seasonal rainfall, and sun and wind exposure all help in avoiding the pitfalls along the path to a successful gardening.

Set out frost-tender shrubs, such as Shark Bay baronia, white shrimp plants, and vireyas, on or about the last projected freeze day in your area and adhere to the spacing recommendations for specific varieties.

For gifts to yourself, as well as friends or neighbors, collect seeds from spent flowers and take semihardwood cuttings from last summer's growth. Root them in flats. If you don't have a cold frame or a hot house, a simple method to propagate seeds is to fill a ziplock plastic bag with about $1/3$ vermiculite or perlite; moisten so that it is wet, but not soggy; put in your seeds; zip up the baggy; and place it on a windowsill where it will receive filtered light. If too much moisture beads inside the bag, open periodically to air the bag out. The germinated seedlings can then be planted in peat pots or planted outdoors after the danger of frost, when they are about 2 inches tall.

WATERING

Supplemental watering might be necessary if the autumn and winter rainfall was below normal, especially if new growth emerges. Keep in mind that soils should never become so dry that a plant's foliage wilts. *Hydrangea macrophylla* is an excellent example of a plant that will collapse if it is not hydrated. But determining the level of soil moisture eludes most new gardeners.

Use a soil probe, a tensiometer, or a trowel to see or feel how moist the soil is. Monitor the moisture content of container soils frequently. They dry much more quickly than soils in the garden, yet it is almost impossible to overwater a plant growing in a container, especially if the medium is porous and the water drains freely.

Use these tests to judge the soil moisture content; if your soil is a sandy loam, take a soil sample from a plant's root zone, not off the surface:

- If a handful of soil is gritty and drops through your fingers, water is not available. (It's time to water.)
- If the soil appears dry and will not form a ball, less than 50 percent of the water is available. (It's time to water.)
- If the soil forms a ball but doesn't hold together, 50 to 75 percent of the water is available. (Wait to water.)
- If the soil forms a ball without a shiny surface but crumbles apart, 75 percent to field capacity of the water is available. (Don't water.)

The movement of water through the root zone is one of the most important considerations of establishing and maintaining plants. If water does not percolate but saturates the soil, anaerobic pathogens, such as water molds, invade a plant's root system and destroy its ability to transport water and nutrients. To avoid this, determine the percolation rate at the planting site by excavating an 18-inch-deep by 18-inch-wide test hole. Fill the test hole with water, let it percolate (drain), then fill it with water again. The second filling should drain at a rate of 1 inch per hour. If all the water has percolated, you can be confident that there will not be standing water in the plant's root zone two or three days after irrigating, but if the pit is still full after eighteen hours, you have excavated a waterproof bowl. In that event, a raised planting bed, French drain, or perforated drainpipe will solve the lack-of-porosity problem by removing the water from the root zone. If the water is percolating but at a very slow rate, consider expanding the planting pit deeper and wider to accommodate the slower rate.

FERTILIZING

For all shrubs, other than California natives and plants that evolved in similar environments, such as plants from the arid regions of South Africa, Australia, and southern Europe, fertilize with a complete, dry organic fertilizer in early spring, early summer, and early autumn, and water in thoroughly with a solution high in humic acid. If you prefer to use a liquid organic fertilizer, apply more frequently—early spring, late spring, midsummer, and early autumn.

The potential for damaging the foliage of plants from fertilizing using a complete organic fertilizer is negligible even if new growth has begun. The nutrients become available as the soil warms and as the plant requires them.

The dry complete organic fertilizers should be distributed in a band just inside the berm that forms the watering basin and then thoroughly watered-in with a solution of humic acid.

The initial spring application of a complete organic fertilizer, such as cotton-seed meal for acid-loving plants like camellias, azaleas, and vireyas, should occur shortly after the flowers are spent. If you fertilize while they are still budding and blooming, the plant will drop its buds and blooms and begin to grow.

MAINTAINING

As the flowers on your shrubs fade, pinch them off using your thumb and forefinger or by using a pair of needle-nosed bypass shears. Their removal will direct the shrubs' energy back into reflowering and growing, and not into developing seeds.

To keep Italian cypress healthy, periodically blow out interior debris by directing a strong stream of water into its dense foliage and branching structure.

Maintain a 2-inch blanket of organic mulch on the ground and below the canopy of all shrubs (keep the mulch 4 to 6 inches away from their trunks). Continue mulching, but cultivate the surface of the ground to suppress weeds and allow air and

moisture movement through the soil.

To save time and wear and tear on your back, use a preemergent to eliminate the next generation of weeds. Do not use a preemergent if you are going to plant seeds in that area. Apply it about twice a year, once in late winter or early spring and once in late summer or early fall.

Take advantage of pliable soils, loosened by autumn and winter rains. Aerating the soils when they are moist is much easier than when they are dry and rock hard. In addition, applying a liquid soil conditioner such as saponin (an extract from yucca) helps keep soils loose; follow the formulator's directions.

Shrubs that bloom on current-season wood, such as fuchsias, shrimp plants, and sky flowers, can be pruned back 40 to 60 percent in late winter or early spring, before the new flush of foliage.

Prune plants that bloom on second-year wood, such as lilacs, after their blooms are spent. There are some hybrids, such as the Descanso hybrid lilacs, that may repeat bloom in fall. If you have a repeat-bloomer, prune after fall.

Some shrubs, such as the shrimp plant, rose of Sharon, and sky flower, tend to get leggy. To encourage more branching structure, which in turn provides more flowers, tip the ends of the branches back by 1 to 2 inches.

In early spring, prune nonblooming shrubs to maintain their form by heading back errant growth; also open their canopies by thinning (lacing) shrubs to allow sunlight to reach the interior portions of plant, encouraging new growth.

PROTECTING

Populations of aphids, giant whiteflies, thrips, and leafhoppers, explode in spring when new growth occurs. Aphids secrete honeydew, which is harvested by ants; after a time, a fungus, black sooty mold, appears and eventually covers the leaf surfaces. Giant whiteflies come from Central America and, once established, are very difficult to control. They lay a pattern of eggs that looks like a target on the underside of a plant's foliage. If you control these pests early in the season, life will be much easier for you and your shrubs. Use a systemic insect control with imidacloprid as its active ingredient if your shrubs are growing in an area where there are no plants with edible parts, Since imidacloprid remains in the plant's system for one year, it is an effective and convenient control. For a more benign but effective solution, use Neem oil, garlic oil, or pyrethrum-based pesticides, or wash off the infestation with a stream of water. Repetitive applications of the natural controls and the syringing should continue until the infestation is under control.

Spring's typically cool and damp weather is the perfect environment for snails and slugs. To stop them dead in their trails, use a molluscicide with iron phosphate as its active ingredient. Iron phosphate is organic, it can be used in areas where plants with edible parts are growing, and is safe around pets and small children. Another advantage is that eventually iron phosphate degrades into fertilizer. Decollate snails also seek out and devour small- to medium-sized brown garden snails. Once decollates have decimated the brown garden snail population, they feed primarily on decaying organic material. Contact your local Extension office to make sure decollate snails are allowed in your county. If you *do* use decollates, *do not* use iron phosphate or any other molluscicide.

Cutworms emerge as adult night-flying clear-wing moths, and they immediately begin laying eggs to continue their life cycle. Distribute parasitic wasps (*Trichogramma brassicae*) to control cutworms.

Ants are a continuing problem and nuisance in our gardens. They "farm" sucking insects, such as aphids and brown soft scales, for their honeydew, which eventually causes an infestation of black sooty mold. The following are homemade, organic formulas to control ants. Mix 1 part boric acid with 2 parts of a sweet sticky liquid (such as mint jelly, honey, or maple syrup), put a dollop of the mixture in a container, and punch an ant-sized hole on the top. Believe it or not, orange peel oil is toxic to ants. Blend a puree of orange peels with water, and pour the mixture immediately into the entrance of ant holes. This is most effective on hot days.

To protect shrubs from parasitic fungi such as mildew, apply Neem oil or a lemon myrtle tea tree extract. Usually these controls require a more frequent spraying regimen, three or four times, a week apart, but it is worth the extra effort if you are trying to maintain an organic garden.

Italian cypress is often subject to twig girdlers, spider mites, cypress tip moths, and cypress cankers. Take a section of a branch that is in transition from dead to green to your local garden center or Extension office for proper identification, and follow their recommendations. For twig girdlers, spider mites, and cypress tip moths, imidacloprid is a systemic control that translocates up to 150 feet into the canopy of a tall shrub or tree. Once the systemic is used, reapplication is not necessary for one year. Apply strictly according to the directions on the label.

The rhythm of the 'Tiny Towers' Italian cypress can be frustratingly slow, taking a decade to reach 8 feet, but patience has it rewards—this plant requires little or no maintenance once it becomes established.

PLANNING

Summer is the best season to survey garden centers, arboretums, botanical gardens, and your neighborhood for plants you might consider for your landscape. Most shrubs bloom during spring and summer, so it is an excellent time to observe their structure and flower color. Photograph combinations of plants that please you and that have a useful scale for residential landscapes, as well as combinations with similar maintenance requirements.

PLANTING

Plant shrubs early in the morning rather than at midday or during the afternoon to avoid rapid moisture loss that results in transplant shock. The following tasks can lessen the shock of transplanting if you *must* plant during the summer heat:

1. Thoroughly water the plants the day before planting, giving them time to imbibe as much water as possible.
2. Remove 60 to 80 percent of the foliage to reduce the water loss through transpiration.
3. Spray an antitranspirant to avoid moisture loss through the leaves.
4. Water-in saponin and a root stimulator containing IBA (indolebutyric acid) or NAA (naphalene-acetic acid). Follow with two more applications of root stimulator, one week apart.

WATERING

Watering landscape shrubs during summer involves routine observation. If the leaves are beginning to wilt, if the branches are flagging, and if the surface of the ground is cracking, it is probably time to water. Checking the soil moisture with a tensiometer (water meter) is a useful method of learning the moisture content 1 to 2 feet below the surface of the soil.

Add a surfactant, such as saponin, to the water stream during the hot, dry, and windy summer months. (Saponin is an extract from *Yucca schidigera*; it can be applied as often as every season.) Surfactants help break the surface tension so water will sheet across the soil particles and be absorbed rather than beading and rolling off. Soils and mulches desiccate and their surfaces repel water before it can percolate. A simple way to add surfactants is with a siphoning device connected at the hose bib.

The most efficient time to water shrubs is in late afternoon or early morning when there is time for absorbing roots to move moisture into the canopy. For container gardening, it *was* the norm to recommend early morning irrigation, particularly during summer, but researchers have concluded that the optimum time to water container plants is between noon and 6 p.m. Indications now show that morning watering stresses plants and retards their growth and that watering containers in the afternoon increases their growth as much as 70 percent and increases photosynthesis, compared to morning watering. Plants apparently appreciate cool afternoon showers on hot, summer days!

Designing an irrigation system is mostly a function of site limitations, soil texture, plant species, and cost. Hand watering is the most efficient way to avoid wasting water. If the waterer is paying attention, he or she will move to the next plant as soon as the current watering basin is full. Drip irrigation is the next best application method. It puts the water only where it is needed. The drawback is the system must routinely be maintained. The least efficient method of irrigating, but the most convenient, is the fixed PVC irrigation system. Its drawback is that there is usually an excess of overspray into areas where there are no plants.

During summer, use drip irrigation systems with emitters that have a release rate of 2 gallons per hour; they are very efficient and an effective method of conserving water during high-demand months. With a programmable irrigation clock, it is possible to accommodate seasonal and climatic variation. This type of system enables you to place water precisely where it is needed and reduces surface runoff. The microtubing attached to the emitter should be long enough to accommodate any future expansion of the basin. For example, if the basin is 4 feet in diameter and 4 inches deep, there should be at least four emitters placed just inside its perimeter. It takes 30 gallons of water to fill this basin. With four emitters, it would take approximately four hours to provide 32 gallons of water. The amount of water can be controlled by frequency and duration. As the shrub expands, extend the watering basin out to the plant's drip line and increase the number of emitters.

Irrigating deeply and infrequently benefits most plants much more than shallow, frequent watering will. The deep-watering routine dissolves and leaches soluble salts down and through the root zone. During summer when watering is more frequent and evaporation is more rapid, salt accumulation can lead to higher pH and EC readings, both of which will cause plant damage such as leaf burn or stunted growth.

Be aware of your regional weather patterns; if a high-pressure cell is projected over your region, expect hot dry weather and adjust your irrigation clock to water more frequently. As with all plants, irrigating shrubs should not be by the clock or calendar, but by observation. Once established, Italian cypress, gumi, and Australian fuchsia are much more tolerant of drought than are other plants, so be particularly careful about overwatering them.

FERTILIZING

Continue applying organic liquid fertilizers once a month or a dry organic fertilizer every six to eight weeks (water-in dry fertilizer with a soil-building product that is high in humic acid to increase the soil's health). Controlled-release fertilizers are also available that require applications every four to six months, depending on the formulations. Fertilizers that are controlled release make nutrients available very slowly; they are convenient to use not only in the garden, but also for container plants.

Avoid using high-nitrogen fertilizers during late summer because rapidly available nitrogen promotes rapid, leggy growth.

MAINTAINING

Remove the weeds and grasses that grew in spring. If there's open space between the landscape shrubs in your garden spot, treat the weeds with a contact or systemic herbicide. If the landscape shrubs are a dense mass planting, the weeds should be physically removed and a pre-emergent weed control applied to eliminate the next generation of weeds.

Continue deadheading spent flowers; flowers divert the energy from seed production (unless there are berries to be harvested, as with the gumi shrub).

Using an adjustable nozzle or a hand-held fan sprinkler, wash off the dust and air pollution debris from the foliage of all plants; be sure to syringe the underside, also.

Summer is the time to allow sunlight to reach latent interior branch buds. The sunlight will stimulate these buds into growth. Also prune out dead or diseased branches and errant growth.

Summer pruning is used to control the size of plants, including large shrubs, standard citrus trees, standard fruit trees, and full-sized shade trees.

PROTECTING

If there are mice and rats, use rat bait in a bait station and manual traps to control them. One successful technique for prompting a rat to commit to the bait on a rat trap is to suspend the bait-loaded rat trap from a string just out of reach of the rat. The bait will taunt the rat to snap the trap. Guillotine traps are the most effective control for insectivorous burrowing moles.

For gophers, use manual traps or bait. To keep deer out of your garden, use motion-activated watering sensors or olfactory repellents; for small areas, set up a perimeter of 6-foot stakes and string monofilament line around the stakes, deer chest high. The deer cannot see the line when they brush up against it, which frightens them away from the barrier.

Unless rabbits, raccoons, skunks, squirrels, and opossums are causing a great deal of damage, adopt the "live and let live" philosophy and allow them to be part of your garden's appeal. We are on the regular route of a trio of raccoons who check in on us every few days to munch on our slugs, snails, and insects. After they wash themselves in our fountain, they often come on our deck to peek in on us as if wishing us a fond farewell before continuing their nocturnal trek through the neighborhood. We look forward to their visits every summer and fall.

Pythium, *Phytophthora*, and *Rhizoctonia* are water molds (fungi) that invade a plant's root system and limit or destroy the ability of the plant's vascular system to transport water and nutrients. Clayey, dense, and continually wet soils are perfect habitats for plant-ravaging fungi. Combat these fungi by applying compost tea, worm castings, and humic acid to the soil.

Spider mites thrive during the hot, humid days of summer, but persist all year long along the coastal regions. They have eight legs and are related to spiders and ticks rather than insects. They pierce the leaf surface and suck out the juices for nourishment. The leaf becomes stippled from their feeding, and if the colony is undisturbed, a silvery sheen will develop. Neem oil is registered as a mite control, as are beneficial predatory mites.

AUTUMN SHRUBS

Summer fades, weather cools, and daylight decreases, nubby-capped acorns of the scrub oak ripen and fade from green to brown. Harbingers of a reflective time, they fall to the water to float or sink.

PLANNING

Autumn is the other best season to plant shrubs. The soils are still warm from exposure to the summer's sun, and root growth accelerates before the onset of winter; even though the outside temperatures drop rapidly, the root systems of deciduous shrubs are still active.

Autumn is the second season of the year (spring being the first) that soil pH levels should be recorded. Salts quickly accumulate in the soil during summer as watering frequencies increase. The pH levels should be at their highest levels during this time. The salts that accumulate in the root zone can become highly toxic to landscape shrubs. High pH levels are indicators of future problems with nutrient absorption. The ideal pH for the majority of the plants used in our landscapes is 6.0 to 6.8. This pH supports nutrient availability for 95 percent of all our plants, including shrubs. To test a soil sample, acquire a pH test kit from your local garden center, or contact your county Cooperative Extension Office and ask whether they offer soil-testing services.

PLANTING

Autumn is an excellent time to plant Burford hollies and 'Tiny Tower' Italian cypress in decorative ceramic pots for the holidays. Burford holly does not need a pollenizer; its berries mature in late autumn, just in time for the holidays. 'Tiny Tower' Italian cypress is the perfect conifer for a container; it takes ten years to grow into a tree, which makes it very easy to maintain and to decorate.

If pH levels are higher than 7.2 to 7.5, take the following steps to lower the levels to 6.2 to 7.0: Add soil sulfur and gypsum or calcium chloride. For soil sulfur, apply 1 to 2 pounds per 100 square feet; gypsum is applied 10 to 15 pounds per 100 square feet, and calcium chloride is mixed 1 quart per $2^1/2$ gallons of water for 1,000 square feet. If the soil lacks organic material, evenly spread 2 to 3 cubic yards of humus mulch, compost, worm castings, or another comparable amendment.

In most mild-winter regions, fall is one of the best times to plant unthirsty native shrubs, such as Christmas berries, mazanitas, and coffeeberries, or non-native drought-tolerant shrubs, such as Australian fuchsias. Planting these shrubs in autumn gives them a head start over those planted later in spring, particularly if you live in a frost-free area. The soil is easy to till, and the cooler days encourage root systems to develop in preparation for winter. (Also see pages 81, 90, and 95 for more shrub selections.)

WATERING

Reduce the amount and frequency of watering according to climatic conditions and the slowdown of the plant's growth rate. Do not overwater during the cooler seasons. Remember the rule: The volume of water a plant requires is the volume of water that transpires off its canopy and evaporates from the ground. So in autumn, when it is cool, daylight hours decrease, and there is adequate rainfall, it is better to turn off the automatic irrigation and turn it on manually if there is a dry spell. If you are uncomfortable guessing the wetness or dryness of the soil, use a tensiometer (moisture meter) to measure the soil moisture level.

Watering guideline:

- If a watering basin is 3 feet in diameter with a 4-inch berm, it takes around 20 gallons to fill it.
- If a watering basin is 3 feet in diameter with a 6-inch berm, it takes around 30 gallons to fill it.
- If a watering basin is 4 feet in diameter with a 4-inch berm, it takes around 30 gallons to fill it.
- If a watering basin is 4 feet in diameter with a 6-inch berm, it takes around 50 gallons to fill it.
- If a watering basin is 6 feet in diameter with a 4-inch berm, it takes around 70 gallons to fill it.
- If a watering basin is 6 feet in diameter with a 6-inch berm, it takes around 150 gallons to fill it.

FERTILIZING

As the weather cools, daylight diminishes, and plant growth slows, it is best to discontinue fertilizing. But fertilization is appropriate on two occasions: First, during early fall, an application of a high-potassium fertilizer increases the sugar content within the plant, which enables it to better tolerate cold weather. This process is called *winterizing* a plant. Second, unless they are shrubs from arid environments or California natives, these plants usually have accelerated root growth in early autumn and in spring, as the soil warms; an application of an organic fertilizer, such as cottonseed meal, is appropriate during their fall growth period.

Do not feed camellias or azaleas nitrogen while their buds are developing or while they are blooming; they will drop their buds and flowers and begin growing.

MAINTAINING

Enhance your prize-winning camellia blossoms by thinning the developing buds. If there are clusters of five or seven buds on a branch, cull two or three of them, making space for the remaining buds to fully open. Disbudding is a technique that will direct the plant's energy towards producing the perfect flower.

If you live in snow country, note on your gardening calendar to drain the irrigation line before the water in the pipes freeze. Also insulate the manifold (valve cluster).

To save time and wear and tear on your back, just after the current crop of weeds is removed, use a preemergent to eliminate the next generation of weeds. Do not use a preemergent if you are going to plant seeds in that area. Apply a preemergent about twice a year, once in late winter or early spring and once in late summer or early fall.

Composting is an integral part of gardening rhythms. There are four key materials in composting: nitrogen, carbon, water, and air. Nitrogen sources are from grass clippings, plant trimmings, vegetative kitchen refuse (never add meat), and livestock manure. While nitrogen sources come from the "green stuff," carbon sources are the "brown stuff of life," which includes dried leaves, chipped branches, bark, or straw. Compost bins measuring 3 feet by 3 feet by 3 feet have volumes of 1 cubic yard, an ideal size for residential gardens. A practical way to construct a compost bin is to use four wooden pallets. Stand them up on their sides, making an open-top boxlike structure. The ratio of green to brown stuff is 50 percent green to 50 percent brown. Alternately layer the accumulated green and brown debris in the bin. Keep the moisture content in the compost between 40 and 60 percent. Since composting is an aerobic process, turn the material over once a week. Depending on the weather, the composting process may take two to four months. If the materials are "cooking" properly, temperatures during composting can range from 120 to 140 degrees Fahrenheit. Once the process has completed, the materials are ready to add to your garden as an amendment to the soil or as mulch to the soil surface.

If large shrubs serve as a visual screen, a sound buffer, or a wind break, there is no need for autumn pruning unless there is errant growth (water sprouts) or flagging (branches fallen away from the center axis of the plant), as in the case with the Italian cypress.

Midautumn is an excellent time to shape espaliered shrubs such as angel earring fuchsias and pink powder puff plants. The window of time for shaping the espaliered plants is after autumn's hot dry winds but before winter's cold snap.

To propagate from cuttings such shrubs as Australian fuchsia, rose of Sharon, and shrimp plant, cut 4- to 6-inch semihardwood sections (these sections are not taken from the branch tips, but about 6 inches down or wherever the woody sections are less flexible). Remove the bottom leaves by snipping, rather than tearing them off. Allow them to callus over for twelve to twenty-four hours. Dip the ends in a rooting hormone, and cluster three cuttings in the middle of a 1-gallon black plastic nursery container (with drainage holes) filled with a rooting medium (50 percent sand, 50 percent vermiculite). Moisten the medium, and place the container in a warm, humid, well-lit area or cover the cuttings with quart-sized plastic bottles. Just cut off their bottoms and put them over your cuttings for an instant greenhouse. Cuttings should root in three to four weeks. Do not pull them out to check whether they are rooting; when the cuttings are rooting, foliar buds appear. After the foliage begins to grow, it is time to transplant your cuttings into individual containers, using an organic potting soil. Plant the cuttings at the same level as they were in the rooting medium (if you want, use a dibble to make the planting hole). Press the soil around the cuttings, and soak thoroughly with a root stimulator three times, one week apart.

PROTECTING

Control camellia blight by continuing the summer routine of deadheading, raking up, collecting, and trashing spent camellia flowers. Also maintain 2 inch of mulch over the root zone.

Control the persistent and damaging presence of spider mites on azaleas, Italian cypress, rose of Sharon, and Australian fuchsias by applying horticultural oil. Check the weather predictions, and wait until there will be three days of clear weather before spraying.

WINTER

The rhythms of winter produce the gumi's wonderful burgundy fruit, the firethorn's orange seeds, and the holly's holiday-red berries. They provide a welcome buffet for resident birds and other wildlife.

PLANNING

Plan and prepare appropriate locations for gift plants or for mature-specimen plants that friends or neighbors offer because they no longer want or have room for them. Established plants give a finished look to the landscape, and gift plants serve as reminders of friends and family.

Study your gardening journal and reflect on the events that occurred over the year to make plans for next year based on those observations. Ask these questions:

- Was the rainfall average?
- Was the pest population ovewhelming?
- Were there new insects or diseases in the garden?
- What new shrubs were planted, and how are they doing?

PLANTING

Early winter is still a manageable time to move coniferous shrubs, especially if the soil temperature is still being warmed by a mulch blanket. If the shrub to move is 3 to 5 feet high and 3 feet in diameter, prepare a planting pit that is 4 feet in diameter and 2 feet deep. Tie a ribbon on the north side of the plant, and maintain the same north orientation when the plant is positioned in the planting pit. Scratch a 4-foot-diameter circle around the plant. Begin excavating the soil so there will be a column of earth and roots 18 inches high standing in the center of the hole. With a heavy-duty plastic sheet or canvas tarp at hand, separate the bottom of the column of soil and roots from the bottom of the hole. Push the plant and its rootball to one side, exposing the bottom of the column, and slide the sheet or tarp under the column of soil. Then tip the plant back to the vertical. Lift and move the plant to the new planting pit, and orient the plant to its original compass direction. If the soil textures of the new and old locations are similar, amending the backfill is not necessary. Shovel in and tamp enough backfill to maintain the top of the rootball at the same level as the adjacent soil. Continue backfilling until half the height of the rootball is reached. Soak the soil in the planting pit with water to collapse any air pockets. Fill in the rest of the planting pit with backfill, saving enough to build a 4-foot-diameter watering basin, formed by a soil berm 6 inches high around the base of the plant. Ensure that the plant is vertical; then give it a thorough soaking by filling the watering basin twice. Give the plant an application of root stimulator; then mulch the surface of the basin with 2 inches of organic material.

WATERING

The rainy season extends from November to the middle of March. Supplemental watering is unnecessary unless there is a prolonged dry spell; in that case, the native and most of the established shrubs will have roots that extend well beyond the plant's drip line and much deeper than the initial planting depth, so a deep soaking once a month should be enough water. In containers and in the garden, the soil and its components serve as a reservoir for nutrients and moisture. If a dry spell does occur, adjust your watering schedule to keep the plants from wilting by applying the water at a slower rate but for a longer time. This adjustment will permit the water to percolate deeper.

It is always more efficient to water deeply and infrequently than to water a little and frequently. So if the rainfall is light, turn on the irrigation system and drive the moisture deeper by rewatering; then delay the next application until the soil is dry 6 to 8 inches deep.

This is a good time to survey, repair, and adjust your irrigation system to accommodate the demands of spring growth and the neglect of winter's isolation.

An old adage tells us that in a sustainable landscape, "the right plant in the right place never needs watering." This is rarely true in California gardens; even native and drought-tolerant plants require water to get established.

The daily volume of water (gallons) that evaporates from the ground around a plant and volume of water (gallons) that transpires off a plant's canopy is the volume that should be replaced. In a loam soil, 25 percent of its volume should be a water reservoir. Factors such as wind, air, and soil temperature; humidity; dew point; and the plant's health all affect the need for irrigation.

FERTILIZING

No fertilizing is necessary during winter; in fact, in the milder regions of California where camellias bloom from fall to spring, if the plants are fed camellia food during the winter season, they will drop their buds and flowers and start to grow again.

MAINTAINING

Rebuild the watering basins, and maintain 2 to 4 inches of organic compost, keeping it 4 to 6 inches away from the base of the plants.

Shred all the branches and trimmings that were collected and piled throughout the growing season. Add the shredded material to compost piles, or use it to mulch.

In late winter or early spring, just after the last frost, shrubs that bloom on current-season wood, such as fuchsias, should be hard pruned back as much as 40 to 60 percent before the new flush of foliage appears.

PROTECTING

Protect tender shrubs from damaging frost by covering them with a cotton sheet or floating horticultural blanket just before the predicted frost, and don't forget to remove the covering during the day. You can also spray the foliage with an antitranspirant.

Camellia blight is a fungus that rots the petals of camellia flowers. The fungus lives in or on the soil surrounding the camellia and disperses spores into the air and onto the camellia's foliage, buds, and flowers. To break the cycle, gather all infected flowers, petals, buds, and fallen foliage and dispose of them into the trash (not in the composter). Blanket the ground 1 foot beyond the drip line of the camellia plant with 4 inches of organic mulch to suppress further fungal development. Keep the mulch 4 to 6 inches away from the base of the camellia.

CHAPTER TEN

California Specialty Fruit Trees

The phrase, "people can make a difference," is particularly applicable to horticulture, and Kate Sessions is one such person. In 1892, in exchange for thirty acres in San Diego's newly designated Balboa Park—where she would establish a private nursery—she promised to plant one hundred trees a year in the park for ten years and another three hundred trees a year throughout San Diego. As a result, she created a horticultural wonderland in Balboa Park and transformed San Diego's scrubby mesas into a botanical paradise. Our (Bruce and Sharon) own lychee tree is said to be from a rooted layer of a tree planted by Kate herself.

From the exotic lychee, dragon fruit, and cherimoya to the more familiar apricot, avocado, and peach, California's hospitable climate and ethnic diversity combine to yield a cornucopia of fruit.

Throughout every season, fruit trees transform our yards into gardens of Eden with their spring blossoms, summer and fall bounty, and blaze of autumn foliage. Even in winter, their silhouetted branches and sun-gilded trunks mesmerize us. In the circle of life, few plants compare to the seasonal rhythms of fruit trees.

In Our Garden

Paradise and fruit trees are one and the same. Fruit trees—with their clouds of fragrant peach, pink, red, and white blossoms—celebrate life's renewal, much like the more earthbound harbingers of spring—crocus, grape hyacinth, and daffodil. Warming spring breezes nudge clinging blossoms into flight in technicolor drifts, making room for budded fruit bursting in anticipation of sun-burnished days. By summer, densely packed leaves blanket limbs, providing shade umbrellas for the fruit. From summer to fall, bountiful harvests generously serve a buffet of sun-ripened offerings for all creatures great and small. Finally in winter, the circle of life begins to close once again, shedding faded foliage that are pale remembrances of past verdant greens or recent autumnal blazes of reds, oranges, and yellows.

Although our selections may be at the top of our list, keep in mind they might not be as appealing to you or might not perform as well in your micro-climate, but hopefully, there are enough choices that several will be perfect for you. We have even included a fruiting cactus in this chapter because its unique fruits are so special and deserving of attention.

AVOCADO
Persea americana

The most frequent question from our radio listeners is how to tell when an avocado is ripe. Avocados ripen off the tree; wait until they have grown to size and taste-test to see if its oil content is ready. Leave it at room temperature or place it in a paper bag with an apple; it should ripen within 2 to 5 days. When the skin gives under gentle pressure, but remains firm, the time is "ripe" to eat.

Central America / Zones 10 to 11 / full sun / height 10 to 25 feet / width 10 to 25 feet / harvest winter to autumn or autumn to spring, depending on variety

LYCHEE
Litchi chinensis

We were thrilled when our first-year lychee bore a sizeable crop of raspberry-colored clusters of pebble-textured fruit. Then seven years passed without a single one. We learned ants were "stealing" the pollen. Now we have ant eradication measures in place by early spring, encouraging floriferous panicles of tiny, chartreuse-yellow blossoms. The reward is exotic fruits that possess the taste of the tropics.

S. China / Zones 10 to 11 / full sun / height 15 to 35 feet / width 15 to 30 feet / harvest summer

PERSIMMON
Diospyros kaki

One brisk autumn morning, Bruce and I were walking through a farming village in Japan when we saw farmhouse after farmhouse gaily festooned with curtains of bright orange 'Fuyu' persimmons, peeled, stacked, and strung. Once every few days, the drying fruits are hand-massaged to keep them pliable. This painstaking ritual continues until the New Year when hosting families serve their "fruits of labor" to visitors as a gesture of hospitality.

Japan / Zones 8 to 11 / full sun / height 12 to 20 feet / width 15 to 20 feet / harvest autumn

SPRING

The rhythm of cherimoya, the "Fruit of the Gods," is a little off beat; when other specialty fruits are blooming and setting fruit in midspring, it drops its foliage and begins a short dormancy.

PLANNING

Be discriminating when you decide on a location in your landscape design for growing one or more specialty fruit trees. One of the foremost considerations is the plant's chill requirements. The deciduous specialty fruit trees, except for the cherimoya, require an accumulation of chill hours, which refers to the total number of hours when temperature is below 45 degrees Fahrenheit less the number of hours above 75 degrees. Chill hours are compiled during autumn and winter. Consider the microclimates of your neighborhood and garden to obtain quality fruit select varieties that will meet the chill-hours requirements. Also, select several kinds of specialty fruits so that you will have fruit maturing from spring to fall and not all at once. Local garden centers display maturity charts and chill-hour recommendations to help you select the appropriate varieties.

Evergreen specialty fruit trees include avocados, which are endemic to southern Mexico and Guatemala and lychees from Southeast Asia. For optimum growth and fruit production, they prefer growing locations that are in full sun, wind protected, and frost-free. Free-draining soil is also an important requirement.

Plan your orchard by drawing a planting plan on $1/8$-inch-scaled graph paper. Space the plants so they do not interfere with each other's canopy and to allow adequate air circulation. A comfortable spacing for standard trees is 15 to 20 feet on-center. For semidwarf varieties, space 12 to 15 feet; space true dwarf trees 8 to 12 feet apart. Dwarf varieties also make ideal container plants. Locate deciduous fruit trees in a lower, colder area of your yard and the cold-sensitive avocados, lychees, and dragon fruit in a higher, frost-free site.

Plan to grow dragon fruit plants in large 15-gallon containers using porous cactus potting soil. They are considered crawlers, so provide a structure such as a trellis for them to grow on.

Select deciduous fruit trees when they are available as bare roots; inventories will not be as large in spring as they were from late autumn to early winter, but it's a good time to look for season-end specials. This is the transition time from bare-root and balled-and-burlapped to container stock. If bare-root inventory is still being offered by your garden supply outlet, be sure the trees are still dormant. If the leaf and flower buds are swelling or showing color, the absorbing roots have begun to grow. If they are, pass on the inventory and wait for the container inventory to arrive, unless they offer an unconditional money-back guarantee.

Plant three semidwarf or dwarf varieties in the same planting pit if you have limited space. These trees are grafted or budded onto dwarfing rootstocks, which do not have as extensive a root system as standard fruit trees.

Salad fruit trees are also available for large containers or for cottage gardens. Different varieties are grafted or budded onto a single rootstock, for example, combining a peach, plum, and nectarine on a single tree.

PLANTING

Plant dragon fruit in black, plastic, 15-gallon containers filled with cactus mix, or if you prefer, formulate your own mix by blending worm castings, coarse perlite, coarse sand, pumice, and loam soil in equal parts.

If the tree needs support to keep it vertical, do not bind the trunk tightly to a single stake. Instead, install two stakes 12 inches away from the trunk and on opposite sides, then stabilize the trunk between the stakes by using a flexible tree tie in a figure-eight pattern. As the caliper (diameter) of the tree trunk increases, loosen or replace the flexible tree tie. (See also Winter Planting.)

WATERING

Thoroughly drench the soil around the rootball of newly installed plants. This drenching collapses any air pockets in and around the rootball.

Apply a surfactant such as saponin (derived from *Yucca schidigera*) or a product containing calcium chloride (derived from leonardite) to increase percolation through the tree's root zone. Early spring is the end of the rainy season, unless there is an El Nino, and supplemental watering every ten to fourteen days might be necessary to maintain the spring flush of growth.

Maintain an even amount of soil moisture around your fruit trees. If the soil moisture fluctuates between wet and dry, the tree will often stress, causing premature fruit drop.

Avocados cannot withstand drought. Any level of moisture content that is below field capacity will begin to stress avocado trees. They also prefer free-draining soil. Even though the majority of the tree's roots are in the top 1 to 2 feet of the soil, water should percolate 3 to 5 feet deep. Ideally, the soil should have a sandy loam texture, plus 20 to 40 percent organic material. When there is a hot, dry spell, avocados drop their fruit as a result of stress (the fruit's peduncle will desiccate, then separate, and the fruit falls). It might be necessary to double the frequency and amount of water to compensate.

FERTILIZING

Apply a liquid organic fruit tree fertilizer, high in humic acid, every six weeks throughout the growing season, or apply a dry organic fruit tree food four times per year. The first application should be in late winter while the tree is still dormant and just before the flower buds swell and show color (the popcorn stage). The second application takes place when the fruit develops to about an inch in diameter. The third feeding should occur in midsummer, and an optional feeding to winterize your trees can be made in late summer.

MAINTAINING

Control the weeds around your trees by maintaining a 1- to 2-inch compost layer, humus mulch, worm castings, or other comparable organic material above the root zone or 20 percent out beyond the drip line of the tree's canopy. If the prior season's weed population was overwhelming, consider applying a granular or liquid pre-emergent weed seed control. Follow the directions for the application rate and timing.

Cherimoya trees are considered evergreen, except for about forty-five days during early spring when they drop their leaves. They thrive in porous, free-draining soil containing 30 to 40 percent organic material. The flowers of the cherimoya have both female and male parts. The first day that the flower opens in the morning, its female parts are receptive to pollination. Then the flower closes around midday and reopens in the afternoon when its male parts are ready to shed pollen. There are usually enough flowers opening and closing that pollination occurs naturally, but hand pollinating increases chances for successful pollination.

Allow avocado foliage to fall and remain on the ground. The leaves create a blanket of decomposing organic material over the root system, stabilizing the moisture content and keeping the weeds down.

Leave avocados on the tree, and harvest them as needed. Determine whether an avocado is ready to eat by removing the button at the stem end and inserting a toothpick into the opening. If the meat is ripe enough, the toothpick will slip in and out easily. They can also be picked before full ripening as long as the oil content in the fruit is high enough. Select one that feels heavy and put it in a paper bag with an apple. The ethylene gas produced by the apple will ripen the avocado in a day or two.

Shape cherimoya trees when they defoliate in early spring. Without foliage, it is easier to see and remove interfering branches.

For most fruit trees, prune back errant growth during the spring flush of new and vigorous growth.

Espaliered specialty fruit trees trained to a trellis, fence, or wall require periodic pruning to maintain the flattened growth form. It keeps the trees low and the fruit within easy reach. Plus it is simpler to cover an espaliered tree with netting to protect the fruit from birds. It is much more challenging and impractical to throw a net around a standard-sized fruit tree.

Lychees are almost the perfect tree when it comes to pruning. If you select the right location for it to thrive, the canopy has a 6- to 8-inch flush of growth twice a year and you should never have to prune it.

Avocados do not have to be pruned unless they pose a hazard or require size reduction. They should have an understory structured like the ribs of an umbrella. If you stand under the canopy of a mature avocado tree and look up, you will see that the scaffolds, the laterals, and even the dead branches combine to support the outer canopy. This growth pattern exposes the outer foliage to the most sunlight and protects the fruit from sun as it hangs under the leaves.

Most of the heavy pruning of deciduous specialty fruit trees occurs in late winter while the trees are dormant. (See also Winter Maintaining.)

PROTECTING

Fruit trees are prime targets for foraging squirrels, opossums, and rats. Wherever there is ripe fruit, they will find them. Wild creatures are part of the natural order of things, and if there is plenty of fruit to share and they are not damaging your trees, enjoy their company and leave them alone. If squirrels and opossums become a nuisance, trap them using a wire mesh box trap with slices of fresh fruit or sunflower seeds as bait and then relocate them to more wilderness-friendly areas, but contact your state department of fish and game for appropriate release sites. For rats, use a rat trap.

Keep birds at bay by exclusion or intimidation. Covering the tree's canopy with protective bird netting will protect the fruit from birds. Intimidate the birds by suspending free-twisting, reflective, aluminum pie pans or aluminum strips around the tree's canopy. Float shiny Mylar® balloons in and around your trees, or make a scarecrow. If there are crows invading your orchard, the University of California, ANR Communications Service ((800) 994-8849) offers a cassette recording of the "Death Cry of a Crow." This distress call frightens the flock into leaving.

Dragon fruits attract snails and slugs. The succulent nature of their stems provides shade and an environment of high humidity and decaying organic material perfect for snails and slugs. If dragon fruit plants are not trained to grow up onto a trellis, branch, or rock outcropping, they grow flat on the ground, creating a cozy habitat for snails and slugs. Control the snail and slug population by using a snail and slug bait, or iron phosphate, or by introducing decollate snails into the environment.

Repel deer by using olfactory repellants (such as odiferous bars of soap, encapsulated garlic extracts, or predatory urine products) or water-activated motion sensor detectors.

Moles are terrestrial and insectivorous and are not a threat to specialty fruits unless their tunneling damages the plant's root system. If you see evidence of damage, then use a guillotine trap.

AVOCADOS

Variety	Fruit Time	Fruit Type	Fruit Size / Fruit Skin	Fruit Color / Tree Size	Fruit Shape / Cold Hardy
Bacon	Autumn-Winter	B	8 to 12 oz. Medium thin	Dark green 15 to 20 ft.	Pear form Very
Gillogly (pp)	Summer-Winter	A	8 to 12 oz. Medium	Green 8 to 14 ft.	Obovoid Tender
Gwen (pat. #5298)	Summer-Autumn	A	7 to 12 oz. Medium	Green 6 to 16 ft.	Obovoid Average
Haas	Spring-Autumn	A	5 to 10 oz. Medium	Black 15 to 25 ft.	Obovoid Average
Holiday	Autumn-Winter	A	19 to 24 oz. Medium	Green 10 to 12 ft.	Pear-form Tender
Nabal	Summer-Autumn	B	12 to 16 oz. Medium thick	Green 20 ft.	Round Tender
Zutano	Winter	B	8 to 10 oz. Medium thin	Green 20 30 ft.	Pear form Very

The term A or B group avocado refers to an avocado's pollinating cycle. Although most avocado varieties are considered self-fruitful, avocado production can be increased 20% by growing an opposite variety amongst the desired crop.

SUMMER

An internal clock alerts the green fig beetle, the banquet maturing on the fig trees leaves little to the imagination. By the end of the day, all that is left are naked pits.

PLANNING

Organize your planting, watering, fertilizing, pruning, and pest control schedules to take summer vacations into account. Have a responsible person monitor your garden for periods of high winds, soaring temperatures, and other possible damaging conditions that might occur while you are away.

Inform the caretaker of the locations of the water meter, gas meter, and any other utilities that affect the residence. Make a list of plants that might need extra water or protection, and ask that those plants be moved into the shade if the sun becomes too intense. Give your security company and neighbors the name and phone number of the caregiver and the approximate time of day he or she will be in the yard. Leave emergency phone numbers and the locations where you can be reached if the caregiver has any questions.

PLANTING

Avoid planting fruit trees during dry, hot weather. If you have selected and must plant your fruit trees under conditions that are hot, dry and windy, dig the planting pit and fill the pit with water to wet the surrounding soil. Amend the backfill with organic material. Add a controlled-release fertilizer (15-15-15) to the backfill. Ensure that the trees are thoroughly hydrated the evening before planting. If there is a choice, wait until late afternoon or early in the morning. There will be less stress from

transplanting shock. Apply an antitranspirant to help prevent transplant shock.

Dragon fruit tree can be transplanted into larger containers anytime unless there is the threat of cold damage. The optimum time to plant is during early summer when the root system has time to reestablish itself. If you plant in fall, they might push rapid, new, and tender growth that would be susceptible to frost damage.

WATERING

Monitor the moisture content of the soil weekly by using a moisture meter (tensiometer) or by the time-tested method of pushing a soil probe 12 inches into the soil. The soil should be moist, but not overly saturated. Based on what you learn from the moisture meter or soil probe, adjust the amount and frequency of water accordingly. During summer, when the temperature is high, the water needs of a tree can double or triple. If a tree stresses from lack of water, its foliage will wilt, the fruit will fall, and it may even prove fatal to it.

"Why do the fruits fall off the tree before they are ready to harvest?" is one of the most frequently asked question on our (Bruce and Sharon) garden program. The most common cause is the repetitive fluctuation of the soil moisture level, when the soil becomes rapidly wet then dries, rapidly becomes wet again then dries. The fruit fall is particularly evident between midspring and early summer.

June drop is another reason fruits may suddenly fall. The phenomenon occurs most commonly during late spring or early summer when there is a rapid change in moisture availability or climatic conditions, or if there is a bumper crop. It is Mother Nature's way of culling to protect the tree. Persimmons, peaches, nectarines, and apricots are among the most susceptible fruit trees to experience June drop.

FERTILIZING

Apply a dry organic fruit tree fertilizer every sixty days starting in late winter, continuing through midsummer. If you prefer a liquid organic fruit tree food, follow the schedule under Spring Fertilizing. For varieties whose fruit mature early, one additional application of a liquid organic fertilizer can be made just after the fruit is harvested.

MAINTAINING

Control sucker growth by applying a plant growth regulator (napthalene-acetate acid, or NAA) to the suckers as they emerge from below the bud or graft union, or from lateral roots near the surface of the ground.

In the past, fruit trees were not pruned in summer, but now it is an accepted practice. Summer pruning reduces the volume and height of the tree's canopy when the canopy starts to become unmanageable and shortly after the fruit has been harvested. Our rule is, "One should be able to harvest the fruit by hand or with a telescoping fruit picker while standing on the ground." It is much too dangerous climbing atop tall ladders and teetering to reach fruits up high.

Remove errant growth such as suckers that sprout from below the bud or graft union or from shallow lateral roots.)

PROTECTING

Use safe summer insect controls and techniques when protecting any plant with edible parts from chewing, sucking, and rasping insects. Wash foliage off early in the morning with a strong stream of water, ridding the foliage of aphids, leaf hoppers, and caterpillars. Apply controls such as a garlic extract or Neem oil.

Cotinis texana, commonly known as green fig beetle, are most active when summer fruits are reaching maturity. Bird damage to the skin exposes the interiors of fruits, and the 1 to $1^1/2$-inch iridescent green beetles swarm around the openings. They sound like buzz bombs and maneuver like helicopters when they are attacking the fruit. The female beetles lay their eggs below the ground, in compost or in dung piles. The eggs hatch and then the larvae feed on roots and decaying organic material. Control the adults by netting and disposing of them, and control the larvae by using *Bacillus thuringiensis* (Bt) on the compost piles where they dwell.

To protect ripening fruit from birds, we have had moderate success floating helium-filled Mylar® balloons. Their reflective surfaces seem to deter birds, especially when we draw large, fearsome eyes on the balloons with a marker. Another option is to hang strips of Mylar®, aluminum foil, or glittering CD discs. Often it is a race to see who gets to eat the fruits first, we or the birds. We usually harvest our fruits when they are still slightly firm and ripen them indoors, but we leave enough for our winged friends, too.

AUTUMN

The bacon, fuerte, and zutano avocados mature during the cooler seasons. Like their other avocado cousins, their flowers are complete but male and female parts function at different times during the day.

PLANNING

The foliage on the selected deciduous specialty fruit trees have petioles (leaf stems) that attach the leaves to the twigs of the tree and conduct water and nutrients used in photosynthesis. At the base of the petiole, an abscission layer desiccates them as the seasonal changes occur. Prior to leaf fall, some nutrients are released to the growing tips and are stored in the leaves. The autumn tradition of recycling the fallen leaves is an event we should embrace.

PLANTING

Specialty fruits, whether deciduous, evergreen, or cactus, can be planted in early autumn if they are being transplanted from containers and have established root systems. But be warned: If warm weather stimulates growth hormones to put out new foliage, the tender growth is susceptible to cold damage. When in doubt, wait until late winter as long as the ground is not frozen, or early spring. The cost of bare-root varieties make them much more affordable, and available inventories are at their peak.

WATERING

Reduce the watering frequency and amount to accommodate the slower growth rate of the trees and the cooler temperatures, but never allow the soil to dry to the point the tree becomes stressed.

If you are using well water to irrigate your plants, autumn is when the water table is at its lowest. When this occurs, the concentration of total dissolved solids (TDS) is high; the concentration of total dissolved solids usually peaks in late summer. Use calcium sulphate or calcium chloride to temporarily loosen clay soils. The results will help irrigation water move through the surface of the soil and into the root zone.

Drain irrigation lines before the ground freezes if you live in an area where water freezes in the irrigation lines.

FERTILIZING

Increasing the sugar level in a plant's system increases its ability to weather winter conditions. Adequate levels of potassium should be made available to accommodate this winterization. Potassium in the form of kelp meal, greensand, wood ash, or sulfate potash (0-0-8) should be applied in early autumn, at a rate directed by the formulator. The potassium will help optimize the winterization of your trees.

Be cautious about using rapidly available mineral or synthetic nitrogen. Its use should be kept to a minimum because of its negative effect on soil microorganisms. Nitrogen stimulates new and frost-tender growth. If the new growth does not have time to harden off, severe damage could occur in the plant's canopy.

MAINTAINING

If summer growth produced suckers from the base of the trunk or from the lateral roots, remove them by pulling or pruning them off. Then apply a plant growth hormone (NAA) to the wound to suppress the regrowth. Sealing the wounds with pruning paint where the suckers were removed has been shown to reduce regrowth somewhat, but the application slows down the natural callusing of the exposed area.

Rebuild and expand the watering basins around the trees in anticipation of winter rains. The basins should have a radius 10 to 20 percent greater than the radius of the drip line of the tree's canopy. Maintain a 1- to 2-inch layer of compost, humus mulch, worm castings, or comparable organic material to stabilize soil moisture and temperature.

Clean out the street gutters, roof gutters, downspouts, exposed French drains, catch basins, dry wells, and flowage easements of leaves, bird nests, twigs, and debris that have accumulated since last winter.

Hard pruning stone fruit trees in autumn is a process that is usually scheduled in late winter or early spring, while the trees are still dormant. But if the tree overgrew during spring and summer and you are the kind of gardener who doesn't like to procrastinate, pruning in fall as soon as it goes dormant is fine. Your pruning chores will be done before the winter holiday season. If your garden requires an additional amount of potassium, it can be derived from the wood ash left over from the burning of garden debris.

Survey your fruit tree to ensure the branching structure is stable and will be able to withstand the freezing cold, chilling winds, foraging deer, and water-saturated soils of autumn, winter, and early spring.

PROTECTING

Deciduous fruit trees—including apples, pears, persimmons, figs, and apricots—are susceptible to disease and insect infestations during the growing season. Many of these pests remain on the surface or just under the plant's trunk and branches during fall and winter. Use a suffocant such as a horticultural oil to control most over-wintering insects and diseases that plague specialty fruit plants.

Peach leaf curl is a fungal disease that affects peach and nectarine trees. The foliage of these trees becomes blistered, deformed, and stressed, eventually falling to the ground. To control peach leaf curl, spray your peach and nectarine trees three times with calcium polysulfide. The first application should be made in autumn after the leaves have fallen, the second application at the end of December, and the third and last time just before the buds swell and show color in spring (the popcorn stage); this last application is the most important. Before all applications, check your local weather conditions to make sure it won't rain within seventy-two hours of the applications. If rain is predicted, wait until there are at least three days of clear dry weather predicted.

For apples, pears, pomegranates, apricots, persimmons, and plums, apply a general clean-up dormant spray such as Bordeaux mix (copper sulphate). Do not apply copper sulphate on your peaches or nectarines; it is not an effective control for peach leaf curl. For peaches and nectarines, use calcium polysulfide following the label directions. Apply at the same intervals as the control for peach leaf curl.

For *all* types of controls, follow the formulator's directions to the letter.

WINTER

The darkened silhouettes of barren apple and apricot trees hold the promise of renewal in spring. Before the sap surges and latent buds swell and show color, prune the tree canopy for spring's arrival.

PLANNING

The following are steps for establishing deciduous specialty fruit trees.

- The movement of water down and through the tree's root zone is one of the most important considerations in selecting a planting location. If water does not percolate down and away but saturates the root zone, anaerobic pathogens, such as water molds, quickly invade the roots and destroy the ability to absorb water and nutrients. Determine the percolation rate by excavating an 18-inch-deep by 18-inch-wide test hole. Fill it with water, let it drain; fill it with water a second time. The second filling should drain at a rate of 1 inch per hour. If water is still standing at the bottom of the hole after eighteen hours, the planting pit should be substantially larger than criteria established under Planting or you should construct a raised bed.

- Select bare-root specialty fruit varieties that are suitable for your location, especially noting the recommended chill hours and whether or not it is self-fruitful or needs a pollinator. Look also for a strong graft or bud union, few or no broken roots, and a branching pattern that will develop into an open-vase-shaped canopy.

- Fruit trees are rated by the number of chill hours needed to bloom and set fruit. For an accurate estimate of chill hours, purchase a recording thermometer available at most agricultural supply stores. Total the accumulated hours below 45 degrees Fahrenheit during fall, winter, and early spring. This will help you select appropriate fruit tree varieties for your area. You can also contact your local county agricultural department for historical chill-hour records.

- Determine how a particular fruit tree is pollinated, and whether or not it is self-fruitful. Many are not self-fruitful and need at least one or two compatible cultivars planted within 100 feet of each other in order to bear fruit.

- Consider how much space is available and what type of fruit tree is best for your needs, whether standard, semi-dwarf, or dwarf.

- Survey your yard for a full-sun and wind-protected location. Locating the tree in full sun is absolutely necessary to optimize fruit production. Calm, wind-protected areas also encourage insect pollinators around your fruit trees.

- Determine the pH of the soil. Nutrient availability for plant growth is adversely affected if the pH is too high or too low. The pH range should be a little on the acidic side or neutral, between 6.5 and 7.0.

- Consult your local garden center, arboretum, public gardens, University of California Extension office fruit specialist, and neighbors for appropriate recommendations of fruits and cultivars that flourish where you live, as well as potential pest and disease problems.

PLANTING

If the above planning criteria are satisfactory, consider the following procedures.

Excavate a planting pit. The pit should be one to one and a half times the depth of the rootball and two to three times as wide. If the texture of the soil is a sandy loam, there is no need to blend an organic amendment into the backfill. If the soil is fine textured, dense, and clayey, increase the size of the planting pit to at least four times the width of the rootball. The backfill should also be blended with organic material, such as compost, humus mulch, planting mix, worm castings, or a comparable amendment. Ultimately, the backfill should consist of 30 percent organic material. Rough up the interior surface of the planting pit by scratching the vertical surfaces with a cultivator.

If there has been gopher activity in the area, line the planting pit with chicken wire, making sure the piece is large enough to encircle the rootball, and gather the chicken wire edges around the base of the trunk. Prefabricated gopher baskets are also available at your local garden center or agricultural supply store.

Shovel some of the backfill mix into the bottom of the planting pit, bringing the bottom level up to the point where the top of the rootball will be an inch above the finished elevation of the native soil (do not let the top of the rootball settle into the planting pit). Planting the rootball a little high compensates for the inevitable settling.

Position the rootball into the center of the planting pit. If the tree has been grafted or budded, position the bud or graft union facing north, away from the sun.

Shovel the backfill mix into and around the rootball, wetting the soil simultaneously. Wetting the soil as you fill in the planting pit collapses any air pockets around the rootball.

Create a watering basin around the base of the tree by constructing a berm, 4 to 6 feet in diameter and 4 to 6 inches high.

Mulch the surface of the ground in the watering basin with 2 to 3 inches of organic material such as compost, humus mulch, compost, worm castings, or comparable amendment.

WATERING

The first step after planting is to fill the watering basin with water and let the water percolate. Fill it again and give it three applications of a root stimulator, one week apart. The initial deep soakings continue to collapse any air pockets next to the absorbing roots, enabling the plant to hydrate more completely.

Reset the times and frequencies on your irrigation clocks to compensate for seasonal changes in the weather. Historically, California's rainy season occurs from late fall to early spring; during this time, you should monitor the soil moisture. If your soils are clayey and it rains a lot, the soil will saturate and anaerobic pathogens will invade the plant's root system. To mitigate the effects of anaerobic pathogens, aerate the soil.

FERTILIZING

Discontinue fertilizing during winter. Applying a rapidly available chemical fertilizer to specialty fruit trees in winter might stimulate new growth, especially if the application coincides with a warm spell, as in the case of an El Nino. Any subsequent cold weather damages the new growth.

MAINTAINING

Spray your cherimoya, avocado, and dragon fruit with an antitranspirant if the weather forecasters are predicting freezing temperatures. The film that is left on the leaf surface functions like a layer of insulation.

Container-grown dragon fruit trained onto trellises can be easily covered with an old cotton sheet for cold protection. Do not use plastic sheeting, clear or black, to cover your plants because plastic is a poor insulator. Another method of protecting your frost-sensitive specialty fruit trees and cacti is to keep a layer of mulch, compost, or worm castings over the root system. If you already maintain a blanket of mulch over the roots, consider increasing the area by 10 percent each year for seven years.

If you maintain a mulch layer on the soil surface, cultivate it periodically to keep the layer from crusting over and restricting the exchange of air in and out of the soil.

Winter is the perfect season to add flocculent to the soil. Gypsum ($CaSO_4$) has been used for decades to improve the soil, but its effect is temporary at best. Other products containing humic acid, mychorrizae fungi, and saponin are much more effective and have a lasting effect.

Deciduous specialty fruit trees, such as stone fruit trees, go dormant during winter to rest and protect themselves from cold winter conditions. Prune during their dormancy before their sap begins to surge in early spring.

Pruning enhances fruit production and helps maintain the tree's structural integrity. The first three years of seasonal pruning establishes the structure of the future shape of the tree's canopy. If a sapling tree has a single leader when you acquire it, prune the top off so that the top branch bud is 3 to 4 feet above the ground. During the second and third winter season, continue to prune the tree, developing an open-vase form by pruning out interfering, diseased, or dead branches. Deciduous specialty fruit trees, such as apples, apricots, and plums, blossom and set fruit on spurs. Spurs are short stubby branches that are viable for five to seven years. Fruiting spurs develop on branches that are at least one year old, so maintaining a framework that will sustain many, many spurs is one goal of pruning.

Dragon fruit plants crawl on supporting structures, such as trees, trellises, and arbors. They are considered epiphytic or terrestrial, and in either case, they need support. Pruning is only necessary when you want to replicate the plant by stem cuttings or to increase fruit production by encouraging additional stems. Prune also if errant growth causes the plant to become unsightly or unbalanced.

PROTECTING

The rodents are sequestered away in the burrows; the caterpillars have spun cocoons around themselves and are now chrysalises; the birds have flown south for the winter; the lizards, frogs, and toads have burrowed into a safe place and are nestled into the ground. All activity has slowed except for the coyotes and deer.

Control deer by stretching 100-pound-test clear monofilament fishing line, deer-chest high, around the part of the yard you want to protect.

Control coyotes by calling the animal control agency or the American Humane Society.

SELECTED SPECIALTY FRUITS

Variety	Fruit Time	Chill Hours Tree Shape	Skin Color Self Fruitful	Flesh Color Comments
Fuji Apple	Summer-Autumn	400 Globe	Green/red Yes	Cream/white Excellent flavor
Goldkist Apricot	Summer-Winter	300 Decurrent	Orange/red Yes	Yellow Heavy bearer
El Bumpo Cherimoya	Winter-Spring	Tropical Globe	Green Yes/no	White Sweet flavor
Pitaya Dragon Fruit	Summer	Tropical Oval	Yellow Yes	White Excellent flavor
Kate Sessions Lychee	Summer	Tropical Round	Red Yes	White Alternate crop
Donut Peach	Summer	400 Doughnut	Peach Yes	White Almond flavor
Fuyu Persimmon	Autumn	200 Up/open	Orange/red Tes	Orange Non-astringent
Santa Rosa Plum	Summer	300 Up/V-shape	Purple/red Yes	Orange/red #1 plum
Eversweet Pomegranate	Autumn	150 Large shrub	Red Yes	Clear Seedless fruit
Double Delight Nectarine	Summer	100 Dwarf tree	Dark red Yes	Yellow The best

MORE PRUNING TIPS

Flush cuts are no longer recommended. Those are cuts made flush with the surface of the supporting branch. Cuts should be made just outside the branch bark ridge (the wrinkle of bark extending from the "V" at its point of attachment) and the collar (the raised bark below the "V"). This exposes the least amount of surface to insect and disease damage. Begin by cutting *up from the lower side* of the branch 10 to 20 percent of the diameter, finish by cutting *down from the upper side* to meet the first cut. This sequence prevents injuring the remaining portion of the supporting branch.

Applying a sealing compound over pruning cuts slows down natural compartmentalization (sealing off areas of injury). If, however, there is damaging insect or disease activity nearby it might be prudent to seal the wound.

See pages 55, 229, 293, 298, 302, 306, and 309 for more pruning information.

CHAPTER ELEVEN

California Trees

Trees are astonishingly diverse and adaptable. One grove of bristle-cone pines—the oldest living of trees—has survived an estimated 4,000 to 5,000 years in the gale force winds of California's White Mountain Range. The world's tallest trees, California's coastal redwoods, flourish under incessant rainfall. And the California fan palm endures searing desert heat.

Sacramento—known as the "City of Trees"—has a unique organization called "The Right Tree in the Right Place Committee." Charged with maintaining the city's urban forest, it works to maintain a diversity of tree species. Some municipalities have allowed one species of tree to cover an entire city—with often tragic results. If insects or pathogens invade one tree, the malady can quickly decimate an entire urban forest.

Just like Sacramento's Tree Committee, we believe there is the right tree for the right place somewhere in your garden.

In Our Garden

Of all the plants we cultivate, trees are the most dominant embellishment and the most permanent. They are the scene-setters and the mood-makers.

No matter the season, trees are among the loveliest of living things. They help produce the air we breathe, trap and hold pollutants, offset the build-up of carbon dioxide, control and stabilize the climate, reduce water loss, feed and shelter wildlife, serve as visual and noise-filtering screens, and supply lumber and fuel.

Trees are also our spiritual sanctuaries, teaching us to reach for the skies. In one of my (Sharon) favorite stories, Jean Giono's *The Man Who Planted Trees*, Elzeard Bouffier spends his entire life transforming a desolate region of barren land and raging winds. By planting a forest of trees, life around him is reborn, filled with gentle breezes rustling though the leaves like the sound of water from the mountains. And in the process, he too is reborn.

As gardeners and lovers of trees, our family has planted many trees. They are the source of gardening inspiration and the connection to our past, present, and future—because without trees, there would be no miracle of life.

FIREWHEEL TREE
Stenocarpus sinuatus

Years ago, our firewheel tree grew slowly, but it was such a handsome tree that we didn't mind its bloomless nature. Just as we were moving, brilliant red flowers with glowing, gold stamens arranged like a wheel burst forth. They resembled crowns of rubies decorated at their points with citrine-yellow stones. Firewheel is a wonderful accent near swimming pools.

E. Australia / Zones 10 to 11 / full sun / height 20 to 30 feet / width 15 feet / flowers summer to autumn

FOREST PANSY REDBUD
Cercis canadensis 'Forest Pansy'

Forest pansy redbud is perfect as an ornamental specimen for small gardens. In early spring, dark-rose painted buds open into clusters of tiny, deep pink, sweet-pea-shaped flowers that bloom profusely on bare branches. By late spring, leaves mature into intense scarlet-purple, heart-shape. Autumn is a blaze of yellows, oranges, and reds. Even in winter, its rounded silhouette brings a quiet focus to the garden.

E. Central USA / Zones 7 to 11 / full sun, part shade / height 12 to 20 feet / width 15 feet / flowers spring

JAPANESE MAPLE
Acer palmatum

Known as the coral bark maple, 'Sango Kaku' is our favorite. With bare, coral-red bark in winter, blazing fall foliage, and fresh, red-tinged spring and summer leaves, 'Sango Kaku' is effectively displayed in patios, in lawns, or among ferns and azaleas. Most of all, it is a welcome sight of brilliant color in the winter landscape.

Korea and Japan / Zones 6 to 11 / part shade / height 12 to 15 feet / width 12 to15 feet / flowers insignificant

SPRING

Rhythms of trees in spring become the heart and soul of our gardens. It is the season of renewal, and trees become havens for skittering squirrels and sound stages for colorful chattering songbirds.

PLANNING

If you select the right tree for the right place, it should serve you well with little or no care. Pause for a minute before you select a tree for your garden; take a drive through your neighborhood, and list the mature trees that exhibit exceptional form, color, and proportion. Give special attention to street trees and trees growing in commercial developments. Most municipalities have planning and maintenance departments, whose certified arborists or landscape architects review and recommend approval or denial of permits. Trees used for commercial developments are usually inexpensive and fastest growing, with aggressive roots; be wary of these species. Seeing mature trees will give you an idea of how their root systems will develop in the local soils and whether they require an inordinate amount of maintenance to remain safe. Trees with exposed surface roots that are causing concrete or asphalt drives to break apart, clogging sewer line, or shattering retaining walls are usually growing in shallow soils or in clayey, dense, poorly aerated soils. They can also indicate poor irrigation practices or perhaps the wrong species for the location.

When selecting trees, be aware of their eventual sizes and characteristics—accentuate their positives and be mindful of their negatives. For example, maidenhair trees tolerate freezing temperatures, withstand extreme wind loads, have beautiful autumn color, adapt to limited spaces, and grow in just about any soil type. But gender matters when it comes to female maidenhair trees. They have an unpleasant odor called *Gingko Stink* when their nuts mature in late summer or early autumn. We advise you to plant only male trees.

Other examples include acacias and magnolias, which grow rapidly (20 percent a year) after they become established but can also be counted on to drop their leaves each time a new flush of growth occurs. Silk oaks, ashes, sycamores, willows, and alders are all deciduous, which makes their presence upwind from a swimming pool a disaster in autumn when their leaves fall.

PLANTING

After you have selected a tree and determined the planting location:

1. Excavate a planting pit that is one to one and a half times the depth of the container and four times the width. If the percolation test results were acceptable and the soil texture is a sandy loam, then minimal soil preparation is necessary. In fact, if the tree is endemic to your area, amending backfill is usually not necessary. But if water percolates too rapidly, blend the excavated soil with organic amendments that will function as a natural sponge. If the water percolates too slowly, increase the size of

the planting pit to accommodate the slower percolation rate. Or install a French drain (a sloping trench filled halfway with $3/4$-inch gravel, which is covered with 6-millimeter black plastic then topped with soil), or use a 4-inch-diameter perforated ABS or PVC drain line (maintaining a minimum 2 percent sloping flow line).

2. Fill the excavated planting pit with enough prepared backfill to ensure the top of the tree's rootball will be an inch above the finished elevation of the native soil. As you fill the planting pit, compress the backfill by tamping down with your feet to reduce settling.

3. Lay a containerized tree on the ground and knock off the container with a mallet. If the tree's rootball has been growing in a fiber pot and is rootbound, stand the tree up and make three evenly spaced vertical cuts down its side. Fold down the three sections of the container's sidewall, and remove the rootball; then loosen the matted roots with a knife or a hand cultivator. Place the rootball into the bottom of the pit; then shovel enough blended backfill around the rootball to stabilize the tree. Soak the backfill with enough water to collapse the air spaces around the roots; shovel in and compress enough backfill to fill the planting pit, and resoak. If the tree was field grown, balled and burlapped, and transported to your local garden center, the planting procedures are the same, except the burlap coverings and bindings are loosened and rolled back from the rootball before the backfilling and initial watering takes place.

Build a 6-inch soil berm, 2 feet outside the drip line of the tree or 6-foot diameter, whichever is wider. This dimension will create an oversized watering basin that will encourage lateral root growth. Fill the basin twice to settle the soil in the planting pit; then apply root stimulator once a week for three weeks. If the tree is young, a year-old sapling, and tied tightly to a single stake, it is probably being girdled, so cut the ties and remove the stake, and then pound in two 6-foot tree stakes $1^1/2$ feet into the ground, each on opposite sides of the tree and about 1 foot away from its trunk. Use flexible garden ties to create a figure-eight pattern around the trunk and the two stakes to support the tree without harming it.

If you have selected a California native tree to plant and the soil is free draining, there is no need to amend the backfill. Just excavate the planting pit to the same dimensions as if you were planting a container tree. If the native tree has been growing in a container for a long time, you can expect the roots to be bound. Alleviate this rootbound condition by shaving off the matted root layer with a knife or loosening it with a cultivator. Removing the matted roots might set the reestablishment of the tree back a few months, but in the long run, the tree will be stronger and healthier when the new roots grow out. Encourage new root growth by applying a root stimulator.

WATERING

"Deep watering promotes deep rooting" is an old nursery adage. Absorbing roots move through the soil cell by cell, ferreting out moisture and nutrients for photosynthesis. Absorbing roots will not move into soils that are dry and airless, so it is important to determine the percolation rate at where the tree is to be planted. See Winter Planning for details. If drainage is good, you will know that there won't be standing water in the root zone and that deep soakings once every seven to ten days during the growing season should be adequate

For established trees, two to four hours after watering, use a moisture meter and probe the soil near the tree's drip line to make sure water has percolated 18 to 24 inches. If the soil is still dry at the probe depth, then the next time you irrigate, extend the watering time.

Japanese maples are very sensitive to salt buildup in the soil. Keep the soil moist, but not soggy. Every other month, add a surfactant (wetting agent) to the irrigation water; this will facilitate dissolving and leaching the salts. If you use a garden hose to water, a simple and practical method to add surfactant to the irrigation water is to attach a siphoning device between the hose bib and the garden hose. Once the siphoning device is in place, fill a bucket with a solution of the surfactant and drop the siphoning tube into the solution; the mixture is added to the water as it flows through the hose. Fertilizer injector systems are available for adding nutrients to the water as the trees are being irrigated.

The karo tree from Australia is a low-care, drought-tolerant tree that can be easily over-watered, especially if it's growing in dense, clayey soil. It is important to monitor the soil moisture before another irrigation cycle is started. If you doubt the moisture content, use a tensiometer (moisture meter).

FERTILIZING

As spring transitions from winter, many trees, especially Japanese maple and forest pansy redbud, require a boost. Their swelling terminal buds indicate that sap is rising within them and that their absorbing roots are expanding in search of water and nutrients. During early spring, apply a complete dry organic fertilizer with equal proportions of NPK (5-5-5), at a rate of $1/2$ pound per inch of trunk diameter measured 18 inches above the ground. For example, at 18 inches above the ground, the diameter of a trunk measures 6 inches, so the tree requires 3 pounds of fertilizer. Evenly distribute the fertilizer in a band just inside and at the base of the berm that makes the watering basins. Then repeat the application in early summer and early autumn to encourage even growth.

If you prefer to use liquid organic fertilizers because of their rapid availability and convenience, winterize the tree by applying five times: late winter, early spring, late spring, early summer, and early autumn. Use the siphoning device (with an anti-siphon safety feature) to add the organic liquid fertilizer to the water as you irrigate.

Controlled-release (CR) fertilizers are another option for fertilizing trees; they are convenient, complete, and reliable. The CR fertilizers evenly mete out nutrients over a prescribed period, so if the formulator's directions are followed, there is scant possibility of trees stressing from overfertilization. On average, CR fertilizers are applied in early spring and then every four to six months.

Also every sixty to ninety days from early spring through early autumn, water-in a soil rejuvenator high in humic acid. (See page 270.)

MAINTAINING

Suppress annual and perennial weeds before the seasonal rains, warming temperatures, and increasing hours of daylight spawn an army of noxious, invading weeds. You can save many, many hours of tedious weed pulling by applying, before the weed seeds germinate, a liquid or granular preemergent weed control or by mulching the exposed soil surface with a 2-inch layer of humus mulch, compost, worm castings, or comparable cover. Another alternative is to hoe them out as they begin to grow.

In early spring, before the sap rises in your trees, prune out all dead, diseased, damaged, or dangerous branches. Accomplishing this task before the new buds begin to swell will provide enough time for the pruning wound to begin callusing. Pruning sealer is not necessary. (See also Maintaining.)

Do not top, thin, or head back (selectively prune) trees growing under elevated power lines; request help from the utility company. Since it is one of the most hazardous of all occupations, leave it to the professionals. Along the same line, trees should not be grown under power lines unless you receive permission to grow a tree in their right-of-way and it is a tree that will grow to the right size and require minimum care.

Trees can be the catalyst for neighborly disputes, as when branches and roots from one neighbor's tree grow over and into the other's property. If this conflict presents itself, don't sever the tree vertically at the property line, it just might topple over. If the tree happens to be a Japanese black pine, its size can be easily controlled simply by pruning off its candles (new growth). Keep a congenial relationship with your neighbor, and discuss the alternatives for solving the problem; otherwise, there are attorneys that specialize in landscape conflicts.

California has one of the world's most diverse permanent bird populations and is part of one of the world's longest migratory flyways. Many clusters of trees become rookeries for the migratory birds, so if possible, don't prune your trees until the fledglings have left their nesting sites (early spring to early summer). Contact your local Audubon Society to find in which months and in what areas birds do most of their nesting. If at all possible, refrain from heavy pruning during their breeding times.

PROTECTING

Warming spring weather makes trees an easy target for chewing, sucking, and rasping insects. Save time, expense, and frustration over the long term by controlling the insect population early. If your trees are growing where there are no plants with edible parts, use a systemic insect control with imidacloprid as its active ingredient. Imidacloprid translocates up into a tree's canopy 80 to 100 feet and remains effective in the tree's system for one year. It's an effective and convenient insect control for ornamental trees.

For natural pest controls, consider Neem oil or a garlic- or pyrethrin-based control. (See also pages 140 and 150.)

Spring's typically cool and damp weather is the perfect environment for snails and slugs. To stop them dead in their trails, pick and squish in the early morning or use a molluscicide with iron phosphate as its active ingredient. Iron phosphate is organic and can be used in areas that have plants with edible parts; it's safe around pets and small children. Another advantage is that eventually iron phosphate degrades into fertilizer. Create snail barriers by wrapping 2-inch-wide copper strips around the trunks of trees (about a foot off the ground).

To protect your trees from parasitic fungi such as mildew, apply a control with Daconil™, but if an organic control is preferred, use tea tree extract or Neem oil. Organic controls usually require a more frequent spraying regimen, about once a week, for two to three weeks or until the fungi are eradicated.

As summer progress, rodents and other furry creatures may invade your garden and forage for food. Capture them with a critter-friendly trap and relocate them to a more wilderness-friendly neighborhood.

If pocket gophers are active in the area, as a deterrent, consider placing the rootball of a new sapling in a gopher basket fabricated using chicken wire or hardware cloth.

Roof rat control includes rat bait placed in bait stations (to protect children and pets from consuming the bait), and live traps.

Guillotine traps are the most effective control for burrowing, insectivorous moles and gophers; or use manual traps or bait. To keep deer out of your garden, use motion-activated watering sensors or try olfactory repellents. Unless rabbits, raccoons, skunks, squirrels, and opossums are causing a great deal of damage to your trees, leave them alone and let them roam at will.

FERTILIZING

The thin veneer of soil, which has taken thousands of years to develop, is where the roots of a plant, helped by beneficial soilborne microorganisms, absorb moisture and nutrients to transport them into the plant canopy. In regions where rainfall is minimal, this soil profile can be as shallow as 2 inches but in regions where rainfall is plentiful and plants flourish, the depth of the soil profile can be in excess of 20 feet. The fertility of the soils is automatically suspect when the soil profile is shallow and there are few varieties of plants.

Natural sources for nutrients, both organic and mineral, benefit the entire soil ecosystem. Soils are alive with trillions of beneficial microorganisms. When natural nutrients are applied to the soil these beneficials are fed, thereby improving soil quality and ultimately providing for the plants growing above. Another advantage of using natural sources is they provide nutrients as plants require them; for instance, if an application of cottonseed meal is made in midautumn and the plant is already entering dormancy, the nutrients would not dissolve and leach out but would be available in spring when the plant breaks dormancy. In addition, if there is a mulch blanket over the root zone and the soil temperature does not drop below 32 degrees Fahrenheit, the nutrients will continue to feed the soil (and roots) through winter.

Knowing when to fertilize seems like a mystery. Here is a clue: If the soil is nutrient deficient there are usually changes in leaf color. Primary nutrients (nitrogen, phosphorus, and potassium) easily translocate (move) throughout a plant, so changes in leaf color—usually a loss of green—occur near the bottom and inside the plant first. Secondary and micronutrients do not easily translocate through a plant's canopy, so their deficiencies (leaf yellowing) usually show up on top and at the ends of the branches. This is a general observation but it has held true in our gardens.

An antiquated, but economical, practical, and expeditious way of applying liquid fertilizers is to use a siphoning device attached between a hose-bib and a garden hose. Once the siphoning device is in place, fill a bucket with a solution of fertilizer, drop the siphoning tube into the solution, and the mixture will be added to water as it flows through the hose. These devices are available at your local garden center. The newer models are designed with a backflow control designed into its system.

SUMMER

The summer season is midpoint of a tree's yearly rhythm; from new leaves and flowers in spring to the reclusive dormancy of winter, summer is the season of photosynthesis, the engine that enables all life.

PLANNING

An integral step in your planning is to decide how large your tree fund should be before you commit to other landscape projects. The cost of a tree can be astronomical—especially if the tree is a specimen Australian firewheel tree with multiple trunks and perfect form. The tree could consume your entire set-aside funding for all your trees and shrubs (and sometimes it's worth the cost!). Specimen trees become the focal points of landscape designs, and supporting plants can always be incorporated later. Remember, we are buying time when we buy an older, larger, more developed tree when we select a specimen, but the younger, less mature sapling is apt to adapt more quickly than the older tree to a new set of growing conditions.

PLANTING

It takes a certain amount of optimism to plant a tree during summer because searing heat can desiccate a newly planted tree, foliage-consuming insects can strip a tree in a week, and unseen underground varmints, such as pocket gophers, can destroy a sapling's root system as they munch their way through your garden.

Steps can be taken to reduce the stresses caused by summer conditions. Reduce moisture loss by removing 40 to 60 percent of the tree's foliage and then spraying the remaining leaves with an antitranspirant formulated from pine pitch. This antitranspirant coats leaf surfaces (bottom and top), effectively shutting down the process of transpiration by sealing the openings (stomata and lenticels) where air and water are exchanged to and from the atmosphere. If an antitranspirant is to be applied, the newly planted tree should be thoroughly irrigated the day before and misted with the pine pitch formulation early in the morning. Do not plant trees during midday heat or when it is dry and windy.

WATERING

Moisture evaporating from surrounding soil and transpiring from canopies are two classic causes of summertime stress in California trees. It is the hottest, driest and windiest time of the year and a time when established trees stress from a lack of water because they are growing rapidly or, if they are established native trees, because their systems have shut down and don't require irrigation.

The majority of an established tree's root system is within 2 to 3 feet of the surface and extends outward well beyond the drip line, in some cases three to five times the radius of the canopy. So trees should be irrigated not only under the canopy, but beyond the drip line, where the majority of the tree's absorbing roots are located. If the surface soil is exceptionally dry, use a surfactant (wetting agent) to facilitate percolation and the leaching of salts from the root zone.

Monitor the soil moisture weekly for three months after planting by using a moisture meter (tensiometer) to probe the soil to depths of 12 and 24 inches. If the soil is dry (2 or 3 on a scale of 10, with 10 meaning the soil is saturated) at a depth of 24 inches, give the entire root zone a thorough soaking, wetting the soil 24 to 36 inches deep. Remember that it is always better to water infrequently and deeply than often and lightly.

As a starting point to determine a watering regimen, consider the soil texture; if the texture is a sandy loam, it will take 1 inch of water on the surface to wet the soil 1 foot down. If the soil texture is a clayey loam, it will take twice that amount: 2 inches of water to wet the soil 1 foot down. These rates are approximations, but a starting point.

Forest pansy redbuds react to alkaline soils and the continual buildup of salts in the soil. Maintaining moist soil keeps the salts in solution so the trees aren't as likely to show salt burn on their foliage. Every other month, add a wetting agent to the irrigation water to help dissolve and leach salts from the root zone.

FERTILIZING

We (Bruce and Sharon) are fortunate to have several ornamental trees in our garden, including an Australian firewheel tree, a Victorian box, and a forest pansy redbud. Early summer is the second time during the year we mete out a complete organic dry fertilizer (5-5-5) to these trees. We prefer a dry fertilizer because the soil is a sandy loam and the dry form does not leach out of the root zone as quickly as a liquid formulation. In the areas of the garden where the soils are clayey, use an organic liquid formulation; for that formulation, early summer is the fourth application. (See Spring Fertilizing.)

Ornamental trees known for their splashy summer blossoms, such as pink trumpet tree, firewheel tree, African tulip tree, and tipu tree, should be fertilized after the flowers are spent and again before midautumn. If you are using the dry form of organic fertilizer, distribute the fertilizer around the inside perimeter of the watering basin (see Spring Fertilizing); then give the entire basin a thorough soaking. If the fertilizer does not wet easily, add an ounce of surfactant to 2 gallons of water, mix it with a stick, and then pour the solution over the fertilizer. Repeat the surfactant application every time the soil or mulch surface crusts and inhibits water absorption.

In addition to selecting organic fertilizers as the source of primary, secondary, and micronutrients for trees, it is helpful to increase the beneficial microorganisms' activity throughout the tree's root zone. They will occur naturally over time, but inoculating the soil with these beneficials accelerates their presences. Soil regenerators high in humic acid promote healthy soils, which in turn promotes healthy trees, so apply every sixty to ninety days from early summer when the soil dries through early autumn.

MAINTAINING

Grasses and annual weeds seem to enjoy the companionship of trees. They can be found growing among the nearby shrubs and ground covers, in watering basins, and up trees' root flares. One of the more aggressive ways of removing these weeds is to employ a serrated line cutter (a weed-whacker), but be aware that mechanical damage done by a line cutter can destroy the cambium cell layer around the tree trunk and destroy the tree.

Large branches fall to the ground during the summer doldrums for no apparent reason. But the reason is probably Sudden Summer Limb Drop, a hazard that occurs when hot air, little air movement, and heavy horizontal limbs, coupled with a minimum of moisture loss through the tree's canopy, increases pressure inside the limb. Suddenly, the limb weakens, then succumbs to gravity, crashing to the ground. To minimize Sudden Summer Limb Drop, do not overirrigate and encourage transpiration by reducing insect and disease damage to the foliage.

The errant rapidly growing shoots that develop near the root flare are called suckers; unless a coppice is desired, shoots should be cut flush at the point of origin and the exposed wound sprayed with a plant growth regulator (alpha-napthalene acetic acid, NAA) to suppress regrowth. Similarly, if rapidly growing vertical shoots go up through the canopy, they can also be pruned out or headed back into the canopy to fill a void.

There are also peculiar mutant growths called chimeras that commonly have no common characteristic with the parent tree. They are primarily curiosities and can be left to develop or can be removed to maintain a uniform character.

Prune back spring- and summer-blooming trees after the flowers are spent. Prune for shape, structure, and safety.

Remove any dead, diseased, or interfering branches. (Also see Maintaining.)

PROTECTING

If your trees become a haven for roosting crows, scaring off the other birds, float a group of helium-filled Mylar™ balloons into the tree's canopy; the sun's flashing reflection frightens crows away. Anchor the balloons in the canopy by tying them to a branch with a black nylon thread.

A few trees, such as California sycamores and crape myrtles, are prone to bouts of powdery mildew, a parasitic fungus, during the hot and humid days of the monsoon season. An effective and benign method of controlling this malady is to wash the spores off the leaf surfaces with a strong stream of water.

Protect newly planted trees from sun scorch by loosely covering the tree's canopy with a breathable horticultural cloth, and protect the tree trunk from scorching by brushing on glossy white, water-based, interior latex paint or dressing the trunk with a protective gauze wrap.

Sometimes we don't have to interfere with protective measures. For example, some trees communicate with each other. When attacked by webworms, willows emit a chemical signal that alerts other willows of the attack. A short time later neighboring willow trees respond by pumping additional tannins into their leaves, which makes it difficult for the attackers to digest their leaves.

AUTUMN

For deciduous trees, autumn is the crown jewel of the year. Their leaves turn red, gold, orange, and burgundy giving us a kaleidoscope of colors. The brilliant colors of fall are like a second spring.

PLANNING

"Bigger is better" is a dictate that does not always ring true, especially when it is concerns selecting container grown trees. An 8-foot tree growing in a 5-gallon container is likely to be rootbound and will probably never develop a proper supportive root system. On the other hand, the root system of a 5-foot tree growing in a 5-gallon container is likely to transition easily out of the rootball and into soil that has a similar texture. (If the roots are bound in their containers and can be seen protruding out of the drainage holes, avoid these trees even if they are cheap, unless they are to become bonsai).

PLANTING

Autumn is a fine time to plant most trees, especially trees that evolved in similar environments. The root systems of native trees and imported drought tolerant trees accelerate root growth from the end of summer to late autumn. Stimulated by summer-warmed soil and the onset of the California's rainy season, tree roots accelerate their growth before they shut down their systems because of winter conditions. Planting in autumn enables trees time to establish their roots prior to spring.

Autumn is also a fine time to transplant sapling and dwarf (2- to 4-foot) trees from one location to another (ground to ground). Before digging the tree, take four pictures:

one from each compass direction. Because a tree is stationary, its survival depends on defensive measures. To defend itself from the elements, including wind, rain, and sun, the tree develops thicker bark on its windward side, drops leaves under its canopy to decompose and preserve moisture, and often manufactures allelopathic compounds to ward off competing plants. When the tree is positioned in the planting pit at the new location, it should be oriented in the same relative compass direction as it was before so its defenses will continue at the new location.

Expect tree roots to expand outward from the root flare a minimum of three to four times the radius of the drip line; although roots have been observed 80 feet deep, the majority of trees' roots are located in the top 3 feet of topsoil. When preparing soil for planting or transplanting a tree, it's most important to expand the width rather than the depth of the planting pit.

Nineteen species of oak, populating California's different regions, represent the biodiversity of our state. The oaks produce acorns that germinate, grow, mature, and most important, become the custodians of the gene pool that perpetuates their species. To propagate an oak, collect acorns in late autumn when their color is changing from green to brown; decap them, then rinse them in a fungus control solution ($1/2$ cup bleach in 1 gallon of lukewarm water). Discard any damaged and floating acorns; they won't be viable. Stratify (chill at 42 degrees Fahrenheit) 2 cups of acorns in a 1-quart plastic sandwich bag for a month before planting. Plant the acorns during the rainy season (November to March) 1 inch deep in porous soil and in a sunny location. It takes from 20 to 50 years before an oak tree produces acorns . It takes from three to six years for an acorn to grow into a sapling.

WATERING

Early autumn invites the ferocious north easterlies that blow down from the Great Basin into southern California—the Santa Anas. In northern California, winds blow from the southern reaches of Oregon's Cascade Mountain Range. These hot, dry autumn winds cause trees to desiccate and become dangerously brittle. When these conditions are predicted, irrigate deeply and expansively the day before the winds ensue.

Established, drought-tolerant, and native trees do not require irrigation during the rainy season (late autumn to early spring). Provide supplemental irrigation if there is a drought and the trees show sign of moisture stress.

FERTILIZING

Autumn is the season to feed trees that are native to California or imported species that have evolved in regions of the world with similar growing conditions. Apply a complete organic fertilizer (5-5-5, 5-3-1) just before the rainy season (midautumn to early spring).

Coast live oaks, Monterey pines, Torrey pines, and Catalina cherries, all native trees, have evolved and adapted to the weather cycle and soil types that occur in California. Other trees such as the karo tree, peppermint tree, and firewheel tree react similarly to the weather and soil types.

During summer when there is little or no rain, these trees slow down their growth systems to conserve moisture. To reduce transpiration, they drop 40 to 60 percent of their foliage, and to reduce evaporation, their autumn leaves decompose and form a blanket of mulch over the root system.

Fertilizing is not necessary for tropical trees; in fact, if the trees received an application of fertilizer in autumn and begin to grow, the new growth is very susceptible to cold damage.

MAINTAINING

Together with a flexible rake, a pitchfork, and a tarp, haul out your chipper, shredder, or power blower and power vacuum to remove the blanket of leaves and debris that have accumulated below your trees. The biodegradable material should be chipped or shredded and then composted to be used as a mulch or soil amendment.

For trees that start their dormancy in autumn, saturated soils in the root zone can lead to tree-destroying anaerobic fungi called water molds. To partially relieve the condition, open the berms that form the watering basins and allow water to drain away from the soil surface around the base of the tree.

Early in autumn apply a granular preemergent to control annual bluegrass in the landscape area around the tree or add it to the mulch blanket covering the surface of the watering basin. (Mulch with a base of corn gluten or pet-safe cocoa beans.)

If the trees in your landscape are conifers or deciduous, they need little or no attention as they become dormant. It's time to adjust your irrigation clock in accordance with the changing weather conditions and growth patterns of your trees.

Autumn *is* the season to prune. Survey the structural integrity of your trees if you live in California's snow country, especially on the slopes of the southern Cascades, below the timberline of the Sierra Nevada, or among the pines of the Transverse and Peninsular range. If you find your trees' condition suspect, but are apprehensive about evaluating and correcting their weaknesses, enlist the services of a certified or consulting arborist to evaluate their conditions. Certified arborists are usually members of the International Society of Arborists and can be contacted on the Web at **www.isa-arbor.com/**. Consulting arborists are usually members of the American Society of Consulting Arborists and can be contacted on the Web at **www.asca-consultants.org**.

Examples that could lead to structural weakness in your trees are errant directional growth, hazardous cantilevers, damaged roots, and uneven weight distribution. Before the weight of a dangerous snow load accumulates in their canopies, you should have an arborist or forester evaluate the strengths and frailties of your trees.

If there are flowering trees in your landscape that bloom in clusters at the ends of their branches—such as crape myrtles, saucer magnolias, jacarandas, and Hong Kong orchid trees—heading back the branches would preclude having flowers the following spring. It is much better to head them back after they finished blooming.

Another example of heading back is the technique of *pollarding*, a procedure that has been used for centuries in Europe, initially for a renewable source for firewood, basket-weaving wood, and now for controlling fast-growing trees such as the fruitless mulberry, elms, and London plane trees. The technique employs the practice of heading back all of the tree's growth to the same point on the primary scaffolds or to the trunk.

PROTECTING

As the daylight hours dwindle and the weather cools, the snails reappear. It is as if these mollusks have an internal clock that rings its alarm when conditions are favorable. Snails put their foot into low gear and slime their way up into the tree's canopy to crunch on the tastiest foliage. An easy and safe way to stop the parade is to ring the tree trunk with a 3- to 4-foot-wide copper band. A mini-electrical current is generated when the slime below the snail's foot comes in contact with the copper.

If your trees have been victims of insect or fungi infestations during summer, apply a clean-up spray to control their next assault—consider horticultural oil.

The phrase "knock on wood" originated with primitive tree worshippers. They believed that knocking on wood would summon the protective spirits of the tree. But knocking your head on a low-growing branch can make you less spirited unless you are wearing a protective hardhat. Tree maintenance personnel have one of our nation's highest workers' compensation rates; that makes it one of the most dangerous occupations a person could be in.

Trees can be very hazardous. The following checklist helps you identify suspect trees.

- If a tree is leaning and its root system is lifting the surface soil, employ a certified arborist to tell you whether this situation is repairable or whether the entire tree and roots system should be removed.

- If a tree's branching structure is positioned over the roof of your house, it can be very disconcerting when the debris from the tree accumulates on the roof.

- If a tree's history indicates that its species does not grow well in clayey soils, it's likely to fall over when the rainy season supersaturates the soil and the soil structure loses its strength.

- If a tree develops into a coppice (an expanding group of trees)—examples include aspen, Chinese trees of heaven, toon trees, and birch trees—the trees can grow over a large area very quickly.

- If a tree has two leaders of equal importance, they can be bolted together with extra-long threaded $5/8$-inch-diameter bolts or the branching structure can be guyed with steel cables and turnbuckles.

- If a tree has been topped and hat racked, (that is, pruned leaving a stubbly portions of the tree's scaffold), the new growth is weak and breaks off during the first windstorm. This new growth emerges from latent buds just under the bark.

- If a tree has weathered the stresses of wind and rain, it should be surveyed for damage before any activity below or near the tree occurs.

- If a tree has suffered mechanical damage from construction activity, being hit by a vehicle, or by weed-whacking near its base, check for injury or insect activity.

TREE SIZES

When size is a requirement, consider: Small trees (12 to 10 feet): hawthorn (*Crataegus* species), crape myrtle (*Lagerstroemia indica*), flowering crabapple (*Malus floribunda*), saucer magnolias (*Magnolia* × *soulangiana*)

Midsized trees (20 to 40 feet): red maple (*Acer rubrum*), red horsechestnut (*Aesculus carnea*), strawberry tree (*Arbutus unedo*), catalpa (*Catalpa speciosa*), sweet gum (*Liquidambar styraciflua*), Victorian box (*Pittosporum undulatum*), littleleaf linden (*Tilia cordata*), scarlet flowering eucalyptus (*Eucalyptus ficifolia*)

Tall trees (40 feet or more): deodar cedar (*Cedrus deodara*), tulip tree (*Liriodendron tulipifera*), southern magnolia (*Magnolia grandiflora*), London plane tree (*Platanus* × *acerifolia*), coast live oak (*Quercus agrifolia*), black oak (*Quercus kelloggi*), valley oak (*Quercus lobata*)

WINTER

Think about deciduous trees and conifers in winter. It's the season when nurseries offer them to us as bare root or balled-and-burlapped. In time, they will mature into summer's shady sanctuaries.

PLANNING

When attentions turn inward during winter, it is time to do a little garden dreaming and evaluation. Think about more or less shade in the garden, the litter of leaves, the hordes of last summer's insects, and the roots surfacing in your lawn. Maybe it's time to plant a new tree next spring or autumn.

To site a new tree in your garden, begin by measuring and recording all the pertinent dimensions and information concerning your garden. Then convert the dimensions to a graphic representation on a sheet of fade-out vellum drafting paper ($1/8$-inch grid). A 1-inch line on the drawing would represent a distance of 8 feet.

First consider the following when deciding and selecting a tree:

Q. What is the tree's average mature height and width?

A. Small trees: 12 to 20 feet; midsized trees: 20 to 40 feet; tall trees: 40 feet or more

Q. What is the tree's mature form?

A. Excurrent trees have a vertical axis.

A. Decurrent trees have the traditional umbrella shape.

Q. Is the tree evergreen or deciduous?

A. Evergreen trees hold their foliage year-round.

A. Deciduous tree defoliate in autumn or winter.

Q. How much moisture does the tree require?

A. Drought tolerance requires only small quantities of water over a long period.

A. Drought avoidance is the ability to become dormant until conditions are favorable.

Q. Is the tree prone to insects or diseases?

A. Sweet gums are prone to mildew; sycamores are prone to sycamore blight; lemon-scented eucalyptus attract the lerp psyllid.

Q. Where should I commit my tree dollars?

A. A $1 tree in a $20 hole is far better than a $20 tree in a $1 hole.

Q. When is the ideal time to plant the tree?

A. Autumn is the beginning of the growing season for native trees.

A. In spring, most trees have until late autumn to reestablish themselves.

A. In summer, there is time to plant and trees are usually on special.

A. In winter, trees are available and inexpensive as bare-root or balled-and-burlapped stock.

Q. What color are its flowers?

A. Many species of trees have varieties that bear different-colored flowers.

A. Pink cloud cherry trees have spectacular spring blossoms, and crape myrtles have beautiful summer clusters of red, pink, white, or lavender flowers.

Q. Does the tree shed seeds?

A. Seeds of the sweet gum tree can be a nuisance.

A. Fruitless olive trees don't shed olives.

Q. Does the tree generate excessive pollen?

A. Acacias disperse pollen for several weeks in spring.

Q. Are its roots aggressive?

A. California and Brazilian pepper trees have extremely aggressive roots.

Q. Does the tree produce allelopathic substances?

A. Allelopathic compounds, manufactured by plants, deter other plants from growing close by; for example, the California black walnut will keep plants that are members of the Solanaceae family from growing anywhere it has roots.

Q. Are its branches likely to break?

A. Branches that grow up at narrowly acute angles are prone to breaking off.

PLANTING

Deciduous trees and field-grown conifers are available in winter as bare-root and balled-and-burlapped (B&B) inventory. Available at economical prices and in a wide variety, bare-root and B&B stock is a popular way of acquiring new trees. From growing fields in the Great Central Valley, deciduous trees are trimmed, rated, dug, cold stored, packaged, shipped, displayed, and sold to consumers to be replanted in new locations. B&B trees, mostly conifers, are field grown in Oregon and shipped south to California communities with similar growing environments and similar soil conditions, both necessary for the trees to reestablish themselves.

The planting procedure for a bare-root or B&B tree is identical to the steps outlined in the Spring Planting, except that bare-root trees should be vertically suspended under a tripod tall enough to maintain the top of the root mass an inch or two above the finished elevation of the surrounding soil. As the backfill is shoveled into the pit and between the roots, add a stream of water to make a slurry that fills the void and collapses the air pockets between the roots. This process negates the need to compress the backfill with the butt end of the shovel's handle, a technique that often injures the tree's roots.

Another difference from standard planting procedure is to leave the top of the burlap covering the rootball intact until spring to protect the root flare; then in spring loosen the ties and fold back the burlap to expose the surface of the rootball. Removing the tie will keep the trunk from being girdled.

WATERING

Watering established trees during winter is usually not necessary, unless there is an abnormal dry spell; in that case, supplemental irrigation might be necessary. Midautumn to early spring is considered the rainy season in California. Native trees such as the coast live oaks have evolved to survive in this annual wet-then-dry weather cycle. Other trees, such as the Australian firewheel tree, peppermint tree, karo tree, and the Costa Rican pink trumpet tree, come from similar conditions and have little problem adapting.

If there is little or no rain during late autumn, winter, and early spring, a thorough supplemental soaking of a tree's root zone, to a depth of 24 to 36 inches, once every forty-five to sixty days should sustain these trees.

FERTILIZING

We do not recommend fertilizing ornamental trees during winter. Deciduous trees are defoliated and dormant during winter, and fertilizing them now might stimulate new tender growth that would be vulnerable to freezing weather. Evergreen trees are, for the most part, in a state of suspended growth except for their root system, which keeps growing while the tree takes advantage of the rainy season.

MAINTAINING

Winter winds can cause irreparable damage to young trees if they are not permitted to flex and be self-supporting. Keeping young trees vertical by tying them tightly to tree stakes will not only weaken the trees but cause the tree trunks to snap as soon as the supports are removed. A young tree should not be staked; if it does require support, refer to Spring Planting.

Pruning trees during winter should not be necessary unless a hazardous condition presents itself. If torrential rain and ferocious winds are predicted, then reducing the sail area (canopy) of trees should be an immediate task.

Unless the structure of a tree becomes precarious because of freeze damage, do not prune off damaged twigs, branches, or scaffolds. Wait until new growth occurs. The new growth will indicate how deep into the tree the damage occurred. Prune out the damaged portion of the tree just above the point where the new growth is emerging.

PROTECTING

If a tree is felled and cut into lengths for firewood, stack it in full sun and away from any structures. Firewood piles can harbor a host of noxious critters: mice, crickets, bark beetle larvae, brown recluse spiders, black widow spiders, and roof rats. One of the benign methods of controlling these pests is to solarize the stacked logs during summer. The process is simple and effective. Completely cover the stacked wood with 4- or 6-millimeter clear plastic, creating a cocoon. During summer, the heat accumulated in the envelope will eliminate the unwelcome pests. (Do *not* apply pesticides to firewood; toxic fumes might disperse while the firewood is burning.)

Protect trees, young and old, from foraging deer. Many home remedies are available; scent repellents, sound repellents, and sight repellents all have their proponents, but the two most effective methods we have found are to physically exclude the deer from reaching their goal by fencing them out or by stretching around the trees to be protected, at shoulder (deer) height, 10 feet away, clear, 100-pound test, monofilament fishing line.

If the weather is mild and boring insects such as bark beetles were active during the year, consider using the pesticide imidacloprid in late winter or early spring, mixed then poured onto the ground near the root flare. The active ingredient will be absorbed and transported into the tree over 80 feet and is effective for a year.

QUESTIONS TO ASK BEFORE SELECTING A TREE

1. Is the tree evergreen (E) or deciduous (D)?

2. Does the tree have a vertical (excurrent (X)), umbrella (decurrent (D)), or (O) form?

3. Does the tree tolerate drought? (Yes (Y) or No (N))

4. What is the average mature height and width of the tree?

5. Is the tree readily available? (Y) (N)

6. Are the branches brittle? (Y) (N)

7. Does the tree have brilliant flowers (Y) (N)? or foliage? (Y) (N)

8. Does the tree require yearly pruning? (Y) (N)

9. Will the tree survive freezing weather? (Y) (N)

10. Does the tree require a host-specific mycorrhizal fungus? (Y) (N)

	1	2	3	4	5	6	7	8	9	10
African Tulip Tree	D	X	Y	50'h–20'w	Y	Y	YN	N	N	N
Firewheel Tree	E	X	Y	30'h–20'w	N	N	YN	N	N	N
Forest Pansy Redbud	D	D	Y	15'h–10'w	Y	N	YY	N	Y	N
Japanese Black Pine	E	O	Y	30'h–20'w	Y	N	NN	N	Y	Y
Japanese Maple	D	D	N	20'h–20'w	Y	N	NY	N	Y	N
Karo Tree	E	O	Y	15'h–15'w	N	N	NN	N	N	N
Peppermint Tree	E	O	Y	20'h–20'w	Y	N	NN	N	N	N
Pink Trumpet Tree	D	D	Y	30'h–40'w	Y	N	YN	N	Y	N
Tipu Tree	D	D	Y	40'h–60'w	Y	N	YN	N	Y	N
Toon Tree	D	D	Y	30'h–20'w	N	N	YY	N	Y	N

CHAPTER TWELVE

California
Tropical Plants

For many, the word *tropical* conjures up images of sandy beaches, azure-blue waters, and swaying palm trees. Gardeners, however, are more apt to imagine lush jungle-scapes teeming with giant banana leaves, frangipani flowers, and neon-colored hibiscus. For Californians in zones 9 or above, there are dozens of tropical plants from which to choose, but even those living in cooler zones can create a tropical oasis by planting cold-tolerant varieties or by utilizing containers to move sensitive tropicals into temporary winter quarters. A greenhouse, conservatory, enclosed courtyard, atrium, or entryway offers yet another solution.

The exotic canna lily looks at home under a Hawaiian sunset, but can survive freezing weather by dying back to the ground and resprouting from its roots. Bromeliads and epiphyllums are epiphytic rainforest plants, but they also adapt to the shaded canopies of trees in southern California. The unusual crown of thorns was hybridized in Thailand, but—with a little care—it will bloom on a California patio.

So dare to dabble in tropicals—you will be in for an exciting journey that will captivate all your senses.

Bruce and I (Sharon) have an eclectic mix of garden areas. There are two raised vegetable beds, a series of three terraced beds for perennials and annuals, and an ever-expanding rose garden next to an ever-diminishing lawn area. There is also a "natural" native habitat, and—for a walk on the wilder side—there are several pockets devoted to tropical plants. Banana and canna plants provide a panorama of brilliant foliage and spectacular flowers. We could not live without the fragrance of angel's trumpet or *Plumeria*, nor could we ignore the exotic beauty of pricklier tropicals, such as the bromeliads and the crown of thorns, as well as the "prickle-free" orchid cactus.

Even in colder regions of California, it is possible to create a tropical garden paradise. Our personal selections are as eclectic as our landscape, but we hope there will be some that will become part of your garden, too.

In Our Garden

BANANA SHRUB
Michelia figo

For years, we've cared for our slow-growing banana shrub. It is not particularly showy, but its fragrance more than compensates. 2-inch long, cup-shaped, yellow blossoms blushed in purplish brown exude a heady, fruity perfume—bananas. For four special weeks in spring, we linger by our banana shrub, promising to let it remain as long as it wishes.

China / Zones 10 to 11 / full sun, part shade / height 8 to12 feet / width 4 to 12 feet / flowers spring

FRANGIPANI
Plumeria rubra

Most of our frangipani are from my (Sharon's) parents and from a long-time listener. Shortly after my mother's death, our long-time listener friend gave me a photo of my parents, both beaming happily. My minister father had officiated at her son's wedding. I often think about how memories perfume the air, just as much as flowers themselves.

Mexico, Panama / Zones 10 to 11 / full sun / height 10 to 40 feet / width 10 to 15 feet / flowers spring to autumn, depending on variety

HIBISCUS
Hibiscus rosa-sinensis culivars

Hibiscus are so commonly used as hedge screens that their brightly colored blossoms are often taken for granted. But a new generation of grafted hybrids barely resembles plain, solid-colored blooms of the standard hibiscus. We meant to purchase only one grafted hibiscus and ended up with three on our patio deck and another three in our tropical garden display.

Asia / Zones 9 to 10 / full sun, part shade / height 4 to 6 feet / width 3 to 5 feet / flowers summer to autumn

For a precious few weeks in spring, the banana shrub shares its gloriously fruity fragrance with all passersby. Wafting on the wings of an afternoon breeze, no one can resist inhaling and savoring its perfume.

PLANNING

If the design of your home and landscape lends itself to a tropical look, study your climate to determine whether tropical plants are appropriate. Along coastal Southern California, parts of coastal Northern California and even a few miles inland, the climate is ideal for growing a wide variety of exotic plants. Plants from the Amazon, central Africa, Southeast Asia, and the Pacific Islands offer overwhelming choices.

Even where regions experience winter frost, it is still possible to design a tropical paradise because many plants tolerate some cold and those that do not can be planted in containers or dug up and stored until warmer weather prevails. When cold weather settles in, potted plants can be moved to more protected areas, to a greenhouse, or indoors. The other option is to select species and cultivars that are hardier under frost conditions such as canna lilies, cast iron plants and bird of paradise. Other hardier tropicals include 'Fire and Ice' heliconia and 'Dancing Lady' or 'Dancing Girl' gingers that withstand temperatures as low as 28 degrees Fahrenheit. Grafted hibiscus bears flowers as long as the day and night temperatures are above 50 degrees. They may even bloom when evenings dip into the 40-degree range, provided the days warm to above 50 degrees. For areas with winter temperatures even lower, the Chinese yellow banana and banana shrub tolerate weather down to 5 degrees.

Most tropical plants require full or partial sun in wind-protected sites. They prefer sandy loam soils (60 percent sand, 30 percent silt, and 10 percent clay) with a high, organic content to retain moisture. Tropicals are often native to regions where there is heavy rainfall and continuously decomposing organic material. Think about bromeliads growing in the canopied understory of Costa Rica's rainforest. Rainfall and foliage fill up the bromeliad cups with vital moisture and nutrients, while spiders, frogs, and other amphibians feast on the insects that might otherwise damage the plants. In this environment, beneficial microorganisms also flourish, further acidifying, aerating, and enriching the soil. Although it is difficult to create a rainforest environment in your own garden, you can grow tropical plants successfully if you provide for their temperature, humidity, soil, and moisture needs.

If the soil in the area to be planted is very dense and clayey, add a water-soluble or granular product containing humic acid (follow the application rate recommended by the formulator), as well as organic amendments such as humus, compost, peat moss, or worm castings. Water it all in with compost tea. Apply gypsum, at a rate of 10 pounds per 100 square feet, three times every four to six months as a temporary remedy. After several seasons of improving the soil with humic acid, organic materials, and compost tea, it should no longer be necessary to use gypsum. Read page 307 under Soil Rhythms and Spring Planting for more details about improving the soil texture. Container planting and raised beds are practical alternatives if you want to plant only a few tropical plants. Soil quality and remedies are limited to small, easily controlled areas, rather than an entire yard.

It is important to test the pH of the soil, if it is too acidic or too alkaline, many elements such as nitrogen, iron, and zinc are not available to the plant. Most tropical plants can survive if the soil pH is between 6.0 and 6.8. Refer to page 307 for methods to adjust soil pH.

Another important consideration is the percolation rate of water through the soil. Tropical plants do not like their roots in standing water. To determine the percolation rate, refer to page 308. Where possible, create a watering basin two to three times the diameter of the plant and one and one-half times the depth of its rootball. Since most tropical plants have root systems near the surface of the ground, encourage the development of lateral roots because air, water, and nutrients are most readily available near the surface.

PLANTING

Late spring is a perfect time to plant tropicals during their active growth cycle. For those who live in hot, dry regions, plant in early to midspring after the last frost date. This will give tropicals enough time to acclimate through the summer so that they can survive the cooler temperatures in fall and winter.

- The composition of the soil should approach 50 percent loam soil (including organic material), 25 percent air, and 25 percent water. These percentages are guidelines, but illustrate the importance of air and water being an integral part of the soil composition.
- A loam-textured soil should also include 20 to 30 percent organic material. The only other additives necessary to mix with the backfill are pH correctives. Soil sulfur or compost acidifies the soil, and dolomite lime corrects soils that are too acidic.
- If the soil excavated from the planting pit is to be used for backfill, and is similar in texture and composition to the plant's rootball, there is no need to blend planting mix or amendment with the backfill. Usually this is not the case. Refer to page 307 under Soil Rhythms.
- Shovel the backfill into the pit, bringing the soil in the bottom of the pit to a level that will lift the top of the rootball 1 inch above the top of the surrounding soil. Tamp the soil firmly as you are filling the planting pit.
- Build a 4- to 6-inch high berm around the plant to create a watering basin. The radius of the basin should be 10 to 20 percent wider than the radius of the drip line of the plant. The soil level in the basin should slope away from the root flare. This slight slope keeps the irrigation water gravitating toward the perimeter of the basin and encourages the roots to grow outward.
- Apply a 1- to 2-inch layer of organic material out to the drip line, but keep it 2 to 4 inches away from the base of the plant.
- After transplanting a new plant, thoroughly soak the root system with a water-soluble product containing

humic acid and apply a plant growth regulator containing indolebutyric acid (or alpha naphthalene acetic acid) three times, one week apart. These applications encourage new absorbing roots to develop.

Containers are practical for growing tropical plants because all that is required is a well-draining, organic potting soil and a 15-, 20- or 30-gallon container, with at least four 1-inch drainage holes at the bottom of the side wall. Add polymers to the mix for water conservation. Follow the directions, however, because adding too much can cause the moistened polymers to bubble over and make it necessary to replant. When used properly, water frequency may be reduced by 50 percent, especially for large-leafed tropicals such as banana plants, angel's trumpets, and canna lilies. If you live in an area subject to frost, make sure the containers are on casters so they can be moved easily to a more protected site or clustered together so they can be covered with a cotton sheet or horticultural blanket. If the containerized plant is placed in a saucer, set two or three bricks between the saucer and the bottom of the pot. This technique is used to keep the irrigation water from siphoning back into the bottom of the container and rotting the root system. Most tropical plants are very sensitive to saturated soils and are susceptible to root rot.

The best time to make cuttings or to transplant mature plants such as plumeria, tropical crown of thorns, or angel's trumpet is in late spring or early summer. Since they exude a milky latex and have thorns (in the case of the tropical crown of thorns), wear protective gloves. The following steps are recommended:

1. Prepare a soil mix that is 2 parts cactus planting mix, 1 part coarse perlite, and 1 part worm castings.

2. Fill a 5-gallon, black plastic nursery container with the soil mix, and moisten thoroughly.

3. Prune off two or three 18-inch sections at the ends of branches that are not in bloom.

4. At the cut end of the branch section, make four evenly spaced slices (90 degrees apart) parallel to the stem length, $1/8$ inch deep and long enough to pass through two or three leaf scars (the ridges that occur when a leaf falls). In the case of angel's trumpet, make the parallel cuts 2 to 4 inches long.

5. Set them aside out of the sun and let them callus over (dry) for three to seven days.

6. Use a dibble to push two or three 1-foot-deep holes in the soil mix, 2 or 3 inches away from the rim of the 5-gallon container (if the lengths are shorter than 18 inches, make the holes about $2/3$ the depth of the cutting length).

7. After callusing, dip the bottom end of the branch section into a rooting solution deep enough to cover the length of the $1/8$-inch cut. Place the cut end of the branch section into the planting hole, and tamp the soil around it.

8. Tie loosely to a stake for support.

9. The branch sections should begin rooting within four to six weeks.

10. Once there is evidence of foliar growth, the rooted branch sections can be separated and replanted in separate containers with new planting mix.

11. Water thoroughly, and apply a root stimulator containing indolebutyric acid or alpha naphthalene acetic acid.

12. Place the rooted plants in full sun.

Orchid cactus or "epi" is also very easy to root in late spring or early summer.

Follow the above directions except use a 50:50 mixture of moistened peat moss and cactus mix as the rooting and growing medium and allow the 6- to 12-inch cuttings to callus over seven to fourteen days before planting. Also, a 1-gallon, black plastic nursery container is the ideal size. After dipping the cut ends in a rooting hormone, plant the cutting and tie it loosely to a stake for support. Sturdy hanging baskets made of wire are perfect for displaying these magnificent bloomers at eye-level. For dry climates, press in sphagnum moss, line the moss with burlap, and fill with the cactus mix or coarse medium bark. To avoid root rot in moist climates, use palm fiber to cover the basket and grow epis bare root. Plant the cuttings and hang the wire basket in a shaded area. Epis tend to burn in full sun, particularly in the central valleys and inland where the heat is very intense.

To repot an established tropical plant, wait two years or more. Depending on the size of the container and the plant, it can be planted in a larger pot, one size up, or returned to the same container after root pruning. Cut away the lower $1/3$ of the rootball, loosen the outer roots with your hands, and plant in sterile organic potting soil or 2 parts cactus mix with 1 part worm castings and 1 part coarse perlite. Give the plant a thorough soaking, and apply a root stimulator three times, one week apart.

For tropicals such as Chinese yellow banana, ginger (fifty-two genera belonging to the Zingiberaceae family), and canna lily, space the plants about 3 to 6 feet apart to allow sufficient space for them to expand. Divide them and other clumping or rhizomatous plants in late spring or early summer. Plant 'Dancing Lady' or 'Dancing Girl' ginger plants in partial to full shade. They flower when temperatures are about 80 degrees Fahrenheit primarily in the summer season. Shell ginger is not as cold tolerant and will not produce blooms the following year if its shoots freeze back.

Canna lilies, ginger rhizomes, and other tropical plants with tuberous roots are available during spring and summer at retail nurseries. Plant them from roots or as container plants in early spring. If canna lilies and ginger rhizomes were lifted in fall or winter and stored through winter, replant them in spring after the last frost. Plant them in full sun with the rhizomes just below the soil surface. Winter-stored plumerias should also be planted in full sun in spring. Refer to Spring Planting for additional information on plumerias.

Birds of paradise are endemic to South Africa and thrive in mild winters, but also do beautifully in containers that can be moved into more protected spots for cold winter regions.

Bougainvillea is another spectacular plant that tolerates drought, is brilliantly colorful, resists insects and diseases, and grows easily in frost-free locales. Since some are vines and some are shrubs, decide where you want them—cascading over walls or fences, or planted as a ground cover or shrub. For a faster start, plant from 5-gallon containers, but if you are patient, 1-gallon containers will eventually fill in the blank spaces, too. Select a site in full sun, but for areas in the desert or interior valley, provide light shade or morning sun. To protect bougainvillea's fragile roots, turn the pot on its side and cut around the bottom of the container. Slip the plant out by gently pushing from the bottom. While cradling the bottom of the roots with your hands, slowly lower the container into the hole and backfill. Plant so that the top of the rootball is at the same level as the surrounding ground. Tamp the soil down around the plant with your hands. Build a watering basin as recommended on page 287.

WATERING

The trick to growing tropicals is to get them quickly established from spring through fall and allow them to rest in winter. To accomplish this, feed and water them regularly during spring and summer. Creating watering basins around tropical plants is an effective way to provide moisture. For fast-draining soil, water most newly planted tropicals every day for three days, then every other day for the next two weeks. Decrease to twice a week for another four weeks. For the next two to three years, water them about once a week. In clay soils, water sufficiently so that the rootball remains moist but not soggy. Most young tropical plants need lots of water to get established as long as there is good drainage.

Use a soil probe or shovel to determine when to water. Go down to the root zone and if the soil is showing signs of drying, water again. The roots of gingers and canna lilies are just below the surface of the soil, but the roots of angel's trumpet reach deeper, 6 to 12 inches. With a soil probe or shovel, take a handful of soil from a plant's root zone, not off the surface. It is time to water if the soil feels dry to the touch and, if squeezed, does not form a ball. When the soil forms a ball, but does not hold together, it has enough moisture. If squeezing the soil releases moisture in the hand, wait a few more days and check the soil moisture again before watering.

Once established, some drought-tolerant plants, like tropical crown of thorns, bougainvillea, and bird of paradise, no longer need to be watered as frequently as before. Often they can survive with supple-mental watering about twice a month during spring. Other water-thirsty tropical plants such as Abyssinian banana, angel's trumpet, canna lily, Chinese yellow banana, plumeria, and grafted hibiscus require continuous moisture, but not saturated soils. As the winter rains subside, increase supplemental watering to accommodate their spring growth.

In its native habitat, orchid cactus has a small, fibrous root system that draws its moisture from the humid air and tropical rains. While considered a succulent, it does not tolerate drought, so keep its roots moist, but not waterlogged. For newly planted cuttings, withhold watering for a couple of weeks to help avoid rot.

Do not water plumeria plants until new leaves form. Watering or fertilizing before their leaves emerge inhibits the development of blooms.

Tropical plants in containers need more frequent watering than those planted in the ground. When they are beginning their growth cycle, they may need to be watered three to four times a week, particularly during periods of little or no rainfall. If the soil feels dry, then water again. The same recommendations apply to newly repotted tropical plants.

FERTILIZING

Feed tropical plants with a liquid organic fertilizer every thirty to forty-five days beginning in early spring. When using a complete organic dry fertilizer, extend the intervals to forty-five to sixty days and water in with a solution high in humic acid during the bloom and growth cycles.

Hibiscus requires a 6-2-6 fertilizer formulation and is available in a complete dry organic food at your local garden center (often labeled as a palm hibiscus food) because they do not tolerate any fertilizer high in phosphorus. As with any dry fertilizer, distribute it evenly under the plant and out to the drip line.

Feed orchid cactuses (epis) with a dry organic fertilizer before and after their bloom cycles. Supplement with an organic water-soluble fertilizer sprayed on their flat stems if they begin to yellow. It is not usually necessary to feed cuttings until there is new growth.

Do not feed plumeria until new leaves appear. After they emerge, use an organic food or a controlled-release fertilizer.

For containers, use a controlled-release or organic fertilizer to supply an even amount of nutrients. Both forms release at a slow rate, discouraging rapid, soft and leggy growth.

MAINTAINING

When blustery winds or salt spray leave pits on the surface of large-leafed tropical plants or tatter their edges (such as banana or canna lilies), set up wind baffles and wash the foliage frequently. Read Citrus Summer Maintaining for information on how to construct a wind baffle. If there is persistent damage, move the plant to a more protected area, such as the leeward side of your home or other structure. Space the plant 3 to 6 feet away from the structure (depending on the species or cultivar) to allow it more room to grow and for good air circulation.

Allow birds of paradise, gingers, banana plants, and canna lilies to develop large clumps for best flower production. Wait three to five years before dividing.

Epis are found naturally in the cracks and crevices of trees. Although they do not climb, they appreciate being in hanging containers, tied up against a tree trunk, or secured in the crevice of a tree branch. Make sure the ties hold them secure but not too tight. Velcro or soft plastic plant ties are available at your retail nursery or agricultural supply store. Most hybrids produce day-blooming flowers, but whether they bloom day or night, their vibrant flowers are short-lived. On the positive side, epis will bloom on and off from late spring to autumn. When cut, they will last one to three days, depending on the cultivar.

The banana shrub's heavenly fruit-scented flowers perfume the late spring air, which more than compensates for their plant's average beauty. Although their blossoms stay with us for only three to four weeks, their heady fragrance is worth waiting for another eleven months.

After the last day of frost, gradually remove the thick blanket of mulch surrounding frost-tender tropical plants. Over a couple of weeks, remove enough to maintain a 1- to 2-inch layer. If there are insect problems in the mulch, replace the entire layer with fresh mulch.

In early spring, pull, hoe, or solarize existing weeds before using a pre-emergent to knock down the next generation. A 1- to 2-inch layer of humus mulch, worm castings, or other comparable organic material is another effective weed control.

Adjust the irrigation clocks to accommodate the change in weather conditions and plant growth. Since most tropical plants are growing during the warm seasons, irrigation timers need to be "tweaked" when spring rainfall is irregular and below normal, as well as when spring rainfall is adequate.

If your tropical plants are leggy, pinch back the ends of the branches to encourage more branching at the lower levels; that in turn gives them a fuller appearance. For example, hibiscus plants develop new branches below pruning cuts.

The result is a fuller plant with more blooms, because they form flower buds toward the end of each stem. Hybrid hibiscus plants are grafted on roots that flourish in California's climate. Remove any growth that appears below the graft because sucker growth diverts energy from the grafted hibiscus. Prune after the danger of frost has passed or whenever the plant needs a light shaping.

If the stems or branches of tropical plants were damaged by frost, do not prune until new growth appears. Sometimes what initially look like dead stems or branches are actually only damaged and recover in the warmth of spring. New foliar growth indicates the point where healthy growth remains and how far down to cut back the dead portions. Prune just above the new growth.

Birds of paradise and other frost-sensitive plants need a "spring cleaning," especially if they were in temperatures below 30 degrees Fahrenheit during winter. Prune off all the frost-burned foliage.

Prune to shape angel's trumpet in spring after the last frost. Refer to Summer Maintaining for more information.

PROTECTING

If insect problems have been severe in the past or if you want a safe, effective preventative, research indicates that worm castings dramatically increase the chitinase levels in plants, which in turn dissolve the chitinous exoskeletons of insects. Since chitinase in plants tastes like sour milk to insects, they quickly move on to someone else's garden. Spraying the soil and plants with compost tea also helps make plants more insect-resistant. Read Herbs and Vegetaables Spring Protecting. The parasitic wasp *Encarsia formosa*, lady beetles, and green lacewings are among the many beneficial insects that prey on pests. They are available at your local retail nurseries and through mail-order insectaries. Follow the release recommendations on the packages so they will linger in your garden long enough to do the most good. Do not apply chemical or organic pesticides unless their labels specify that the formulation is not harmful to beneficial insects like bees. The organic pest formula on page 203 is safe to use around beneficial insects. Since ants attack beneficial insects to protect their honeydew food source (from aphids, whiteflies, etc.), keep the ant population in check with commercial or homemade ant baits.

Despite the best preventative measures, pests and diseases can continue to pose problems, especially in spring and summer. Control ants and aphids early because their populations explode during the warmer months. Although ants do not harm plants, they farm aphids for their honeydew and move them around from plant to plant. To effectively get rid of aphids, you have to get rid of the ants. There are many commercial products formulated so that the toxic bait is carried back to the nest by the worker ants, eventually killing the entire nest. But for a homemade remedy, mix 1 part boric acid and 2 parts mint jelly. Puncture four $1/4$-inch holes around the sides near the bottom of an empty plastic container, snap the lid shut and place next to an ant nest. Another ant control is to puree orange peels with enough water to liquefy it; then pour the liquid immediately into the ant hole. You can also wash aphids off with a strong stream of water or spray the foliage with the organic pest formula on page 203 or Neem oil. A tablespoon of orange oil (d'limonene) added to the formula will get rid of the ants on contact. The d'limonene does not have any residual effect and will need to be reapplied whenever you see more ants. Insect controls containing pyrethroids, such as cyfluthrin, are synthetic versions of natural insecticides produced from the blossoms of certain varieties of chrysanthemums. They can be used to kill many different insects, including aphids, leafhoppers, cabbage loopers, chinch bubs, cutworms, earwigs, leafminers, mealybugs, thrips, and whiteflies, if you prefer a chemical remedy.

White, cotton-candylike streams suspended underneath hibiscus, canna lily, and angel's trumpet leaves are caused by giant whiteflies. They are much more difficult to eradicate compared to ordinary whiteflies. If they persist after using the organic pest formula on page 203 for several applications, it may be necessary to use a systemic insecticide containing imidacloprid. Based on the chemistry of nicotine, this pesticide is relatively nontoxic to mammals but very effective on insects. Imidacloprid is also effective against scale and gall midge.

The gall midge is a tiny fly that lays its eggs in flower buds. One of its favorite flowers is hibiscus. When the eggs hatch, wormlike larvae munch on the young buds, causing them to fall off before they open. When the bud falls, the larvae go under-

ground to pupate and reappear as adult flies in three weeks. Imidacloprid is available in ready-to-use sprays and in soil- drench form, follow the label directions carefully and do not use near plants with edible parts.

Fungal diseases such as mildew and rust may become problems during the warm seasons. Read Summer Protecting for more information.

Control brown garden snails and slugs with nontoxic iron phosphate or decollate snails. Decollates are predacious snails that attack and consume small- to medium-sized brown garden snails. It is necessary to check with your county agricultural department before you acquire decollate snails because they are prohibited in some northern California counties. Avoid the use of iron phosphate or chemical molluscicides if you have decollate snails.

For controlling gophers, use baitless gopher traps or gopher bait; for moles, use a guillotine mole trap. You can also plant angel's trumpet where gophers keep tunneling and destroying other plants. Angel's trumpet is toxic to gophers, but is also poisonous to humans and pets. So be careful where you plant it. See Autumn Protecting for controls of browsing deer and rabbits.

MORE PRUNING TIPS

Applying a sealing compound over pruning cuts slows down natural compartmentalization (sealing off areas of injury). If, however, there is damaging insect or disease activity nearby it might be prudent to seal the wound.

If you have flowering shrubs and trees that bloom in clusters at the ends of branches, heading back the branches in autumn or winter precludes having flowers the following spring. The optimum time to prune these trees and shrubs is shortly after their blossoms are spent.

Pruning to allow light to penetrate the canopy of a plant stimulates new growth, improves air circulation, and facilitates pest control. This is often called *lacing*.

See pages 55, 229, 261, 298, 302, 306, and 309 for more pruning information.

When is a rose not a rose? When it is a hybrid *Hibiscus rosa-sinensis* showing off its spectacular 6- to 10-inch flowers in the summer heat. It is the tropic's answer to the rose.

PLANNING

Summer is the best time to select tropical plants at your local garden centers or at plant sales. Read your local newspaper for announcements of sales. Join a local tropical plant society or garden club. There are myriad organizations for orchids, plumerias, bromeliads, epis, palms, and rare plants, as well as general garden clubs, horticultural societies, and the University of California Cooperative Extension office. All offer resource advice, a wealth of information, and fellow gardeners willing to share their knowledge with you. Become a member of a nearby arboretum or botanical garden, and subscribe to their newsletters to learn about their special events. Also, subscribe to California gardening magazines such as *Garden Compass*™ or *Sunset Magazine*. *Garden Compass* offers a special tropical issue once a year—the July/August issue, which features the latest, most exciting, and most applicable tropical varieties for California, along with book reviews and articles about current tropical websites. In addition, most garden magazines feature event calendars that often include tropical plant seminars, sales, and shows. Send for mail-order tropical plant catalogues, and visit tropical plant websites for more information.

When making vacation plans, include visits to arboretums or botanical gardens with tropical collections to see what might work well in your landscape. The following is a brief list of suggestions to get you started in California: Descanso Gardens in La Canada, Huntington Botanical Gardens in San Marino, the Los Angeles County Arboretum and Botanic Garden in Arcadia, Lotusland in Montecito, South Coast Botanic Garden in Palos Verde, Quail Botanical Gardens in Encinitas, the San Francisco Conservatory of Flowers, Sherman Library and Gardens in Corona Del Mar, the San Francisco Botanical Gardens at Strybing Arboretum, the University of California Botanical Garden in Berkeley, the University of California Arboretum in Davis, and the University of California Botanic Gardens in Riverside.

Remember to ask a friend or neighbor to water your plants if you do not have an automatic irrigation system. Tropical plants are growing and blooming in summer, and most need extra watering care, especially those in containers.

PLANTING

Tropical plants like bougainvillea, hibiscus, ginger, plumeria, angel's trumpet, bromeliad, and banana plant can be planted in summer except in interior valleys or other areas where intense heat may scorch their foliage. Follow the general planting guidelines under Spring Planting.

For hibiscus, dig a hole twice the size of the rootball and mix 1 part soil with 1 part organic material such as humus, worm castings, or compost. Add a preplant fertilizer to the soil mix, or plop a biodegradable packet of preplant fertilizer in the bottom of the hole. As with most tropical plants, make sure the top of the original rootball is at the same level as the surrounding soil. Backfill with the soil mixture, water as you are backfilling to eliminate any air pockets, and tamp the soil around the plant. Use a root stimulator with indolebutyric acid or alpha naphthalene acetic acid three times, two weeks apart.

Bromeliads belong to a vast number of genera that include over 2,500 species, cultivars, and hybrids. Most do not tolerate frost and prefer to be planted under the shaded canopy of a tree. Epiphytic species (plants that derive moisture and nutrients from the air and rain and live on other plants, but not as parasites) do best in very light, well-draining planting media such as cactus mix. Grow epiphytes in the nooks and crannies of tree branches. Terrestrial species may be grown in 2 parts cactus mix combined with 1 part worm castings, humus, peat moss, or compost; plant them under the protective canopies of trees. For winter areas that dip below 55 degrees Fahrenheit or summer regions that heat to over 90 degrees, plant them in containers that can be moved to more protected areas during periods of temperature extremes. Shortly before or soon after a bromeliad's colorful bracts are spent, it will produce new "baby" offshoots. Most bromeliads are monocarpic, meaning they die after flowering and after producing new plants from offsets. Some parent plants remain alive for quite a while longer, but will not bear any more colorful bracts. Read Autumn Planting for planting offsets.

Continue to take cuttings from tropical plants such as plumeria, tropical crown of thorns, and angel's trumpet to propagate more for yourself or for your friends. Refer to Spring Planting for details on propagation techniques.

Plumeria (also known as frangipani) does not develop many roots compared to their mature size, and even large plants are easily transplanted during warm weather. Make sure the soil is fast draining and sandy loam in texture. Refer to Spring Planting for more information.

Divide tropical plants such as Chinese yellow banana, ginger (fifty-two genera belonging to the Zingiberaceae family), canna lily, and other clumping or rhizomatous plants in late spring or early summer.

WATERING

As the weather turns hotter and drier, monitor the soil moisture and supplement watering at shorter intervals. Keep all newly planted tropicals well watered because summer weather encourages growth and causes stress when there is an inadequate supply of water. Drooping leaves or leaf drop are signals that thirsty plumeria, canna lily, banana plant, angel's trumpet, and hibiscus need deep and regular watering. Canna lilies demand so much water during the warmer seasons that they are often grown along the edges of shallow ponds or in water gardens with water barely covering their soil.

On the other hand, not all tropical plants are thirsty. Some, such as the blue hibiscus, bougainvillea, bird of paradise, and tropical crown of thorns, tolerate drought once established. If they are planted in well-draining soil, water them every ten to fourteen days during the summer months. Once established, they prefer to be kept on the dry side.

During hot summers or periods of drought, fill bromeliad cups with just enough water so that it overflows into their surrounding soil. Mist during periods of low humidity, and keep their cup reservoirs filled with water.

Water epis frequently during hot weather, but keep them relatively dry when cool temperatures prevail. They like to be kept moist, but not waterlogged.

FERTILIZING

While tropical plants may have different individual needs based on the species or cultivar, generally they need fertilizer while they are growing, particularly at the beginning of summer.

Continue feeding your plants with a complete dry organic fertilizer; water it in with a solution high in humic acid every forty-five to sixty days. If using liquid organic fertilizers, apply about once a month during their growth and bloom cycles.

Container-grown tropicals also need regular feedings. If you're using a water-soluble organic fertilizer, feed plants every two weeks while they are growing and blooming. They are particularly thirsty and hungry during these periods. Read Spring Fertilizing for additional information.

The following recommendations are based on certain plant needs. Feed hibiscus an organic hibiscus food once a month. Similarly, bromeliads appreciate a monthly feeding, but fertilize them with a water-soluble organic feeding during summer. Discontinue fertilizing plumeria during their bloom season, and feed them one more time after their flowers are spent. Once bougainvilleas are three to five years old, discontinue fertilizing them in summer. Some tropicals with high acid needs, such as anthuriums and banana shrubs, appreciate a supplemental feeding of cottonseed meal (follow the recommended application rates on the package) before flower buds form or after their blooms are spent.

MAINTAINING

If you have an automatic irrigation system, check it over to make sure it is functioning properly, especially before going on a vacation. Determine how long the timers need to be on in order for the water to reach to the root depth of your tropical plants (that depth is relatively shallow for rhizomatous plants such as gingers and canna lilies, but 6 to 12 inches for angel's trumpet), and adjust accordingly.

Clean up fallen flowers and clipped-off foliage, stems, or branches regularly because they harbor such pests as borers and insect larvae.

To maintain moisture in the soil and to keep the root system cooler during the heat of summer, make sure there is a 1- to 2-inch layer of organic material surrounding your tropical plants. This is also an effective method to control weeds.

Keep weeds away by hand-pulling, or use a mulch with corn gluten. Corn gluten helps suppress weed germination. For stoloniferous weeds such as Bermuda grass, it is best to use a systemic weed killer rather than hand-weeding. Just the tiniest remnant of a stoloniferous weed will produce more, and hand-weeding or cultivating may actually help to spread it. Follow the formulator's directions, and refer to Roses Spring Maintaining for more hints about applying systemic weed killers.

If your potted bromeliads have been indoors, move them outdoors under the protective canopy of a tree to give them a summer vacation. Wait until the evening temperatures are above 60 degrees Fahrenheit.

Tropical flowers are often at their most fragrant and beautiful during summer. Harvest tropical flowers in the morning when their stems have the highest moisture content. Continue the time-honored Hawaiian tradition by fashioning plumeria into leis and offering them as gifts of welcome and friendship to neighbors and family. In the evening, angel's trumpet saturates the air with its heady perfume, but because of its toxicity, do not use angel's trumpet in flower arrangements. Float cut plumeria and hibiscus in ponds, pools, or brandy snifters (or other clear glass bowls) for short-lived but beautiful displays. The magnificent Chinese yellow banana blooms are actually buttery-yellow, stiff bracts that can last up to six months on the plant. Rather than cut them, we prefer to let them remain on the plant so that we can enjoy them from summer through late fall.

Prune for shape as errant growth occurs. Large-sized foliar tropical plants such as canna lily, Chinese yellow banana, and Abyssinian banana often have unsightly older foliage during summer. Remove the older growth to encourage new growth in the center of the plant.

When banana shrubs are planted in full sun, they will develop multiple trunks with a rounded to urn-shaped canopy that may need periodic trimming for shape. It is best to tip-prune their uppermost leaves after their spring bloom to develop more side branching. If planted in the shade, a banana shrub will grow with a central leader and need little or no pruning.

Continue to prune angel's trumpet during summer. They look their best when pruned into an umbrella shape so that the pendulous flowers hang freely like giant bells.

Woody shrubs such as the blue hibiscus can get a bit leggy with skimpy branching. Prune back every month from spring to fall by selecting two to three of the longest branches and cutting their lengths back 50 to 60 percent.

PROTECTING

Watch out for aphids, mealybugs, scales, spider mites, whiteflies, and loopers. Spray with *Bacillus thuringiensis* (Bt) if there are caterpillars feasting on tropical foliage, or handpick and destroy them. To wash off aphids or whiteflies, spray with a strong stream of water. Sticky traps are also a safe way to get rid of whiteflies. For spider mites, use a miticide; for aphids, scales, and mealybugs, use the organic pest formula on page 203. If there are no plants with edible parts nearby, a systemic containing imidacloprid is effective for one year. As with any chemical, read the application directions carefully before using the product.

Spider mites proliferate in dry weather conditions, leaving a silvery sheen or stippling on all portions of leaves. They are very difficult to see with the naked eye, but you can spot their tell-tale fine, white webbing on the undersides of leaves. Control mites by spraying them with a strong stream of water, horticultural oil, or miticide. Most insecticides are ineffective against mites because they are spiders, not insects.

Thrips, small yellow or brown insects, are most common during the warm summer months. They cause deformed leaves, and buds and flowers are riddled with mottled brown spots. Spray with the organic pest formula on page 203, or use Neem oil or a pyrethrum-based spray.

Plumeria and many other tropical plants are susceptible to plumeria rust, leaf spot, powdery mildew, and fungal rots. Remove and dispose of the infested foliage. Control with the organic formula on page 203. If the problem is particularly severe, double the amount of the lemon myrtle tea tree oil in the formula and apply twice a week. Fungal rots are typically due to overwatering or poorly drained soil. Decrease watering; apply compost tea, humic acid concentrates, and worm castings to increase the population of beneficial microbial activity, including mycorrhizal fungi. Read Spring Protecting for additional information on building healthy soils. If there is continual die-back due to fungal disease, it may be best to dig up the plant, dispose of the soil surrounding it, and allow the ground to remain fallow for a couple of seasons. For containers, empty the soil and throw it away. Clean the pots thoroughly using a mixture of bleach and water (10 parts water to 1 part bleach) or a commercial product such as Physan 20™ (available at most retail garden centers or agricultural supply stores). Use a well-draining, sterile medium such as cactus mix. You can also add 10 to 20 percent organic material such as humus, compost, or worm castings to the mix.

Gingers and other rhizomatous tropical plants are often attacked by root-knot nematodes, resulting in stunted growth. If the roots show signs of swelling or gall development, they are most likely due to nematodes, microscopic worms that enter through the root system. Since their life cycle depends on warm temperatures, they proliferate and do the most damage during the warmest months of the year. Dig out and throw away the infested plant, and clear out any weeds because nematodes breed in them. Allow the ground to remain fallow for a season or two; add generous amounts of organic materials, humic acid concentrates, and compost tea to the soil to increase the beneficial microorganisms in the soil. For application rates of compost tea, refer to Herbs and Vegetables Spring Protecting.

Bromeliads are protected from most insect infestations because of their symbiotic relationship with frogs, lizards, birds, and spiders. To maintain this mutually beneficial relationship, avoid chemical pesticides whenever possible. Instead, use the organic pest formula on page 203 if insects are causing extensive damage.

Snails and slugs can defoliate angel's trumpet leaves and other tender tropical foliage in a very short period. Use decollate snails in the war against the brown garden snail in the counties of Fresno, Imperial, Kern, Los Angeles, Madera, Orange, Riverside, San Bernardino, San Diego, Santa Barbara, Tulare, and Ventura. For other counties, iron phosphate is an effective organic snail and slug control. Do not use iron phosphate or any other molluscicide if you have decollate snails. Of course, summer evenings are pleasant enough to go snail and slug hunting at night with a flashlight. Take along a bucket of soapy water (they can still survive in plain water) to dispose of them.

MORE PRUNING TIPS

Severe pruning of plants is generally not necessary, however there are a few times you should pull out the pruning saw, bypass pruners, or loppers and without hesitation prune suckers off trees unless you want to develop a coppice. Suckers grow fast and furious from lateral surface roots or from the area between a root flare and a bud or graft union and they have been known to sprout up from surface roots 15 to 20 feet away from the parent plant. After pruning off the sucker, apply a sucker suppressant (NAA) which will reduce regrowth.

See pages 55, 229, 261, 293, 302, 306, and 309 for more pruning information.

AUTUMN

Most tropical blossoms accept autumn's shorter days and cooler evenings by falling away. The tropical crown of thorns is one of just a few that continues to bear its hydrangea-clustered flowers in stubborn defiance.

PLANNING

Update your garden journal by organizing all the accumulated clippings, photos, and ideas for future tropical plantings. Think about where you might like to plant more tropical plants in your garden next spring. Review your notes to recall why some of the tropical plants flourished and why some struggled. If they were planted in the ground, perhaps they would do better if transplanted in containers or transplanted to a different part of the garden. Mark the plants in question. They can be moved as long as your locale remains mild through winter, or wait until spring.

If you live where winter freeze or cold weather is common, begin making room indoors, in the greenhouse, or in a protected spot outdoors for frost-sensitive plants in containers. Before moving the plants, look for any signs of disease or insect infestations and treat them now to prevent future problems. While you are looking over your potted tropicals, check to see whether any are rootbound. They may need to be moved up a size.

Gather supplies for repotting: potting soil, soil amendments, and more containers.

PLANTING

Continue to propagate by cuttings outdoors as long as temperatures are above 65 degrees Fahrenheit. If not, propagate them indoors or in a temperature-controlled greenhouse or conservatory. If you live along the coast where mild weather is typical in autumn, it is still possible to plant tropicals in containers or in the ground, such as bougainvillea, hibiscus, and plumeria in early fall. For interior regions of California, wait until spring because fall planting leaves them susceptible to frost.

Depending on the amount of space available, allow bromeliad pups to remain attached to the parent, or carefully remove them and plant them in commercial, cactus mix. Cut the offsets when they are $^1/_3$ to $^2/_3$ as large as the parent plant. Use a coarse, fast-draining potting mix such as cactus mix, and keep the pups upright. As long as the pups are large enough, they can be transplanted anytime from spring through fall. Move them to a more protected area when temperatures dip below 55 degrees or soar over 90 degrees.

When their clumps are small, birds of paradise can be easily divided with a sharp shovel. Once their clumps are immense, they may have to be dug up in sections to be further divided. Or use a chainsaw to get a good-sized section. Replant the clumps in spring or autumn.

Canna lily and ginger have rhizomatous roots; when they become too crowded, the bloom production declines. Spring and autumn are the times to repot or divide to ensure next year's flowers. Slice through the rhizomes with a sharp spade or knife. Cut them into 8-inch-diameter sections, and trim off any damaged or dead roots. Plant at a shallow depth, with the rhizomes just below the soil surface, but their roots completely buried. They appreciate a rich, well-draining soil. The faded flowers can be snipped off, but leave the stalks and foliage. They need their leaves for winter. 'Dancing Lady' gingers, on the other hand, stop growing and begin to die back when fall days shorten and temperatures begin to dip.

WATERING

Adjust the watering to accommodate the change in weather conditions and the slower rate of plant growth. If there is an extended period of warm and dry weather, continue regular, supplemental watering. Tropical plants in particular cannot tolerate hot, dry winds. If such winds are predicted, use an antitranspirant and make sure the plants have been thoroughly watered the night before. Water less when the weather begins to cool down.

Decrease supplemental watering once the rainy season begins and temperatures cool. As some plants begin to go into dormancy, such as plumeria, canna lily and ginger, it may be necessary to protect them from torrential rainfalls. If they are in containers, move them under eaves. If this is not possible, open up their watering basins and put a temporary tarp or plastic around the base of the plants that extends out to their drip lines to protect them from over-watering. Weight the edges of the temporary covers with bricks. Make sure you remove the coverings as soon as the rains stop.

FERTILIZING

Fall is the time to withhold fertilizer, particularly if you live in the desert or inte-

rior valleys. If you are in a frost-free area, feed them one more time with a water-soluble organic food in early autumn. Do not feed them a controlled-release food because that might encourage soft, tender growth in the later months of fall, which will make them susceptible to early frost. Tropical plants need to slow down their growth so they can survive light frosts.

Yellowing foliage may be due to leaf chlorosis. Apply a chelated iron product in midspring and again in early autumn.

MAINTAINING

In preparation for the winter rains, rebuild the watering basins and replenish the mulch so it remains at 1 to 2 inches.

For frost-sensitive tropical plants that are planted in the ground or in large, difficult-to-move containers, increase the layer of mulch to 4 to 6 inches out to the drip line of their root systems. Do not pile it directly around the base of the plant. Instead, leave a 2- to 4-inch space so that moisture will not accumulate directly around the plant.

If an early freeze is protected, use an antitranspirant or, if the plant is small enough, cover it with a cotton sheet. Move containers to a more protected location when practical. Bromeliads in containers acclimate very well to indoor life as long as they have bright, indirect light.

Canna lilies, gingers, and other rhizomatous plants should be dug up in autumn and stored indoors where temperatures typically dip below freezing during winter and early spring. Remove the dead leaves and flowers, and make sure the plants are free of pests and disease. When there are signs of pests and diseases, spray with the organic pest control formula on page 203. Allow the plants to dry out a bit before storing them in a frost-free place. They are best stored with some compost or organic potting soil covering their rhizomes and wrapped loosely in burlap. Sprinkle occasionally with water to prevent the roots from drying out completely. For mild-winter areas, keep them in the ground, but cover with a 2- to 4-inch blanket of mulch after pruning off the dead leaves and spent flowers.

Where winters are wet and cold, lift out plumerias and store them in a cool, dry place. If left outdoors under these conditions, plumerias are prone to root rot. Follow the same procedures for digging up canna lilies. They need no care during winter dormancy. Replant after the last frost in spring. Even in mild-winter regions, if heavy rains are predicted, move potted plumerias to a more protected spot. If they are planted directly in the ground, make sure the water drains away from the plants. In warm, dry locales, allow the plants to go dormant after their flowers are spent and their foliage begins to fall to the ground. Do not water or fertilize.

Keep weeds away from your tropical plants by pulling them out; follow up with a preemergent week control such as mulch products using corn gluten. Corn gluten helps suppress weed germination. For stoloniferous weeds such as Bermuda grass, it is best to use a systemic weed killer rather than hand-weeding. Follow the formulator's directions, and refer to Ground Covers Spring Maintaining for more application hints.

Fall cleanups are just as important as spring and summer. Gather up fallen flowers and clipped-off foliage, stems, or branches regularly because they harbor pests such as borers, insect larvae, snails, and slugs.

Once canna lilies begin to look tired and dried out, cut them back just above their crowns. By spring, their foliage will emerge once again. Clip off dead bird of paradise foliage, and snip off their spent blooming stems.

Generally speaking, there should be no need to prune or fertilize tropical plants. Pruning and fertilizing only encourages new growth, which is then susceptible to frost damage.

PROTECTING

Local wildlife creatures are busily searching for food in preparation for the less bountiful, upcoming winter months. Raccoons, skunks, and opossums dig up the soil in search of grubs and other larvae; they are not intentionally trying to damage your tropical plants. Get rid of the food source by saturating the area with water and then picking the larvae off as they rise to the surface. You can also put up physical barriers to keep the critters away. If they continue to damage and destroy your plants, select a product containing a synthetic pyrethroid such as cyfluthrin to kill the larvae. Another option is to live-trap the wild things and relocate them to a less urban area. Check first with the California Department of Fish and Game to make sure live-trapping and releasing of specific wild animals is allowed. If not, hire a specialist licensed to remove wildlife—or accept and appreciate their visits. A walk on the wild side offers many rewards and is, after all, part of outdoor life.

Pocket gophers and moles are another matter. They can decimate an entire garden with their tunnels. Use manual traps or bait stations for gophers, and set a guillotine trap to eliminate insectivorous moles. Manual traps or bait stations are also effective against rats and mice.

For additional information about managing insects, diseases, rodents, and weeds, visit the University of California's

Integrated Pest Management program on their website at *www.ipm.ucdavis.edu.*

To discourage nibbling deer and rabbits, use water-activated motion detectors or olfactory repellents, or protect individual tropical plants with tubes of small-mesh, stiff-wired fencing. Euphorbia, angel's trumpet, bougainvillea, and hibiscus are known to be deer-resistant plants, but if they are hungry enough, deer will eat just about anything. Deer do not like to brush up against monofilament line because they cannot see it and it scares them. Set up a series of 6-foot stakes around the perimeter of the planting bed area and string monofilament line deer chest high around the stakes. The final and most expensive solution is to put up a permanent 8-foot fence around your garden. Since most city ordinances usually allow a maximum height of 6 feet (a height most deer can jump over), many owners are putting up double 4-foot fences parallel to each other with a 4-foot space between them. Apparently the space between the two fences is too narrow to allow a double jump and too wide for them to jump over in a single bound.

Powdery mildew is one of the most common fungal diseases affecting tropical plants. It is easily recognized by the light gray or white powdery substance that covers leaves. Several different kinds of fungi cause this problem, but if you spot it early enough, simply wash off the plants and remove the affected foliage early in the morning. This allows enough time for the plant to dry out before evening. Throw the leaves away to avoid spreading the spores, and spray the plants with compost tea or a lemon-myrtle-based organic fungicide. Read page 203 for the organic pest formula. To prevent future outbreaks of powdery mildew, plant tropical plants with sufficient space for good air circulation. Also avoid fast-release chemical fertilizers.

Whiteflies and caterpillars are still active in the warm autumn season. They migrate from plant to plant, damaging new and established tropical plants. When caterpillars are found munching their way through large-leafed banana, canna lily, bird of paradise, and angel's trumpet, spray with Bt or hand pick and destroy them. Bear in mind that caterpillars may be the larvae of butterflies; if you want to protect the butterflies, you may have to put up with worm-eaten foliage.

TREE PRUNING TIPS

- Trees pruned in the spring upset nesting birds.
- Trees growing under power lines should be pruned by utility companies.
- Trees pruned in the spring upset nesting birds.
- Trees growing under power lines should be pruned by utility companies.
- To control the height and shape of pine trees, remove their candles (new growth).
- Trees growing in your garden that have branches or roots growing beyond your property line are likely your responsibility.

See pages 55, 229, 261, 293, 298, 306, and 309 for more pruning information.

WINTER

The barren antlers of plumeria remind us "for everything there is a season;" for most tropical plants, winter is the season to rest. Winter's quiet rhythms allow plants to rebound again in spring.

PLANNING

Read up on the selections available in catalogues and websites, and check out some books from the library on tropical plants. Make note of necessary conditions, and see whether they match your climate zone. There are more than 200,000 species of known tropical plants, with many more to be discovered. Angel's trumpets, gingers, bananas, birds of paradise, cannas, hibiscus, epis, plumerias, and bromeliads are among the most flamboyant plants in the world. They make you dream of lush foliage waving in the gentle breeze and the warmth of perfume-saturated summer days. So dream on as you thumb through catalogues, visit websites, and check out library books specializing in tropical plants. In winter, tropical dreams are still possible.

While researching tropical plants, you may be surprised to learn how many can solve some difficult challenges in your garden. If you need plants that are tough survivors, demand little care, thrive under filtered light, and produce dramatic flower spikes that last for weeks and weeks, plant bromeliads. Many species and hybrids grow under trees where little else can, and they bring brilliant color to the shade. Since they do best in temperatures between 50 and 90 degrees Fahrenheit, plant them in containers that can easily be moved indoors or to a more protected location where winters or summers fall outside their comfort zones. Other plants to consider are the somewhat hardy 'Dancing Lady' or 'Dancing Girl' gingers because they also do best in shaded nooks. For plants that don't need much space, bear clusters of hydrangealike flowers almost year-round, survive on benign neglect with very little water and fertilizer, and tolerate salt spray and alkaline soils, pick the tropical crown of thorns. Plumeria thrives in frost-free climates and also withstands slightly alkaline soils and sea spray. Use standard hibiscus as dense hedges if you live along the mild climates of coastal California or along the "banana belt" in Northern California. Grafted hibiscus blooms in morning sun or partial shade and is ideal in containers planted on decks and patios or around the swimming pool. Grafted or hybrid hibiscus is considered the tropical counterpart to roses. It blooms from spring through autumn if fed and watered regularly.

If you are going away for the winter holidays, ask someone to water your "houseguest" tropicals while you are gone. When it is not possible to have someone check in on your plants, water them thoroughly, allow them to drain, and then water again. If there is a tub or sink near a window that provides medium light, line the bottom with several sheets of newspaper or paper towels. Set down bricks on the paper to support all your plants. Plug the drain and add enough water to barely cover the bricks; then set the plants directly on the bricks. For small plants, use margarine tubs or other similar-sized plastic containers to employ the wick watering system. Poke a hole in the lid, fill the tub with water, and put the lid back on. Push a piece of string or yarn into the drainage hole of your plant with a knitting needle, chopstick, or pencil. Shove it several inches into the soil. Push the other end of the wick through the hole in the lid and set it in the water. Moisten the wick by watering the plant; it will continue to transfer water from the top to the pot. Do not turn the heat off if winter temperatures dip below freezing. Leave the heater set at 65 to 68 degrees Fahrenheit for most tropical plants that are spending the winter indoors.

PLANTING

If you see a greenhouse-grown tropical plant that you absolutely must have, keep it indoors through winter in an area that receives bright, indirect light. Anthuriums are often available during winter and prefer regular moisture and humidity. Set them on a humidity tray (read Maintaining), and mist with a spray bottle every few days. As with any indoor plant, do not place near heating or air conditioning vents. Take them outdoors during spring and summer when evening temperatures have warmed to about 60 degrees Fahrenheit. Most anthurium hybrids prefer bright filtered light outdoors and bloom intermittently when spring evenings are cool.

The banana shrub can be planted just about anytime because of its tolerance to cold weather (down to about 5 degrees Fahrenheit). If the ground is workable, plant banana shrub in late winter or early spring. Plant anytime in containers; just be sure to provide well-draining, acidic soil.

WATERING

Decrease supplemental watering during winter rains. Stop watering drought-tolerant tropicals, such as bougainvilleas in winter or tropicals that go dormant, such as ginger, canna lily, and plumeria. Epis also go dormant during cool weather and do not need any supplemental water, unless winter remains warm and dry. During winter rains, reduce the water collected in bromeliad cups or empty them periodically to prevent rotting. For drought-tolerant or dormant tropical plants, open up the watering basins; if this is not possible, temporarily cover their planting areas with tarp or plastic and secure the edges with bricks or blocks. Remove after the rains have stopped.

If winter rainfalls are normal, hibiscus should not need supplemental watering, unless it is in a container. Then allow it to dry out slightly before watering again. During periods of torrential rainfall, move the containers under eaves or other protected spots to keep them from getting oversaturated.

Keep indoor plants evenly moist, but never allow them to stand in water. Remove any excess water in the saucers or trays immediately. Since most tropical plants are sensitive to salt, water them with de-ionized water (available at grocery stores for steam irons). If you must use tap water, fill a gallon jug and allow the water to sit for a few hours so that the chlorine evaporates. Bromeliads are particularly sensitive to salt and chlorine. Besides humidity trays, mist with a spray bottle every two to three days to increase humidity.

FERTILIZING

Feed container tropical plants, such as bromeliads and anthuriums, if they are still growing or blooming indoors or in a greenhouse. Use a water-soluble organic fertilizer about once a month. If they are not in a growth or bloom cycle, leave them alone.

MAINTAINING

Use an antitranspirant to protect frost-tender tropical plants; if they are in containers, move them to a greenhouse, conservatory, or more protected site. Plants such as Abyssinian banana and angel's trumpet die back to the ground when temperatures fall below 30 degrees Fahrenheit, but if it is not a prolonged freeze, they may come back. Successive freezes, however, will eventually take their toll; the plants may get weaker and die completely after a few years. If possible, plant them in containers and move them to a protected space indoors or in a greenhouse during winter.

Banana shrub remains evergreen in frost-free regions, but will go dormant during winter freezes and can survive temperatures down to 5 degrees. Tropical crown of thorns drops all its leaves when temperatures dip below 32 degrees. If the temperature remains at freezing for several days, bring the crown of thorns indoors.

Forced-air heating decreases humidity. To counteract dry air, set up humidity trays for plants brought indoors. Use saucers or trays and fill with pea gravel. Add enough water to cover the gravel. Place bricks on the gravel and set the plants on them so they won't have their roots sitting in water. These trays and saucers dramatically increase the humidity surrounding your plants.

Mark the spots where your dormant gingers are "resting" because they will probably be the last to poke out in spring and you don't want to dig around or step on them in the meantime.

If an early frost catches you unprepared, do not trim back frost-damaged plants immediately. They may grow new foliage and suffer additional damage if there are more freezing periods. For minor tip die-back on the leaves, stems, or branches, trim them off lightly, but if all the foliage turns brown and falls off or the top and side branches are killed, wait until new growth begins in the warmer spring months to determine how far back to prune. At that time, cut off only the dead portions, just above the green parts. When everything above ground, including the branches and trunk, is killed, but the roots are still viable, remove the dead growth. This is often the case with canna lilies. The plants die with early frost, but their roots bear sprouts in spring. When the sprouts emerge, allow one or two of the most vigorous to remain and prune out the rest.

PROTECTING

In warm-winter areas, snails and slugs may still be slithering and sliding about during the rainy season. Continue to apply iron phosphate, particularly after rains, but if there are decollate snails, do not use any molluscicide.

For controls against deer, raccoons, rabbits, and other wild critters, read Autumn Protecting.

Whether banana shrubs and other tropical plants remain evergreen or are dormant, look for scale infestation; control it with horticultural oil.

Bringing outdoor tropical plants indoors can "bug" you because many are hitchhiking on the foliage and stems and in the soil. Spray the plants and the soil with the organic pest formula on page 203 before bringing the plants indoors or into the greenhouse. Despite preventative measures, some insects may still appear or insect eggs hatch. Isolate the infested plant from the others, and treat it immediately. White, cottony insects known as mealybugs may suddenly mass in colonies, sucking the sap from leaves, causing them to yellow and eventually weakening the entire plant. If there are only a few clusters of mealybugs, give them an alcohol rub with a cotton swab dipped into rubbing alcohol. Make sure you get them all, under the leaves, on top, and between the stems and leaves. Spraying them with water in the sink, bathtub, or shower can also be helpful, or take them outside temporarily and spray with the pest formula on page 203. Taking them outdoors prevents any spray from staining your furniture or floors. Bring them indoors when the plant is dry. Repeat the treatment if they return.

One of the toughest insects to control indoors and outdoors is the whitefly. Referred to as "plant dandruff" because they are tiny flies that flutter off in great white clouds when an infested plant is shaken, their complex life cycle takes about forty days to complete, and each stage differs in its tolerance to insecticide remedies. To make matters worse, several stages can coexist with each other. The eggs are laid underneath leaves and hatch in five to seven days. As translucent crawlers, they are actively moving about searching for food sites. Once they settle down and feed, they morph into sedentary scalelike creatures. Several days later, they emerge as adult flies. A combination of remedies over this forty-day period is important to prevent the development and re-infestation of whitefly. Use yellow sticky traps to attract the adult whiteflies, wash off the eggs and scale that are on the undersides of leaves and stems, and spray the entire plant with the organic pest formula on page 203. Neem oil and horticultural oil are other safe controls. If the infestation is stubbornly pervasive, consider houseplant spikes containing the systemic imidacloprid, but follow the formulator's directions carefully.

Fungus gnats are small gray or black flies that are $1/4$ inch long. They feed on moist soil rich in organic matter and won't hurt mature plants, but can transmit plant diseases. Mostly they are a nuisance because they are attracted to carbon dioxide and have the annoying habit of flying in your face. Gnats love moisture, so reduce watering to allow the soil to dry out about an inch. Water less frequently, and apply the organic pest formula on page 203 to the plant and Bt as a soil drench to control the larvae. Also place yellow sticky traps horizontally on the pots to attract the adult gnats.

To control fungal problems, read Summer Protecting.

MORE TREE PRUNING TIPS

Plant height can be controlled by summer pruning. The first three to five years of pruning should form a tree's structure to make the size and form manageable. For instance, if a sapling has a single leader when it is planted, prune the top off so that the top branch bud is three to 4 feet above the ground. The second and third year, prune to develop an open vase-shape canopy by keeping the branches that are approximately in a spiral pattern on the trunk. To control the height and shape of pine trees, remove their candles (new growth).

See pages 55, 229, 261, 293, 298, 302, and 309 for more pruning information.

SOIL RHYTHMS

Soil development represents one of the slowest rhythms that occur in nature. It can take thousands of years before rock weathers enough to become soil. To replicate the characteristics of the soils found in the home region of garden plants would be next to impossible. A practical alternative, however, is to create a soil structure that avoids compromising the health of the plants.

TEXTURE

Most plants prefer soils that are friable and with a loam texture. Loam soils amended with organic material become moisture and nutrient reservoirs and environments that encourage beneficial microorganisms.

Heavy, dense, and clayey soils limit a plant's access to air and water. They also limit beneficial aerobic microorganisms, such as ecto- and endo-mychorrizae fungi, from assisting the roots. If the soil in your garden is clayey, amend the soil with animal manures, shredded green plant material, or leaf mold. As these materials decompose, they produce an organic "glue" that binds fine soil particles together, forming aggregates of the surface soil particles.

pH

Ideally, garden soils should have a pH (soil reaction) reading between 6.5 and 6.8. When the planting site has been decided, but before the planting pit has been excavated, use a pH meter, a pH test kit, or a soil test to determine the soil reaction. If the readings are higher than 8.0 or lower than 5.0, many necessary elements will not be available to the plants; that is, the plants will not be able to utilize them. Potassium (K), nitrogen (N), iron (Fe), Zinc (Zn), and Manganese (Mg) are among those elements that are not available to plants if the pH is greater than 8.5. Even if these elements are present in the soil, many plants cannot assimilate them until the pH is in the availability range of 6.5 to 7.2.

If the soil pH is *below* 5.0, begin raising it to a range between 6.5 and 6.8 by applying dolomite lime at a rate of 7 pounds per 100 square feet, unless there are plants such as azaleas, rhododendrons, and vireyas (4.5 to 6.0), camellias (5.8 to 6.55), and blueberries (4.0 to 5.5). The change happens slowly so monitor pH every month and one half until the level falls in the range of 6.5 to 6.8.

If the soil reaction (pH) indicates a level *above* 7.2, begin acidifying the soil by tilling it to a depth of 8 to 12 inches; then, evenly distribute soil sulfur, gypsum, and peat moss (or a comparable soil amendment) over the area. For soil sulfur, spread 1 to 2 pounds over 100 square feet; for gypsum spread 10 to 15 pounds over 100 square feet; for the peat moss, evenly distribute 2 to 3 cubic yards over an area 20 by 50 feet (1,000 square feet). Calcium chloride can be used instead of gypsum. Compared to dry gypsum, calcium chloride is easily applied; 32 ounces of calcium chloride cover up to 1,000 square feet depending on soil and pH conditions. Once the amendments are spread evenly, till all the ingredients into the soil again. Rake the amended soil smooth, removing all large rocks and solid clods of earth. Soak the soil thoroughly to collapse any air pockets in the root zones. The process of adjusting alkaline and acidic soils is a slow process because the change occurs as soil microorganisms modify the materials.

BENEFICIALS

We have found it very helpful to inoculate the backfill with beneficial microorganisms, such as endo- and ecto-mycorrhizal fungi. These beneficials increase by 100 to 300 times a plant's roots ability to absorb moisture and nutrients from the soil. Dry or liquid organic fertilizers are available with mycorrhizal fungi added. Compost tea and humic acid also encourage the proliferation of mycorrhizal fungi.

COMPOST

Composting is an integral part of gardening. There are four key materials in composting: nitrogen, carbon, water, and air. Nitrogen sources are derived from grass clippings, plant trimmings, vegetative kitchen refuse, and livestock manure. While nitrogen sources come from the "green stuff," carbon sources are the "brown stuff of life," which includes dried leaves, chipped branches, bark, or straw. Compost bins measuring 3 feet by 3 feet by 3 feet have volumes of 1 cubic yard, an ideal size for residential gardens.

A practical way to construct a compost bin is to use 4 wooden pallets. Stand them up on their sides making a boxlike structure. The ratio of "green and brown stuff" is 50% green and 50% brown. Alternately layer the accumulated green and brown debris in the bin. Keep the moisture content between 40 to 60%. Since composting is an aerobic process, turn the material over once a week. Depending on the weather, the composting process may take 2 to 4 months. If properly "cooking," temperatures during composting can range from 120 to 140 degrees F. Once the process has completed, it is ready to add to your garden as an amendment to the soil or as mulch to the soil surface.

WATERING RHYTHMS

PERCOLATION TEST

A simple test can determine how quickly water percolates (drains) through the soil. The result of a perc test is one of the most important considerations when selecting and planting. At the proposed planting site, excavate a pit 18 inches wide by 18 inches deep. Fill the pit with water, let all the water percolate into the surrounding soil, and fill it again. The second filling should percolate at a rate of one inch per hour. If the water has completely drained in 18 hours, all is well; just expand the planting pit width 3 to 4 times the diameter and $1^1/2$ times the depth of the plant's rootball. Expanding the width encourages natural lateral root growth and since the majority of a plant's roots are within 2 to 3 feet of the surface, it is most important to have a concentration of roots where air, water, and nutrients are most readily available.

IMPROVEMENTS

Improve the moisture holding capacity of your soil by increasing the organic content to 20 to 30 percent. Ideally, the root zone should be 25% moisture, 25% air, and 50% structure (loam soil). When all of the soil particles are wet and all of the gravitational water has flowed down and away through the root zone most plants should thrive.

Drip irrigation is a very efficient way to water. Instead of filling watering basins with a garden hose, the slow application rate of a drip system will not waste water and saves an enormous amount of your time. It is an effective method for water conservation during the months when water demand is high. With a programmable clock, it is possible to accommodate any seasonal variation or climate change. This system enables you to place water precisely where it is needed and reduces surface runoff. The microtubing attached to an emitter should be long enough to accommodate any future expansion of the basin. For example, if the watering basin is 4 feet in diameter and 4 inches deep, there should be at least 4 emitters placed just inside its perimeter. It takes 30 gallons of water to fill this basin. Using 4 emitters, it will take approximately 4 hours to provide 30 gallons of water. The volume of water applied is controlled by frequency and duration settings in the irrigations clock. As the tree or shrub expands, extend the watering basin out to the plant's dripline and increase the number of emitters.

Use these Websites as tools to help schedule watering times:

- **www.mwdh2o.com/**
  Metropolitan Water District's (MWD), Watering Calculator
- **www.nws.noaa.gov/**
  National Oceanic and Atmospheric Administration's Weather Page
- **www.cimis.water.ca.gov/cimis/ welcome.jsp**
  California Irrigation Management Information System (CIMIS)

PLANTING RHYTHMS

Prepare for planting by excavating a planting pit 1 to $1^1/_2$ times the depth and 3 to 4 times the diameter of a plant's rootball; save the excavated soil for backfill, then create a rectilinear form (4 flat sides). Assuming the native soil is denser than the soil in the rootball, a rectilinear form directs newly planted roots towards the corners of the pit and then into the native soil, rather than circling around the inside surface of a cylindrical pit. Loosen the inside surface of the pit with a hand cultivator or a knife, which will further encourage the absorbing roots to grow into the native soil.

After planting, build a 4- to 6-inch high berm around the plant to create a watering basin that has a diameter 10 to 20 percent wider than the diameter of the plant's canopy. The soil level in the basin should slope away from the root flare. This slight slope will keep irrigation water gravitating toward the perimeter of the basin, which will also encourage the roots to grow outward.

TREE PRUNING RHYTHMS

Summer pruning is used to reduce the height and volume of a plant's canopy, so maintaining the plant can be accomplished without standing on a ladder. This pruning should be done in mid- to late summer. First, prune out the dead, diseased, damaged and interfering wood. Next, head back the remaining branches, maintaining the natural form of the plant. Lastly, groom the tree to encourage new growth to grow in uniformly by pruning just above a bud that points toward the open space.

If you live in California's snow country, survey the structural integrity of your trees. If you find your trees' condition suspect and you are apprehensive about evaluating and correcting their weaknesses, enlist the services of a certified or a consulting arborist and have that person evaluate their conditions. Certified arborists are usually members of the International Society of Arborists and can be contacted on the web at **www.isa-arbor.com/**. Consulting arborists are usually members of the American Society of Consulting Arborist and can be contacted on the web at **www.asca-consultants.org**.

Examples that lead to structural weakness are errant directional growth, hazardous cantilevers, branch or root damage, uneven weight distribution, or insect or disease problems. Before the weight of a dangerous snow accumulates in your trees' canopies, have an arborist or forester evaluate their strength.

See pages 55, 229, 261, 293, 298, 302, and 306 for more pruning information.

We have so many selections to recommend that we had to include this page of more great ones to plant!

CITRUS

Calamondin, Variegated

(*Citrus mitis* 'Calamondin Variegated')
Unknown parentage / Zones 9to 11 / full sun / height 10 to 12 feet / width 8 to 10 feet / harvest autumn to winter

Grapefruit, Oroblanco

(*Citrus paradisi* 'Oroblanco')
China / Zones 9 to 11 / full sun / height 10 to 14 feet / width 12 to 16 feet / harvest winter to spring, winter to summer, or spring to autumn depending on cultivar

Lemon, Variegated, Pink Eureka or Pink Lemonade

(*Citrus limon* 'Variegated Pink Eureka')
China / Zones 9 to 11 / full sun / height 8 to 12 feet / width 8 to 12 feet / harvest autumn to winter, autumn to summer, or year-round depending on zone

Orange, Common Valencia

(*Citrus sinensis* 'Valencia')
South China, Vietnam / Zones 9 to 11 / full sun / height 15 to 20 feet / width 15 to 20 feet / harvest winter to spring, spring to summer, or spring to autumn depending on zone

Orange, Sweet, Blood Orange

(*Citrus sinensis* 'Moro')
Southeast Asia / Zones 9 to 11 / full sun / height 18 to 20 feet / width 12 to 18 feet / harvest winter to spring

Orange, Sweet, Cara Cara Navel

(*Citrus sinensis* 'Cara Cara')
Venezuela / Zones 9 to 11 / full sun / height 4 to 15 feet / width 4 to 15 feet / harvest winter to spring

ORCHIDS

Beallara Orchid

(× *Beallara* 'Howard's Dream')
(*Odontoglossum* × *Cochlioda*) × (*Miltonia* × *Brassia*) / Zones 10 to 11 or indoors / bright dappled light / height 18 inches / width 18 inches / flowers late spring or summer / plant in fine grade orchid bark / 50F to 85F

Cattleya (Mini-Cattleya)

(*Laeliocattleya*)
Laelia × *Cattleya* / Zones 10 to 11 or indoors / bright dappled light / height 4 to 12 inches / width 4 to 24 inches / flowers spring and summer / plant in medium grade orchid bark / 55F to 85F

Chocolate Orchid

(× *Oncidium* 'Sharry Baby')
Oncidim hybrid origin / zones 10 to 11 or indoors / bright dappled light / height 10 to 30 inches / width 10 to 24 inches / flowers late spring to summer / plant in medium grade orchid bark / 50F to 85F

Coconut Orchid

(*Maxillaria tenuifolia*)
Mexico to Nicaragua / zones 10 to 11 or indoors / bright dappled light / height 6 to 10 inches / width 6 to 10 inches / flowers late spring or early summer/ plant in medium grade orchid bark / 50F to 85F

Cymbidium

(*Cymbidium* × *hybrida*)
Asia and Australia / zones 9 to 11 / bright dappled light / height 12 to 48 inches / width 8 to 36 inches / flowers winter/ plant in equal parts bark and soil mixture / 35F to 85F

Epidendrum

(*Epidendrum* × *hybrida*)
Central and South America / zones 9 to 11 or indoors / full sun to part shade / height 8 to 36 inches / width 8 to 36 inches / blooms constantly in temperate climates / plant in medium grade orchid bark / 40F to 85F

ALSO IN OUR GARDEN

Nun's Orchid
(*Phaius tankervilleae*)
Africa, Madagascar, India, SE Asia / zones 10 to 11 or indoors / full shade outdoors, bright indirect light indoors / height 12 to 40 inches / width 8 to 32 inches / flowers late winter to early spring / plant in equal parts bark and soil mixture / 40F to 80F

Pansy Orchid
(*Miltoniopsis* × *hybrida*)
Central America / zone 11 or indoors / full shade outdoors or bright, indirect light indoors / height 8 to 16 inches / width 8 to 16 inches / flowers winter / plant in medium grade orchid bark / 45F to 75F

Spider Orchid
(*Brassia* × *hybrida*)
South America / zones 10 to 11 or indoors / bright dappled light / height 8 to 12 inches / width 8 to 16 inches / flowers spring to summer / plant in medium grade orchid bark / 45F to 85F

SHRUBS

Angel Earrings Fuchsia
(*Fuchsia* × *hybrida* 'Angel Earrings')
Brazil / zone 10 / partial sun / height cascading / width 3 to 4 feet diameter / flowers spring, summer in red & white

Australian Fuchsia
(*Correa puchella*)
S Australia / zones 9 to 10 / sun / height 3 feet / width 4 to 5 feet / flowers summer to spring in pink

Camellia
(*Camellia japonica*)
Japan / zones 8 to 10 / partial sun / height 4 to 20 feet / width 4 to 10 feet / flowers winter, spring in crimson red, pink, white, yellow, and multicolor

Common Lilac
(*Syringa vulgaris* × *hybrida*)
Europe, NE Asia / zones 6 to 9 / sun / height 6 to 15 feet / width 4 to 8 feet / flowers spring, fall in pink, blue, and white

Gumi
(*Eleangnus multiflora*)
Japan, China / zones 4 to 9 / sun / height 4 to 8 feet / width 4 to 6 feet / flowers spring in creamy white / red berries

Satsuki Azalea
(*Azalea satsuki* × *hybrida*)
Japan / zones 6 to10 / partial sun / height 3 to 6 feet / width 3 to 4 feet / flowers spring in white, pink, red, and multicolor

Shark Bay Boronia
(*Boronia crenulata* 'Shark Bay')
W. Australia / zones 9 to 10 / sun or partial shade / height 3 to 6 feet / width 4 feet / flowers summer in pink

Shrimp PlanT
(*Justicia brandegeana*
[syn. *Beloperone guttata*])
Mexico / zones 10 to 11 / full sun along the coast, partial shade inland / height 3 feet / width 2 feet / flowers summer in salmon, white, yellow, rust, and pink

Tiny Tower Italian Cypress
(*Cupressus sempervirens* 'Monshel')
Mediterranean / zones 9 to 10 / full sun or partial shade / height 20 plus feet / width 2 feet / conifer

Vireya
(*Rhododendron vireya*)
SE Asia / zones 10 to 11 / partial shade / height 4 to 8 feet / width 3 to 6 feet / flowers summer in orange, yellow, red, and pink

adventitious: Describes a structure that develops in an unusual place, such as roots that develop from a trunk's base.

alkaline soil: Soil with a pH greater than 7.0.

alkaloids: Compounds such as atropine, caffeine, morphine, nicotine, quinine, and strychine produced by members of the poppy and nightshade family.

allelopathic: Describes a plant that releases a toxic chemical that inhibits growth in other plants.

all-purpose fertilizer: Powdered, liquid, or granular fertilizer with three primary nutrients—nitrogen (N), potassium (P), and phosphorus (K). It is suitable for maintenance nutrition for most plants.

alternate bearing: Describes fruit or nut trees that produce heavily one year and little or none the next.

alpha-naphthalene acetic acid (NAA): A plant growth regulator (auxin).

annual: A plant that completes its life cycle within one year.

anther: The pollen-bearing part of a stamen.

aerial root: A root that absorbs moisture from the atmosphere, rather than the soil.

auxins: Plant growth regulators whose functions include fruit formation, root development, and seed germination inhibition.

***Bacillus thuringiensis* or Bt:** A bacterium, lethal to many kinds of caterpillar pests, and used to control them.

back bulb: An orchid pseudobulb that has lost its leaves and only the bulbous base remains.

backfill: The soil mixture used to surround a rootball in a planting pit.

balled and burlapped: Describes a tree or shrub grown in the field whose rootball was wrapped with protective burlap and twine when the plant was dug up to be sold or transplanted.

bare root: Describes plants that have been packaged without any soil around their roots. (Often young shrubs and trees purchased through mail-order arrive with exposed roots covered with moist peat or sphagnum moss, sawdust, or similar material, and wrapped in plastic.)

beneficial insects: Insects or their larvae that prey on pest organisms and their eggs. They may be flying insects such as ladybugs, parasitic wasps, praying mantids, and soldier bugs, or soil dwellers such as predatory nematodes, spiders, and ants.

berm: A narrow raised ring of soil around a tree, used to hold water so it will be directed to the root zone.

biennial: A plant that completes its life cycle within two years.

bipinnate: Describes a leaf that has divisions that are themselves once or several times compound.

borer: An insect or insect larva that bores into the woody parts of plants.

bract: A modified leaf structure on a plant stem near its flower that resembles a petal. Often it is more colorful and visible than the actual flower, as in bougainvillea.

brown rot gummosis: A disease characterized by the formation of patches of gum on a fruit tree, the result of insects, microorganisms, or weather; when left untreated, it causes bark to scale, fall off, and ooze from the infected site and will eventually lead to the tree's demise.

bud union: The place where the top of a plant was grafted to the rootstock; usually refers to roses.

bulb: A short, modified, underground stem usually surrounded by fleshy, modified leaves that contain stored food for the shoot within. True bulbs have pointed tops, short underground stems on basal plates, and new growths, called bulblets, which form from offshoots of the parent bulbs. The term is used loosely to describe bulblike plants (such as corms, rhizomes, and tubers), as many plants are technically not true bulbs.

canopy: The overhead branching area of a tree, usually referring to its extent including foliage.

chelate: A compound that attaches to a nutrient molecule to facilitate absorption.

chitinase: A digestive enzyme that degrades chitin, i.e. the exoskeleton of beetles

chlorotic yellowing: Yellowing between leaf veins.

ciliated: Edged with hairs along the margin or edge, usually forming a fringe.

cold hardiness: The ability of a perennial plant to survive the winter cold in a particular area.

cole crops: Vegetables belonging to the Brassica family; broccoli, cabbage, kohlrabi.

color packs: Sectioned plastic containers used for growing annuals and perennials.

compost: Organic matter that has undergone progressive decomposition by microbial and macrobial activity until it is reduced to a spongy, fluffy texture. Added to soil of any type, it improves the soil's ability to hold air and water and to drain well.

corm: A structure that grows upwards and is similar to a bulb, except that each summer a new corm grows on top of the original one. As the parent corm disappears, the roots of the new corm grow downward into the hole left by the decayed corm.

corolla: The petals of a flower considered as a group or unit.

corona: A crown-shaped, funnel-shaped, or trumpet-shaped outgrowth of certain flowers, such as the daffodil or the spider lily. Also called crown.

cultivar: A cultivated variety. It is a naturally occurring form of a plant that has been identified as special or superior and is purposely selected for propagation and production.

deadhead: To remove faded flower heads from plants to improve their appearance, abort seed production, and stimulate further flowering.

deciduous plants: Unlike evergreens, these trees and shrubs lose their leaves in fall.

dehissance: The separation of the outer seed covering.

desiccation: Drying out of foliage tissues, usually due to drought or wind.

diazinon: An amber liquid, $C_{12}H_{21}N_2O_3PS$, used as an insecticide.

dimorphic: Existing or occurring in two distinct forms.

dioecious: Having the male and female reproductive organs borne on separate individuals of the same species. Both male and female plants are needed for pollination and seed production.

disbud: To take out the center flower bud shortly after the side buds emerge so that the plant's energy is directed toward the side buds.

division: The practice of splitting apart perennial plants to create several smaller-rooted segments. The practice is useful for controlling the plant's size and for acquiring more plants; it is also essential to the health and continued flowering of certain ones.

dormancy: The period, usually winter, when perennial plants temporarily cease active growth; a rest period. Go dormant is the verb form, as used in this sentence: Some plants, like spring-blooming bulbs, go dormant in summer.

drip line: The area on the ground formed directly under a plant's perimeter.

drupe: A fleshy fruit, like a peach, plum, or cherry, with a single hard stone that encloses a seed.

drupelets: Individual bumpy, fleshy, seed-containing units that make up a whole berry.

earwig: An elongate insect of the order Dermaptera with a pair of pincerlike appendages.

en masse: In one group or body; all together.

epiphytes: A plant that grows on another plant upon which it depends for mechanical support but not for nutrients.

espalier: A tree or shrub that is trained to grow in a flat plane against a wall, often in a symmetrical pattern.

establishment: The point at which a newly planted tree, shrub, or flower begins to produce new growth, either foliage or stems. This is an indication that the roots have recovered from transplant shock and have begun to grow and spread.

estivation: A state of dormancy or sleep, protecting animals from heat or drought.

evapotranspiration: The movement of water from the earth into the air by evaporation from soil and transpiration from plants.

evergreen: Describes perennial plants that do not lose their foliage annually with the onset of winter. Needled or broadleaf foliage will persist and continues to function on a plant through one or more winters, aging and dropping unobtrusively in cycles of three or four years or more.

floral node: A point along the floral stalk that contains a latent bud, usually designated by a scale-like leaf bud.

floret: A tiny flower, usually one of many forming a cluster, that comprises a single blossom.

foliar: Of or about foliage.

frass: Sawdust-like debris that accumulates below the holes caused by insects or larvae that bore into the woody parts of plants.

freestone: Describes a fruit with flesh that separates easily from the stony pit.

germinate: To sprout; germination is a fertile seed's first stage of development.

girdling: a process that results in the removal or decay or the outer tissues of a stem or trunk, limiting growth by damaging the vascular transportation system of a plant.

glaucous: Smooth, with a waxy blossom such as a *Hoya carnosa*.

glucocides: Form the link between mono- and polysaccharides and are found in tannins and anthocyanins.

graft (union): The point on the stem of a woody plant with sturdier roots where a stem from a highly ornamental plant (or plant with superior fruit quality) is inserted so that it will join with it. Roses and fruit trees are commonly grafted.

hardpan: A layer of hard subsoil or clay.

herbaceous: Describes plants having fleshy or soft stems that die back with frost.

holdfasts: Tendrils with disc-like suction cups or rootlets that enable a plant to attach to just about anything.

hybrid: A plant that is the result of intentional or natural cross-pollination between two or more plants of the same species or genus.

indolebutyric acid (IBA): A plant growth regulator (auxin), that promotes root development though cell elongation.

inflorescences: Flower clusters.

June Drop: A common fruit tree malady: the sudden shedding of immature fruit, nature's way of adjusting the crop size to the tree's capability to produce good fruit.

keiki: An orchid plantlet that is born on an orchid shoot; translates to "baby" in Hawaiian.

latex: The colorless or milky sap of certain plants that coagulates on exposure to air.

lathe house: A shade structure with sides and overheads made of separated wooden slats

leach lines: Sewer discharge lines.

lignotuber: A swollen portion of the root flare that is just above or below the ground. It functions as a moisture and nutrient storage reservoir during times of drought. Even after a natural disaster, such as a fire, the lignotuber allows the plant to regenerate.

mobil nutrients: A nutrient that a plant can transport from one place to another.

molluscicide: An agent that kills mollusks, including slugs and snails.

monocarpic: Describes plants that flower and bear fruit only once.

monocotyledon: A flowering plant, like grasses, orchids, and lilies, that has a single leaf in the seed.

monopodial growth: Plant growth along a vertical axis.

mulch: A layer of material over bare soil to protect it from erosion and compaction by rain, to maintain soil moisture, and to discourage weeds. It may be inorganic (gravel or fabric) or organic (wood chips, bark, pine needles, chopped leaves).

mycoplasmic organism: A microscopic organism that exhibits both fungal and bacterial properties.

mycorrhizal fungi: Beneficial fungi that function symbiotically with plants roots.

naturalize: (a) To plant seeds, bulbs, or plants in a random, informal pattern as they would appear in their natural habitat; (b) to adapt to and spread throughout adopted habitats (a tendency of some nonnative plants).

nectar: The sweet fluid produced by glands on flowers that attract pollinators such as hummingbirds and honeybees.

Neem oil: An insecticidal, fungicidal, and miticidal oil derived from the Neem seed.

nitrogen-fixing bacteria: Bacteria that converts gaseous nitrogen into a form that is absorbable by plant roots.

offset: A shoot that develops at the base of a plant and may root to form a new plant.

operculum: A lid that covers each bud and pops off when its stamens unfold during its flowering period.

organic material, organic matter: Any material or debris that is derived from plants. It is carbon-based material capable of undergoing decomposition and decay.

palmate: Describes fronds that are round or semicircular in outline.

parthenogenic: Reproducing asexually

peat moss: Organic matter from peat sedges (United States) or sphagnum mosses (Canada), often used to improve soil texture.

pedicel: In a cluster of flowers, a stem bearing a single flower.

pellicle: The papery divider between nut meat halves.

percolation: Passing or oozing through porous material, as in water passing through soil.

perennial: A flowering plant that completes its life cycle in more than two years. Many die back with frost, but their roots survive winter and generate new shoots in spring.

petiole: The stalk by which a leaf is attached to a stem.

pH: a measurement of the relative acidity (low pH) or alkalinity (high pH) of soil or water based on a scale of 1 to 14, 7 being neutral. Individual plants require soil to be within a certain range so that nutrients can dissolve in moisture and be available to them.

pinnate: Describes fronds that are linear or oblong in outline with segments arranged like the pattern of a feather.

pollen: The yellow, powdery grains in the center of a flower. A plant's male sex cells, they are transferred to the female plant parts by means of wind or animal pollinators to fertilize them and create seeds.

pollinator: The (male) plant that supplies the pollen to fertilize the female plant of a dioecious pair; also called pollinizer.

pollinizer: Pollinator.

pony packs: Sectioned plastic containers used for growing annuals and perennials.

pre-emergent: A herbicide that prevents seeds from germinating.

probusci: Mouth parts of an insect; piercing or sucking insects have elongated probusci to penetrate plant tissues.

pseudobulb: An orchid appendage that appears as a bulbous base with lanceolate or ovate leaves protruding above.

pyrethrin: An pesticide derived from the extract of the chrysanthemum flower.

rectilinear: A shape bound by four straight lines and with 90-degree corners.

remontant: Reblooming, as a remontant rose.

rhizome: A swollen energy-storing stem structure, similar to a bulb, that spreads horizontally underground or on the surface with adventitious roots and sprouts stems, leaves, and flowers from the rhizome's upper sections.

rootbound (or potbound): The condition of a plant that has been confined in a container too long, its roots having been forced to wrap around themselves and even grow out of the container.

rootstock: The lower part of a grafted tree or rose.

russeting (or silvering): A blemishing of the rind on lemon trees, caused by mite infestations.

scarification: To cut or scratch the skin of.

scion: The top part of a tree or rose that has been grafted onto a rootstock.

self-fruitful: Describes a fruit tree that pollinates itself.

semievergreen: Tending to be evergreen in a mild climate but deciduous in a rigorous one.

shearing: The pruning technique whereby plant stems and branches are cut uniformly with long-bladed pruning shears (hedge shears) or powered hedge trimmers. It is used when creating and maintaining hedges and topiary.

slow-acting fertilizer: Fertilizer that is water insoluble and therefore releases its nutrients gradually as a function of soil temperature, moisture, and related microbial activity. Typically granular, it may be organic or synthetic.

sow bug: A small terrestrial crustacean; also known as wood louse.

spathe: A leaf or bract subtending a flower grouping.

spray: A cluster of flowers in different stages of development on a single stem.

stamen: The pollen-producing reproductive organ of a flower.

stasis: A period of no growth and minimal metabolism.

stolon: A specialized above-the-ground stem that produces roots and shoots at the nodes.

stomata: Leaf pores.

sucker: A new growing shoot. Underground plant roots produce suckers to form new stems and spread by means of these suckering roots to form large plantings, or colonies. Some plants produce root suckers or branch suckers as a result of pruning or wounding.

sympodial growth: Plant growth along one or several horizontal axis. In orchids, growth by pseudobulbs.

tillering: Sending forth shoots from its base (as grass does).

tomentose: Fuzzy in texture.

tuber: A swollen underground storage structure that produces pulpy, instead of scaly, stems. Tubers normally grow just below the surface of the soil and, like bulbs, store food for the plants. The buds on tubers become stems, leaves, and flowers, and clusters of roots form at the base. They multiply by division, and as they divide, the parent tuber deteriorates.

turgid: Firm due to internal water pressure.

umbel: A flat-topped or rounded flower cluster; the flower stalks rise from about the same point.

variegated: Having various colors or color patterns. The term usually refers to plant foliage that is streaked, edged, blotched, or mottled with a contrasting color, often green with yellow, cream, or white.

vectoring: Carrying diseases from plant to plant.

vellum: The outer coating of an orchid root that aids in water and nutrient absorption as well as dessication prevention.

xeriphytic: Having to do with water-conserving landscaping.

xeriscape: A seven step landscape system designed to conserve water.

Asakawa, Bruce, and Sharon. *Bruce and Sharon Asakawa's California Gardener's Guide*. Nashville, Tennessee: Cool Springs Press, 2001.

Attenborough, David. *The Private Lives of Plants*. Princeton, New Jersey: Princeton University Press, 1995.

Bagnasco, John. *Plants for the Home*. Minneapolis, Minnesota: The Retail Group, Inc., 1976.

Bailey, L. H. *A Standard Cyclopedia of Horticulture*. 3 volumes. New York: The Macmillan Company, 1958.

Beales, Peter. *Classic Roses*. New York: Henry, Holt & Co., 1997.

Beidleman, Linda H., and Eugene N. Kozloff. *Plants of the San Francisco Bay Region*. Berkeley, California: University of California Press, 2003.

Bennett, Jennifer. *The Harrowsmith Book of Fruit Trees*. Willowdale, Ontario: Firefly Books, 1991.

Brenzel, Kathleen Norris, Ed. *Sunset Western Garden Book*. Menlo Park, California: Sunset Publishing Corporation, 2001.

Bryant, Geoff. *Rhododendrons and Azaleas*. Willowdale, Ontario: Firefly Books, 2001.

Byczynski, Lynn. *The Flower Farmer*. White River Junction, Vermont: Chelsea Green Publishing Co., 1997.

Cairns, Thomas. *The Easiest Roses to Grow*. San Ramon, California: Ortho Books, 2002.

Cairns, Thomas, ed. *Modern Roses XI: The World Encyclopedia of Roses*. New York: Harcourt Brace/Academic Press, 2000.

Cowling, Richard, and Dave Richardson. *Fynbos: South Africa's Unique Floral Kingdom*. Vlaeberg, South Africa: Fernwood Press, 1995.

Dardick, Karen. *Estate Gardens of California*. New York: Rizzo International Publications, Inc., 2002.

Dardick, Karen. *Simply Roses: Essential Guide to Easy Gardening*. New York, New York: St. Martin's Press, 2004.

Dobson, Beverly R., and Peter Schneider, eds. *Combined Rose List 2004: Roses in Commerce*. Mantua, Ohio: Peter Schneider, 2004.

Ecke, Paul Jr., and O.A. Matkin, eds. *The Poinsettia Manual*. Encinitas, California: Paul Ecke Poinsettias, 1976.

Edinger, Phillip, ed. *Roses*. Menlo Park, California: Sunset Publishing Co., 1998.

Euser, Barbara J., ed. *Bay Area Gardening: Practical Essays by Master Gardeners*. San Rafael, California: Writers Center of Marin County, 2002.

Facciola, Stephen. *Cornucopia II: A Source Book of Edible Plants*. Vista, California: Kampong Publications, 1998.

Flint, Mary Louise. *Pests of the Garden and Small Farm*. Berkeley, California: University of California Press, 1998.

Flores, Barbara. *The Great Sunflower Book*. Berkeley, California: Ten Speed Press, 1997.

Galle, Fred C. *Azaleas*. Portland, Oregon: Timber Press, 1991.

Gilmer, Maureen. *The Complete Guide to Northern California Gardening*. Dallas, Texas: Taylor Publishing, 1994.

Giono, Jean. *The Man Who Planted Trees*. Chelsea, Vermont: Chelsea Green Publishing Company, 1985.

Griffiths, Mark. *Index of Garden Plants*. Portland, Oregon: Timber Press, 1994.

Grissell, Eric. *Insects and Gardens*. Portland, Oregon: Timber Press, 2001.

James, I.D. *Orchids*. Willowdale, Ontario: Firefly Books, 2001.

Johnson, Warren T., and Howard H. Lyon. *Insects That Feed on Trees and Shrubs*. Ithaca, New York: Cornell University Press, 1979.

Kaplan Prentice, Helaine and Melba Levick, *The Gardens of Southern California*. San Francisco, California: Chronicle Books, 1990.

Kenyon, John, and Jacqueline Walker. *Vireyas*. Portland, Oregon: Timber Press, 1997.

Larkcom, Joy. *Oriental Vegetables*. London, England: John Murray Publishers, Ltd., 1997.

Levick, Melba, and Joan Chatfield-Taylor. *Visiting Eden: The Public Gardens of Northern California*. San Francisco, California: Chronicle Books, 1993.

MacKenzie, David S. *Perennial Ground Covers.* Portland, Oregon: Timber Press, 1997.

Macoboy, Stirling. *What Tree Is That?* Sydney, Australia: Lansdowne Publishing Pty. Ltd., 1996.

Masumoto, David Mas. *Epitaph for a Peach: Four Seasons on My Family Farm.* San Francisco, California: Harper Collins Publishers, 1994.

Meeker, John. *The Mexican Kitchen Garden.* Kansas City, Missouri: Andrews McMeel Publishing, 1998.

Ogren, Thomas. *Allergy-Free Gardening.* Berkeley, California: Ten Speed Press, 2000.

Olson, Jerry. *Growing Roses in Cold Climates.* New York: McGraw-Hill, 1999.

Phillips, Roger, and Martyn Rix. *The Botanical Garden: Volume I Trees and Shrubs, and Volume II Perennials and Annuals.* London, England: Macmillan, 2002.

Pizzetti, Ippolito, and Henry Cocker. *Flowers: A Guide for Your Garden.* 2 volumes. New York: Harry N. Abrams, Inc., 1975.

Preissel, Hans-Georg, and Ulrike. *Brugmansia and Datura: Angel's Trumpets and Thorn Apples.* Westport, Connecticut: Firefly Books Ltd., 2002.

Quest-Ritson, Charles. *American Rose Society Encyclopedia of Roses.* New York: Dorling Kindersley Publishing Inc., 2003.

Rice, Graham. *Discovering Annuals.* Portland, Oregon: Timber Press, 1999.

Riffle, Robert Lee. *The Tropical Look.* Portland, Oregon: Timber Press, 1998.

Rogers, Allan. *Peonies.* Portland, Oregon: Timber Press, 1995.

Saunt, James. *Citrus Varieties of the World.* Norwich, England: Sinclair International Ltd., 1990.

Smaus, Robert. *52 Weeks in the California Garden.* Los Angeles, California: Los Angeles Times Syndicate, 1996.

Smiley, Beth, and Ray Rogers, eds. *Ultimate Rose.* New York: Dorling Kindersley Publishing, Inc., 2000.

Smith, Lyman B. *The Bromeliads.* Cranbury, New Jersey: A.S. Barnes and Co., 1969.

Smithen, Jan, and Lucinda Lewis. *Sun-Drenched Gardens: The Mediterranean Style.* New York: Harry N. Abrams, 2002.

Susser, Allen. *The Great Citrus Book.* Berkeley, California: Ten Speed Press, 1997.

Tankard, Glenn. *Tropical Fruit.* Ringwood Victoria, Australia: Penguin Books, Ltd., 1990.

The Garden Conservancy. *The Garden Conservancy's Open Days Directory West Coast Edition: The Guide to Visiting Private Gardens in California, Oregon and Washington.* Cold Spring, New York: The Garden Conservancy Inc., 2003.

Thomas, Graham Stuart. *The Garden Through the Year.* New York: Thames and Hudson, 2002.

Thomson, Paul H. *Pitahaya: A Promising New Fruit Crop for Southern California.* Bonsall, California: Bonsall Publications, 2002.

Van Aken, Norman, and John Harrisson. *The Great Exotic Fruit Book.* Berkeley, California: Ten Speed Press, 1995.

Varney, Bill, and Sylvia. *Herbs: Growing and Using the Plants of Romance.* Tucson, Arizona: Ironwood Press, 1999.

Vertrees, J.D. *Japanese Maples.* Portland, Oregon: Timber Press, 2001.

Walheim, Lance. *Citrus.* Tucson, Arizona: Ironwood Press, 1996.

Walker, Jacqueline. *Hibiscus.* Willowdale, Ontario: Firefly Books, 2001.

Welsh, Pat. *Southern California Gardening.* San Francisco, California: Chronicle Books, 2000.

Xerces Society and The Smithsonian Institution. *Butterfly Gardening.* San Francisco, California: Sierra Club Books, 1998.

Eric, Sharon, and Bruce Asakawa

Bruce and Sharon Asakawa and their son, Eric, combine their knowledge and experience to bring readers *California Gardening Rhythms*—the "when-to" book of seasonal gardening.

Both Bruce and Sharon Asakawa have been active partners in the green industry since they married in the early 1960s. Bruce's parents founded Presidio Garden Center in 1950, which became one of the premier retail nurseries on the West Coast. After working for his parents, Bruce studied landscape architecture at Cal Poly, Pomona, a field that combines his interests of horticulture, art, design, and nature. Later, Bruce developed and taught horticulture classes for the University of California Cooperative Extension, which led to the beginning of his radio career. Sharon joined the family business and eventually managed the floral department, where she gained a great deal of knowledge about California gardening.

Today, Bruce and Sharon are two of the co-hosts of the *Garden Compass*™ radio program, they are associate editors of *Garden Compass*™ *Magazine,* and both lead garden tours to sites across the world. In addition to this book for Cool Springs Press, they wrote *Bruce and Sharon Asakawa's California Gardener's Guide* (Cool Springs Press, 2000).

Eric Asakawa is a manager for Armstrong Garden Centers in the San Francisco Bay area. Eric has his fingers on the pulse of what consumers and readers want in the garden world. Eric became interested in the world of plants and gardening by an early fascination with orchids—a fascination which continues to this day. Eric and his wife, Stephanie, have a son, Samokai, who will doubtless carry on the family tradition some day.

Bruce and Sharon Asakawa live in Bonita, California. Eric Asakawa and his family live in Larkspur, California. Daughter Tasia and her family live in Oxford, England.